Władysław Strzemiński

theory of seeing

Muzeum Sztuki w Łodzi • 2025

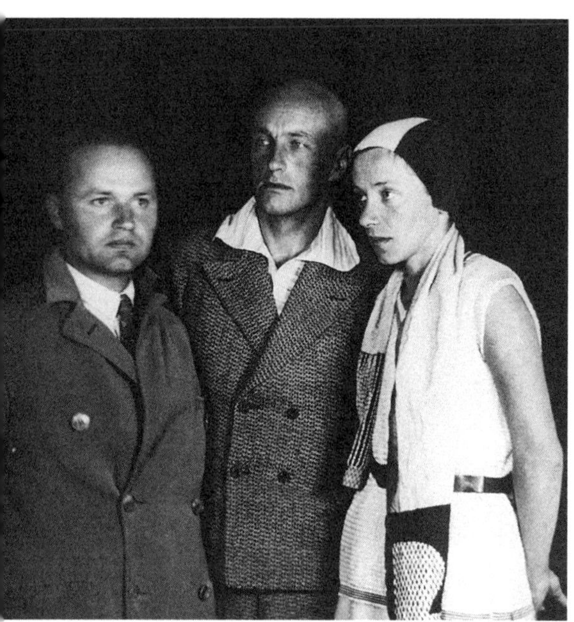

Julian Przyboś
Władysław Strzemiński
and Katarzyna Kobro
ca. 1930–31

table of contents

foreword

Daniel Muzyczuk

Three years after the end of World War II Władysław Strzemiński returned to an avant-garde movement that had long since died in Poland. He set to work on designing the Neoplastic Room, for the new seat of the Muzeum Sztuki in Łódź—in an urban palace that had belonged to pre-war textile factory owners before it was nationalized and converted into exhibition rooms. On its second floor the director of the museum organized an exhibition presenting the linear evolution of modern art starting from impressionism and concluding with abstract art. The culmination of the narrative came with Strzemiński's Neoplastic Room, meant to stand as proof that avant-garde art had been successfully emancipated from objecthood. He constructed a space that was meant to create the ideal conditions for contemplating the work of his peers.

The renewal failed. Only two years after the opening of the museum, the show was altered. The room was painted white and figurative paintings replaced more progressive works. It was the result of the 1949 introduction of socialist realism as the official state doctrine of art, which deemed abstract pieces counterrevolutionary. Strzemiński was removed from his post at the Higher School of Plastic Arts and Design in Łódź and died of pneumonia in 1952. He did not see the restoration of the room that would happen only eight years later, when abstract works were again allowed to be presented in state institutions after Stalin's death.

A more liberal politics opened the door for another of Strzemiński's late works: a treatise on the history of art. The book that was published in 1958 was not a finished text. It was composed by his students out of their lecture notes. Like the Neoplastic Room, the book needed to be reconstructed from parts—both of these events were steps in the larger process of restoring the broken continuity of modernism in Poland. The legendary status of the present volume is thus based partly on the circumstances of its posthumous publication, as the most substantial statement from a key artist of the Polish constructivist avant-garde. The Neoplastic Room was one of the artist's attempts at writing art history. *Theory of Seeing* is another.

Strzemiński became an artist as a consequence of the collapse of his military career. He was an officer of the Tsarist Army and worked as a sapper. After sustaining severe injuries in battle, he was forced to reinvent himself in Moscow during the revolution. He also became involved with art administration. Between May and November 1918, Strzemiński worked under Vladimir Tatlin's direction at the Department of Fine Arts of the IZO-Narkompros in Moscow, the arts division of the education commissariat responsible for setting up a network of museums and cultural organizations. At the beginning of 1919, Strzemiński was elected to the Moscow-based Fine Arts and Craft Committee, where he became the head of the All-Russian Central Exhibitions Bureau. He went on to run the Art Section of the combined Museums and Fine Arts Subdivision of the GubONO (Governorate Branch Department of People's Education) in Smolensk.[1] Now living near Vitebsk, Strzemiński was able to maintain close relations with Kazimir Malevich and other colleagues from "The Champions of the New Art" (UNOVIS) . The discussions taking place at the new avant-garde art institutions touched on the aims of museums, but also, importantly, on the place of art in social and political life. The sculptor Katarzyna Kobro joined him there and together they produced propaganda works and stage designs and educated younger artists.

Staying in Malevich's circle influenced more than the couple's artistic practices. Suprematism became an important example of a theory of art produced by an artist, encouraging Kobro and Strzemiński to develop their own thinking. At the same time Malevich was establishing a teleological horizon upon which all progressive tendencies

1 See Jarosław Suchan, *The Avant-Garde Museum*, in: *The Avant-Garde Museum*, eds. Agnieszka Pindera and Jarosław Suchan, (Łódź: Muzeum Sztuki, 2020).

converged in Suprematism. The interwar period abounds in undertakings like this, with artists creating competing frameworks for a comprehensive view of trends in art. An important element of this type of text is how they characterize groups by presenting their contribution to developments in art, understood as a collective search for consecutive formal solutions. Similar attempts were made by El Lissitzky and Jean Arp, in the 1925 book *Die Kustismen,* and by Theo van Doesburg across a series of writings.

Strzemiński was a prolific writer who saw art criticism as another means of establishing a stable ground for progressive art. The first article he published after his arrival to Poland was a report on the development of new art after revolution. "Notes on Russian Art," (1923) revolved around a description of three groups of artists and their leaders: Mikhail Larionov, Vladimir Tatlin, and Malevich. Strzemiński does not hide his sympathies: he sides with Malevich and Suprematism and condemns Tatlin's Productivism. In this view, the latter had assumed the role of a "social activist or critic," and was too far removed from the responsibilities of an artist. Strzemiński's position raises further theoretical considerations, positioning art as autonomous from, but exerting an influence upon the sociopolitical, ruling out the possibility of artistic ideas being implemented directly in everyday life. This understanding of art's autonomy should also be seen as the source of his persistent interest in the idea of building a public art collection. For him, a museum should be a space where the laboratory of art can be presented without the burden of utility. Grupa "a.r.", a collective of artists and poets that included Strzemiński, Kobro, Henryk Stażewski, Jan Brzękowski and Julian Przyboś, formulated this rule in one of their bulletins:

> The social impact of art is therefore indirect: elevating certain emotional and voluntaristic attitudes, it permeates from leisure to labor, into the full scope of human life. . . . Abstract art is a laboratory for exploring form. The results of these explorations emerge as an indispensable element of everyday life. However, a need to immediately apply abstract works of art does not follow, because the paths of art are not always straight.[2]

2 *Biuletyn grupy "a.r.,"* no. 2 (1930).

The group focused on publishing and building a collection of modern art. Stażewski and Brzękowski visited the studios of artists in Paris and asked for donations to a public collection that would become the backbone of Muzeum Sztuki. The group strengthened the alliance between artists and poets through a series of books that formed the library of the "a. r." group. The nine volumes published between 1930 and 1935 included two pamphlets, four poetry books, and three texts dedicated to theory. The first of these were leaflets that explained the program of the group. The poetry books were all authored by either Brzękowski or Przyboś and all featured contributions by visual artists. Furthermore, the series featured an important theoretical work on sculpture—*Composing Space/Calculating Space-Time Rhythms*, co-authored by Strzemiński and Kobro.

Marian Minich, the first director of the institution that houses the International Collection of Modern Art of the "a.r." group, opened an essay describing his work to exhibit the collection of the Muzeum Sztuki in Łódź with a "dedication" to Strzemiński:

> The most important critiques of existing traditional museum displays have come not from art historians, but mainly from theorizing painters representing art leaning toward Constructivism. This was surely due to their tendency to analyze artistic issues intellectually, fuelled by their knowledge of mathematics and geometry as the basis for an analytical and synthetic interpretation of creative processes, as well as the tendency to choose and construct closed formal elements, existing within an absolute, infinite space, and later functionalism, the merging of science and art etc.[3]

Indeed, we have traces of the fervent discussion that took place between the collection's founders and the art historian – the director of the museum himself, on the direction of the institution[4]. After World War II, however, all their disagreements seemed to be resolved and, for a brief moment, the artist and the director worked shoulder to shoulder to construct the inaugural show.

3 Marian Minich, "O nową organizację muzeów sztuki," in *Sztuka współczesna*, vol. 2, ed. Józef Dutkiewicz, (Krakow: Wydawnictwo Literackie, 1966), 70.

4 See Marian Minich, *Szalona galeria*, (Łódź: Wydawnictwo Łódzkie, 1963)

At the time, Strzemiński's theory of the evolution of artistic forms had likely already reached its full development, and it is hard not to see its influence on Minich's layout of the galleries. These rooms of the museum unfold following a systematic and stylistic method, ranging from landscape painting, through Symbolism, Impressionism, Expressionism, Formism, Cubism, Constructivism, to a Neoplastic room, and then Surrealism in a small room. Minich writes of the first exhibition:

> The aim was to show how the constant transformation of social structures colors and differentiates the psyche of the contemporary artist and man as economic and social changes take place, as various fields of knowledge, technology, and inventions develop, causing continual progress of art, new variations of, essentially, 'Realist' vision.[5]

The key notion here is of course the specific understanding of "realism," connecting the implementation of the method with its source in Strzemiński's theory. The artist did not see realism as a form of representation, a style, or a pictorial technique capable of revealing the world in its recognizable facticity. Strzemiński laid the ground for this theory as early as 1936, in an article entitled "Aspekty rzeczywistości" (Aspects of Reality). The essay was an attempt at accounting for surrealism as a regressive tendency. He sketches a vision of the development of modern art as a progressive understanding of the interconnected nature of reality. With the invention of oil painting all objects became well separated from each other, establishing a gaze that revealed the sharp edges of things. This tendency reflected the emergence and growth of capitalism, following the tension laid on the value of the commodity. The most radical break with this disposition came with impressionism, drawing from studies of the physiology of seeing to blur borders between objects, fully withdrawing from an art based in drawing and treating the image as a composition of color fields instead. For Strzemiński this process is also connected with social

5 Marian Minich, "Muzeum Sztuki w Łodzi," in *Rocznik Muzeum Sztuki w Łodzi. 1930–1962*, eds. Marian Minich, Maria Rubczyńska, and Janina Ładnowska (Łódź: Wydawnictwo Łódzkie, 1965), 2.

development and the understanding that different and seemingly distant aspects of societies are all interconnected. This knowledge is not only reflected in the work of the artist but it also has a physical aspect because it is developed in the faculties of the eye itself. Strzemiński first described the accumulation of visual stimuli that turns into knowledge as "visual contents." In *Theory of Seeing*, the idea of contents will be replaced by a more Marxist notion: visual consciousness. The process of gaining it is described in physiological terms:

> The motion of the eye, the trace of the glancing gaze, the biological line of the contracting and expanding muscles are connected with the shape of the elements of form seen in nature, creating a common rhythm of form. This rhythm is, to a large extent, the rhythm of autonomous movements of the muscular-nervous system. It is a rhythm of physiology, connecting the contents of individual gazes. This rhythm of the descending and ascending line of the pulse and of the movement caused by individual and biological reactions of the muscles—subordinates the visual contents of individual gazes—transforming them, creating a constantly changing rhythm of irregular symmetry.[6]

This is how biology is bound up with social structures, hence *Theory of Seeing* was the story of the eye passing through different economic structures.

The book is also deeply embedded in Marxism. Recently Polish scholars have debated whether or not the text's materialist dialectic was a disguise or Strzemiński's fundamental methodology, capable of accounting for the structure of the theory. It is hard to defend the former view, advanced by art historian Iwona Luba. She contends that Strzemiński needed to conceal his true theory in order to deliver it to the students without losing his position,[7] and that he saw the impending threat posed by the consolidation of official ideology and needed to disguise his thought as something other than it was. Hence he employed not only the Marxist vision of history but also a notion of

6 Władysław Strzemiński, "Aspekty rzeczywistości," in *Pisma*, ed. Z. Baranowicz (Wrocław: Zakład Narodowy im. Ossolińskich, 1975), 267 (trans. DM).

7 Iwona Luba, "Wprowadzenie," in Władysław Strzemiński, *Teoria widzenia* (Łódź: Muzeum Sztuki w Łodzi, 2016).

realism that could mislead the powerful advocates of socialist realism. Tomasz Załuski[8], Agnieszka Rejniak-Majewska[9] and Luiza Nader, on the other hand, argue that the theory outlined in the present volume was inherently and sincerely rooted in Marxism.[10] Strzemiński's analysis was firmly grounded in political economy already in the 30s, when he would not have had to camouflage differing views. In Russia, he was immersed in discussions of the Marxist history of art and its role in social progress. His own ideas of organicity were most likely inspired by Alexandr Bogdanov[11]. Moreover we can trace his dynamic understanding of realism from his involvement with UNOVIS at the latest. After all, Malevich used the phrase in the title of his essay "From Cubism and Futurism to Suprematism: New Realism in Painting," published in 1915 in Saint Petersburg on the occasion of the *0.10* exhibition[12]. Therefore we should see the return to realism as the key category rather as a polemical tool than a smokescreen.

Strzemiński explains realism as the accord between the current state of social development, which affects visual consciousness. and the tools used to represent reality:

> The idealist aesthetic deploys a fixed notion of Realism that does not capture the changeable essence of how we see. It does not see Realism as having been formed through the process of the protracted cognitive work in our vision, or as the result of man's work to move toward a deeper and deeper knowledge of truth, but as

8 Tomasz Załuski, "Władysław Strzemiński po wojnie: modernizacja, marksizm, socrealizm," in *Socrealizmy i modernizacje*, eds. Aleksandra Sumorok and Tomasz Załuski (Łódź: ASP im. Władysława Strzemińskiego w Łodzi, 2017).

9 Agnieszka Rejniak-Majewska, "History of an Eye According to Strzemiński," in *Afterimages of Life. Władysław Strzemiński and Rights for Art,* ed. Jarosław Lubiak (Łódź: Muzeum Sztuki, 2012)

10 Luiza Nader, *Afekt Strzemińskiego „Teoria widzenia", rysunki wojenne, Pamięci przyjaciół-Żydów* (Łódź: Muzeum Sztuki and IBL PAN, 2018).

11 See Andrzej Turowski, *Budowniczowie świata. Z dziejów radykalnego modernizmu w sztuce polskiej,* (Kraków: Universitas, 2000), and Załuski, "Władysław Strzemiński."

12 Daniel Muzyczuk, "Developing a Narrative of Modern Art: On the History of a Certain Concept," in *The Avant-Garde Museum*, eds. Agnieszka Pindera and Jarosław Suchan (Łódź: Muzeum Sztuki, 2020).

> a given, that is binding for all times. One historical stage of Realism is taken for Realism's absolute... The changes in art that idealism explained away as purely arbitrary were, in reality, connected with the historical development of visual consciousness. This visual consciousness, different in each historical period, was an expression of the attainable limits of Realism in that particular historical age.[13]

Realism is always progressive and in constant conflict with formalism. It seeks the truth of artistic form, as opposed simply to the play of appearances. The emphasis on the latter leads to the usage of regressive formal solutions and has a specific social role. The conflict between realism and regressive formalism mirrors the conflict between progressive forces within society and the interest of the ruling class:

> Progress does not run in a straight line, through the gathering of experience and techniques, but through the change of one historical system into another, through the change of one form of exploitation to another. Each successive system, changing forms of exploitation, brings progress in relation to the preceding one—it is, however, limited by the necessity of maintaining the forms of its class rule. It conditions another, regressive function of each of these systems: exploiting the progress achieved and the objective truth discovered in order to suppress progress and falsify reality.[14]

Reproducing the worldview of the past instead of promoting new forms of seeing is an instrument of maintaining power. Strzemiński definitely saw socialist realism as an iteration of this phenomenon. He therefore made an attempt to reconcile Marxist theory with avant-garde art on the basis of the physiology of seeing and its role in the development of consciousness. Art in this system has a double role. On the one hand the progress of art is a symptom of larger social development. From this perspective it is passive. On the other hand, art affects the beholder, sometimes raising them to higher stages of visual consciousness. As the active agent it has a role in emancipating the viewer.

13 Władysław Strzemiński, *Theory of Seeing*, in the present volume, 33 – 34.

14 Ibid. 44.

As the eye accommodates to more progressive forms of seeing, the subject gains social consciousness. Strzemiński's theory constantly unfolds across two planes: the macro scale of phylogeny and the micro scale of the subject's ontogeny. The eye of the individual needs to gain consciousness of the previous stages of seeing to emancipate itself from the regressive constraints that are binding contemporary society. It is the subject of both biological development and history at the same time. There is an interesting aporia that opens through this act. Paweł Mościcki observes a certain impossibility in organizing a history of seeing: "Although the motor of peripheral vision which is responsible for the dynamic structure of the perception of an image recurs frequently in *Theory of Seeing*, it turns out that the impossibility of viewing history peripherally complicates, if not refutes, Strzemiński's argument and its philosophical inspirations."[15] Realism is a constantly fleeting point in an otherwise unpresentable process. It is a critical category that determines the contents of contemporaneity. Realist art hastens the replacement of formalism with new progressive forms, and thus influences the pace at which social structures are reformulated. Giorgio Agamben imagines being contemporaneous as seeing the darkness of the stars travelling so fast that their light will never reach us.[16] That might be the reason why Strzemiński tried so hard to record the minute imprints of light on the retina—the afterimages; the smallest unit of memory, which teach the eye to recognizing repetitions of form and shape. Even once the afterimages are gone, the knowledge persists.

Reading *Theory of Seeing* today, it is this aspect of realism that comes to the fore. In the age of a renaissance of the notion of real abstraction it offers a contemporary answer to the question of how art can become an emancipatory experience. After all art is both a symptom and an active actor of economic restructurizations. It also finds an unexpected resonance with the aesthetics of Jacques Rancière. Like the French philosopher, Strzemiński recognized that art operates in a space formed by the contradiction between the autonomy it asserts

15 Paweł Mościcki, "Being On Time Too Late. On Władysław Strzemiński's Encounters with History," in *Afterimages of Life*, 336.

16 See Giorgio Agamben, "What is the Contemporary," in *What Is an Apparatus? and Other Essays*, trans. David Kishik and Stefan Pedatella (Stanford, CA: Stanford University Press, 2009).

and the social fabric into which it is inextricably interwoven, playing an active role in emancipating its spectators. Art builds a community based on a distribution of sensibility and therefore art does not need to touch on political subjects to be political[17]. Post-Brechtian aesthetics sees realism as an opening up of form and technique to the non-identitarian character of social relations.[18] One finds a similar spirit articulated in the cinema of alter-realism that spans the work of filmmakers like Jean-Luc Godard, Harun Farocki, and Alexander Kluge. They all use realism as a method that simultaneously exposes and undermines the division of labor. Just as capitalism evolves and alters the form in which the relation between owners and workers appears, the notion of realism needs to be understood as dynamic, constantly readjusting to social totality. Strzemiński's unfinished book remains a visionary document for a progressive art that constantly invents new ways of emancipating its viewer.

The translation of *Theory of Seeing* was initiated by Jarosław Suchan, director of Muzeum Sztuki between 2006 and 2022, whose dedication to promoting the work of Strzemiński and Kobro helped revive international interest in Polish Constructivism. With this publication, we hereby contribute another vital element to this work.

2022—2025

17 See Jacques Rancière, *The Emancipated Spectator*, trans. Gregory Elliott, (London: Verso, 2009), 56.

18 See John Roberts' contribution to Octavian Esanu, ed., "Realism Today?," *ART-Margins* 7, no. 1 (February 2018): 58—82. Online at: https://research.gold.ac.uk/id/eprint/25992/1/Realism_Roundtable.pdf.

preface

Julian Przyboś

Władysław Strzemiński – the innovator

I first met Władysław Strzemiński in 1922 or 1923 at the editorial offices of Tadeusz Peiper's *Zwrotnica*, in Kraków. It was a time when young poets and painters were eagerly attuned to news of new tendencies in art and were straining their eyes and reaching out their hands to seize the visions glimmering in their minds as a result of countless artistic proclamations and manifestos. Strzemiński had come from Russia, where he had worked with Malevich, and the observations he published in *Zwrotnica* concerned Suprematism. It was a discovery for me — as, at that time, I only knew about what was happening in the West. I did not know that a new art had also been born in revolutionary Russia, from which we were cut off. Kasimir Malevich, a Pole, was its outstanding representative and theoretician there, and the young Strzemiński, his collaborator.

The "Suprematism" proclaimed by Malevich was a bearer of one of the ways of radically purifying traditional notions of art: it reduced painting to the simplest of elements; it revealed the most obvious fact — that the picture is a rectangular plane. As of the moment when Malevich drew a square inside an empty square, rather than painting, or, when he placed a white rectangle within a white field, the crisis of the old way of looking at the painterly canvas reached both its apogee and its turning point. By studying the interactions of these simplest elements, one could begin to construct a new seeing in visual art. Malevich, however, did not go beyond this purifying criticism:

he only went so far as to assemble straight-edged geometric figures inside the rectangle so as to achieve "dynamic tension" within the composition. In this way, he paved the way for Strzemiński's "Unism" and Mondrian's Neo-Plasticism. Despite his revolutionary radicalism, Malevich had not freed himself completely from an unproductive aestheticism: he regarded his two-dimensional compositions, as well as his compositions of geometric solids, as creations in their own right, incapable of having practical consequences. The ultimate objective was to be their aesthetic contemplation; Malevich's geometric solids were to have no consequences for spatial compositions; for architecture. The Suprematist's aesthetic contemplation may thus have had something of the character of the intellectual predilection that had led Plato to call the circle the most perfect of figures. It was precisely this quality that imprisoned Malevich in the limiting confines of combinations of geometric forms, unverifiable as to their effect on the spectator through possible practical applications: practical, as a new principle of the painterly construction, or practical as an inspiration for so-called applied art, conceived of in the broadest possible terms. Malevich's conception had only a negative, destructive bearing on the history of aesthetics.

Strzemiński was trained as an engineer. He saw the universe of forms and colours as comprehensively linked to man's activity as a whole. From the analytical and critical tendency in art, from studies intended to determine the parts that make up how an object is seen on a two-dimensional surface, he took only its striving — at first as unclear as that of Malevich — for a way of grasping in mathematical terms the laws that connect forms to one another. He did not stop at Malevich's experiments, which rather than leading to the organisation of the picture and space, had halted mid-way, nor at mathematically calculated compositions such as Mondrian's. He thought that the invention of forms and arrangement of colours that he perceived in painterly and sculptural compositions should enter man's everyday life by way of their reproduction in objects of everyday use.

He placed the highest demands on his art, unattainable to an average talent. He demanded that every painting should be an invention, that it should discover a principle of composition of colours and forms not known before. In essence, he demanded that every painting should mark the beginning of a new art movement, a new school.

In this consistent striving for an ever more exact, almost mathematically verifiable seeing, he arrived at the series of paintings that he called Unist. What was Unism? It was the absolute rejection of any illusion in the picture. The rectangle of the painted canvas did not evoke any association with anything existing; no form stood out or appeared detached, whether from the picture plane, from other forms, or from the boundaries of the picture. Were one to compare the paintings of abstract painters to Unist compositions, one would be struck by a glaring difference in the very principle of the understanding of the picture. Abstract compositions render form distinct; there is in them a drama of contrasts of forms and an expression of their suitability. There is nothing of this sort in the Unist painting. It is ruled by the perfect unity of forms with one another and with the rectangular canvas. In abstract painting, one can never achieve a complete break from allusion to objects, as there is no abstract form that does not remind one of some shape or other from the world of objects. An example: a circle can evoke endless associations: with the sun, a disc, a loaf of bread, a shield, a hat, etc. The Unist painting goes further: without evoking any associations with objects or any narrative — it is the extreme, the ultimate example of pure art. But how many pictures can one paint that would be alike though not the same? For his part, Strzemiński managed to paint around a dozen before he realized that he had reached the limit. The limit of the development of modern art, which led to the elimination from the picture of everything that was not simply painting, i.e. the arrangement of colours in perfect unity with the two-dimensional surface. He achieved "pure" painting, the absolute unity of colours and forms with the two-dimensional surface and with its boundaries.

Having reached the limit and enriched by the discipline he had acquired — such as had never been practised before — Strzemiński was able to return to the study of nature. The landscape series, produced after the Unist period, is united by such a concise, focussed, synthetic model of seeing, that the astonishing simplicity of the pictures is striking. Their impact might be compared to the amazement that sometimes overcomes us when looking at children's drawings. But the simplicity of Strzemiński's drawings is sophisticated; not a single line — not even the smallest fragment of a line — in these mature drawings, repeats the course of any other line in the drawing.

I have the drawing *Morze* [The Sea] (reproduced some time ago in *Odrodzenie*). The curves, with which he has depicted waves, appear to be the result of some superhumanly patient mathematical calculations, verifying the work of the eye and direct seeing — they create the impression of moving waves and a more direct impression of the sea than I have experienced when looking at any seascape. And yet, this drawing bears no trace of naturalist illusionism, and the untrained eye could take it as an abstract play of curved lines. Such compositions would not have been possible without Unism.

Like the Unist pictures, Strzemiński's later painting, which he called realist, also had no previous counterpart in modern Western painting. Whereas the search for the purely painterly in the West stopped short at "objective" painting (what we [in Poland] loosely call abstraction), taking as his point of departure an analysis of the elements of the flat picture, Strzemiński went beyond abstract forms. Rather than a composition based on the contrast of forms and colours, he created in the Unist picture such a unity of seeing these elements that traditional notions of composition, the play of forms and colours, become meaningless; the picture becomes such a synthetic projection of seeing that it is impossible to detect its components. To render an understanding of this way of seeing more accessible: imagine that from the window of an express train moving through a variety of ever-changing surroundings, your eye's retina catches glimpses of thousands of diverse landscape, and that later you wish to see them **all** in an instant, suddenly arrested in a single window frame. If you have an eye, which can combine images, overlay them, exchange colours and lines, shuffle them endlessly — you will eventually arrive at an image free of defined, individual lines and colours, not so much an image composed of all those seen previously, but one that is a sum, a verification, a reduction to **almost** a single colour, **almost** a single form. It is this **almost** that expresses Unist seeing: the most ascetic, simplest and, at the same time, the most encompassing and comprehensive. I repeat, therefore, that Strzemiński has gone beyond the limit of abstractionism that remains an obstacle in the development of modern Western painterly seeing.

Having moved on to "realism," after his Unist period, he also produced paintings unlike any contemporary representational paintings I am aware of in France. They are studies from nature, but one is tempted to say that they are so **unistically** purged of the arbitrariness of form and colour that, at least to the untrained eye, they produce the impression of non-objective painting, "abstraction." Surprisingly, though, these paintings and drawings have not lost a sense of the appearance of the concrete object, but rather convey the character of the represented model in an extraordinarily clear, singular, particular way. In the paintings and sketches made shortly before the war and during the [German] occupation, Strzemiński's people and landscapes are uncommonly forcibly expressive. These are abstract yet representational paintings, executed with the most general of synthetic lines and colour, and yet they give the objects a particular and unique expression. For instance, the drawings from the *Deportacje* [Deportations] series, depicting the tragedy of the Ghetto, or the *Ruiny* [Ruins] series. The artist knew how to imbue his human figures with shattering expression (without demarcating eyes, mouth, or features) with a single, wavy line defining a contour, seemingly similar in different drawings. Exhibited just after the war in Łódź, these drawings made a stronger impression on me — why should I not admit it? —than Picasso's *Guernica*.

Strzemiński — relentlessly inquisitive in his investigation of the components of visual art — was not what is called an aesthete; he was a man with a strong sense of the social, an artist who saw art and life as closely interconnected. At the time of his early theoretical activity in the *Blok* and *Praesens* groups, he proclaimed an art whose practical consequences embraced all areas of everyday life. Strzemiński proclaimed the idea that every work of art, painting or sculpture, should be an invention of form, having ultimately a practical purpose many years before Mondrian, who only declared in 1942 that in the future artistic sensibility would express itself in creating objects of everyday use, so that painting and sculpture would disappear. The formal invention known as the painting should not simply serve as a work to be looked at in a museum. Its social goal should be to enter into everyday life by being put to use in the production of everyday objects. The idea of integrating life through art was born in Poland.

Strzemiński devoted much of his time to putting the idea into practice. He lectured at the Printing School,[1] and he deserves recognition

1 The Szkoła Dokształcania Zawodowego dla Drukarzy no. 10 in Łodź.

as a reformer in the graphic design of books in Poland. The "*a.r.*" Library (artyści rewolucyjni [revolutionary artists])[2], from a group that included poets alongside artists, published a number of his books, developing the idea of a total, integral art, taking examples from architecture, sculpture, and graphic art. He developed this idea through particular examples in the book *The Composition of Space, Calculations of Space-Time Rhythm*, the communiqués of the "a.r." group, and, later, in the periodical *Forma* [Form]; for instance, in his architectural compositions, he used colour to define the rhythm of man's movement and repose; he designed a modern alphabet and shop signs, after the war, he published an innovative plan for urban development for Łódź, entitled "Functional Łódź" in the periodical *Myśl Współczesna* [Contemporary thought]. Sadly, Polish urban planners did not take up these ideas. When building the MDM,[3] they preferred to mindlessly copy poor foreign models. After the war, Strzemiński expanded the reach of his universalist ideas and creative practice to embrace industrial design and artistic propaganda. He endeavoured, honestly as always — and, as always, in accordance with the demands of the time — to offer a model of painting, which, losing nothing of modern painterly seeing, would fulfil a directly propagandist role,

2 The "a.r." Library — Biblioteka "a.r." — was an editorial project by the "a.r." group (short for artyści rewolucyjni [revolutionary artists] or awangarda rzeczywista [real avant-garde]) acting on the initiative of Władysław Strzemiński in the years 1929—1936, whose other members were Katarzyna Kobro, Henryk Stażewski, and two poets: Jan Brzękowski and Julian Przyboś. The Library intended to publish the most important theoretical texts of the European avant-garde, such as Albert Gleizes, Filippo Tommaso Marinetti, and Piet Mondrian. As a result of financial difficulties, the Library of "a.r." came to be comprised of just six volumes, of which no. 1 was Julian Przyboś's [collection of] poems, *Z ponad* [From above] (1930), whose cover and graphic design were by Strzemiński. No. 2 was Katarzyna Kobro and Władysław Strzemiński's *Kompozycja przestrzeni. Obliczenia rytmu czasoprzestrzennego* [The composition of space. Calculating space-time rhythm] (1931). No. 6 was Strzemiński's *Druk funkcjonalny* [Functional print] (1935).

3 Marshal Street Residential Quarter (Marszałkowska Dzielnica Mieszkaniowa, MDM) — a large socialist-realist residential complex in central Warsaw, developed according to a collective urban and architectural plan, constructed in 1950—52 in turn under architects Józef Sigalin and Stanisław Jankowski; listed by the National Heritage Board in 2015.

encouraging [viewers] to [participate] in particular works related to building socialism. *Żeńcy* [The Reapers] is one of the proclamation-paintings, social idea-paintings with which I am familiar. He based the composition of figures on an association of forms that intensify the painting's propagandist expression: the sun is also a four-leaf clover, the head of a peasant woman makes allusion to a potato, while the grains of wheat are also loaves of bread, etc. Yet the painting has nothing grotesque in the manner of Arcimboldo, since all these formal allusions are not mechanical additions of one object to another but are a fact of seeing, a visual phenomenon. Strzemiński designed interiors in this period and produced the polychrome relief *Colonial Exploitation* for the "Egzotyczna" café in Łódź. The relief was destroyed by his opponents.

"Theory of Seeing" is a collection of lectures in art history. As we know, Strzemiński was not given a Chair in Painting. Small-minded people were afraid of this man's powerful personality, and they tried to push him to the margins of the Łódź School. The subject that he was asked to teach [art history] was one that is somewhat marginal in academies of art around the world — something of a hobby, taught by aesthetes. Strzemiński was able to breathe new meaning into this most academic of subjects and to revolutionise its teaching. Instead of biographies of artists, interlaced with descriptions of their paintings, his students analysed their painterly seeing. To test whether his students had managed to discern the fundamental components of a period style, he assigned them appropriate compositions. He did not treat this as a means of teaching painting but as a practical test of the student's understanding.

He often told his students that these lessons were no longer lessons in painting, that all this knowledge was no longer useful to an artist.

Strzemiński's "Theory of Seeing" is not a painting textbook; it does not teach the reader how to become a painter. The theory teaches an understanding of the evolution of man's visual consciousness and of the development of modes of representing what is seen that are associated with this evolution. One may be able to understand in theoretical terms the seeing of, say, Matisse, but it is more difficult to grasp Matisse's visual consciousness (and this is something more than "sensitivity" to colour and form). "Theory of Seeing" does not teach how to paint, but it shows how artists used to see and paint. How to paint now is not something that can be taught. And — unlike those professors who teach their personal manner — Strzemiński never did this. Because it is where copying and repeating the old way of seeing end that art begins.

Along with this, another fundamental principle of Strzemiński's theory is his assertion that progress in seeing is achieved through the study of nature; the genuine painter paints only what he sees (and not what he "feels"). So-called "thoughts" in painting are meaningless if the painter fails to see new visual aspects of reality. Strzemiński proclaims realism, but a realism in constant development, a realism different in every period. Cubism, examined in historical perspective, is the realism of its time, whereas Impressionist painters, painting in the same period, must already be regarded as epigones, hence, non-realists.

While teaching in the period from the first years after the Liberation to 1950 Strzemiński paints several oil paintings that are the crowning achievement of his art, an achievement exceeding all his previous painting in so far as their exploratory novelty is concerned. These paintings realise the ultimate unity of seeing that he strove for in the long years of his investigations and discoveries, in a way that is different from those of his Unist period or the post-Unist landscapes. He aimed to embrace all aspects of what is seen in his seeing. In his post-Unist gouaches, watercolours, and drawings, Strzemiński turned to the study of nature. He achieved this unity in his last oil paintings, not by uniting a characteristic expression of the represented object with its abstract generalization, but in a strikingly different way. He reached the very source of colour and light. Like Van Gogh in his last, insane period, Strzemiński painted the sun. But while Van Gogh showed it on the canvas — naively — as a whirling yellow sphere, Strzemiński made the painter's crazy dream rational. He painted not the **image** of the Sun but its **afterimage**, showing the colour inside the eye after looking at the Sun. The Sun really burns, captured forever by man's eye, in the two paintings produced when he was Professor at the Łódź school, that I know. These paintings are like protuberances[4]

4 Protuberances — a term taken from astronomy, describing the phenomenon of the sun's activity, its bright structure — a cloud of hot, rarefied gas, visible above the disk of the Sun; here: reference to the solar painting compositions, also called *Afterimages*, dating from Władysław Strzemiński's final period.

of colours, like living, madly rushing, explosions of light, colours, and shapes, like an endless race of afterimages. There is nothing like it in Polish painting or in contemporary painting around the world. This was the creative peak of Strzemiński's art. The peak, soon followed by the fall. The fall, caused by those blind to art, who came to power in cultural policy.

Artist-innovator and social activist, always sensitive to the needs of the time, he was accused of "formalism." Dismissed from his school, he was condemned to poverty. He was unable to finish "Theory of Seeing." In 1951, exhausted by starvation, he collapsed in the street. He was diagnosed in hospital with rapidly developing tuberculosis and died in December 1952.

It is our duty to show those of his works that escaped destruction. To spread and develop his creative thinking, seminal for original modern art in Poland.

1957

introduction

seeing

Our seeing has not been given to us ready-made and unchanging. Our eye developed from less perfect forms to what we have now as a result of lengthy biological evolution.

But seeing is not just the passive reception of visual sensations. We analyse the received sensations, confront them with corresponding fragments of reality, make sense of the emergent interrelations and causes: what sort of sensations they are and what they say about the objectively existing world. In addition to the passive, physiological reception of visual sensations, there is the active, cognitive work of our intellect. There is the mutual influence of thinking on seeing and seeing on thinking. Thinking poses questions for seeing to answer. Seeing accumulates a stock of observational material, which is validated and universalised in the process of thinking. Thanks to the constant corrections of thinking in relation to seeing, we are able to make ever better use of received visual sensations. We do not let them slip away, we do not let them pass fruitlessly by, because we recognise what each of them means and to which fragment of reality it corresponds.

There are thus two evolutions in the domain of seeing. One is the evolution of our visual apparatus, the development of the eye, which was at one time – in the simplest forms of life – merely a collection of skin cells more sensitive to light than other skin cells. Passing through a range of models and varieties, it became what it is now – the normal human eye. We know that, in a relatively recent phase of the evolution of the species, the eye could not see colours, that the eye of a mouse, for instance, sees a blurred image of objects, the better to discern movement in their background. There is, thus, biological evolution: the development of seeing through the development of the eye.

Alongside this first process, there is another: the development of skills that make use of seeing. Deduction, on the basis of visual sensations, becomes increasingly precise. Thinking and seeing develop through mutual influence. Their development does not take place in isolation from real, formative living conditions but on a social basis, depending on the needs of the labour process. That is why, by setting new tasks, each successive social system leads to the development of new skills in the use of visual sensations. This is why the second process, unlike the first, biological, one, is historically determined. Just as language developed in relation to successive social systems, so, too, the faculty of seeing, visual consciousness, cannot be formed outside its relation to history, the specific development of the forces of production and the class struggle. In this way, the process of the development of visual consciousness mirrors the process of historical development.

If man sees more than an eagle – even though his eyesight is less sharp – it is because man has a wider range of interests and in effect carries out a wider and more precise analysis of his visual sensations, and because he does not pass over those that would not interest an eagle. That is why man **sees** less, but his seeing provides him with more **information** about the world than the dog's far superior sense of smell, because the correcting function of the human mind takes into account the components of sensations that would be passed over by the dog (e.g. the scent of flowers or chemicals).

Taking as a basis the historical development of visual consciousness, we cannot accept, as idealists do, the existence of a single, timeless, ahistorical image of reality, based on the same visual principles, by virtue of which the eye of every normal man sees reality. It is not the biological reception of visual sensations that determines how the real world is seen, but the co-operation of seeing and thinking – the historically determined development of visual consciousness. It is not the abstract void of "normal" seeing but the ever-developing historical, concrete fact of visual consciousness.

Seeing is not only the passive, biological act of receiving visual sensations, it is not a purely mechanical reflection of the world, forever the same and unchangeable — like a mirror image. We acquire knowledge of the world not by merely seeing it but by thinking and recognizing what each visual sensation is telling us and which fragment of our knowledge of the world our eye is delivering — in a word, by analysing visual sensations, generalizing and repeatedly testing them. The scope of our seeing is determined not by some "natural," "normal" seeing, but by the mutually related and interdependent processes occurring between biological seeing and our thinking. It is in this way that visual consciousness arises, which determines the number of components of the world our eye has perceived.

It is not what the eye catches mechanically that matters in the process of seeing, but the **consciousness** man has of his seeing. Increased visual consciousness is thus a reflection of the process of human development.

So-called **professional visual competence** is simply one form of visual consciousness. The eye of the experienced textile worker will notice ten times more faults in the fabric than the equally (biologically) able eye of someone of another trade. But that same eye of the textile worker will see nothing when faced with a cornfield — will not be able to say anything about the humidity of the earth, the ripeness of the corn, the transpiration of the air, or the quality of the soil. The mechanical visual sensations are in all three cases the same, but the scope of seeing is different. This is because, guided by thinking, eyesight has been attuned to the reception of sensations that it passes over in other cases. The range and quantity of what is seen is determined by visual consciousness as formed by real conditions of existence. Not some "normal," arithmetically average, abstracted seeing, but seeing shaped by existence and determined by the sociohistorical structure.

realism – the image of reality

Idealist aesthetics has recourse to concepts of unchanging, "eternal" nature, and of a preconceived, unchanging, ahistorical man with a preconceived, unchangeable, "eternal" way of seeing nature. It occasionally lays aside this "eternal" seeing in favour of pragmatic "normal'" average seeing. In both cases, it insists on the unchanging, constant, ahistorical seeing of unchanging nature. Taking into consideration only the apparatus of seeing and not taking account the directing and organizing role of thinking and experience, it concludes that we see a constant, unchanging, invariable image of the world from which we receive an unchanging fixed quantity of constant visual sensations.

It may be the case that seeing has not changed for a long time, that the mechanism of the eye's functioning remains the same as it did several thousand years ago. But what matters to us is not what the eye grasps mechanically, but the consciousness man has of his seeing. He has only really seen what he is aware of having seen. The rest remains unrecognized beyond his consciousness and therefore goes unnoticed. Experience shows that we notice only the phenomena in nature upon which we focus our attention. It is as though our thinking poses in advance the questions to which our eyesight is to provide answers. The range of observation to which, by seeing, we are to provide an answer either confirming our previous assumptions or contradicting them, is marked out. The labour of thinking, in co-operation with the direct activity of seeing, is decisive for the wealth and diversity of our observations.

That is why the image of nature is not one and the same always and for everyone. Its limits are decided by the historically determined development of visual consciousness. Idealist aesthetics formulated the object, reality, sensations solely in terms of the object, and not as a human activity and practice – not subjectively. That is why it referred to the image of the world (constant and unchanging) rather than to human cognitive activity, intent upon an ever more complete understanding of this image. Nature was referred to as to something given once and for all and absolutely unchanging, whereas there was no discussion of the human activity of seeing and the socio-historical process of the development of visual consciousness and of coming to understand nature. Only when we consider seeing in its developmental dynamics, in its dialectical unity with thinking – can we understand that the image of the world is subject to change and development and is comprised in our visual consciousness.

The image of nature "as it is," arises only from the conscious components of seeing. The unconscious components go unnoticed, are treated as an obstacle, an imperfection in seeing, a distortion of the real world and of real, not illusory, objective nature. Not subjected to the thinking process – they have failed to disclose the truth about reality (inherent to them) and were therefore rejected as marginal.

Thus, we distinguish between **seeing** (in the biological sense) and the **consciousness** of seeing. In so far as the former is dependent on slow biological evolution and presumably remains unchanged for long periods of time, the latter develops over the course of history. Man's ability to make use of his seeing develops and the quantity of consciously seen visual phenomena increases. The image of the world seen by man changes and develops. The process of the development of visual consciousness is a **historical** process, **historically conditioned** by the demands of socially determined processes of labour in different successive historical systems. Thus, the image of the world that we see through our real visual consciousness is not unchangeable, not the only "true" reality, given once and for all, in some abstract void outside history, but a changeable image, dependent on historical development, on social systems arising in its course and, ultimately, on the class struggle shaping history. Visual consciousness develops in active periods of history and remains unchanged in periods of stabilization or even regresses with the regression of historical and cultural structures. The expanding base of visual consciousness constitutes the essential foundation for the development and transformation of our knowledge about the world. This is how we see the world – not biologically, but historically. We see realistically – with our real, conscious eyes.

The idealist aesthetic deploys one, fixed notion of realism, one that does not capture the changeable essence of our seeing. It does not see realism as having been formed through the process of human seeing's protracted cognitive work, or as the result of man's work moving towards an increasingly deeper knowledge of truth, but as a given, once and for all, as binding for all times. One historical stage of realism is, in this case, taken for realism's absolute.

Conceiving of realism in relation to human activity, seeing it as being the outcome of a development in visual consciousness, we must, in practice, acknowledge its infinite possibility of development. Every genuine, conscious visual sensation contributes a new element of knowledge about the world and enriches the domain of realism that has hitherto existed. Thus, in speaking of the historical process of the development of realism, we should, in each concrete instance, define the visual sensations on the basis of which it emerged and the scope of the visual consciousness that shaped it.

Realism is not a Platonic metaphysical absolute but the historically evolving process of the development of the human cognitive faculty.

means of expression and form

The idealist aesthetic is incapable of explaining the mechanism for change in visual art. It deploys notions of an unchanging, constant nature (expressed exclusively in the form of the object) and of a single, pre-determined, unchanging realism, and so it cannot explain why visual art manifests itself in different forms in different periods. If the model of seeing nature is always unchanging — and as a result the same identical model of realism with the same visual essence is binding in all ages — then why did the Greeks paint differently from, say, people who painted in the nineteenth century? The result was a purely arbitrary, a-causal account of the changes taking place. The idealist aesthetic could explain neither the necessity of the changes nor their sequence. For the most part, the following model has been accepted: there is nature, and there is a "pure" realism, most precisely and most completely reflecting nature. This realism is the norm, binding all people and all times. But the artist (for unknown reasons) does not apply this realism. It is not known why he moves away from the true and complete realism, distorts and deforms nature. The idealist aesthetic does not explain and is unable to explain why the artist moves away from a "full and true image of nature" and why he "deforms" it. The idealist aesthetic mainly invokes "an inner life" and "the spirit" of the artist• or mysterious "intentions," also apparently originating from this "spirit."•• At times, it just reduces the problem to purely technical changes in interpretation.••• In short, changes come from the artist's "spirit," and their inevitability is neither explained nor justified. Neither is the need to shift away from realism and nature, nor the point of this shift, of these changes and deformations. From such a perspective, we find in the entire history of art only a small number of points at which realism existed. Everything else is

• "...equivalent not in nature, but in the artist's 'inner being'." [see A. Breton, "Le surréalisme et la peinture," *La Révolution surréaliste* (Paris), no. 4 (1925) — IL]

a departure from nature, deformation, interpretation, and so on. The "spirit" of deformation reigns over the "matter" of realism. We can neither foresee nor understand the whims of this spirit.

This inability of idealist aesthetics to explain changes in art is the result of its ahistorical position. Only when we capture the changes in art as historical changes, as successive phases of historical development – and connect them with the historical change of social conditions as a whole – will we find the causal leads that idealism was unable to deliver. The error of idealism was that it took realism, the seeing of reality, to be static, detached from history – and not as the process of an ever fuller and more precise cognizance of the world, a process developing over the course of history. Its realism was uniformly defined and identical in all times. Existence did not determine consciousness, nor did the purport of realism differ in every age. The variability of epochs, the variability of their historical purport, had no influence on the character of realism that at once expressed and was formed by its age. Realism has its historically determined limits in every age, as a result of the material basis of existence – its achievable limits of cognition. Idealism did not take this into consideration. Its realism was unchanging and existed outside time.

Idealism thus presented as dissent from the only "true" realism whatever was changeable and conditioned by the cognitive limits of the age in realism, failing to understand that its "true" realism was in fact equally relative and determined by the cognitive limits of its own age.

If the painting of the Greeks was different from nineteenth-century painting, this was not because the Greeks "departed" from realism and deformed it, but because there were different forces of production and a different socio-historical system in the age of the Greeks, and so the cognitive limits determined by the age were different. These limits determined the character and model of realism of the age.

The changes in art that idealism explained away as purely arbitrary were, in reality, connected with the historical development of **visual**

•• ...examining the "intentions" of the artist will allow us..." [source of citation unknown – IL].

••• "...'the means of presenting' the invariable realities of nature." [source of citation unknown – IL]

consciousness in that period. This visual consciousness, different in each historical period, was an expression of the achievable limits of realism in that particular historical age.

The purely visual character of the changes taking place in visual art can be explained only by analysing changes in the process of seeing itself. Change in visual art has its material basis in the activity of the brain and optical nerves. Change and the development of formal transformations derive from the physiological process of seeing and the work of the brain associated with it. **Visual consciousness** is born of the relationship between seeing and thinking.

Any attempt to exclude the material basis of the visual function and to connect existence with formal changes directly ultimately leads to idealism. The objective world is activated through the optical organs and stimulates their activity. The conditions of existence influence formal changes in visual art indirectly, rather than directly, by acting on the brain and on the process of seeing.

If we assume a particular model of visual consciousness – then we will have a particular model of visual art. We choose an appropriate set of means of expression to express our visual consciousness. Every model of visual consciousness demands its own corresponding means of expression. Every visual phenomenon can only be expressed through particular formal components capable of this expression. Every new set of means of expression is also a new set of formal means. The development of formal means is thus the result of a change in the visual base, a change in the model of seeing that defines the relationship between man and nature. New means of expression are thus determined by the number of conscious components of seeing that express them and call into being new formal entities. Formal transformations in art do not arise as a result of voluntary impulses, as idealists claim, but as a result of developments in observation, of transformations in visual consciousness.

The historical changeability of forms in visual art reflects the historical development of visual consciousness.*

But visual consciousness does not develop automatically in and of itself. Its development reflects transformations in the socio-historical base. Each period of history poses new challenges for society, compelling it to take stock of new subject matter, born of the experiential essence of the given age. To see the new essence of the new subject matter one has to change one's mode of observation. To perceive in old subject matter a new historical context, one has to **see** the genuinely new components of seeing it contains. Attempts to define evolution by way of a direct influence of social conditions on formal changes that ignores their material optical basis lead to the conclusion that the psyche is independent of the brain and the eye, hence – to idealism.

- There are, however, particular cases to which this does not apply. For it may happen that a painter with a belated, underdeveloped model of visual awareness deploys a means of expression that comes from newer models of seeing. The work of art can always be analysed in order to define the nature of the visual consciousness from which it derives, to determine the limits of its realism and to define the means of expression corresponding to its actual model of seeing. This will confirm that the borrowed means of expression, which had, for other painters, expressed the reality of what they observed, does not express any truth in this particular case. Instead of being the means of expression, these are only formal means, used in a formalist way.

The problem of formalism should be treated in connection with history, dialectically. Instead of a clear-cut idealist definition of realism as something given once and for all and recognized by a "healthy" subjective instinct – and formalism as everything else – these phenomena should be considered in the process of their historical development.

Having acquired his visual consciousness through the long-term observation of the shape of clouds, of the colour of the sky, of the air and so on, that form part of his work, the peasant is able to predict the weather. And so the peasant's visual consciousness is none other than an extrapolation from the age-old labours of his class. The same visual sensations will say nothing to a man with a different model of visual consciousness, as he will be unable to capture the of this real truth.

There is one criterion. That which corresponds to visual consciousness is realism. The means that express the truth of visual consciousness are realist means of expression, though, subjectively, they may not be so for everyone. E.g. for people with a lower degree of visual consciousness, its more advanced models will appear to be unreal.

In order to avoid this typically idealist subjectivisation of realism (and formalism) an analysis of the work of art should be carried out to determine the model and the range of visual consciousness upon which it is based, to define what actual, real components of observation have contributed to it. Then we will be in a position to determine which components of form express this actual, real observation, and which have been used without any grounds.

contour seeing (seeing in the Stone Age)

external contour

To reveal the history of the development of visual consciousness, especially in its early stages, we must turn to the art of primitive peoples, on the one hand, and to children's art, on the other. We will see that there is a considerable convergence between the way children see and that of primitive peoples, and that visual consciousness, that is to say the range of phenomena that man perceives and becomes conscious of, develops gradually. This process is accelerated in the child as a consequence of environmental pressure.

The earliest model of visual consciousness is seeing outlines. At this level, man is only aware that every object has its external boundary – and expresses the object by a single contour line. Of the many characteristic features of the object, he is only aware of the boundary line, outlining its circumference.

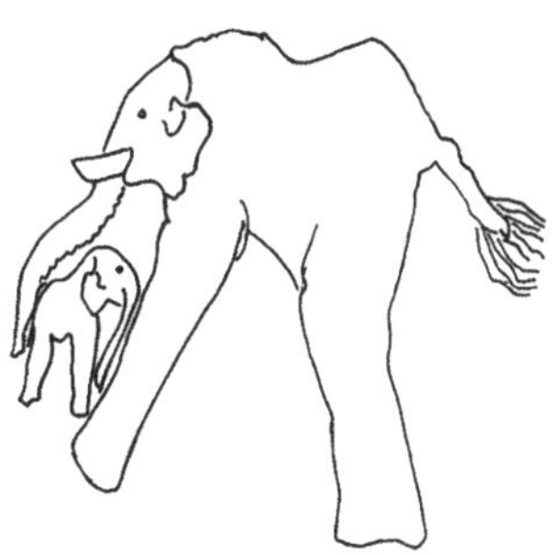

1
Engraving on a rock, Northern Africa, early Neolithic age

2
Child's drawing

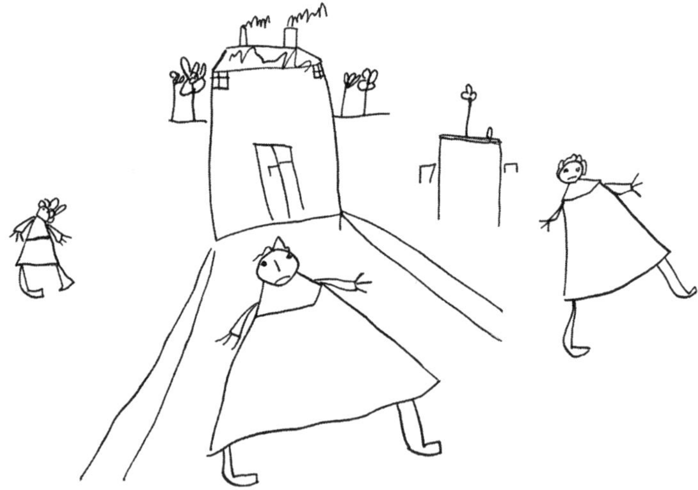

This exclusive consciousness of only one component — contour — the reduction of nature as a whole to solely this alone — is manifested in the fact that the contour is, as it were, also called upon to express other elements of form — not only those that are directly contoured. For example, in order to express that a whole object is yellow, its contour line is drawn in yellow, instead of filling the whole object with yellow colour, which would seem natural to us today. The colour of the contour line was to indicate the colour of the whole object. We find this model of seeing principally in the Palaeolithic era. Such is also the starting point for a child's drawing. No wonder, then, that when an individual at this stage of visual consciousness finds in his hands a photograph, he will see nothing more than dissolving patches of light and shade, as he will be searching for a clearly delimiting contour line, corresponding to his visual consciousness. Experiences of this kind are recounted by explorers of primitive countries, even those in which seeing had entered a superior, more advanced stage. This model of contour seeing is related to the historical formation of the primitive community. It is here that we must look for an explanation of how and to what degree it reflected the existence of its social base. The subject matter of this art was connected with the struggle for survival. The drawings of animals have a specific character. They are animals that one fights, defeats, and consumes. Their every potential, lurking move threatens death and must be understood.

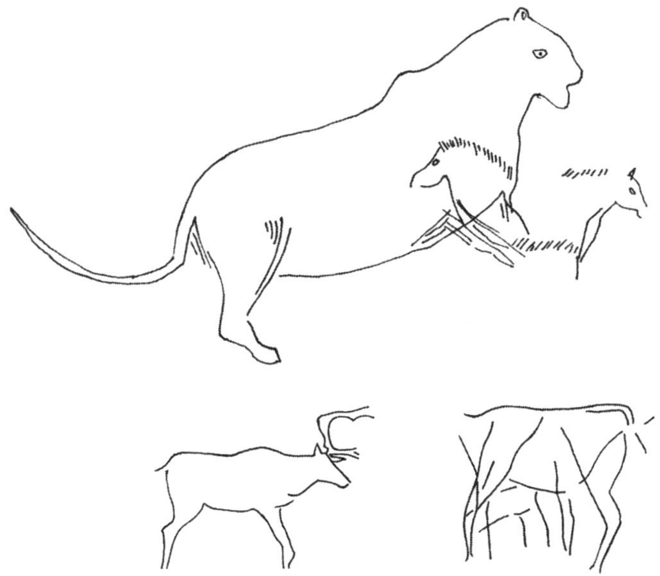

3
Engraving on a rock, Font-de-Gaume, Palaeolithic

4
Engravings on a rock, Norway, Neolithic

One has to understand the lactation of a reindeer, the rhythm and character of its movements, since the ability to supply food depends on it.

Of the multitude of various visual sensations, only those that detect danger and the presence of food are valuable and socially beneficial — those that directly assist in the struggle for survival. Seeing, used as a tool in the struggle for survival, rejects all unnecessary, complicating visual sensations, confining itself to those that allow one to tell whether an object exists or not — to the contour delimiting the object.

The contour, resulting from socially determined needs, is the simplest and, chronologically, the earliest means of expression of human visual consciousness. The realism of contour seeing is the first and the simplest model of realism.

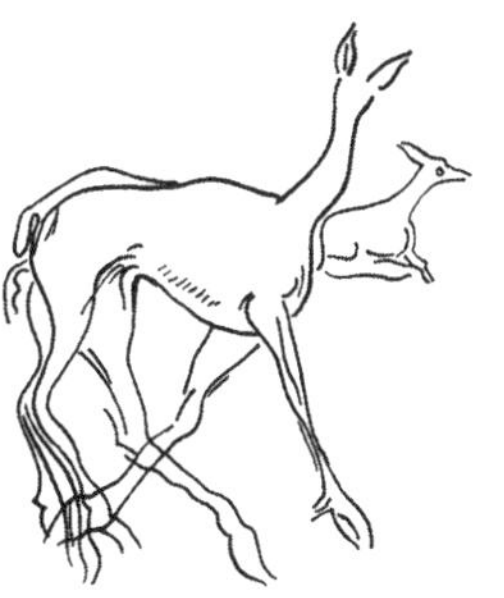

5
Engraving on a block of ston, Les Eyzies, Palaeolithic

contour within contour

In time, with the development of observation, contour drawing was no longer adequate. The contour line, delimiting the circumference, could not express new, conscious realisations that not only the circumference exists, the external boundary of the object, but that there is also something happening inside the circumference.

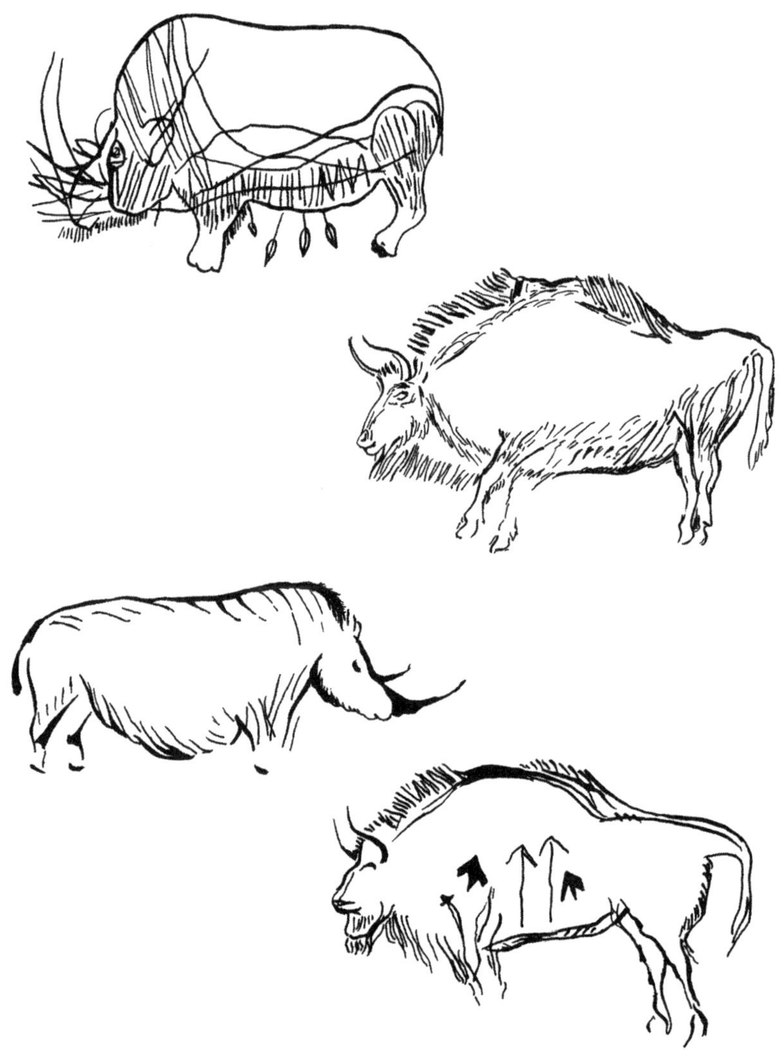

6
Engraving on stone, Le Colombier, Palaeolithic

7
Cave painting, Niaux, Palaeolithic

8
Cave painting, Font-de-Gaume, Palaeolithic

9
Cave painting, Niaux, Palaeolithic

The second stage of contour seeing marks a further evolution. The contour is filled with a line drawing. It becomes a drawing that describes not only the boundary of the object but also the object as a whole, using the means of linear contour seeing. This is undoubtedly a development of contour seeing – within the same category of seeing.

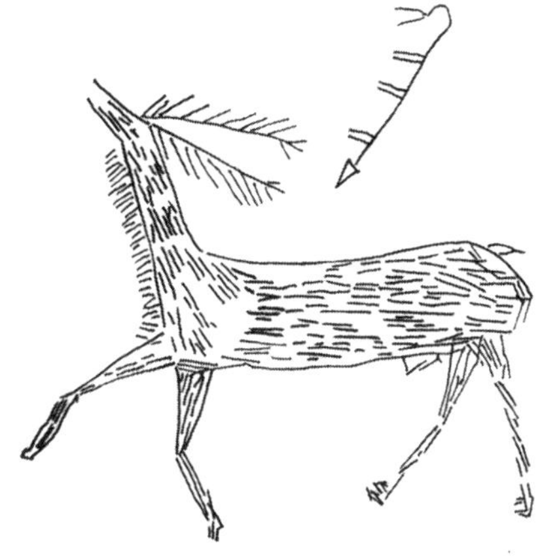

10
Painting on a buffalo-hide cloak, Mandan tribe, North American Indians arts

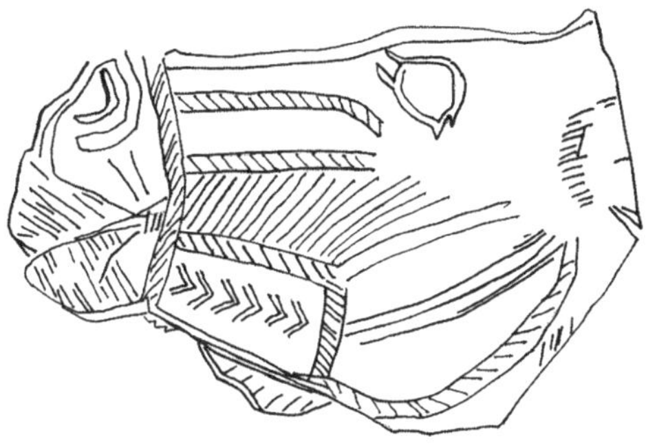

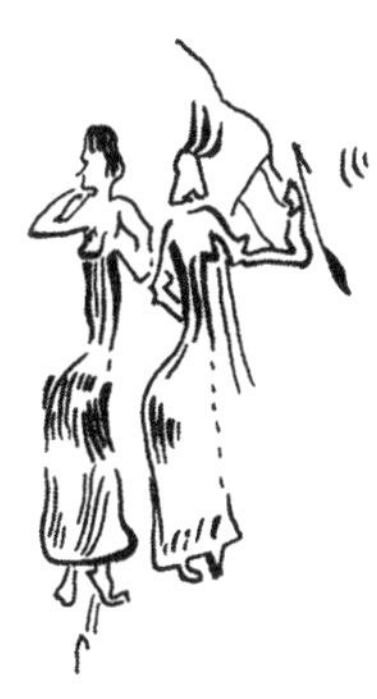

11
Engraved bone, Saint-Michel d'Arudy, late Palaeolithic

12
Rock painting, Alpera, late Palaeolithic

This new model of visual consciousness develops as a result of the accumulated observations still within the primitive community system but is only fully developed in Heliolithic cultures, based on agriculture and animal herding. It was only then that there arose conditions that made a longer, calmer, more detailed mode of observation possible (ill. 10). The contour from the preceding period, in which the object was defined by a sensitive and changeable line, could no longer be the bearer of the load within it. A complex line drawing that fills the contour of the object requires simplification and a certain schematisation of the external contour. Otherwise, it produces an illegible, tangled whole. The development of observation inside the contour requires a reduction in the external contour, its improved legibility.

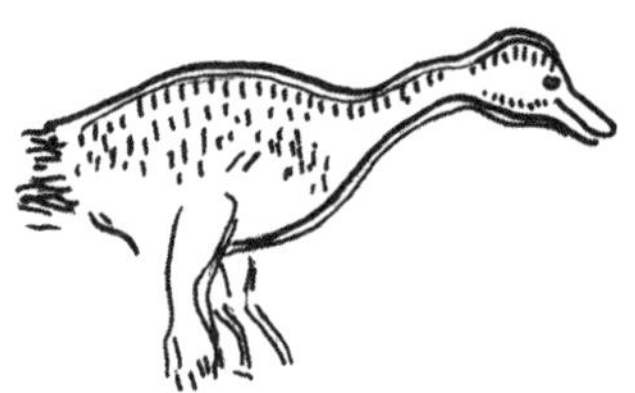

13
Engraved bone, Gourdan, late Palaeolithic

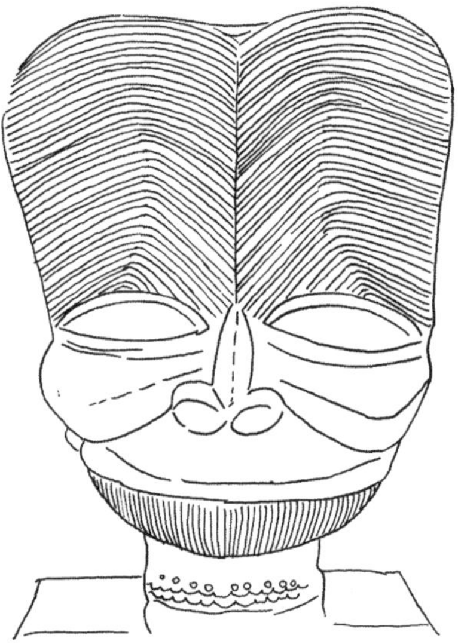

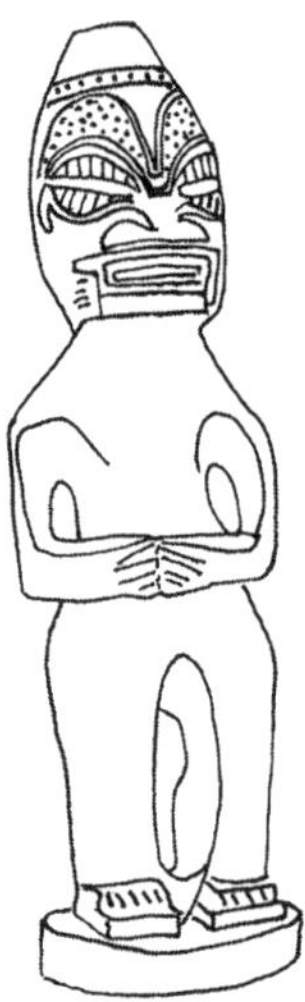

14
Mask, Nigeria

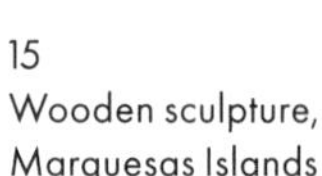

15
Wooden sculpture, Marquesas Islands

In place of the concrete drawing of the preceding period, there appears a schematic and geometricized drawing that is easy to reproduce. By repeating the same figure many times, we produce an ornament. A schematic representation replaces that of a living, individual man or animal. The living creature is rendered devoid of its individuality and becomes merely an ornamental fragment. The ability to transmit abstract concepts and general notions replaces the concrete and the pictorial in drawing. The schematic drawing reflects the thinking process that creates general concepts. The result is the emergence of ornamentation.

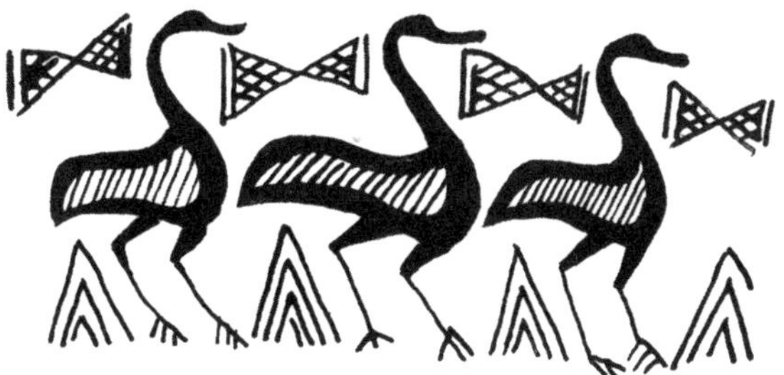

16
From a vase, Greece, ninth–eighth c. BCE

Art historians have generally noted this sequence (geometric drawing following realist drawing) without being able to explain its causes. It was usually explained that "they tired of it." That is why geometric art and abstract art followed realist art, and, then again, in turn, ceded to realist art. And so on and so forth. This is how the "eternal" schema emerged that is so beloved of idealists and so devoid of any perspective as to progressive cultural development: the schema of the "futility" of all endeavours. Analysing this problem more concretely than do art historians, we will understand that the "realism" of the Palaeolithic era is not some absolute, full, timeless realism, but one that is severely limited in its observation by the concrete, historical realism of contour seeing, and that this realism extends no further than the contour line itself, that all this realism is simply absent inside the contour line (precisely where the whole object is to be found).

We will also understand that the next period is not some general departure from "realism" to "geometricism," but arose on the basis of a closer scrutiny, arose through widening the scope of this same realism. Seeing more and observing more, the artist of the Heliolithic age had to confine his observations (within the contour) to a more defined, decisive, geometric contour line in order to avoid the chaos and complexity of entangled lines.

The difference between the "realism" of the Palaeolithic era and the "geometricism" of the Heliolithic era should not be presented in terms of a simple negation. The difference is not an opposition but a dialectical negation, which is to say that it is one in which the development of the same evolutionary tendency leads to its negation. It is thus a contradiction of opposing similarities, a contradiction within unity. A quantitative development in observation leads from the contour drawing to the drawing of contour within contour. It is, however, increased observation that causes the qualitative change of the means of expressions, their transition to a geometric stage, and therefore – the negation of the previous tendency in the development.

Visual consciousness at any stage of its development or in any of its parts is not simply a gift of nature. Visual consciousness is the product of humanity. Humanity formed its visual consciousness in the process of labour in specific conditions – and it is transformed with the arrival of new forms of social conditions, in accordance with new thinking in these conditions. All varieties of visual consciousness are artificial; all are acquired by humanity, and their character is artificial regardless of the fact that they are passed on, as a heritage, from one generation to the next. The sources of visual awareness lie not in external conditions of nature, not in ourselves, but in the community, in its material foundation, in technology and social structure.

From the time of the Heliolithic cultures, the development of humanity begins to proceed differently than before. Every period has its social-historical system, constructed antagonistically – engaged in the class struggle. Humanity enters the era of class oppression and exploitation. Progress does not run in a straight line, through the gathering of experience and techniques, but through the change of one historical system into another, through the change of one form of exploitation to another. Each successive system, changing forms of exploitation, brings progress in relation to the preceding one – it is, however, limited by the necessity of maintaining the forms of its class rule. It conditions another, regressive function of each of these systems: exploiting the progress achieved and the objective truth discovered in order to suppress progress and falsify reality.

This dual character of each successive culture cannot be framed in terms of a simple opposition. Reactionary and progressive elements are inextricably linked. It is a dialectical unity of opposites. That is why art in these cultures, reflecting their antagonistic structure, is itself constructed antagonistically. When it achieves new, objectively true components of visual consciousness, it deploys these to produce a false image of the world that serves to prop up the class structure. Widening the actual scope of seeing, it simultaneously creates a vision of the world that affirms the logical basis for the existence of the given ruling class.

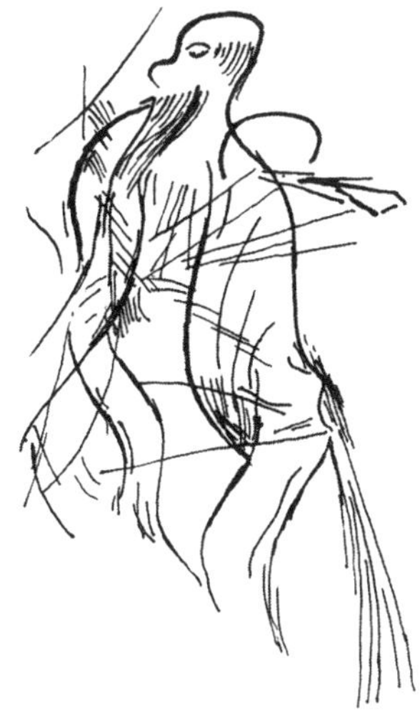

17
Engraved bone,
Lourdes,
late Palaeolithic age

Naturally, Palaeolithic art has no such antagonistic character. Its visual consciousness is oriented towards the direct seeing of reality within limits defined by its historically determined possibilities. However, under each subsequent historical system we can detect the objective progress of visual consciousness and a picture of the world that is untrue, falsified in the interests of the class whom this seeing serves. The opposition between realism and formalism persists in all antagonistic systems, reflecting their antagonistic, contradictory structure. However, just as the classes representing each of these systems change, realism and the formalism that opposes it, also change. The realism of one period is not the realism of another – with time, each is historically superseded in favour of a more complete realism. However, formalism always remains formalism, giving a false image of the world, mendacious in class terms. The difference between particular formalisms lies in the fact that the interests of the classes calling them into being are different, and so each class deforms reality differently, in its own interest. This is why each of these formalisms is different, historically conditioned, and grounded in class. It is the decisive conflict of the age that defines how the deformation of the image of reality develops. The decisive conflict of the age defines the character of its formalism. The objective progress of the Heliolithic age is its visual consciousness, expressed by contour within contour.

Visual consciousness went beyond the representation of the circumference alone to the whole surface of the object, representing it through the coursing of lines across the surface of the solid. This objective development in visual consciousness was taken up and exploited, having as its aim a tendentious explanation of the world in line with exploitative interests that appear in the first antagonistic historical system.

The first exploitative class emerged when certain duties were taken over by experienced and wise people, organisers of labour (planting time etc.): shamans, sorcerers, magicians, pagan priests. This first social division finds its artistic expression in the opposition between ornamental, repeated rows of human figures, devoid of individuality, and the shaman's sinister, frightening mask, a totem sign, or an image of god. This mask is always alone, singular — never repeated in recurring rows.

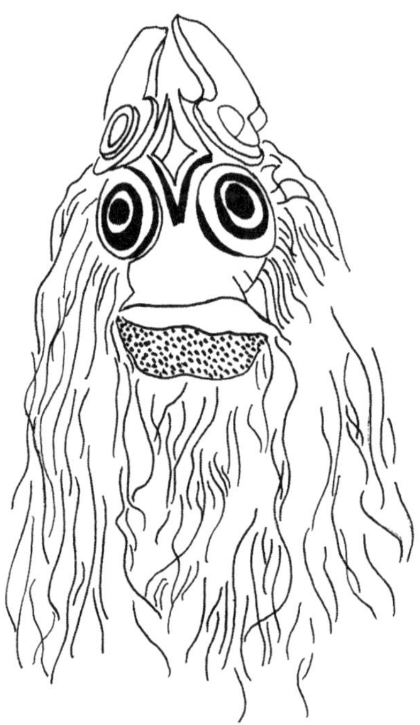

18
Dancing mask,
Cameroon

This is how we are given the opposition between the one (the sinister shaman) — and the many (the exploited human masses). In order to express both of these, it was necessary to reach for the means of expression embodied in a new, superior visual consciousness. This new, superior visual consciousness embodied possibilities capable of expressing a new antagonistic system being formed. The greater scope of seeing, seeing the whole surface of the object — rather than merely the contour, as before — results in a schematic drawing of the figure that is devoid of individuality and can be repeatedly multiplied with ease. In place of concrete pictorial drawing, drawing becomes general and abstract (e.g., rather than John, Peter, and Alexander, a way to designate three people emerges). Thus the process of the emergence of general concepts and abstract thinking was, essentially, a reflection of the process of the emergence of the antagonism between the shaman (and the first god, made in his image) and the marginalised community, cast in the role of a common crowd.

But in both cases we see an unquestionable, verifiable evolution in seeing. The shaman's mask is so expressive because it shows the whole face rather than simply its outline. A deeper analysis of the actual, real forms of the face made deformation possible, giving the face a sinister expression — thanks to a better, more complete, and more accurate seeing.

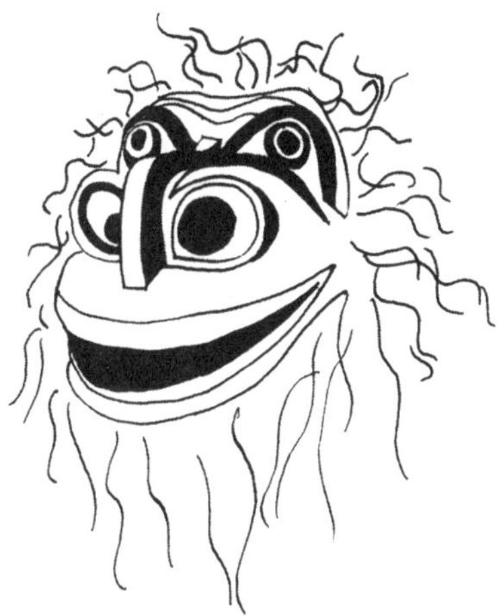

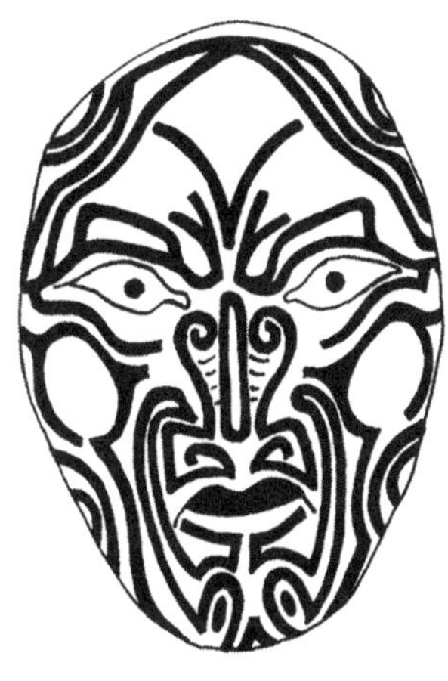

19
Dancing mask,
Kwakiutl tribe,
North American Indians

20
Tattoo,
Southern Oceania

21
Painting, Navajo tribe, North American Indians

22
From a vase, Tiryns, thirteenth c. BCE

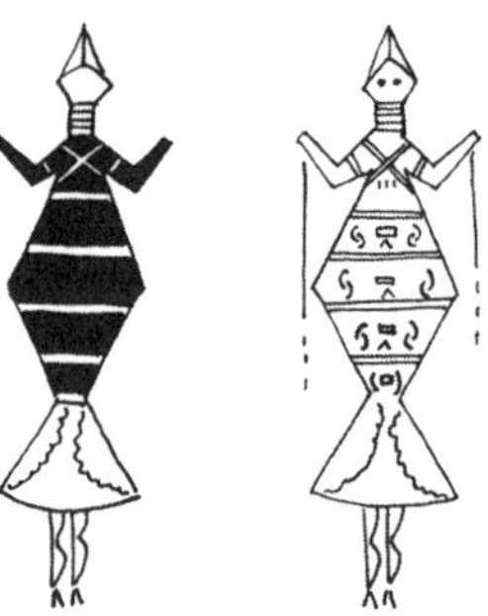

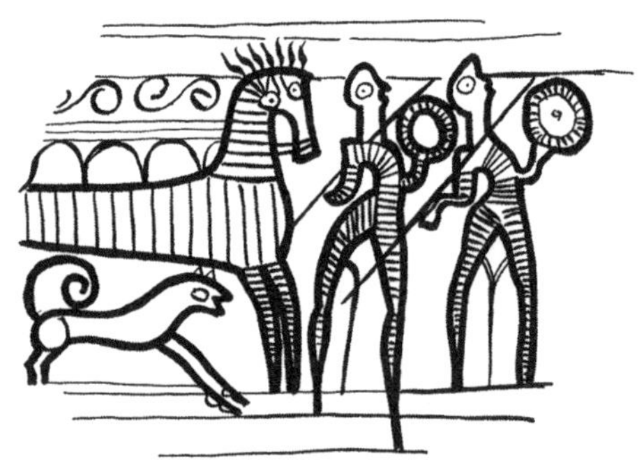

23
Dancing mask, Haida tribe, North American Indians

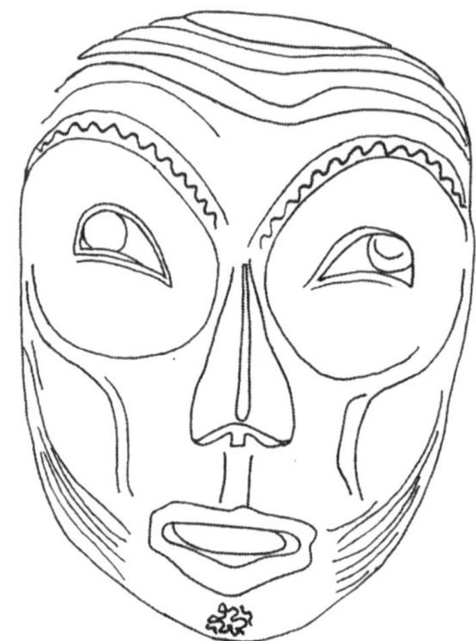

In this way, the existence of an antagonistic social structure led to the emergence of two distinct forms of deformation, two distinct varieties of formalism:

1. The formalism of identical rows of figures, devoid of individuality and expression – **ornamental formalism**;
2. The formalism of the individual, the unique figure with an excessively emphasized individuality and expression – **expressive formalism**.

These two distinct formalisms are inextricably linked and constitute opposing reflections of the same antagonistic system. The developing opposition between the community and the man of experience, the organiser of production (in the first stage) or the sorcerer, shaman, diviner (in the second), gave rise to the process of formulating general concepts and logical thinking. Visual consciousness was a reflection of this process, expressed by contour within contour, in correspondence with the emergence of Heliolithic cultures. The transition to this model of visual consciousness would have been impossible without the development of thinking. Moreover, without this consciousness and the form of drawing that corresponded to it, abstract thinking would be impossible, as would the formulation of new concepts.

Depending on conditions, Heliolithic cultures adopted different forms of social organisation — from a single settlement to bodies politic with millions of inhabitants such as Egypt, Babylon, the Mayas, the Aztecs, and Peru. But wherever the decisive social conflict was a conflict resulting from the rule of the priest as organiser of production and ideological leader, we see the same drawing of contour within contour and the same visual consciousness. Only the degree of development is different — from the primitive to highly developed forms. Nevertheless, the observation of the object's surface and its expression through line drawing remains the basic form of seeing. And the fundamental pith of consciousness remains the social conflict between the shaman and the community. This opposition determines the character of the formalism of the period. The opposed poles of the formalism of the time are the depiction of the community in ornamental rows of recurrent figures, lacking any individuality, and the representation of the "one" as a superhuman figure, full of expression and foreboding.

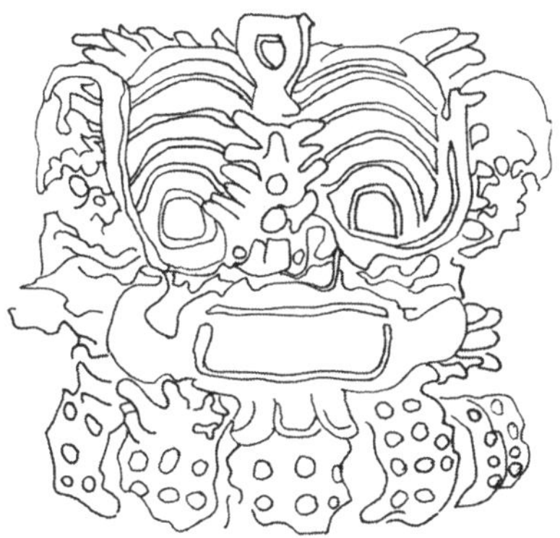

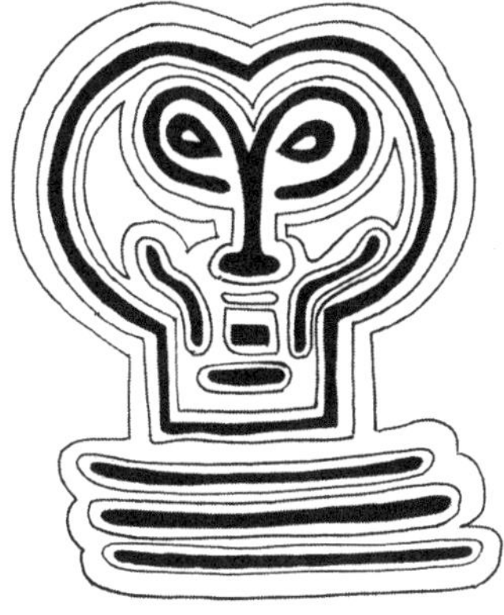

24
Censer, Guatemala, Maya art

25
Painting, Easter Island

26
House pillar,
New Caledonia

27
Pendant from an altar,
New Guinea

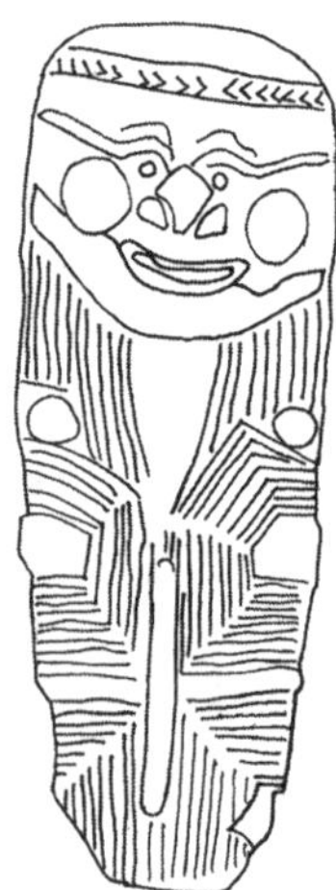

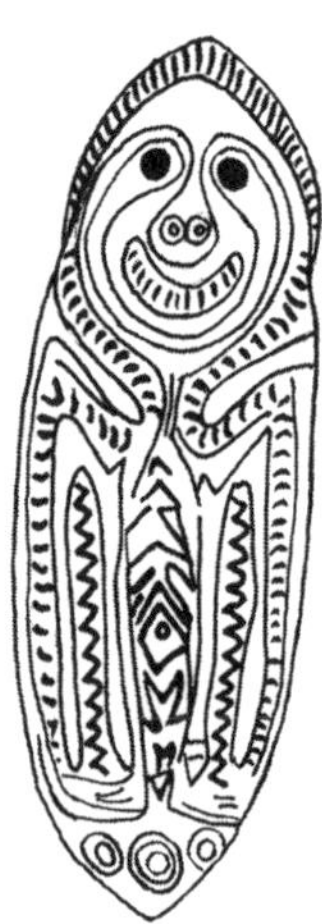

The [quantity] of observations diminishes under the weight of this formalism. Drawings dating from the beginning of the Heliolithic age extract more of nature's distinctive features, look more closely. The longer Heliolithic culture lasts, and the more superior the organizational forms it attains, the clearer the predominance of elaborate calligraphic ornament over the straightforward characterization of nature. Contour within contour seeing, which was to be a more complete way of seeing nature, of extracting a greater number of observed elements – crossed over into its own negation. It became an ornamental degeneration of nature and an obstacle on the road to observation.

28
From a vase,
Cyprus

29
Ornament,
Far East art

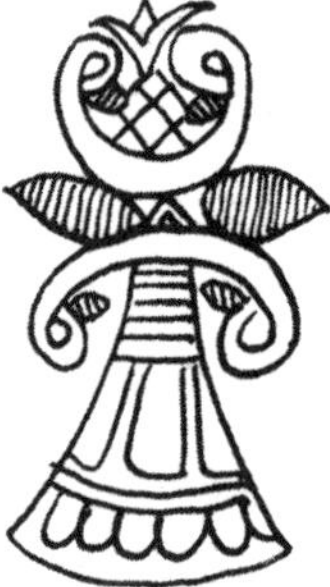

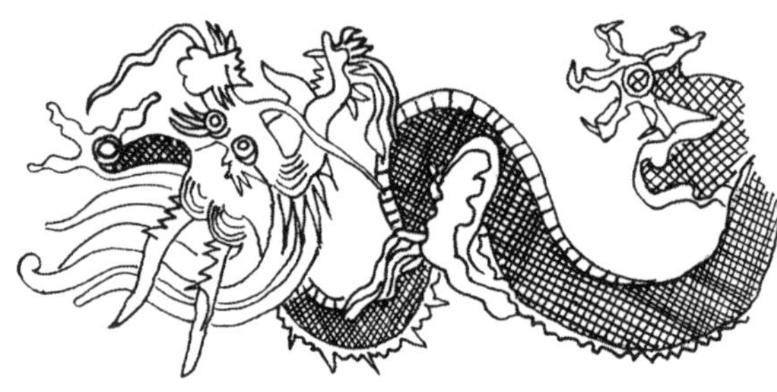

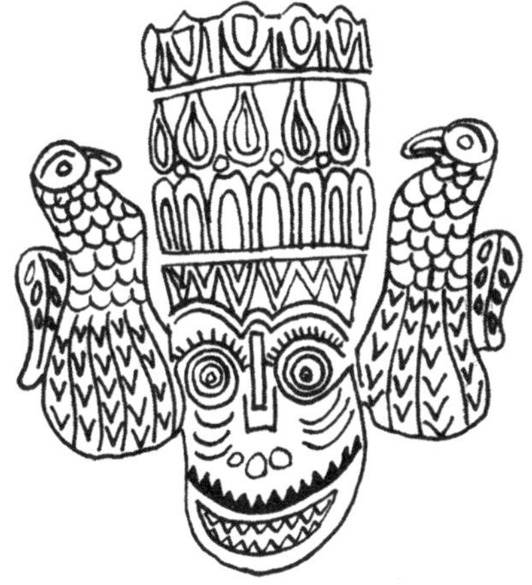

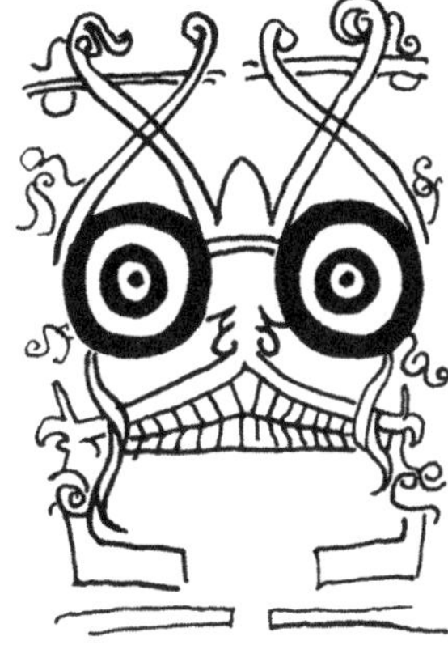

30
Mask,
Ceylon

31
Painting on a shield,
Borneo

Looking at this model of drawing, the question arises: is there any perspective here, i.e., any objectively justified relationship between dimensions? At first glance, the size of objects appears arbitrary. One object may be large, another very small. This would seem to be a negation of every perspectival law, or that perspective did not exist at the time.

To orient ourselves in this matter we have to consider the question of perspective in each particular period.

In practical terms, the question of perspective arises when we need to determine the place and size of several objects. As a matter of fact, perspective, at least in its inferior forms, does not exist where there is only one object. The perspectival representation of nature develops in relation to the emergence of general concepts and abstract thinking. It opposes the concrete pictorial representation of a single object with a conceptual relationship among several objects.

This is why, in the Palaeolithic era, we find concrete drawings of only one object. If several objects are represented, this is simply because there was free space. These are drawings of detached objects, not connected by any common action.

The question of the interrelation of several objects only appears at the end of the Palaeolithic era, in connection with the emergence of magical cults and the formation of new historical systems. However, their interdependence is defined in ways that differ so greatly from our contemporary perspective that, at first sight, it looks as though perspective is absent. Looking more closely, though, we see that there is a very clear idea and approach to the represented objects here — but that the criteria of the approach are too distant and foreign to us. The perspective is an intentional one in which the size of the object is determined by the artists' intention in regard to particular objects. For instance, amongst the herd that is represented, only the bison that he intended to hunt is large. The rest are small bulls, which he does not intend to hunt. The stronger the intentional connection to the object, the larger the object. For this reason, e.g., an arrow can be larger than a bison, as he attributes special significance to its merits. The objects are not commensurate, as in later art, but perspective is present, defined by the author's intentions and emotional relationship to the given object.

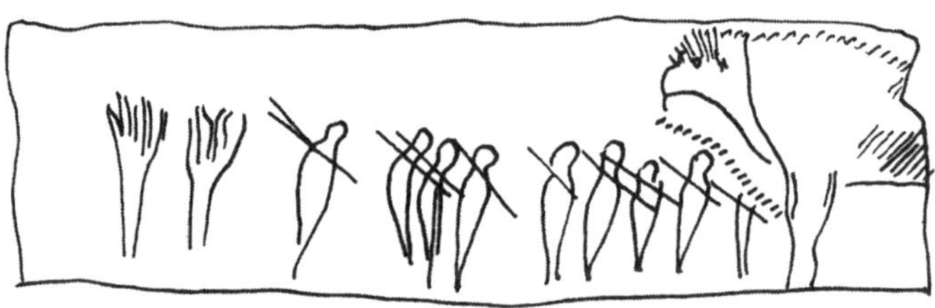

32
Engraved bone,
Les Eyzies,
late Palaeolithic

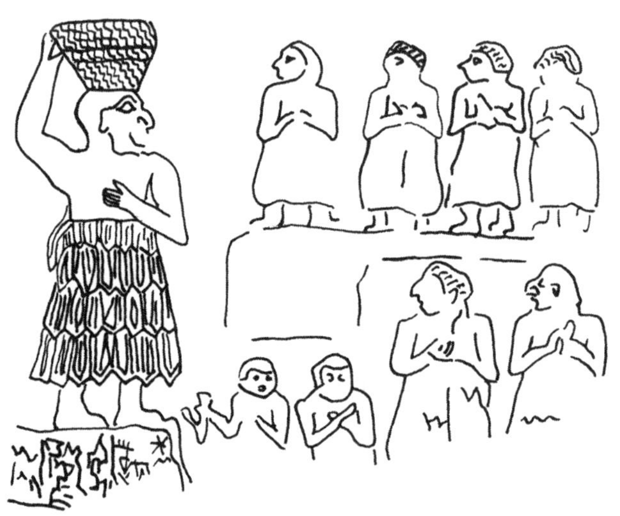

33
Relief,
Sumerian art,
third millennium BCE

Developed on the basis of primitive, incipient magic cults (facilitating hunting etc.), intentional perspective was only fully formed in mature Heliolithic cultures, where contrasts of size served to express and consolidate social antagonism. The monumentality of art – monumentality as a universalised experience and recapitulation of intentional perspective – becomes the main characteristic of mature, highly developed Heliolithic cultures (Egypt, Sumer-Akkad, Babylon, the Indies, Mexico, and Peru).

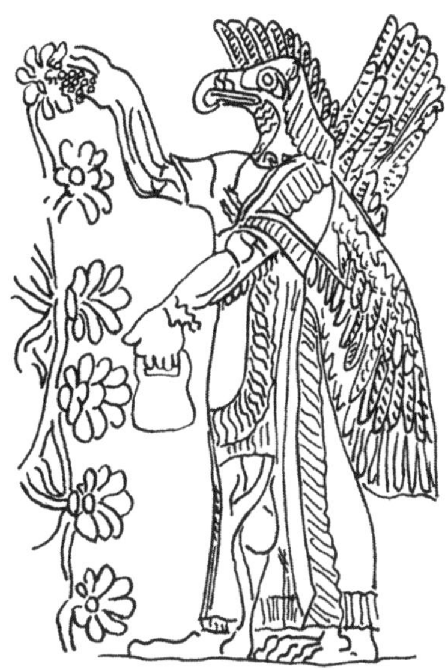

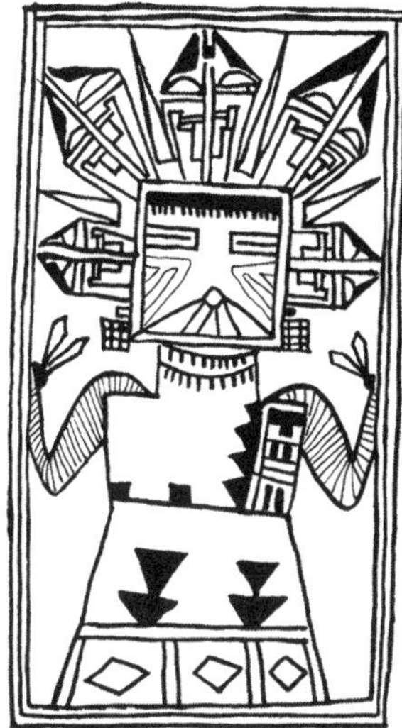

34
Relief, Assyria,
first millennium BCE

35
Altar plaque,
Hopi tribe,
North American Indians

silhouette seeing

A growing awareness of the presence of formal elements describing the object within the boundary line does not only lead to visual consciousness as expressed by line drawing inside the circumference contour. Visual content can also be formulated in another way — as **silhouette seeing.** Rather than a contour filled with line drawing, there comes an awareness that the entire space inside the contour is a uniform material mass, and that the contour is only its external boundary. While line drawing (contour within contour) could better describe the object's surface, it failed to highlight the uniform material structure that causes it to stand out from its surroundings.

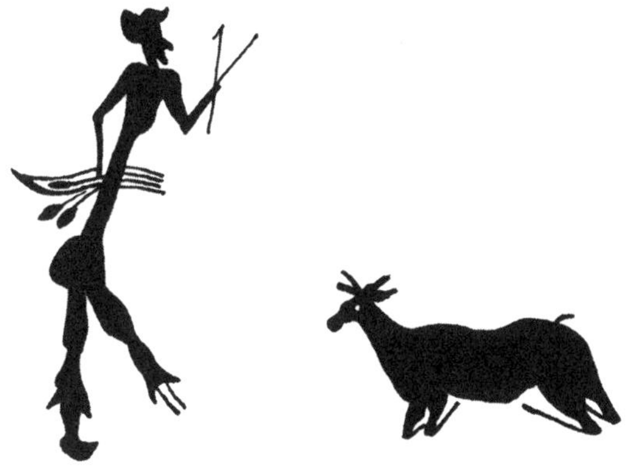

36
Painting on rock,
Tortosillas,
late Palaeolithic

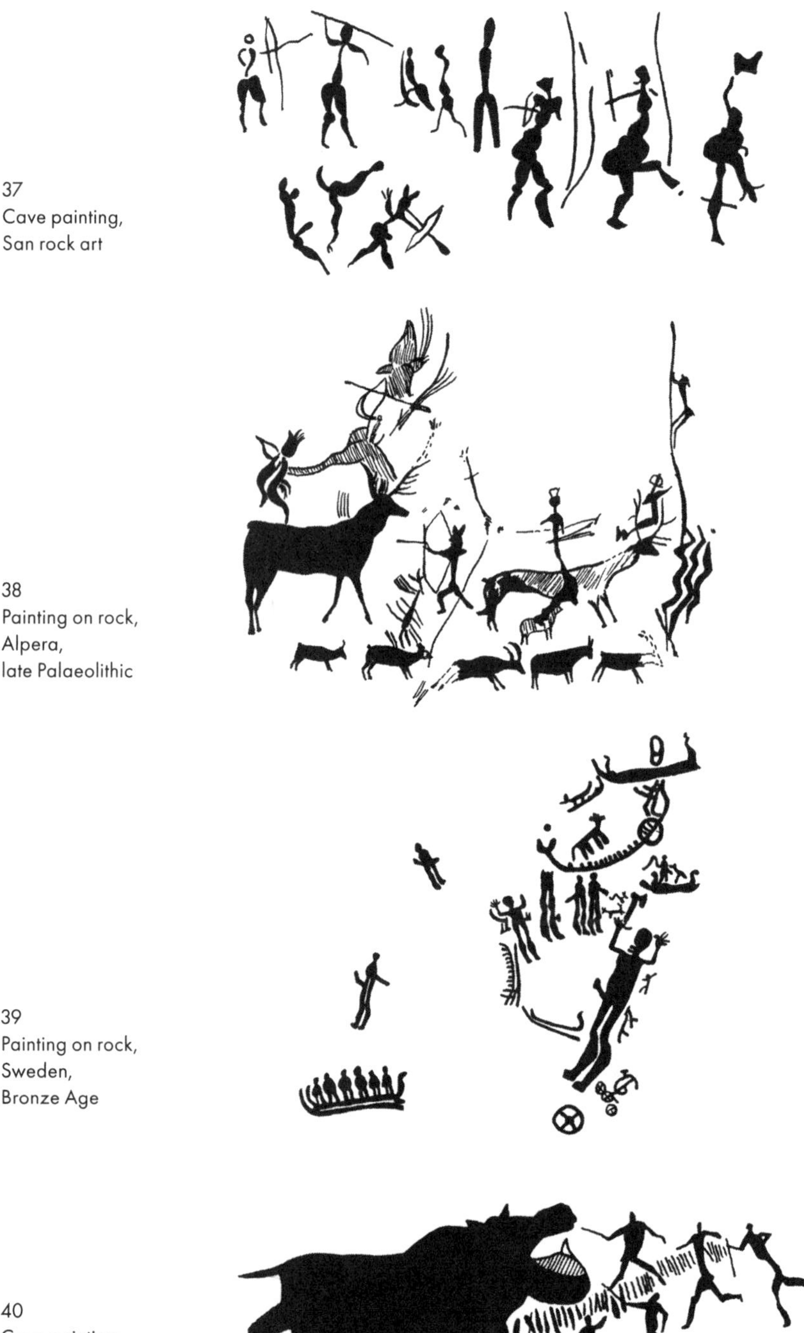

37
Cave painting,
San rock art

38
Painting on rock,
Alpera,
late Palaeolithic

39
Painting on rock,
Sweden,
Bronze Age

40
Cave painting,
San rock art

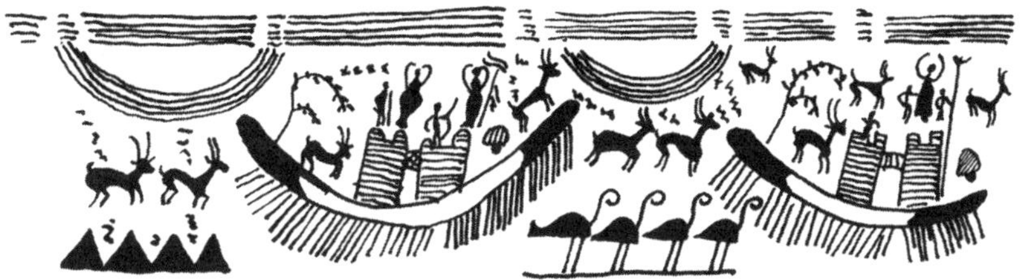

41
From vase,
Egypt,
Predynastic Period

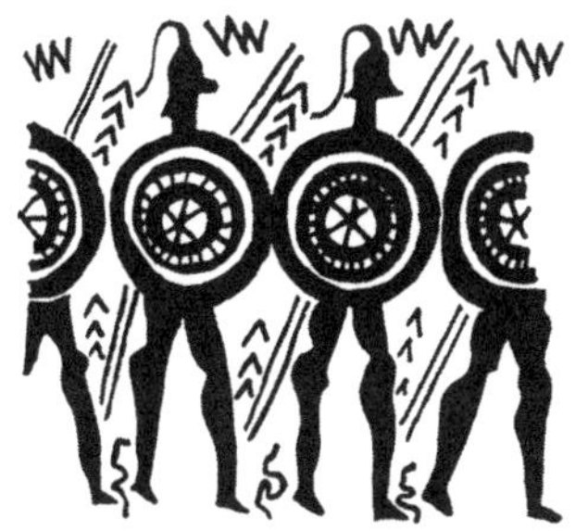

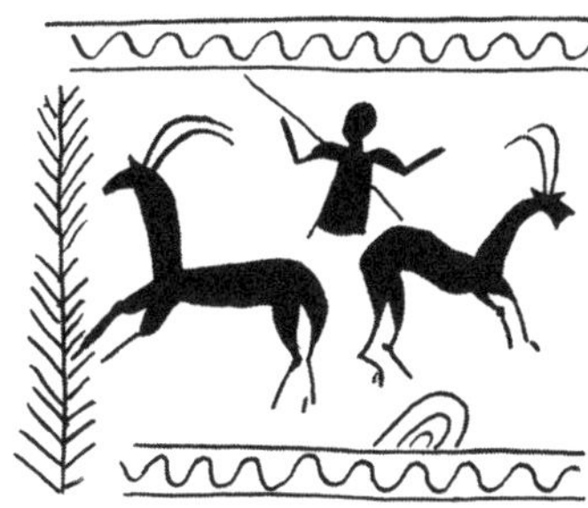

42
From vase,
Greece,
ninth–eighth c. BCE

43
From vase,
Crete,
Sub-Mycenaean
period

It would be a mistake to think that there is only one, single, continuous line of development, leading — in all countries and all historical systems — from the external contour, through the line drawing inside the contour, to the silhouette. In reality, we can see that this is not so. There are two separate lines of development. One of them leads from the external contour to the line drawing inside the contour. The other — passes directly from the pure contour to the silhouette. These are two separate ways of expressing the purport of the object within its boundaries. The awareness of contour within contour entails further observations of the object and expresses more elements of its surface. Silhouette drawing would thus be a model of realism of diminished observational scope, which would entail a quantitative weakening of realism.

Differences only emerge later. Contour within contour has limited possibilities for development. The number of components of reality that can be expressed through line alone is comparatively small. Once these are exhausted, this model of visual consciousness ceases to develop, since it is no longer capable of extracting any new components of seeing. Formalist, increasingly elaborate schemes of ornamental composition follow instead of a development of seeing and a fuller expression of reality. This is the case in all the stagnant Heliolithic cultures that endure too long (Tibet, Peru, Mexico). It serves the interests of the increasingly powerful priestly caste rather than serving the progress of realism. Although in its early phases silhouette gives a less exhaustive image of reality, nonetheless — as will be discussed later — it possesses a considerably greater potential for development. We might be so bold as to claim that it was for this reason that the transition to silhouette-seeing took place in societies that were inferior in cultural terms to those that transitioned to contour within contour. Some societies transitioned to contour within contour, producing Heliolithic art. Others, which were inferior in terms of cultural development, transitioned to silhouette-seeing, transitioning from the primitive-community system to another (non-Heliolithic) historical system.

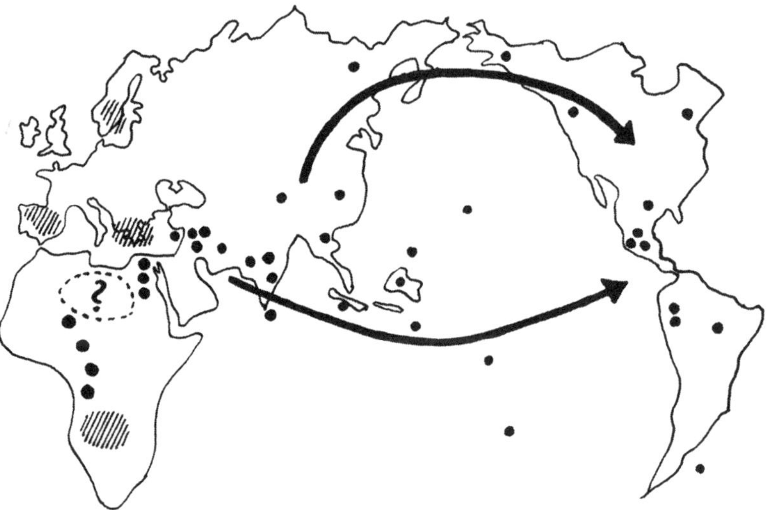

When one looks at the distribution on a map of Heliolithic art, as expressed by a visual consciousness of contour within contour, by ornamental rhythms, by the formalism of frightening deformation, by the monumentality of art — one sees that the principal territory of Heliolithic art coincides with territories of the ancient cultures of the East (Egypt, Mesopotamia, India, China), i.e. with the territories where agricultural communities developed, in the valleys of flooding rivers, where foreseeing floods, determining planting and reaping times, and the provision of water (irrigation) called for the uniform professional leadership of an increasingly powerful priestly caste.

This established historical pattern (of the cultures of the ancient East) requires some adjustment through the addition of the following qualifications:

1. The similarity of Nigerian art to prehistoric Egyptian art points to continued close contact. The influence could not have come by the roundabout route of the Egyptian conquests in Nubia, but directly from Egypt to Nigeria (Timbuktu). Favourable conditions may have existed towards the end of the Ice Age, when rainfall was higher, the climate more moderate, and the numerous Sahara rivers (wadi), which have now dried up, were still active. But this means that we have to shift the entire prehistoric period in question from the fourth millennium BC to the tenth – eighth millennia, when the entire territory of Northern Africa, with its many rivers (at that time, flooding rivers), constituted a uniform territory of Heliolithic culture, influencing the adjacent territories of Congo and Cameroon.
2. Heliolithic culture was disseminated from the Asian continent by sea to the Asian and Oceanic islands, and was spread by land from the coasts of Asia to the American mainland. Failing to find a natural economic base there (lack of agriculture or flooding rivers), it is simplified and degenerates, preserving only some aspects of Heliolithic culture: the rule of priests (sorcerers, shamans, etc.) expressed in the frightening deformations of masks, the cult of blood sacrifices, even extending to cannibalism (soil is most fertile where blood has been spilled).
3. Heliolithic culture develops fully in those places where it finds favourable conditions (the necessary collective organisation of agriculture, irrigation systems, etc., as in Peru and Mexico), working through the issues of the Heliolithic cultures of the ancient world in its own way. Everything that had been put into practice in Egypt and India – monumental constructions, the expressionist deformations of the figures of gods, the representation of the surfaces of objects by line drawing – is repeated in an independent, distinct way in Mexico and Peru.

In territories lying beyond the reach of Heliolithic cultures, however, a new, distinct model of visual consciousness of the silhouette emerges. These are the territories of Spain (Albacete, Valencia, Cantabria), Sweden, Greece (pre-Mycenae), and South Africa (Bushmen culture) – territories that were peripheral to those of the Heliolithic cultures. This art had not yet produced its own formalism and was thus an art created by a society that was as yet non-antagonistic – a society that had achieved the highest, historically conditioned level of development possible within the framework of the primitive-community system. In territories where visual consciousness was that of the silhouette, art is the common reflection of the collective struggle for survival (hunting and herding). Its development of seeing and its developing visual consciousness aim for a fuller capturing of this struggle (seeing man and his movements, seeing the animal, etc.). In Heliolithic cultures, however, the realism of seeing develops within the framework of certain limits to understanding the truth. Under pressure from the social structure, seeing what is inside the contour, observing the surface of the object so as to characterise the object and its features more fully, comes to be directed towards making the deformation of reality ever fuller and more precise, taking advantage of all the new advances in seeing. The development of realism thus already contains the seed of its negation. In antagonistic systems, the sources of formalism lie within realism itself rather than outside it. This is the dialectical unity of opposites.

We see the emergence of two distinct models of visual consciousness in the transition from prehistory to history. The seeing of farmers and hunters reflected the common relations among those branches of tribes of those times that had become settled and other branches that remained nomadic.

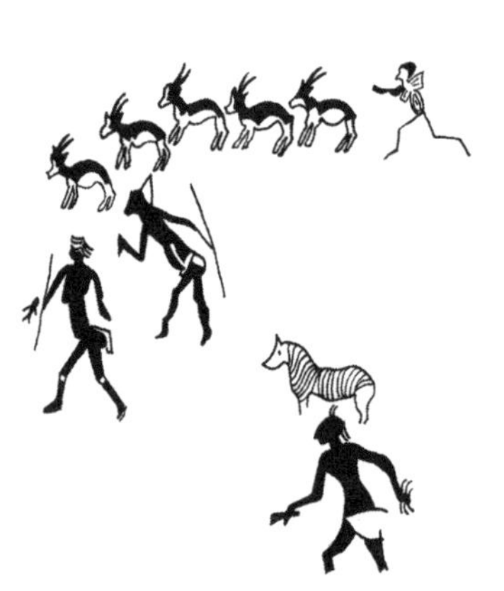

44
Rock painting,
southwest Africa

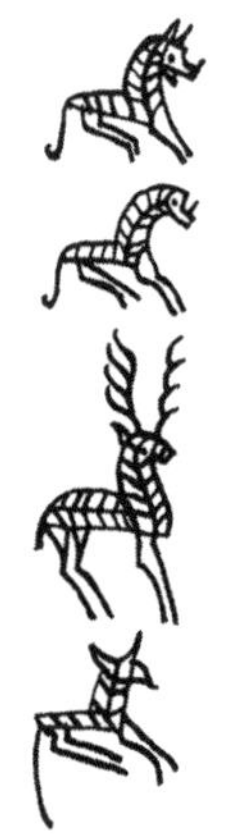

45
From belt buckle,
Caucasus,
thirteenth–sixth c. BCE

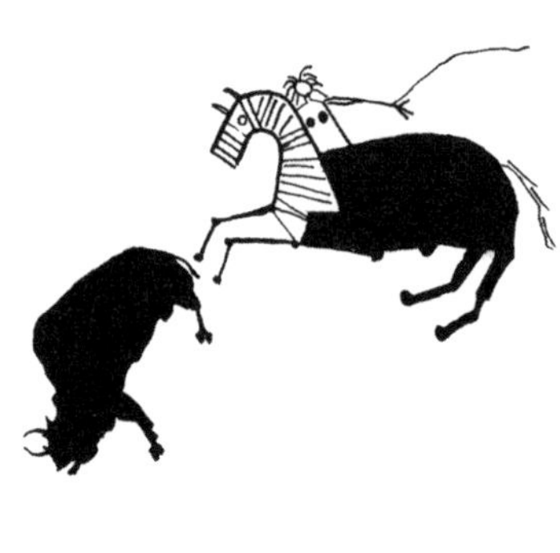

46
Painting on a buffalo-hide cloak,
Mandan tribe,
North American Indians

With the achievement of a new silhouette-seeing, a new model of perspective arises that corresponds to it. This perspective consistently emerges from the specific properties of silhouette-seeing.

How must we use our eyes in order to see a flat silhouette view of an object on the picture plane? We can achieve this by projecting the object onto the screen of the picture through the method of **orthogonal parallel-projection perspective**. Every point of the object will then correspond to a particular point in the picture.

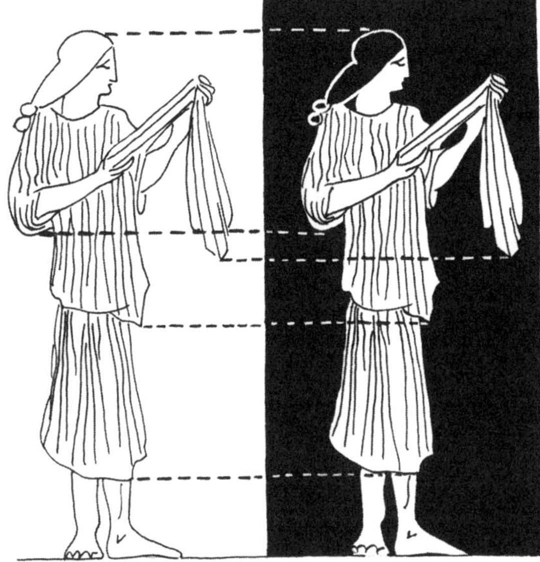

47
From amphora, Greece, fifth c. BCE

We see this perspective on Greek vases. The orthogonal parallel perspective replaces the intentional perspective that was generally characteristic of Heliolithic culture.

In this perspective, the dimensions in the picture correspond to the dimensional relations that exist in nature. From a perspective governed by subjective emotions, we move to a perspective determined by objective moments of seeing. We move to a principle of the **commensurability** of the dimensions of objects. Thus, the change in the mode of visual consciousness calls for the restructuring of all the formal means of expression.

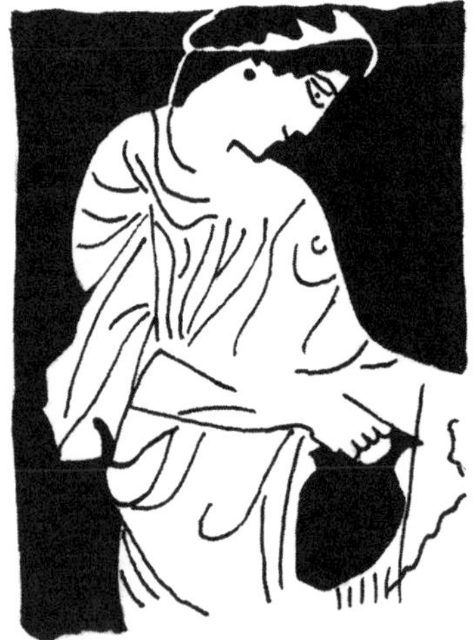

48
From crater,
Greece,
fifth c. BCE

Along with the perspectival system, the colour system is also restructured. The issue of colour schemes (as understood today, i.e. the harmonious juxtapositions of colours) did not exist in contour seeing. The role of colours was to display the author's emotional relationship to the objects represented by means of the attention called for by the colour of the contour.

The system of colour schemes in silhouette-seeing aims to make represented objects stand out from their background. The relationship between the colour of the silhouettes and the colour of the background is decisive for the impact of the picture, and thus for colour harmony.

In the system of orthogonal parallel projection, all objects appear to be standing on common ground.

In this view, the ground looks like a straight line with silhouettes of figures standing upon it. The perspective of orthogonal parallel projection presents nature as a series of objects standing on **common ground**. From this arises the main aesthetic problem, characteristic of art based on silhouette-seeing: the interrelation of figures included in the row. The **rhythm of the parallel row** is the main problem of the aesthetics that emerged along with silhouette-seeing.

There are parallel, rhythmic rows in painting as well as in sculpture and architecture. Individual components of sculptural form

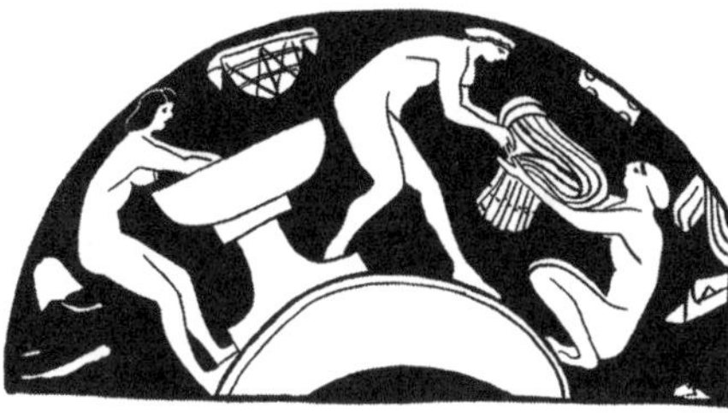

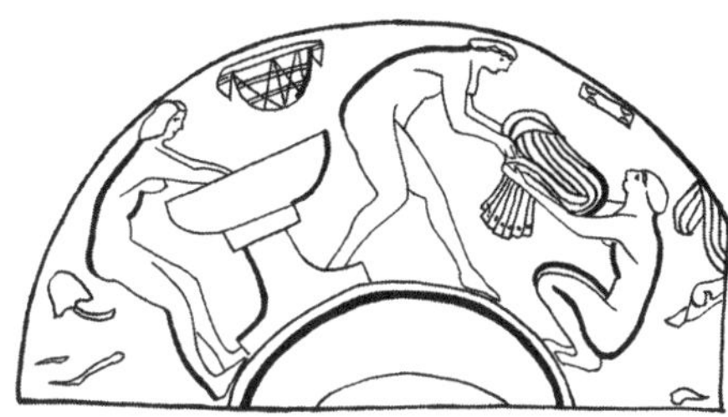

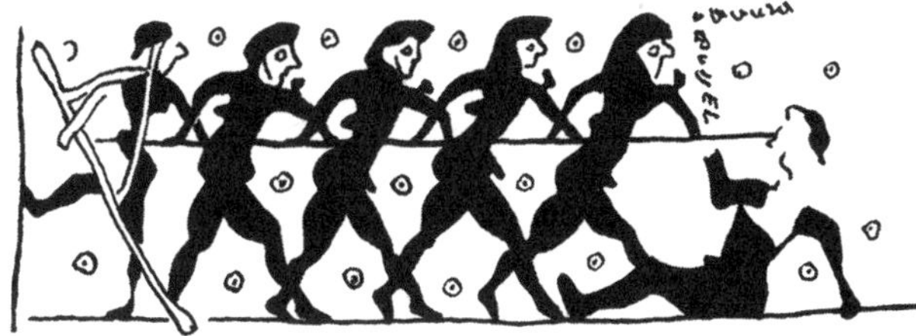

49
From kylix,
Greece,
fifth c. BCE

50
From crater,
Greece,
seventh c. BCE

correspond to the silhouette's linearities in painting and echo the rhythm of parallel, rhythmic rows in architecture.

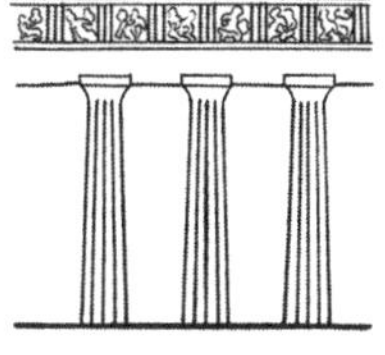

This process of architectonisation, i.e. connecting various shapes and objects distant from one another through a rhythmic interrelation, relies on taking certain formal elements from one object and blending them into the form of another. In this way, it is as though individual objects were lending one another particular formal elements. Repeated in the rows of objects, these formal elements create the common link of the architectonic rhythm.

The method of architectonisation was not conceived of in isolation from the real conditions of existence and seeing. It has a fully verifiable and experiential basis in the phenomena of our seeing. These phenomena are **afterimages**, related to the physiology of the visual processes. The photochemical processes that take place in the eye limit its ability to see and lead to secondary processes associated with its purely material structure.

Looking at any object, we receive its reflection in our eye. The incident light brings about corresponding chemical processes in the retina, whose effects linger. The moment we stop looking at the object and transfer our gaze elsewhere — an **afterimage** of the object arises in the eye, a trace of the object that is the same shape but of a complementary colour (an effect of the regenerative processes of the eye).

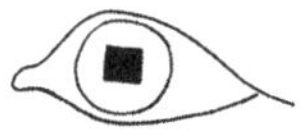

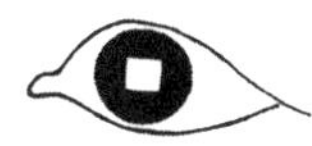

This explains shifts in formal elements, their "seeping through" from nearby objects. It is a direct, chemical, and physiological effect of the overlaying of gazes transferred from one object to another (even involuntarily).

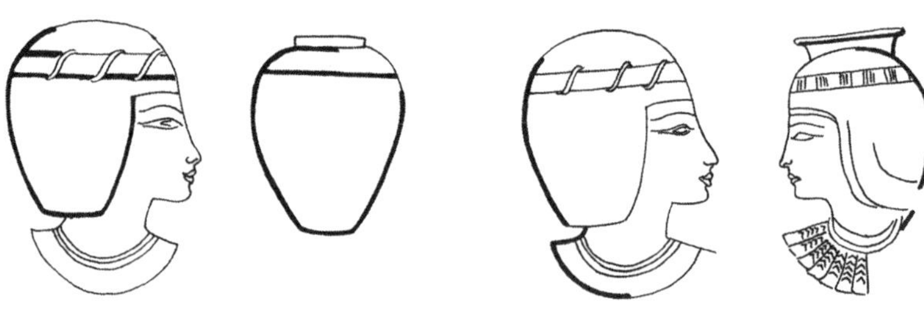

51
Relief, Egypt,
second millennium BCE
and vase,
Predynastic period

Ancient Egyptian sculpture developed entirely in relation to ceramics. Its architectonisation is a ceramic architectonisation.

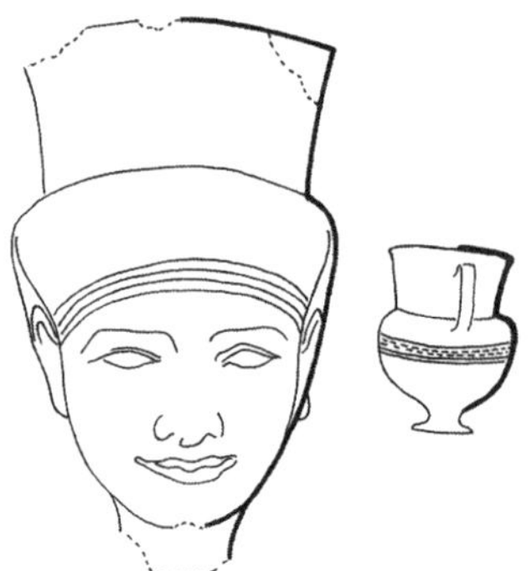

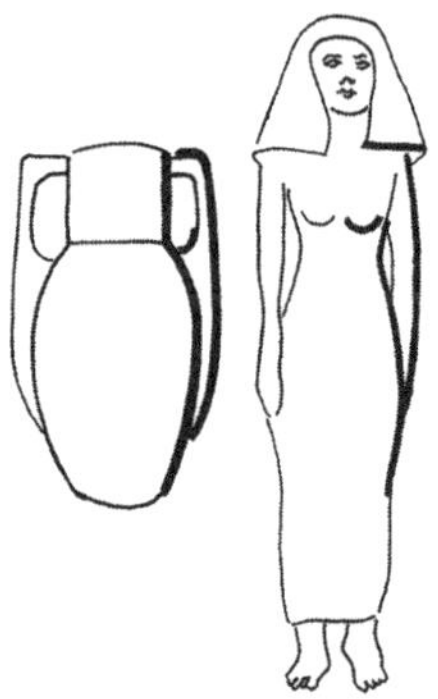

52
Sculpture and pottery,
Egypt,
second millennium BCE

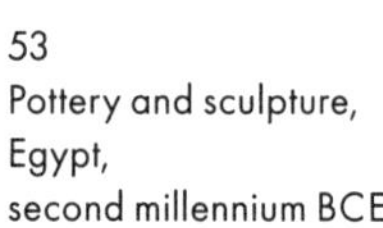

53
Pottery and sculpture,
Egypt,
second millennium BCE

The streamlined forms, so characteristic of forms made in clay, their particular ability to universalise, their lack of straight lines and right angles – are features common to clay ceramics as well as to Egyptian sculpture as a whole, regardless of the material of which it is made. Whether wood or sandstone, granite or limestone – sculpture preserves a trace of its earlier origins, of when it was being made in the ceramics workshop, when it was subordinated to the form imposed on it by clay, and when it absorbed the formal elements of the afterimage, transferred from the ceramic products in its vicinity.

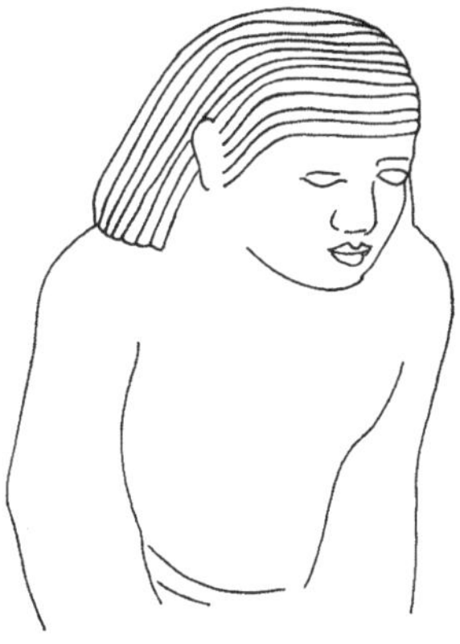

54
Granite sculpture,
Egypt,
third millennium BCE

Both the shapes of the ceramic vessel itself and the decorations on the vessel were subject to this transfer.

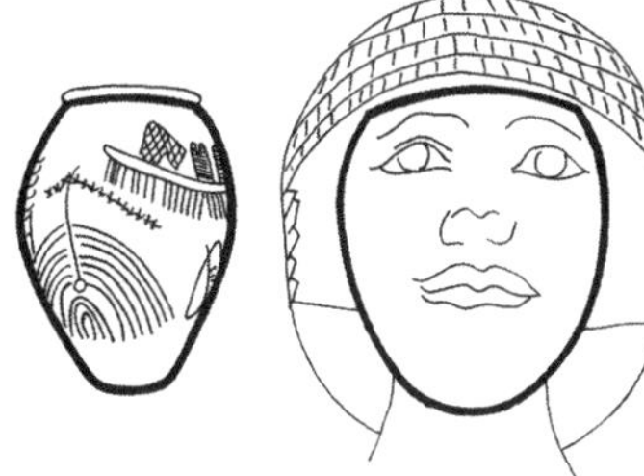

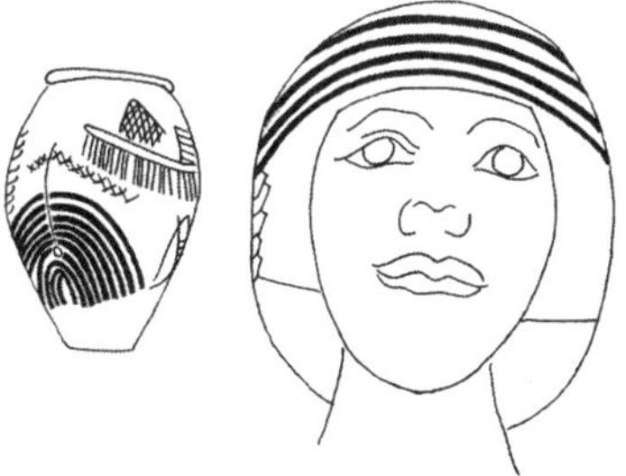

55
Predynastic vase and a limestone sculpture,
Egypt,
third millennium BCE

In this sense, one may claim that the origins of Egyptian sculpture lie in prehistory (in the Egyptian Neolithic period, significantly earlier than the Neolithic period in the northern hemisphere) and derives from ceramics as the most perfected branch of technique of those times.

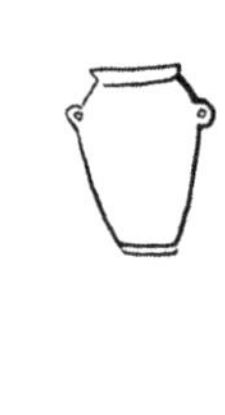

56
Sculpture of ivory and vase,
Egypt, Predynastic period

Such links to ceramics persist throughout this entire historical period. Even when the architecture of pyramids is replaced by the architecture of colonnaded temples, Egyptian sculpture preserves its characteristic shapes, determined by ceramics. The architectonisation of the human figure into architecture does not occur directly – as it does in Greece, for example – by a direct carrying over of form from architecture to the human figure, by endowing the human figure with formal elements taken from architecture.

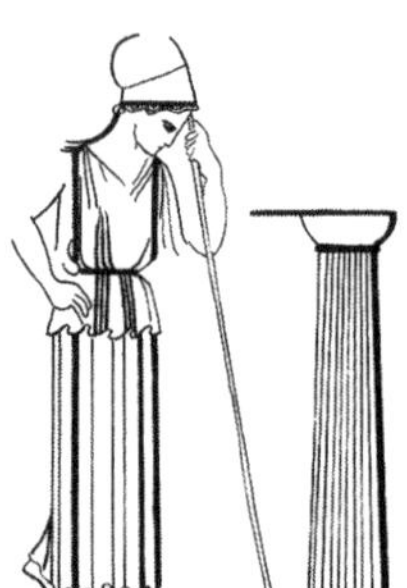

57
Relief, Greece,
fifth c. BCE

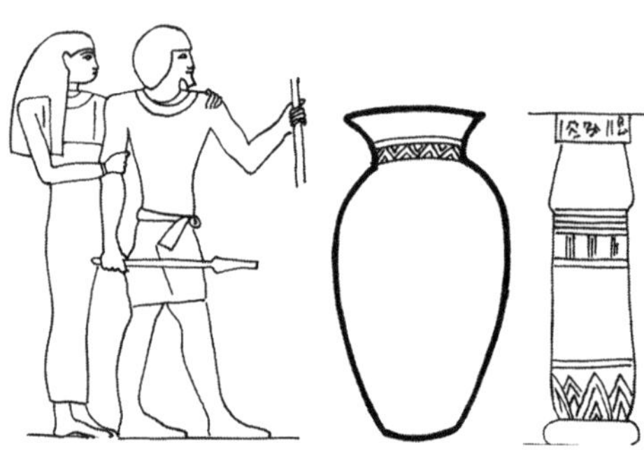

58
Relief, Egypt,
third millennium BCE,
pottery and
a papyrus column

There is always that intermediary element – ceramics – in Egyptian art. Sculpture, linked to ceramics through architectonisation, undergoes a further process of architectonisation to architecture. This demonstrates that colonnaded architecture did not emerge as an organic development in Egypt but appeared later, when sculpture had succeeded in consolidating and working out its own form, which was derived from ceramics. Colonnaded architecture was the result of cataclysms and clashes, of the developmental contradictions of the times, of the contradiction between those tribes that had settled and those that remained nomadic – the principal contradiction that determined the development of the ancient cultures of the East. Hence, the architectonisation of Egyptian sculpture to colonnaded architecture (e.g. Theban architecture) is never as complete as it was, for example, in Greece. Despite the use of formal transfers, a certain strangeness always remains. A ceramic can never be turned into a beam or a column. It always remains a pot.

59
Limestone sculpture and a papyrus column, Egypt, second millennium BCE

60
Wooden sculpture and a papyrus column, Egypt, second millennium BCE

61
Pottery and granite sculpture, Egypt, third millennium BCE

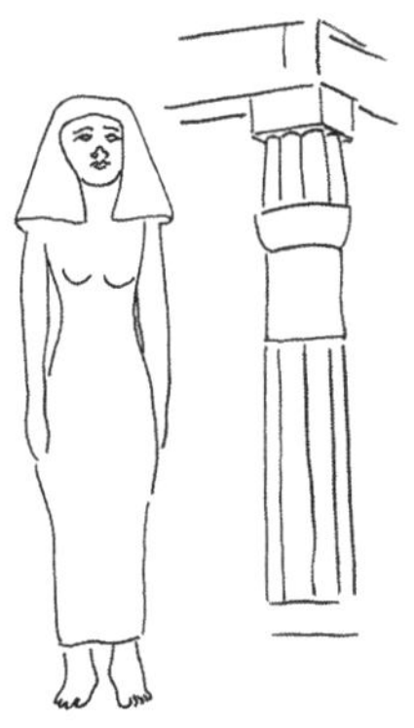

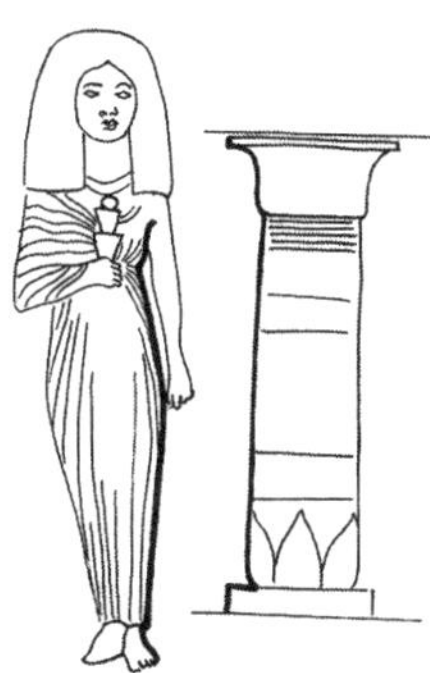

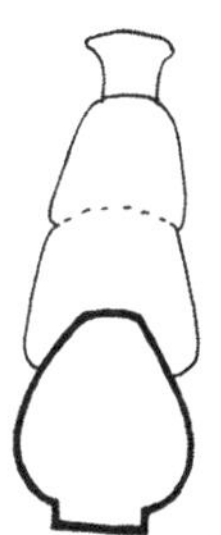

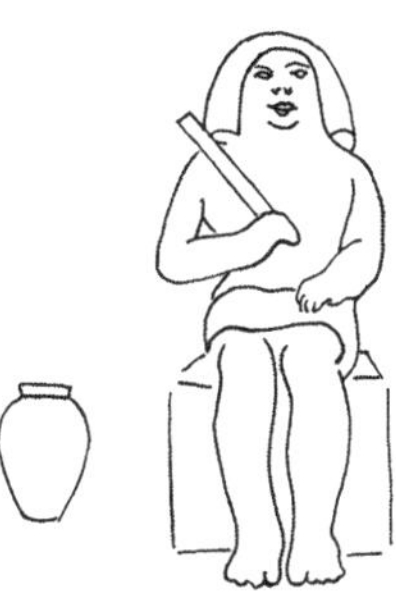

However, if we are looking for an architecture that can be completely and wholly linked to Egyptian visual art, we find this in Nigeria. This would imply that there was once a uniform Egyptian visual art (on the brink of pre-history) that was shattered as a result of historical events. Architecture was pushed to the West, while sculpture and painting had to adapt to a new, imported architecture. But this also suggests that contacts between Egypt and Nigeria were easy and frequent, and that the two territories were once a uniform cultural region (in the transition from prehistory to history); that the Sahara was not then what it is today.

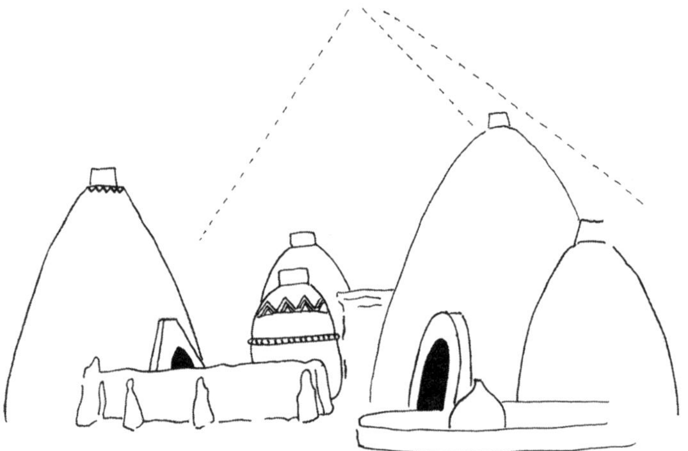

62
Houses and crop silos, Nigeria

Afterimage phenomena are a real, visual, and verifiable basis for the development of the method of architectonisation, with its carrying over of particular fragments of form from one object to another. The method of architectonisation is therefore only a generalization of afterimage experiences, their formulation in certain practical rules. In the course of its development, numerous norms were formulated, defining the method of architectonisation of the work of art. This was not because some new element, detached from nature, stole in to the observation of nature, but because a new form of observation was added to the hitherto existing observation of the object itself — **the observation of observing man**, of his psycho-physiological reactions in the course of observation. Afterimage phenomena are none other than the reaction of the observer to the field of the objective world being observed — and are as verifiable and real as the very objects that evoke these reactions.

If the application of the method of architectonisation results in the production of new works of art that more eloquently express harmony and beauty, this is because the practical scope of observation of the object has been expanded by the practical scope of observations of the eye and mind of the observer, and not because a non-objective, illusory, and unreal beauty has been merged with the objective beauty of nature. Afterimage-seeing and the method of architectonisation associated with it are not a combination of real and unreal, but simply an expansion of the previously existing visual base. Rather than artificially, anti-dialectically isolating the object alone, it is considered in connection with the person of the observer, in its cognitive dynamism. A greater expression of beauty appears because afterimage-seeing enables a wider range of actual observation, expanding rather than narrowing observation, and not because speculative elements, detached from nature, have been added to the actual observation of nature. Harmony and beauty are not the result of the negation of real seeing but of a greater conformity to our real seeing.

Formal changes, the emergence and development of architectonisation, are simply the outcome of a change in the model of visual consciousness. The transition to silhouette seeing inevitably brings about the architectonisation method, with its carrying over of formal elements from one object to another. It is easier to observe afterimage phenomena in silhouette-seeing than in other models of seeing. The object stands out from the background particularly clearly in silhouette-seeing. We grasp it perfectly clearly at a single glance.

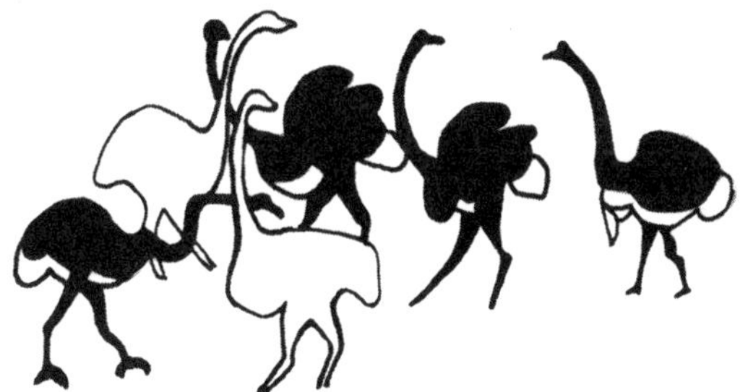

63
Cave painting,
San rock art

The precision of seeing the emergent afterimage corresponds to the precision of seeing the silhouette. Afterimage-seeing followed on naturally from the precision of the synthetic silhouette-seeing formulated by the first hunters and herders — nomadic tribes. A quick, volatile, and synthetic seeing of both the image and the afterimage constitutes the material and social base of the method of architectonisation in those branches of the tribes of the Ancient World that remained nomadic (in the early days of history).

Linear afterimages can be carried over within the limits of the work of art itself, just as they can to connect a work of art to others in the vicinity.

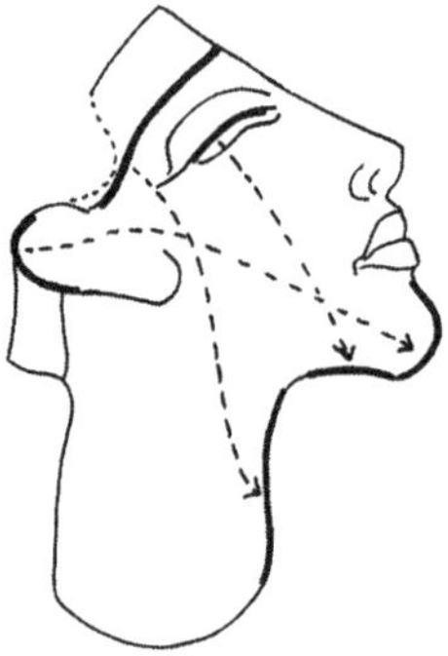

64
Sculpture,
Egypt, second
millennium BCE

Extrapolating from the experience, instead of carrying over lines themselves, one can also carry over their dimensions.

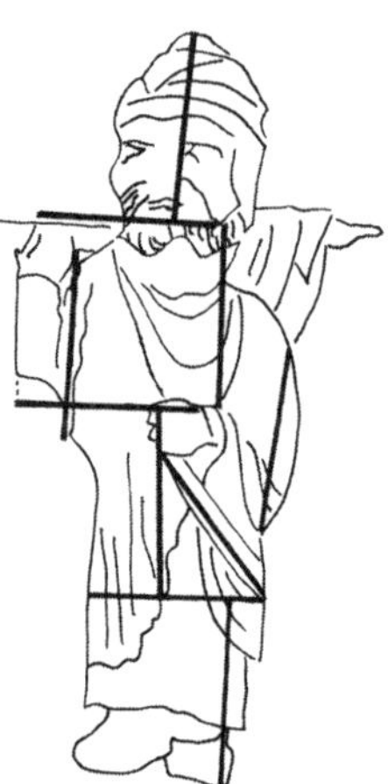

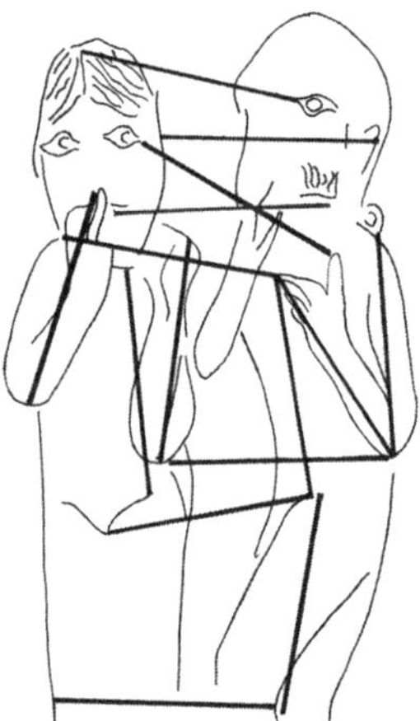

65
Sculpture, Arles,
twelfth c.

66
Sculpture,
Cluny,
twelfth c.

The carrying over of dimensions can also be seen in Egyptian art. The method of architectonisation was applied both within the work of art and outside it in order to connect it with the environment to which its dimensions had been carried over. But we also see another sort of transfer in Egyptian art.

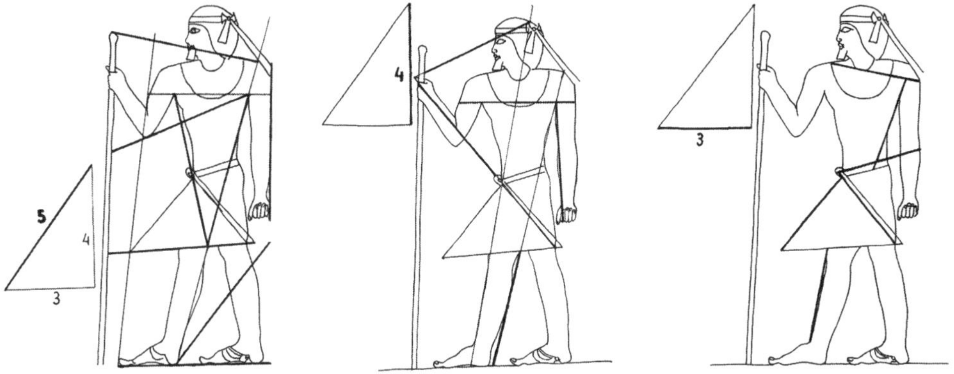

Analysing the dimensions defining the rhythm of the relief, we see that they can be defined in the numerical sequence 5:4:3 – i.e., the Pythagorean right-angle triangle. However, we also find the same series in other works of Egyptian art. The sequence 5:4:3 is the principal sequence defining and governing Egyptian art. The schema of the triangle is the fundamental scaffolding on which all works of art were built in Egypt, and the proportions 5:4:3 binding within it are those that unify Egyptian art into a single whole. All works of art from the territory of the entire country were connected to one another by way of the method of architectonisation, constituting a unified set, whose qualities clearly marked it apart as the national art.

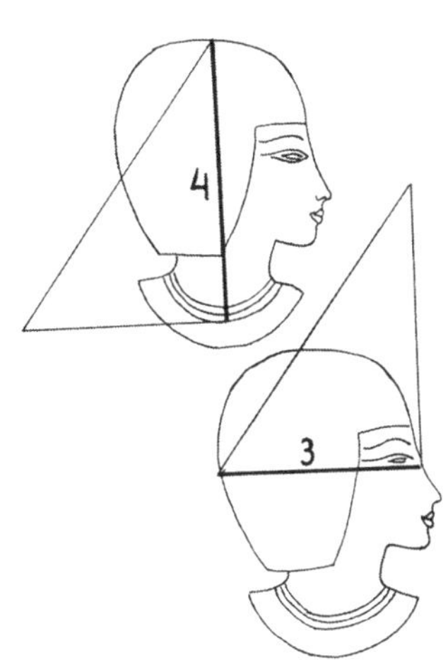

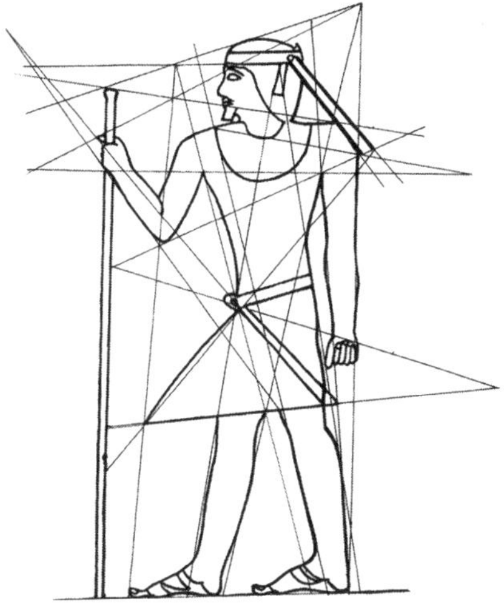

67
Relief,
Egypt,
second millennium BCE

68
Relief,
Egypt,
third millennium BCE

From pyramids to every sculpture and relief, we come across the same schema of the triangle. It is the most widespread form in which the phenomena of afterimages occur – no longer transferred within the limits of the field of view and the limits of human eyesight, but formed within limits that only memory can grasp, of distances travelled and the span of human life, spent in a world of these same triangles and these same sequential proportions, 5:4:3.

We can only grasp the significance of the triangle, of its proportions and its relation to the most essential aspects of Egyptian life, when we realise that this triangle was a measuring triangle having 5:4:3 proportions, and that the Egyptians measured not with tape but with the triangle (which is stable and retains its right angle), and that every parcel of land had to be surveyed and its measurements recreated after each flooding of the Nile. The triangle was deeply embedded in the life of the Egyptians, determining the existence and welfare of every Egyptian (on a plot of land reconstructed and measured afresh each year). And with the help of all sorts of afterimages (mental, associative, and visual), this basic triangle was carried over into Egyptian art in its entirety

Similar universal compositional clues, also derived from findings of afterimage experiences, are to be found in the different conditions of mediaeval Europe. Here, though, the carrying over of equivalent dimensions from one work of art to another developed into a system of squares rather than triangles.

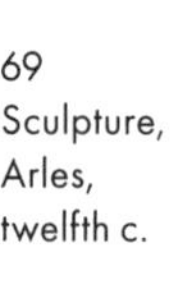

69
Sculpture,
Arles,
twelfth c.

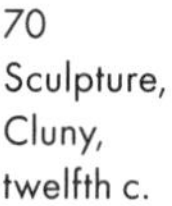

70
Sculpture,
Cluny,
twelfth c.

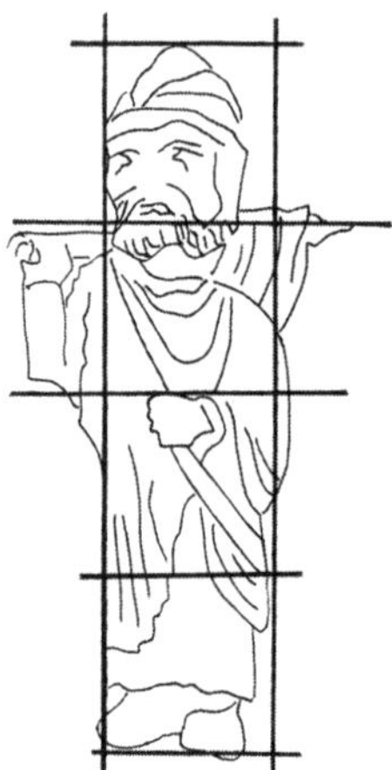

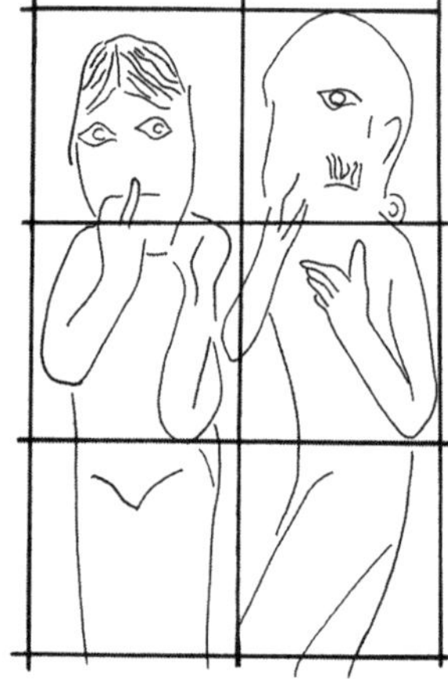

The main aesthetic issue in architecture, as in sculpture and painting, comes to be the rhythm of parallel rows. A reciprocal exchange of the particular formal elements that compose these rows is required to connect the autonomous rows in a rhythmic whole of a higher order. For instance, the verticals of columns enter sculpture and painting as rows of verticals in the folds of hanging drapery. The rounded forms of human figures are interpreted in the curvature of the Ionic capital. The rhythmic forms and parallel rows of sculpture and painting absorb and subordinate themselves to forms carried over from architecture by way of this reciprocal exchange. Architecture becomes the main art form, determining form in sculpture and painting. So the result of the search for a rhythmic unity linking sculptural, painterly, and architectural forms in parallel, autonomous rows is thus the emergence of the issue of the architectonisation of all visual art, its subordination to architecture, its infusion with formal elements carried over from architecture.

We thus see how the formation of a new visual consciousness brings with it a complete reconstruction of all formal means of expression. This is specifically manifested in the reconstruction of the perspectival system, changes in colour schemes, the question of the rhythmic association of horizontal rhythmic rows, and the question of the architectonisation of visual art. **Transformations in art have their source in changes in visual consciousness,** and the same formal questions emerge wherever the visual consciousness of the silhouette is the common ground.

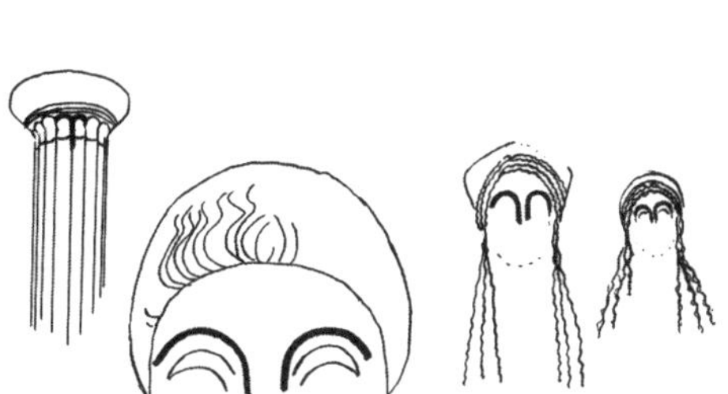

71
Doric architectonics

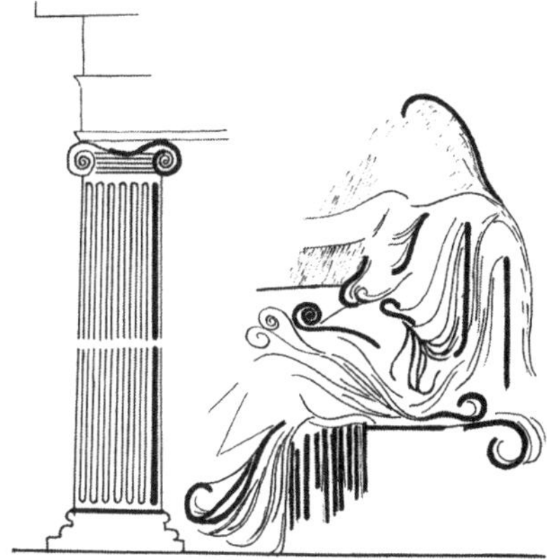

72
Ionian architectonics

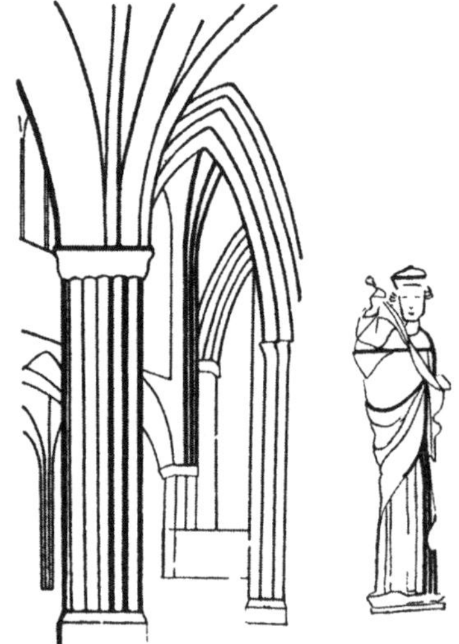

73
Gothic architectonics

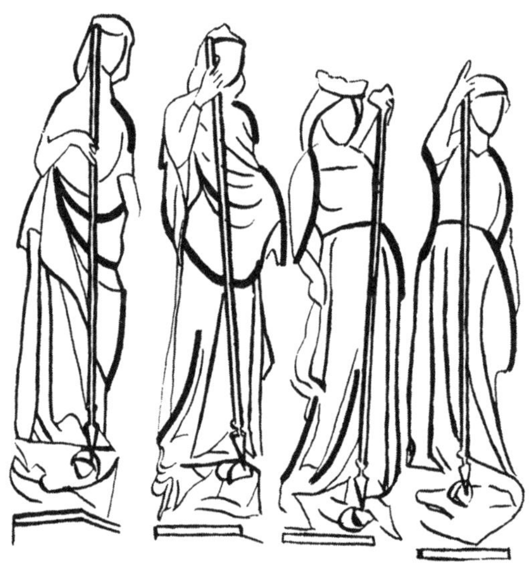

74
Gothic order,
sculpture,
Strasbourg,
thirteenth c.

The visual consciousness of the silhouette was even the decisive common ground in the Gothic era, some two thousand years after Greece, leading to the emergence of the same aesthetic problems: the rhythm of parallel rows and the architectonisation of visual art.

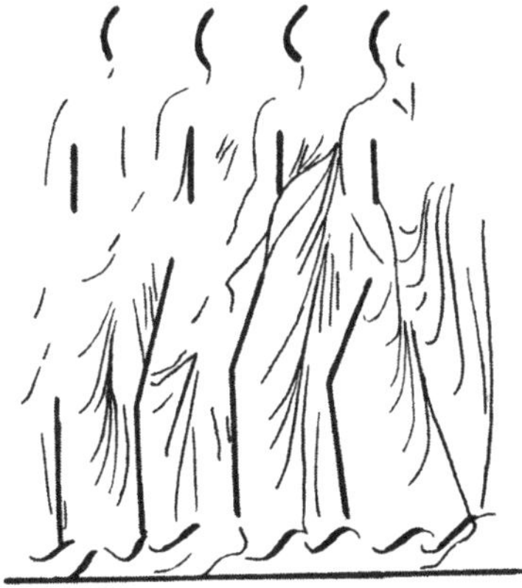

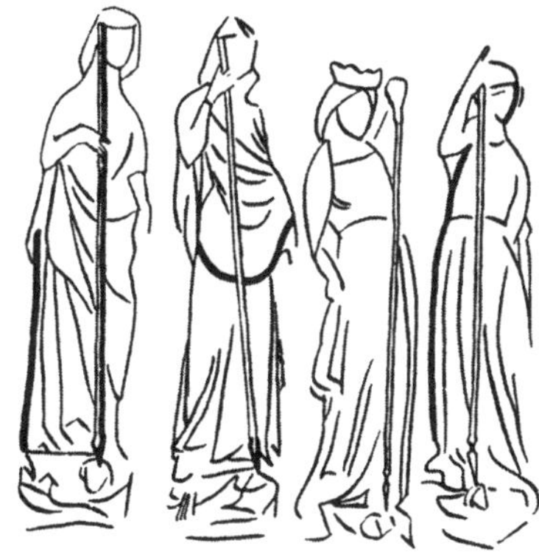

75
Classical order, Parthenon, fifth c. BCE and Gothic order, Strasbourg, thirteenth c.

Silhouette-seeing was formed during the transition from the prehistorical to the historical age. Another form of visual consciousness, expressed by contour within contour, also develops in the same period, in different territories. These two models of seeing — the seeing of settled farmers and the seeing of hunters and herders — reflected the fundamental conflict shaping the beginnings of the new era: the conflict between settled tribes and tribes persisting in their nomadic life.

The community of farmers, still organized as a primitive community but ruled and exploited by an emerging priestly caste, had to defend itself against the plundering attacks of neighbouring nomadic tribes, which were also organized as primitive communities but were increasingly under the rule of the leaders of campaigns to steal, plunder, and wage war. Nomads stole, plundered, and took over the culture of agricultural tribes, taking them as their slaves. Farmers preserved their culture by defending themselves and by attacking nomads — taking them as their slaves, plundering, and robbing them. In both these cases, this led to the emergence of a new historical system — the **slavery of the Ancient World**.

Nomadic tribes take on the character of military democracies, democracies of free and equal people (slave owners). Silhouette-seeing continues to develop under this system, along with its orthogonal and relational perspective, in which the size of every represented object corresponds to the actual relationships of sizes in reality.

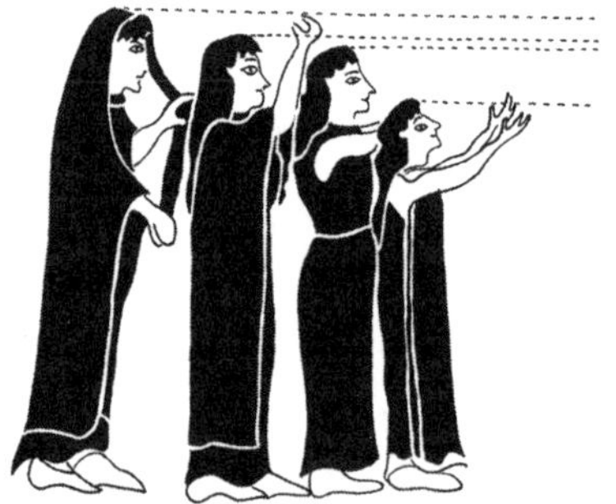

76
From crater,
Greece,
sixth c. BCE

The development of agricultural tribes took another route. Over the course of numerous defensive and offensive wars, military power increased and led to a conflict between a growing secular power and the priestly power that had existed up to this point. The victorious military leader conquers and unites all the hitherto independent tribes and communities in his territory and founds a state. To justify and consolidate his victory over a locally dispersed priestly caste (each community had its own god), he announces that he is the deity, or the son of the godhead (of the state as a whole). This moment of historical fraud is the basis of all the historical states of the **ancient East•**.

This is why the slavery system that developed in the states of the ancient East was based not on military democracy but on the foundations of and in relation to the preceding system of the Heliolithic priestly caste.

The disintegration of the primitive community took place under the pressure of a double yoke: the growing power of the subjugating royal machinery and the subordinate priestly caste that served it, which received its share of profits in exchange for its support of the monarchy. The historical opportunities for the development of the forces of production were conditioned by this double pressure — developed but at the same time hindered by the backwards organization of the state and the ruling class structure, whose remains it was saddled with.

• In different circumstances and in a different form, the same goal resulted in the burning of the historical books of the Qin Dynasty in China (third century BCE). Shi Huangdi, the winning Emperor and "Son of Heaven," murdered about four hundred scholars, supporters of the priests. This was to obliterate the traces of the previous priestly governance and present the power of the emperors as the eternal power.

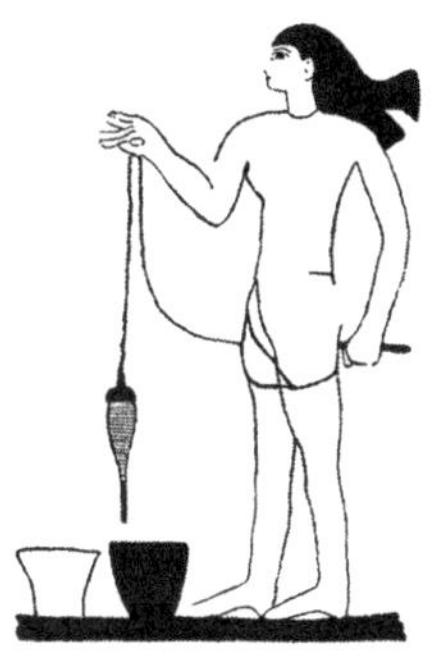

77
Tomb painting,
Egypt,
second millennium BCE

This is why silhouette-seeing could not fully develop in these states. Instead of the development of pure silhouette-seeing, both models of seeing were in use at the same time: contour and silhouette in the same picture.

We also see the coexistence of two different perspectives (intentional and orthogonal parallel). Each of these expresses a different level of knowledge and development. In intentional perspective, the size of represented objects has no relation to their actual objective size but results from a subjective, magic, or emotional relationship to the represented object, while in orthogonal parallel perspective the principle of a strictly proportionate relationship of objects is binding. The relationship between the scale of objects is the same as in reality.

The contradictions of development that were not resolved in the states of the ancient East were reflected in the contradictory, unnatural co-existence of two contradictory, different kinds of perspective. Figures were arranged in several rows. Each row was governed by strictly proportionate relationships. But the relationship between the rows was purely emotional.

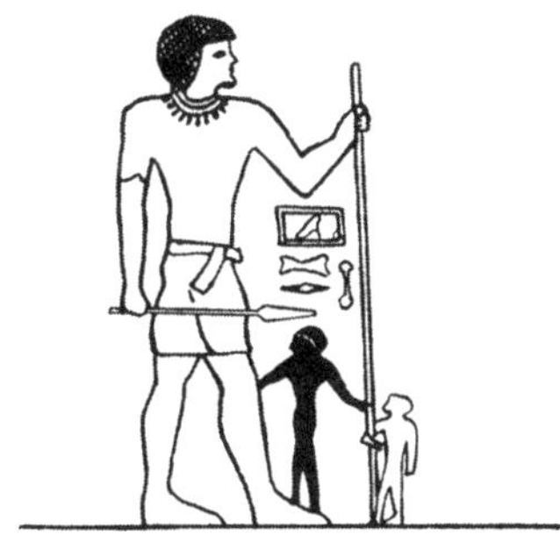

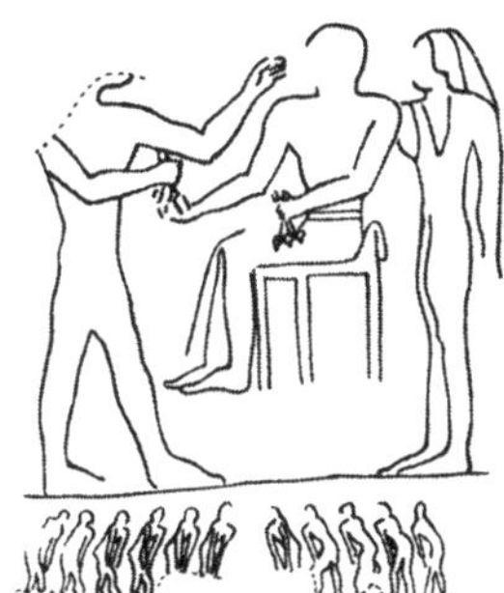

78
Relief,
Egypt,
third millennium BCE

79
Relief,
Egypt,
third millennium BCE

For example, the Pharaoh was always the largest, regardless of his actual height, his subjects the smallest and the size of state officials was somewhere in between. The principle of commensurate size was binding within a particular row and caste. This was the reflection, in visual art, of the principal historical fraud on which these states were founded as a consequence of unresolved developmental contradictions.

The consciousness of silhouette-seeing develops differently in every territory. Wherever the primitive community of hunters and herders makes the transition to the system of military democracy, the result is the development of silhouette-seeing. From a random placement of silhouettes in space, it moves to a strict and precise parallel orthogonal-projection perspective. Figures are positioned along the same common ground line and are subject to the same, common scale of dimensions.

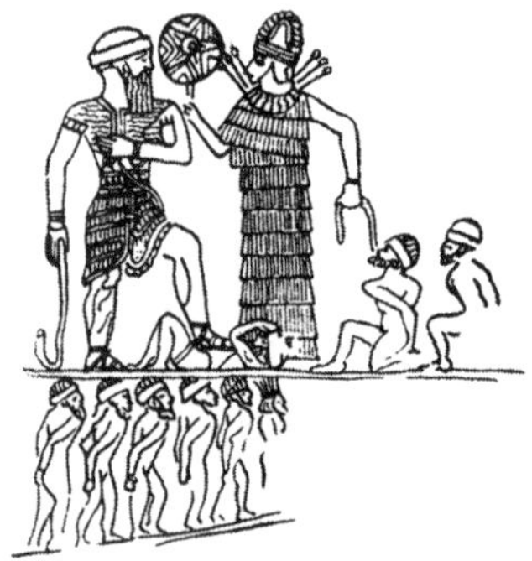

80
Relief,
Sumerian art,
third millennium BCE

In states building their slavery systems on the basis of as yet unresolved class rule, however, we see the non-organic and contradictory co-existence and overlapping of the two models of visual consciousness. In Heliolithic culture, contour-seeing and intentional perspective co-exist with silhouette-seeing and the perspective of parallel rows. The pressure exerted by the social structure makes it impossible to attain the level of realism already achieved in this period. The pressure exerted by the backwards social structure, hindering the growth of the forces of production, also hinders the development of visual consciousness, introducing those elements that have, over the course of their historical development, already passed over from realism to formalism. Being a reflection of historical-social underdevelopment, their formalism has as its aim to distort the image of reality in such a way as to lead to the emergence of suggestions favourable to the further existence of the reactionary classes. This kind of formalism is easily detectable by simple comparison with the progressive art of the progressive systems of the times. This formalism can be simply defined as a remnant of Heliolithic contour-seeing within the framework of the visual consciousness of the silhouette.

But there was also another formalism, being developed on the basis of the new achievements of realism of the times – on the basis of a full, highly developed consciousness of silhouette-seeing. In antagonistic social systems, every new, superior, model of realism, every superior model of visual consciousness inevitably brings forth its own inextricably linked formalism, which obscures reality and makes it impossible to see in full. In antagonistic social systems, the sources of formalism are to be sought in the achievements of realist-seeing, rather than elsewhere. This reveals the historical limitations of development. Realism and formalism constitute a dual unity of opposites. To understand the essence of the formalism of a given period, we have to examine its visual consciousness, its historically accomplished level of realism and to deduce from this the formalism of the period.

The development of silhouette is best considered in relation to Greek art, since it was this system of military democracy, unencumbered by the remains of Heliolithic culture, that gave rise to an art of the purest sort of silhouette-seeing.

What did silhouette-seeing achieve in terms of realism in relation to the preceding period?

1. **silhouette**, ascertaining that outlining the boundaries of the object does not exhaust its characteristics, that the solid materiality of the object lies within the contour.
2. **the commensurability** of objects, defining their size on the basis of their actual, measurable ratio, based on scale, rather than on personal (intentional) interest;
3. **orthogonal parallel-projection perspective**, placing objects on the same horizontal line of common ground;
4. **the phenomenon of afterimages** as a reflection in the consciousness of the objective fact of the chemical reactions taking place in the eye as part of the regenerative processes of vision.

These same achievements of realism also condition the formalism of silhouette-seeing:

1. **parallel row composition**, inextricably linked to parallel orthogonal-projection perspective;
2. **architectonisation of rhythm**, resulting from afterimages being transferred from one shape to another. The visibility of a flat patch of silhouette is greater than that of other kinds of forms. So the action of the image and afterimage are most strongly pronounced and most noticeable in the silhouette. If one accepts the silhouette, one must also accept the afterimages that are its consequence — and these lead to architectonisation and an increased expression of beauty (the classical beauty of Greek art).

It is this deformation, this transformation of the **realism** of seeing to the **beauty** of seeing that constitutes the essence of Greek art. The need for aesthetic experience, the need for beauty and harmony for inner moral cleansing — this was the direction taken as a result of the pressure of the antagonistic social system of the Greeks, of a society of free people (slave-owners).

Realism in Greek art develops in line with social development and the transformation of a military democracy into a democracy of craftsmen by way of the class struggle between the aristocracy (landowners and slave owners) and the demos (craftsmen, manual labourers, and slaves), becoming an ever broader and fuller reflection of the surrounding world, whose beauty and harmony is simultaneously augmented. It is characteristic of this art created by a democracy of craftsmen that it moves from abstract figures (archaic) to increasingly ordinary figures, not distinguished by an idealized beauty, although they are subjected to such strong afterimage rhythmicisation that the whole produces an impression of unforgettable beauty and harmony. The reality of everyday life, losing nothing of its concreteness, is transposed into the world of beauty. The formalism of art transforms reality into that which is demanded by the society that creates it. Seeing the world as beauty and harmony was what the class interests of the democracy of craftsmen demanded. Seeing the world and seeing harmony — are the opposite sides of the same unity, the unity of developing realism and of the formalism developing alongside it. This was how the progressive democracy of free Greek craftsmen, struggling for a full and harmonious development of every man living by his labours, presented a world constructed on the opposition of free people and slaves. It presented an antagonistic world as a world without contradictions, as the beautiful world of comprehensively and harmoniously developed man. Such was the class-conditioned origin of Greek formalism.

With the democracy of free craftsmen replacing military democracy, we see with increasing frequency the characteristic line that gives Greek art the singular beauty that expresses it.

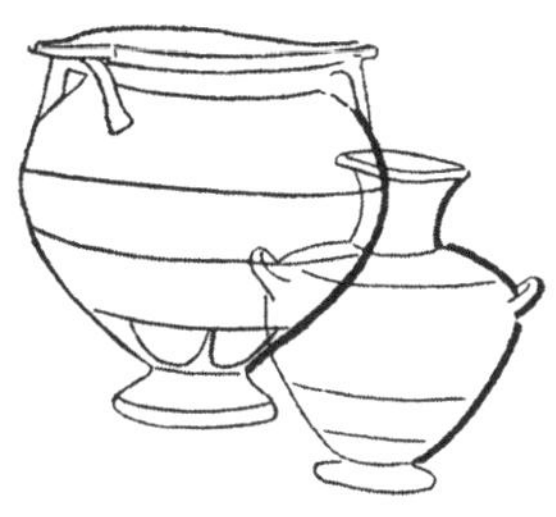

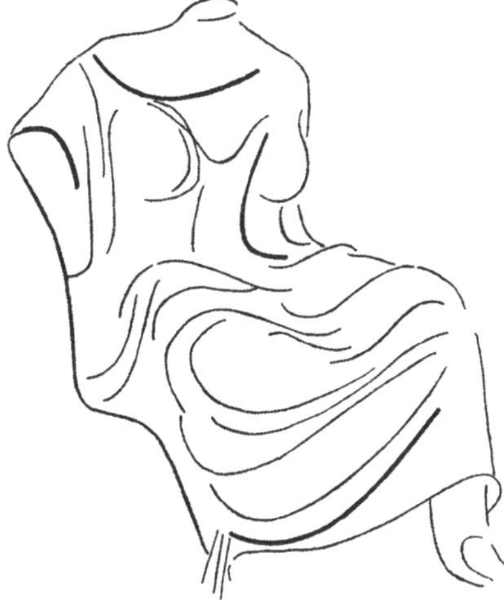

81
Vases,
Greece

82
Sculpture,
Parthenon,
fifth c. BCE

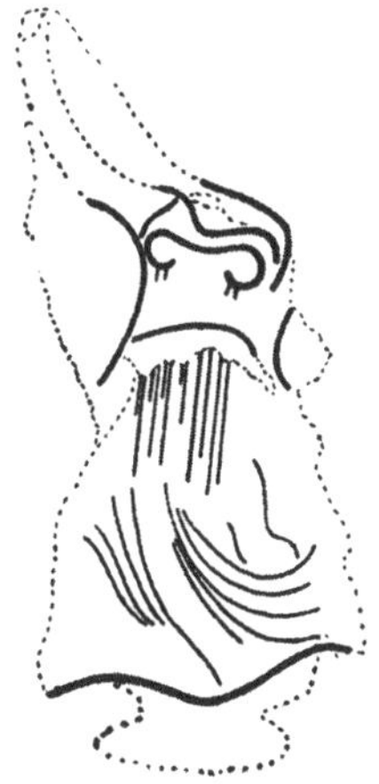

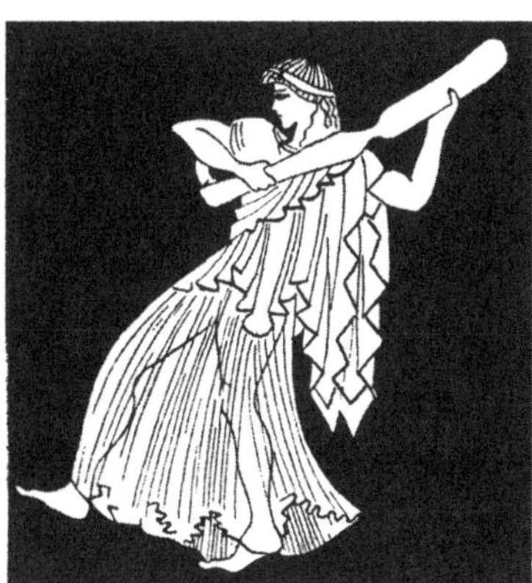

83
Sculpture,
Greece,
fifth c. BCE

84
From vase,
Greece,
fifth c. BCE

We encounter this line everywhere: in the profile of a vase, in the lines of an ornament, in folds of drapery, and in the lines of the human body.

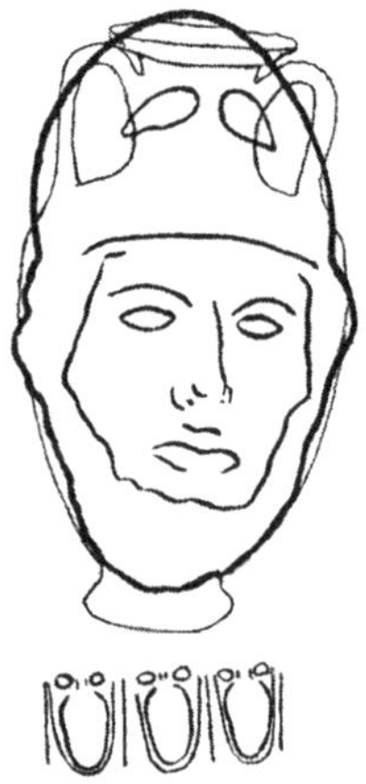

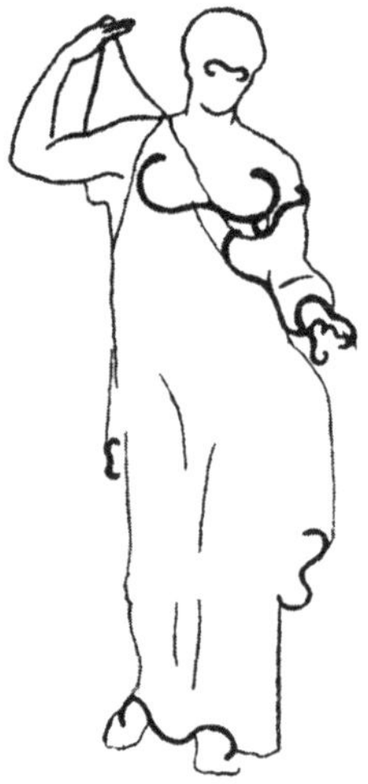

85
Sculpture,
Greece,
fifth c. BCE

86
Sculpture,
Greece,
fifth c. BCE

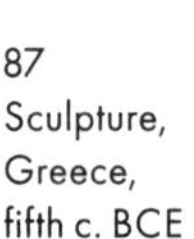

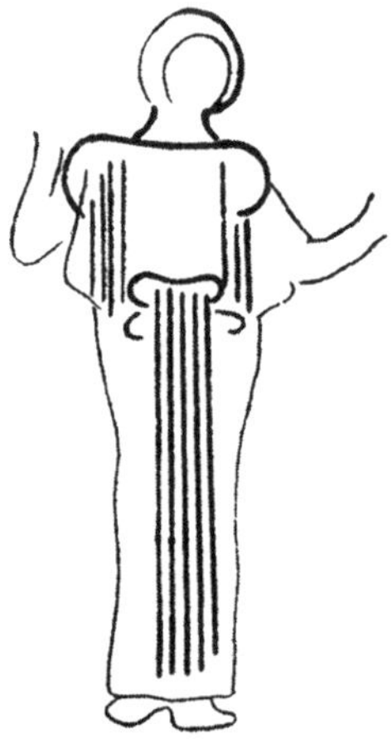

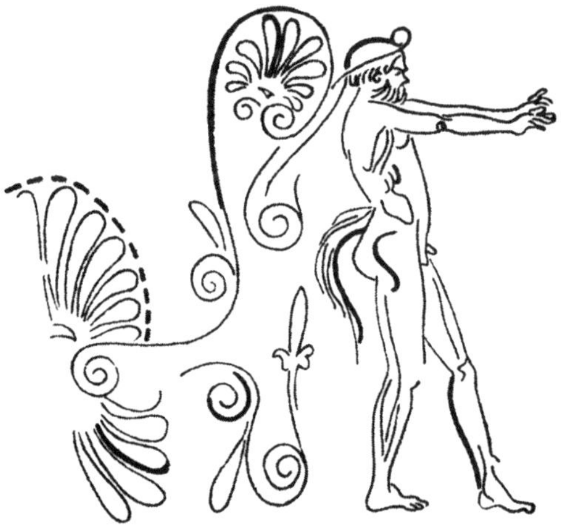

87
Sculpture,
Greece,
fifth c. BCE

88
From a skyphos,
Greece,
fifth c. BCE

This line is not simply the contour line but also appears in cross-sections. It defines not only the contour but also the convexity and characteristics of the three-dimensional form.

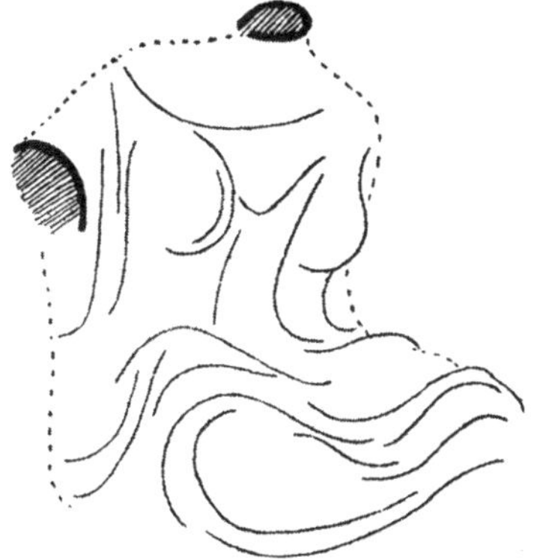

89
Sculpture, Parthenon, fifth c. BCE

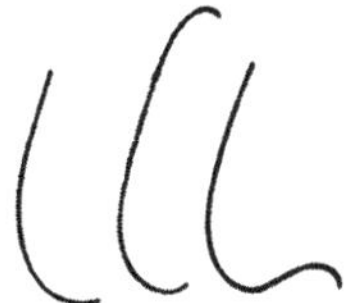

This line is everywhere. It delineates and defines every shape in Greek art at the peak of its development. A cross-section of a spiral is such a line, whether by itself or going on to become another spiral line.

We need to uncover the human significance underpinning such a widespread use of this line. A cross-section of a spiral is the line traced by launching a stone or a shot, a measure of the force used to overcome adversities, obstacles, and resistance. If we take two adjacent cross-sections of the spiral, however, we have a measure of human effort intensifying, reaching the peak of its strength, and then diminishing. An effort constantly being renewed and battling with the obstacles standing before it. An effort being renewed constantly and falling, only to rise again. The effort of a living creative man, his thoughts and muscles. Man who is the measure of all things.

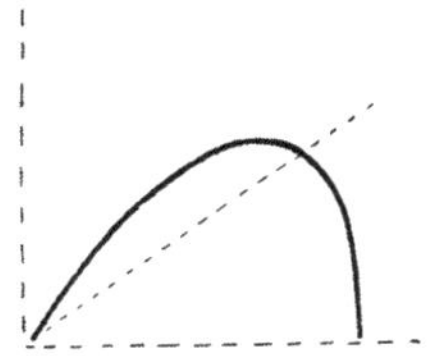

This is how the formalism of Greek art turns into its dialectical opposite — becomes the most profound essence of its realism: a realism of the truth about man, who has harmoniously developed his abilities; a realism that erases the boundaries between physical and intellectual labour; a realism of man forever living and creative — for whom the source of life is his creative effort and work.

At some point, pure silhouette-seeing ceases to correspond to the developing visual consciousness. Man begins to see more than the silhouette can offer. Observations slowly accumulate, and the way out of the current state of visual consciousness is sought. Usually, in such breakthrough periods, the advance is associated with the means of the preceding period. Man begins to make use of elements of contour-seeing to develop further observations.

Silhouette continues to exist, but it is overlaid with contour drawing. A transitional model of seeing emerges, characteristic of Greek painting (the vase) and of the Phidian period in general.

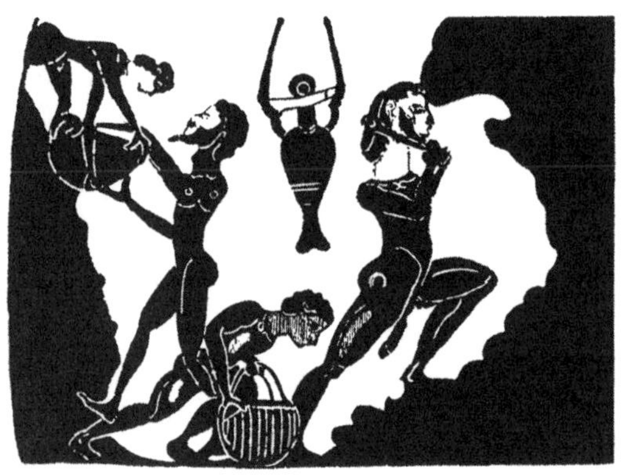

90
From a pinax, Corinth, sixth c. BCE

The architectonisation of the work of art and the use of formal transfers are most fully expressed in this period. The line drawing, overlaid on silhouette, complements it and shows what a silhouette alone cannot express. What we have here is a common historical phenomenon whereby, in order to achieve new objectives that are ahead of the times, there is recourse to a certain sort of masquerade that presents what is new as a simple return to the past. This is how, in a given case, in order to achieve new means of expression one looks to the preceding period. The means of expression of the **previous** period are appropriated so as to express **new** visual content. In this way a combined **silhouette-linear** form of expression emerges, which, in reality, equates to a model of seeing that goes beyond flat silhouette-seeing. This form already contains the germ of three-dimensional visual consciousness: the relationship between the plane of the silhouette and the contour defines the depth of the object — the depth of the third dimension.

As observation develops, the quantity of lines increases, generally accumulating at the edges of the object — there lies their greatest thicket.

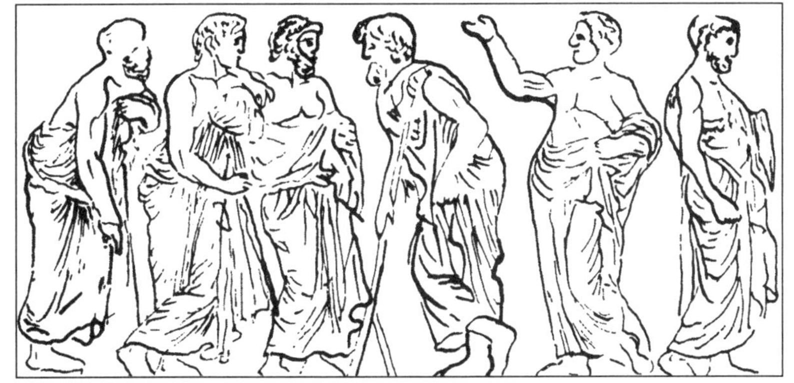
91
Relief,
Parthenon,
Greece,
fifth c. BCE

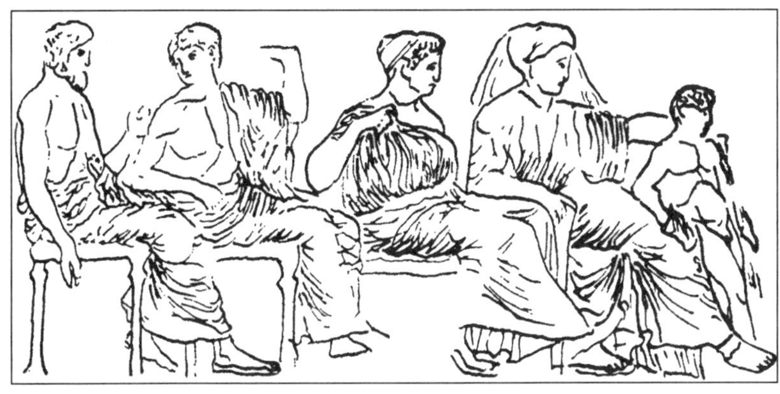
92
Relief,
Parthenon,
Greece,
fifth c. BCE

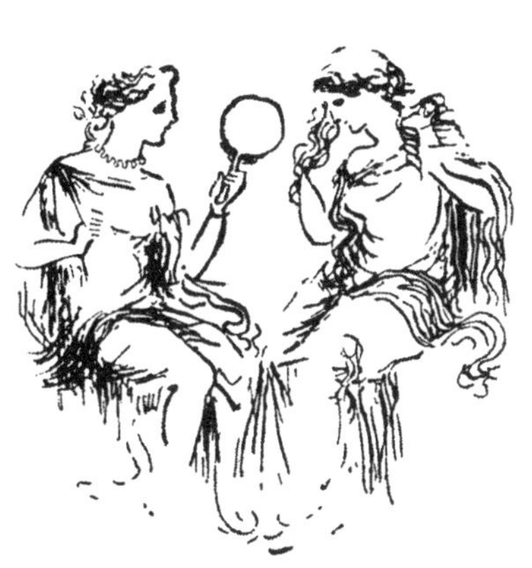
93
From the cover of a mirror,
Greece,
fourth c. BCE

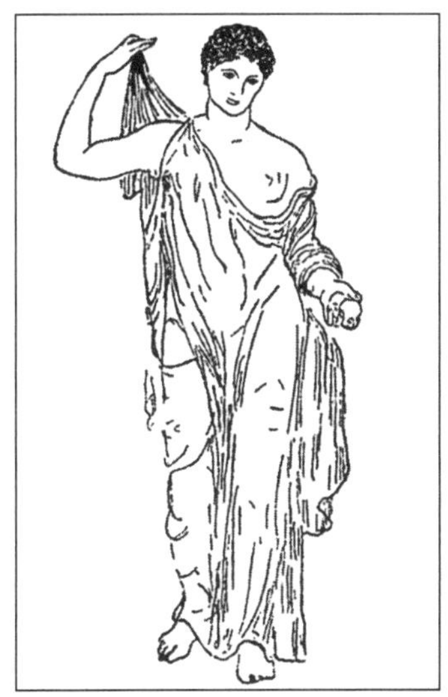
94
Sculpture,
Greece,
fifth c. BCE

solid-form seeing (commodity-seeing in the age of developing commodity exchange)

Intent upon uncovering a means of expression capable of showing the convexity and three-dimensionality of the object, observation initially drew on prior experience: the experience of **silhouette** (that the object inside its contour is treated as a uniform mass) and **contour within contour** (that the convexity of the three-dimensional form within the contour could be expressed synthetically by way of appropriately directed lines).

We see an accumulation of linear characteristics **superimposed** on the silhouette throughout the entire period of classical Greek art.

This is just a step away from merging these lines and shading the object or solid form. In this way, Greek painting enters a new period of visual consciousness based on observing the phenomenon of the solid form and an understanding of how to render it. This occurred during the Peloponnesian Wars. Fully-developed examples of this sort can be found in the art of Alexandria. Anecdotes tell how revolutionary and new these changes were, such as the one about a painter who painted fruit so real that birds pecked at it, while another painter's drapery appeared so natural that a colleague — another painter, therefore a visually experienced person — wanted to sweep it to the side.[5] All these anecdotes testify to a great breakthrough in painting — mastering the means of rendering solids.

5 The reference is to two competing Greek painters of the fifth century BCE, Zeuxis of Heraclea and Parrhasius of Ephesus.

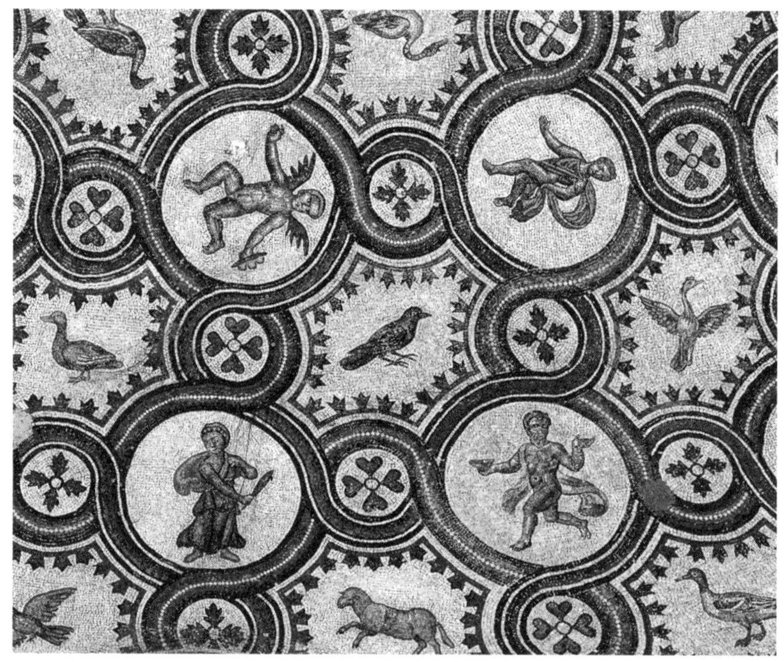

95
Mosaic,
Rome,
fourth c. CE

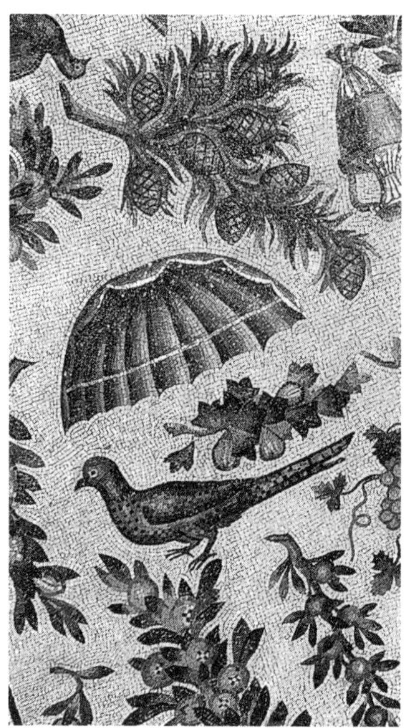

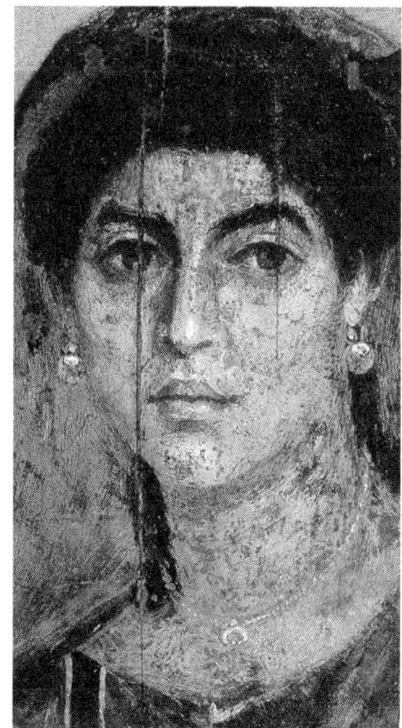

96
Mosaic,
Rome,
fourth c. CE

97
Tomb portrait,
Egypt,
first c. CE

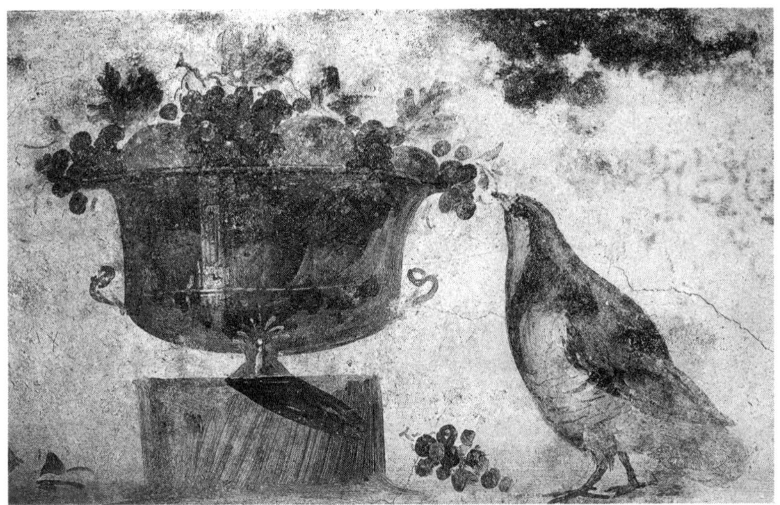

98
Wall painting,
Rome,
second c. CE

The change in visual consciousness necessarily led to the transformation of formal means of expression in art: in the first instance – perspective. Out of the whole complex of the object's features, silhouette-seeing took into account only its flat silhouette, placed on a level ground, shared by all objects. This form of consciousness was incapable of perceiving phenomena representing depth. Depth was felt, but there was no consciousness of precisely what data associated with seeing would serve to express the third dimension or how to position the solid form in receding space. The solid form was initially positioned in parallel-line projection perspective. The object was convex, modelled with shading, but placed on a flat background. This solved the problem of the single solid form, but it did not solve the problem of the three-dimensional space in which the objects were located. A new visual consciousness – the consciousness of spatial depth – rendered it necessary to accumulate observations serving to express the depth that was being sought. Up until then, the consciousness of a flat silhouette with a superimposed line-drawing had been accepted as the complete image of the object. With the end of the classical Greek period, in the transition to Hellenism, visual consciousness developed in so far as new components began to be sought, ones which not only brought out the object's flat contour but also its depth – the sides that lie beyond the front of the object and are invisible from the front.

New components of observation appear alongside the existing scrutiny of the flat front of the object — as a result of looking beyond the face of the object at its sides.

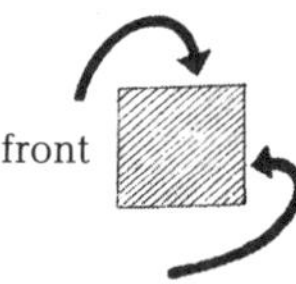

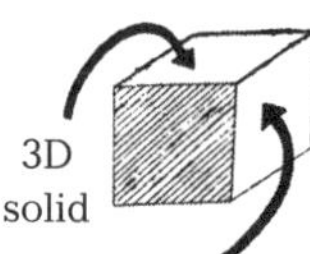

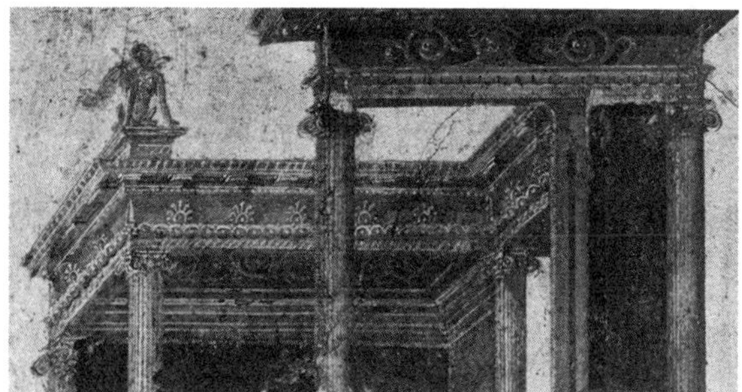

99
Wall painting,
Pompeii,
first c. CE

In this way, the following variants of **oblique perspective** came to be formulated (in place of parallel-line-projection perspective):

1. **Oblique parallel projection perspective**, where the spatiality and depth of the object were expressed by observing them from an oblique angle so that we see the front and depth of every object at the same time. Objects further away are located higher in the picture than those in closer proximity, but their size remains unchanged. They remain commensurate, as in silhouette perspective. We come across this perspective in Persian, Japanese, and Chinese art.

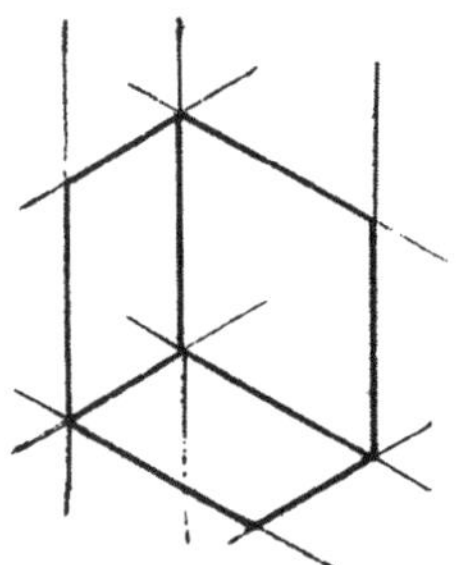

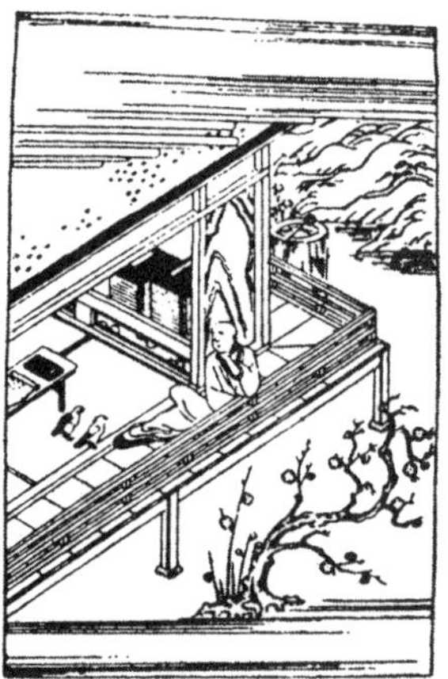

100
Woodcut,
Japan,
eighteenth c.

2. **Converging projection perspective** developing in states with a Hellenistic culture. The diminishing of the size of objects with distance, placing objects on different levels (the higher the further away) made the formulation of a new model of perspective possible — three-dimensional linear, which is currently considered to be traditional perspective. This is no longer a perspective of commensurate dimensions. The sizes of objects are subject to change depending on distance. One cannot juxtapose one object with another to compare them and to establish their size; one has to sketch out a whole complicated geometric construction and only then can one define, indirectly, by mathematical reasoning, the real sizes and proportions of objects located at different distances.

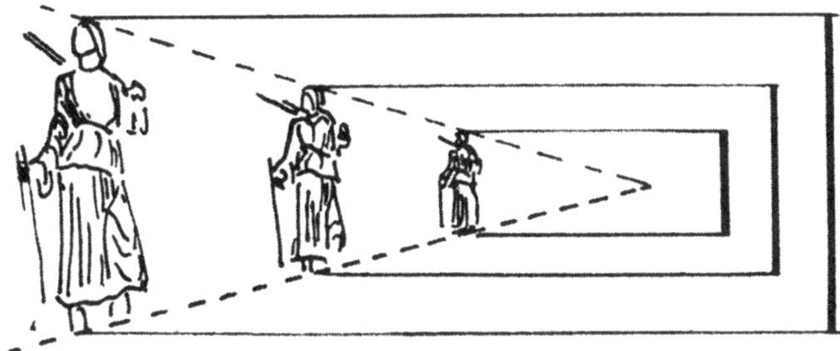

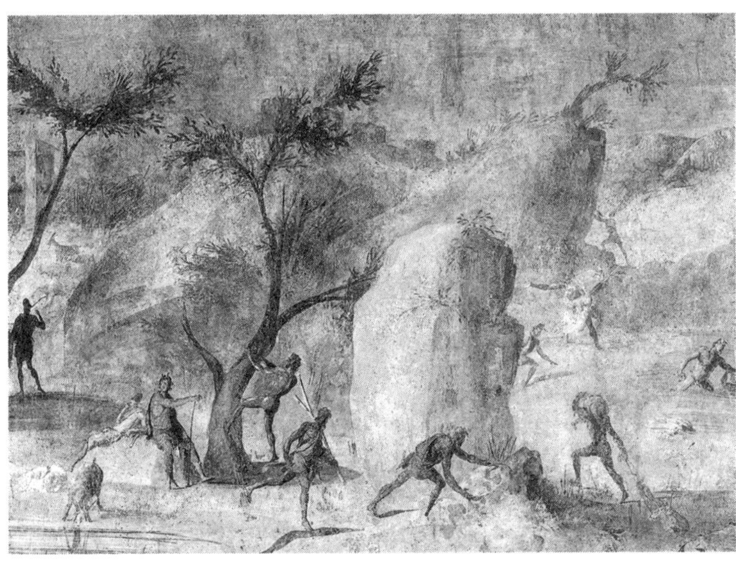

101
Wall painting,
Rome,
40–30 BCE

Currently, everyone thinks that this is natural perspective, fully conforming to human seeing; that this perspective is innate to man; that it was only because of underdevelopment that it was not attained right from the cradle of mankind; that it has been universally accepted by the people at large as natural and innate.

We know, however, that nothing is innate. Everything emerges as a result of the process of historical transformation. In this same way, three-dimensional **convergent** perspective was not accepted as a natural manifestation but rather acquired the right to existence though a series of struggles.

It was not an innate perspective for everyone. There were people for whom the previous perspective was better suited to their visual consciousness and expressed the truth for them, whilst the new perspective — expressing illusions and visions — was untrue. It is only through the force of habit that we consider that, for instance, three-dimensional **convergent** perspective is unrivalled and innate. The contemporaries of the period in which it was born were not in agreement as to its value. Plato wrote in *The Republic*:

"Is a bed that is closer or further away not the same size? And so should we not draw this bed as the same size? Is it not an illusion to draw a bed standing further away in smaller dimensions? Are those painters, who draw in accordance with this perspective, not producers of illusion, and so liars?" (Citation not literal.[6])

In this example, Plato represented the views of people associated with silhouette-seeing; three-dimensional **convergent** perspective was not at all innate and natural for him but a novel perspective that shocked him and did not correspond to the truth of his visual consciousness.

6 Source text: Plato, *The Republic* 598 A. Strzemiński was probably citing from memory. It is also possible that it was his own translation from a critical edition in another language — this would explain why he used a non-Polish title *(Republika)* in the original Polish text. In the English translation of Plato, the fragment runs: "Does a bed really differ from itself when you look at it from the side or from straight in front of from any other point of view, or does it remain the same but appear different? And so with other things." Plato, *The Republic*, Book X, trans. A.D. Lindsay with intro. by A. Nehamas and notes by R. Bambrough (London: Everyman's Library, 1992), p. 285.

Colour, in this period, no longer stops short at differentiating between the silhouette and the flat background, but becomes spatial colour. The juxtaposition of colours was subordinated to the need to grasp three-dimensional space. The range of colours was expanded, enriched, and refined. While in silhouette-seeing, it was enough to paint the background one colour and the objects another, taking care that colours were distinct from one another, here, in this new perspective, it is no longer enough to juxtapose two colours. It became necessary to use a variety of modulated colours. The objective is not only the shading of the figure but a tuning of colours such that one is pushed forwards and the other pushed back. These are colour juxtapositions of a broad range: warm (red, yellow), cold (blue, green). Darkening, brightening, bleaching. A very rich colour scale is produced (Pompeian frescoes).

The change from a visual consciousness of the silhouette to that of solids had the following consequences:

1. the transformation of the perspectival system from orthogonal parallel-projection to oblique three-dimensional,
2. a change in colour system and the enrichment of the colour scale.

A change of aesthetic criteria takes place at the same time, however. The ideal of beauty is different from that of the preceding system. As we have seen, silhouette consciousness brought forth two problems that were defining for the aesthetic of the silhouette eras:

a) parallel rhythms, linking horizontal rows,
b) the architectonic unity of sculpture, painting, and architecture.

Rhythm and architectonics were thus the criteria of beauty that emerged from this model of seeing. In order to understand the beauty of the Parthenon frieze or of the Notre-Dame portal, for instance, we have to approach their evaluation with the appropriate measure. The criteria derived directly from the visual consciousness of the times constitute this measure. Formal elements and the methods of their evaluation, along with the ideals of beauty prevailing at the given time, are all the result of the model of seeing.

In solid-form seeing, ideals of beauty were derived from the character of formal elements – being their concrete realization to the highest standard. The formal elements were the soft shading of form and a rich, varied palette of colours. This form inevitably resulted in a striving for subtlety, gentle and toned down softness, charm, an intimate lyricism. These ideals of beauty were the crowning achievement of the visual form of the time, its most perfect embodiment. Thus the process of formal change responded to the historical process of the development of visual consciousness. The consequence of these formal changes was a change in the ideals of beauty, conditioned by the course of history. We see here a direct causal relationship between the prevailing model of visual consciousness and the formal elements that express it. The linear form corresponds to silhouette-seeing, since attention is fully focused on outlining the silhouette and the formal play revolves entirely around bringing out the linear rhythm of parallel rows. Out of a rhythm of parallel rows that links sculpture, architecture, and painting in a single whole, there arise an architectonics whose evaluative bases are rhythm, linear dynamics, and the compositional unity of formal expression. Thus the model of visual consciousness determines the character of formal means and defines aesthetic criteria.

The same causal relationship can be seen in solid-form seeing. Here, it is the convex elements of the relief that are the most significant, rather than the linear elements. Three-dimensional, convex form, varying degrees of distance of closer or more distant objects can only be represented by way of shading and a varied intensity of colours. Greater or lesser intensities of the same colour, transitions from one colour to another, the juxtaposition of colours placed side by side in the picture but expressing varying degrees of distance — all this demanded as its principal means of expression a rich and varied colour range. Colour becomes the principal formal element, in all its wealth and diversity. Thus the transition to a new model of visual consciousness creates a corresponding new range of formal means. The focus is on convex, rather than on linear, form — as the only form capable of expressing three-dimensional spatial relations. This form, in turn, defines the character of aesthetic criteria. Instead of an aesthetics of rigorous architectonic rhythms, instead of an aesthetics of strict compositional unity, we now have an aesthetics of varied colour, toned-down passages, a lyrical aesthetics of intimate charm — the charm of a life of consumption. Hence a new aesthetics arises on the basis of this new model of visual consciousness, with new values and new criteria of beauty. The consequence of a change in the model of visual consciousness is a change in the ideal of beauty.

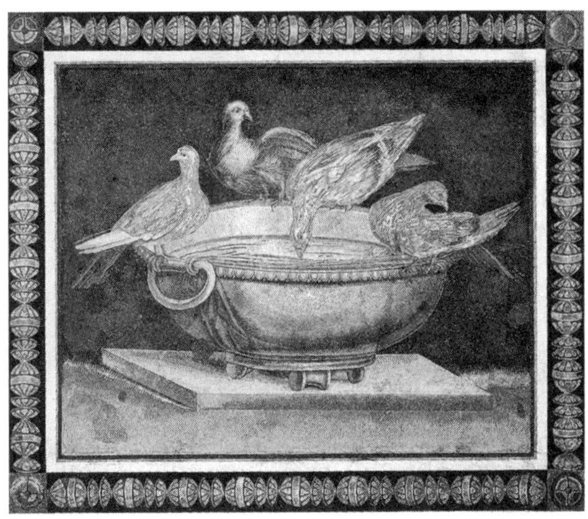

102
Mosaic,
Rome,
second c. CE

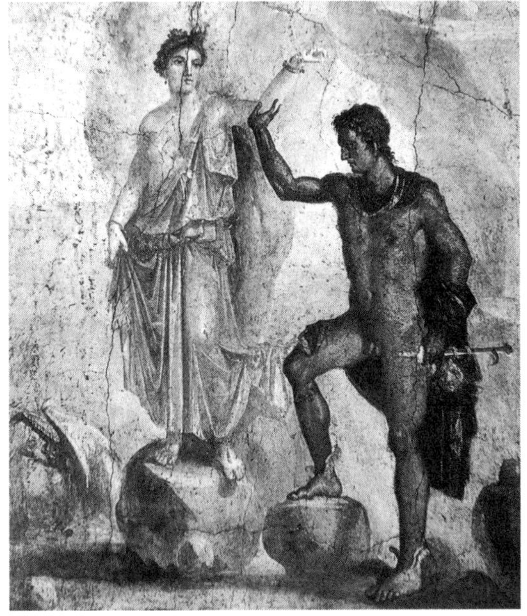

103
Wall painting,
Pompeii,
first c. CE

This conformity between the objective development of visual consciousness (the development of the scope of realism) and the social essence condensed in an ideal of beauty, was only possible because both visual consciousness and emotional essence are a reflection of more profound and essential matters – a reflection of the historical process in all its complexity. They expressed both its progress and its inherent class contradictions.

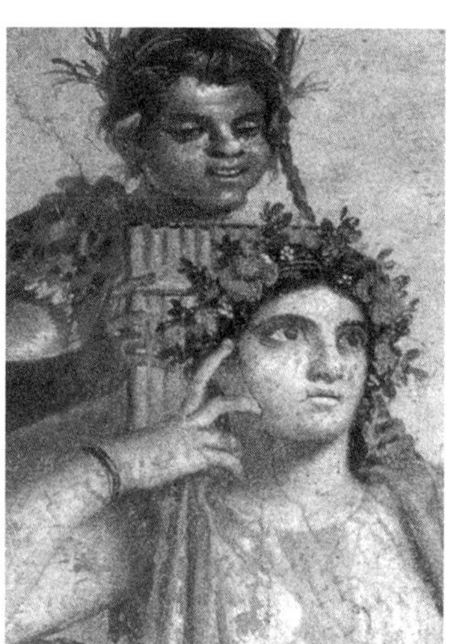

104
Wall painting,
Herculaneum,
first c. CE

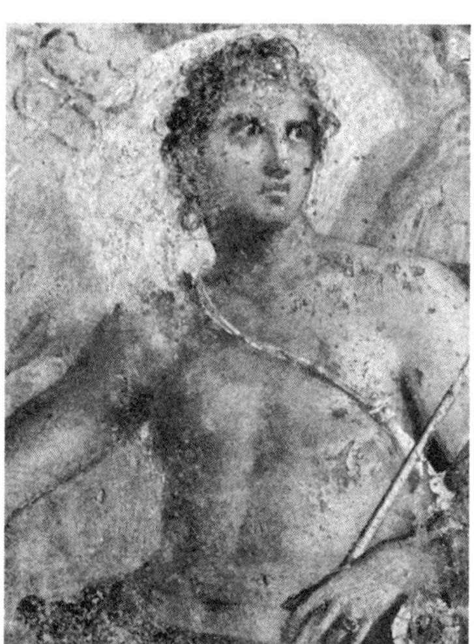

105
Wall painting,
Pompeii,
first c. CE

In order to express intimate, consumerist purport, painting had to master the colour and chiaroscuro techniques that resulted from the visual consciousness of the solid. To pass from silhouette seeing to solid-form seeing, it had to undertake the arduous task of attaining a new, superior model of realism. This objective progress coincided with the development of the new purport and experience of the **new** social system that was developing. Both these seemingly independent, evolutionary lines converged at one point. This occurred because both the developing scrutiny of three-dimensional space and the change in emotional purport preoccupying society were simply two reflections of the same process of historical transformation of ancient society.

The development of the forces of production (in the transition to Hellenism) was expressed in the development of observation, in the development of spatial thinking, and in the transition from a hitherto flat representation of space and silhouette-seeing to an articulation of spatial depth and three-dimensional form, as well as in the developing components of observation expressing the third dimension of space. These observations were linked to the thought process and were formulated into generalizing rules.

However, **this same** development of the forces of production brought about shifts in class within ancient society, the fall of some groups, the emergence and rise of others. These new social groups, which arose within slave-owning society, introduced a new ideological purport and a new range of emotional experiences, resulting from their conditions of existence. With the progressive development of these groups and their rise to rule over society, this purport of theirs was imposed universally, becoming the principal purport imposed on society as a whole.

The development of the forces of production entailed the development of observation, the expansion of its range, and the transition to a superior model of visual consciousness. For their part, the class relations that emerged on the basis of these forces of production defined the essence of the purport of art as socially experienced.

The process that determined the transition from silhouette-seeing to the visual consciousness of the solid form was the continued development of ancient slavery, its transformation from the system of the democracy of craftsmen (small slave-owners) to intensive models of owning great numbers of slaves. The transformation of a classical Greek culture into Hellenistic culture (Rome, for its part, was none other than a local variety of Hellenism) was conditioned by the development of intensive models of slave ownership and the transition to commodity production and to commodity exchange•. The development of the forces of production was a result of the following:

1. mass **commodity production** by large workshops (ergasteria) based on slave labour that replaced the hitherto existing small craftsmen's workshops where craftsman worked alongside slaves;
2. mass **commodity exchange** across the expansive territories of newly founded states;

• In old Roman law, an almost perfect expression of legal relations, resulting from that level of economic development that Marx calls "commodity production." [In the fragment quoted by Strzemiński, Marx used the terms: "commodity production," "manufacture of commodities." See K. Marx, *Wage Labour and Capital*, introduced and trans. F. Engels (1847) first published in German in the *Neue Rheinische Zeitung*, nos. 264–267 and 269 (April 5–8 and 11, 1849).

3. increased employment as a result of the mass production of slaves• as commodities (captured in numerous wars in the period from the fourth to the first century BCE);
4. the development of science, which emerged as a theoretical universalisation of the productive activity of the preceding period and stimulated the contemporary development of production by way of its achievements.

It is worth noting the particular scope of these sciences. It was mainly those sciences that either directly examined three-dimensional space (Euclid's solid geometry, stereometry) or examined natural phenomena, conditioned directly by three-dimensional space (astronomy, mechanics, geography) or indirectly (biology, medicine), that developed in the Hellenistic era (mainly in Alexandria). The common basis on which the development of science in the Hellenist period was based was the classical three-dimensional space of stereometry – the abstracted, "ideal" space of Euclid, detached from matter and time and existing only for itself. The common basis of the Hellenist sciences was the geometry of three-dimensions – the same three dimensions being targeted by the development of visual consciousness. The diagram of a geometric solid form in Euclidean stereometry was analogous to a three-dimensional drawing in Hellenistic painting.

Scientific investigations stimulated artists, increasing their sensitivity to those sensory experiences and observations of nature that express spatial depth. This scrutiny was not passive but occurred simultaneously with thinking – associating, universalising individual observations and encapsulating them in principles and rules. It was only the combined work of mind and sight, becoming consciousness of the essence of one's observations, that made the formation of **three-dimensional** visual consciousness possible. Only thanks to the participation of thinking in the process of receiving visual sensations was it possible to associate miscellaneous observations with one another and to universalise these into a single theory. Advanced thinking –

• "The slave did not sell his labour-power to the slave-owner, any more than the ox sells his labour to the farmer... He is a commodity that can pass from the hands of one owner to that of another. He himself is a commodity." K. Marx, "What are wages? How are they determined?," in K. Marx, *Wage Labour and Capital*, trans. and with an introduction by F. Engels, 1847, in *Works of Karl Marx 1847*, accessed 31 October 2016, https://www.marxists.org/archive/marx.

developed and practiced through generalization and the ability to abstract — were required in order to express depth on a plane.

It was the development of the forces of production, stimulating science and flexible thinking, that made the transition to a visual consciousness of three-dimensional form possible. Without the practised ability to create complex mathematical constructions, without the **mathematical** imagination of three-dimensional space, its **artistic** representation would be impossible.

The three-dimensional, convex, solid form of the object as it now appeared made possible the best, most precise representation of the commodity properties of this object — its size, convexity, colour, weight, etc. In its three-dimensional form, it becomes almost palpable, it can almost be grasped and weighed. This commodity form of nature depicted in works of art corresponds to the period of commodity exchange. The objective progress of developing visual consciousness in this period served to express the qualities of commodities in commodity exchange. The material value of the commodity found its expression in the material, three-dimensional, convex representation of the object, which was made possible by the attainment of three-dimensional, spatial visual consciousness.

The transition from the purport of the preceding period, embodied in its uniform architectonic harmony to the commodity purport of the Hellenistic period, was an ideological expression of the changes taking place at that time in slave-owning society. In addition to the principal conflict between slaves and slave-owners, there was a struggle among various groups of slave-owners. In the formative period of classical Greece, there was a class struggle between the progressive democracy of craftsmen and the landed aristocracy, based on the old ancestral system. The development of (small-scale) slave-ownership in this period strengthened the power of the craftsmen's democracy, providing it with a material basis for existence and with financial independence. The small workshop, in which the craftsman worked along with members of his family and a few slaves, constituted the material basis for the emergence of a political struggle for democracy and for the holistic, harmonious development of the free man. A Greek craftsman living from the fruits of his labour (and that of his slaves) had grounds to believe, by virtue of this work of his, that he represented the aspirations of **all** people (with one small exception — slaves).

In so far as the developing slavery system was a factor propelling the development of democracy in the period of the democracy of craftsmen (and the visual consciousness of the silhouette that corresponded with it), the situation changes in the period that follows. Hitherto united, democracy is shattered by the increase in slavery, by its concentration, the transition from craftsmen's workshops to ergasteria. Plutocracy replaces democracy, being more competitive, ruining the middle class and making slaves of the hitherto free poor. Plutocracy gives rise to another social ideal, the ideological expression of its class position. The elevation of plutocracy above hitherto existing democratic society is expressed in the destruction of the prevailing aesthetic ideals of democracy. The slave system, whose development initially strengthened ancient democracy, then turned against it, empowering the plutocracy. Political and active man is replaced by private, propertied man. Rather than collective activity, by nature **political**, it is the private, egoistic use of commodities (or a conscious renunciation of these) that becomes the new purport introduced by the Hellenist plutocracy.

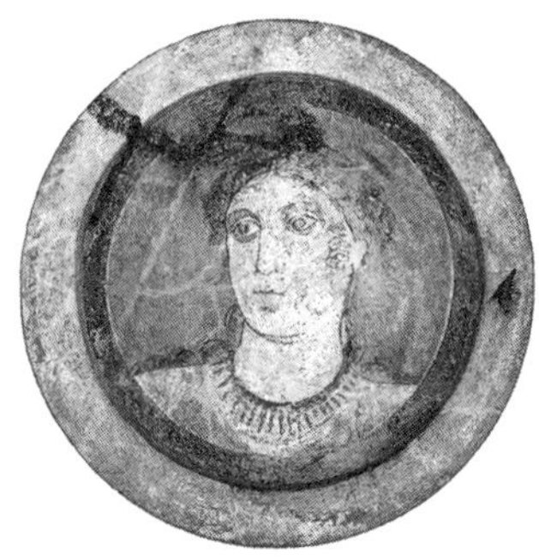

106
Portrait,
Sicily,
Hellenistic art

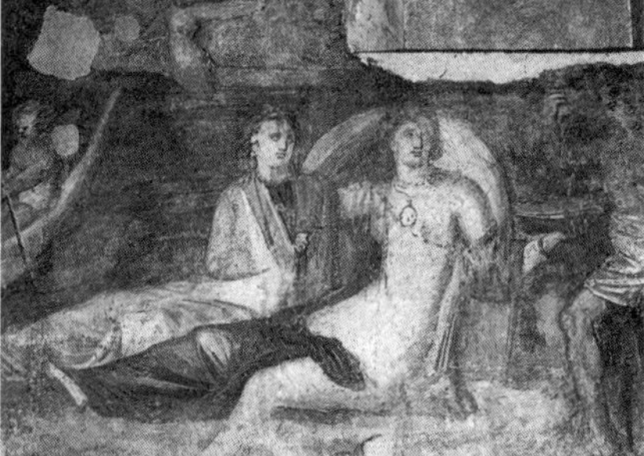

107
Wall painting,
Rome,
second c. CE

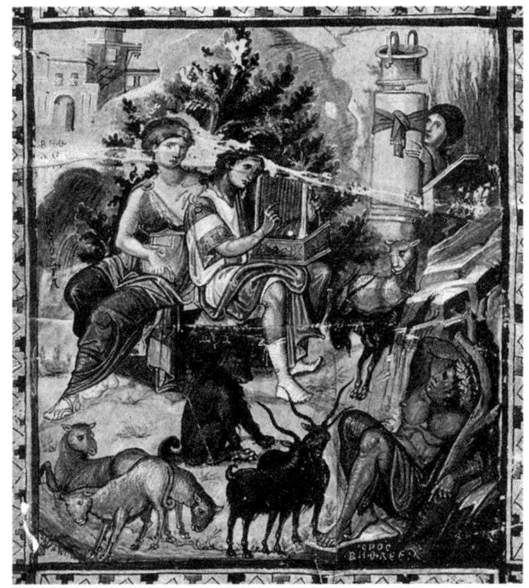

108
Miniature from Greek psalter, thirteenth c.

The class interests of the plutocracy dominant in the Hellenistic period impose on society their own corresponding purport. This is expressed in the very manner of representing objects as well as in the subject matter represented. To represent the egoistic possessiveness of the propertied classes as the supreme value and the bliss of life. To represent that which the non-propertied classes had been deprived of as wise renunciation and the attainment of true joy. The same commodity was at once the supreme worldly good, joy, when possessed by the wealthy man, and joy (for whoever who did not possess it), when he renounced and did not possess it. The philosophy of the Hellenistic era is as a whole, in essence, the teaching of the rational use of commodities. Stoics, Epicureans, and Cynics disagreed with one another only as to the degree of consumption of commodities permissible and the extent of their renunciation. Social passivity, inner life, varying degrees of asceticism, peace and spiritual harmony, moderate renunciation in the name of reason, spiritual independence — these are the main purport of all these philosophical systems — schooling the oppressed classes in how to surrender and passively endure the oppression of the ruling classes. Generally speaking, this is a philosophy that seeks an ideal balance between the use of commodities and their renunciation. Scales — the universal tool of commodity exchange – provided the material basis for this philosophy. Philosophical systems that seek this equilibrium, revolving around the problem of measure, are the reflection of these scales transposed into the realm of ideas. The scales of the merchant and the wholesaler entered the mind of the thinker and, shedding their weight, dimensions, and other material properties, became a philosophical system.

The human body itself, represented as an expression of the infinite abilities of universal human development in the previous period, now becomes a passive commodity whose beauty can be evaluated, purchased, and consumed.

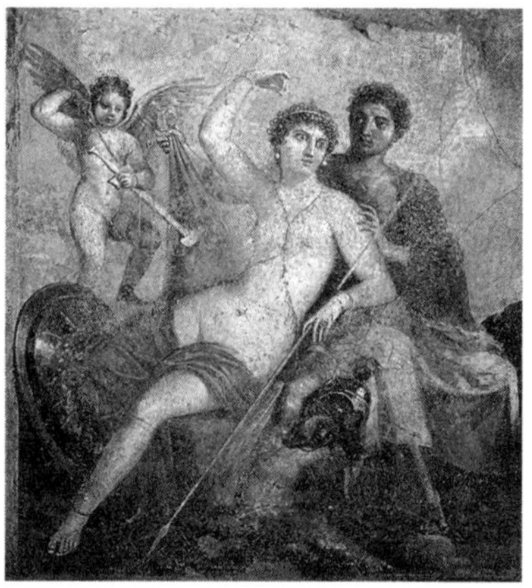

109
Wall painting,
Pompeii,
first c. CE

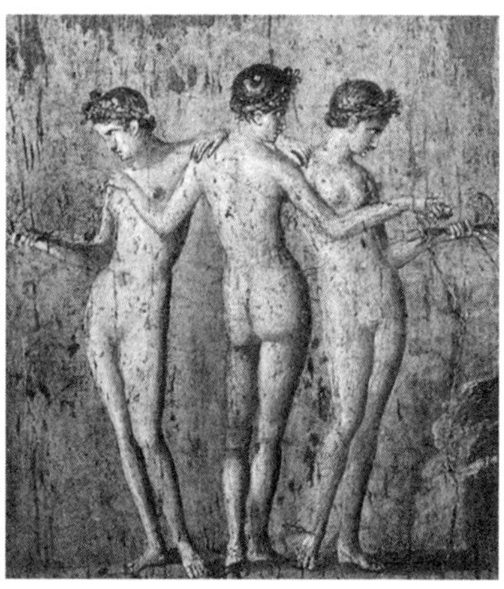

110
Wall painting,
Pompeii,
first c. CE

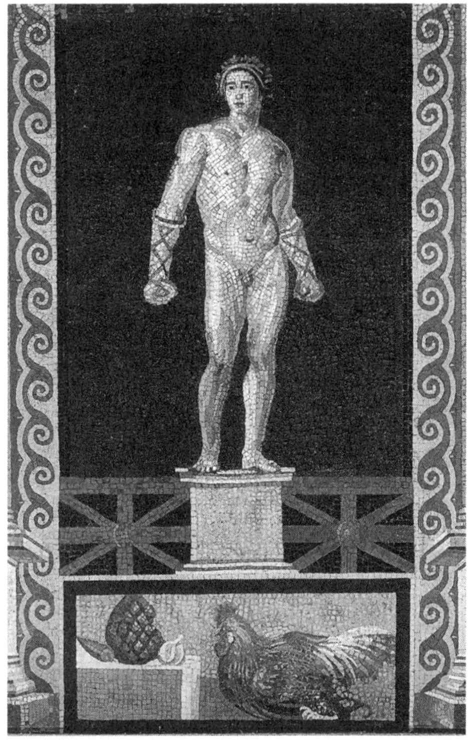

111
Mosaic,
Rome,
first c. CE

This is how the deformations determined by class in Hellenistic art functioned. Conditioned by the development of the forces of production, visual consciousness developed, and the inferior model of silhouette realism was transformed into a superior model of realism — that of the solid form and space. But this same development of the forces of production resulted in a change in social structure. The new ruling class brought with it new social purport proper to itself. The new formalism, determined by class, is inextricably linked to the new, objectively superior realism. The properties of the **formalism of commodity production** cannot be expressed in any realism other than the historically corresponding realism of solids and space. In antagonistic social systems every realism is inextricably linked with its corresponding formalism.

All the components of observation that make up three-dimensional seeing find expression in deploying those means that best characterise the commodity-oriented, consumerist **formalism of the age of commodity exchange**. This formalism is the deformation of nature through commodification, the use of real, objective components of seeing the world, expressing the commodity characteristics of various objects, their status as commodities. That only these elements were observed was the result of historical development and of the developing visual consciousness of three-dimensional space, of the solid form – its size, weight, colour, and structure. All these aspects of nature, actually observed, essentially constitute the commodity characteristics of objects. Realism and formalism are inseparable, dialectically linked.

An interruption in developmental continuity occurs with the fall of Greek and Roman culture.

There follows a retreat in the model of visual consciousness and its formal means in visual art. This retreat was not the same in all territories.

In place of a varied and subtly graduated colouring and three-dimensional space, analogous to that in Pompeian frescos (in around the first century this model prevailed across the field of Greco-Roman culture as a whole), Byzantium regressed to the model of seeing represented in Alexandrian portraiture, that is to say, to a solid object differentiated from a flat background – to a seeing only just emerging from the earlier conception of the silhouette.

This retreat of the principal model of seeing also entailed a change in the universal ideal of beauty. The retreat taking place becomes a retreat to architectonic art. In place of colour composition and the intimate lyricism of softly gradated colours, we see the return of linearism and architectonism. Shape is no longer defined through shading and the gradation of colour but through an emphasis on the line describing it. These lines combine to form rows of rhythmic arrangements, and by absorbing shapes from the surrounding architecture, they give painting a disciplined character, subordinated to the architectural whole. Art returns to the architectonics it previously left behind – a retreat of some five hundred years.

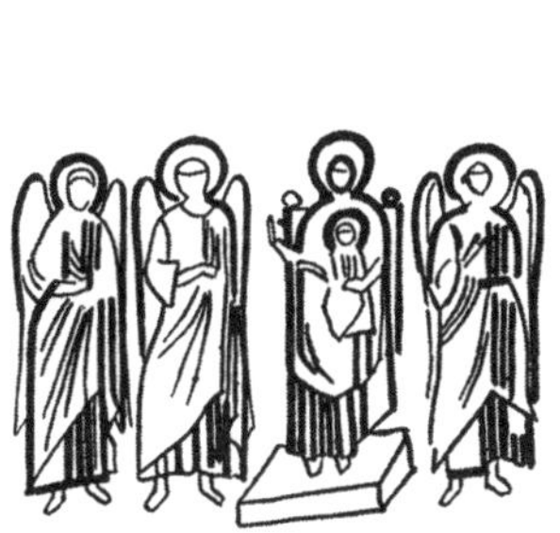
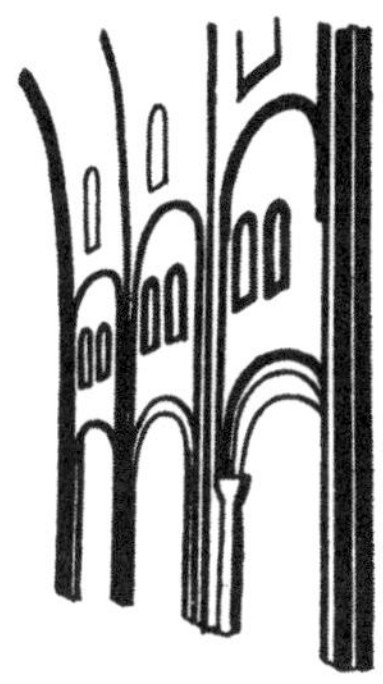

112
Rhythmic motif,
Byzantine style,
Ravenna,
sixth c.

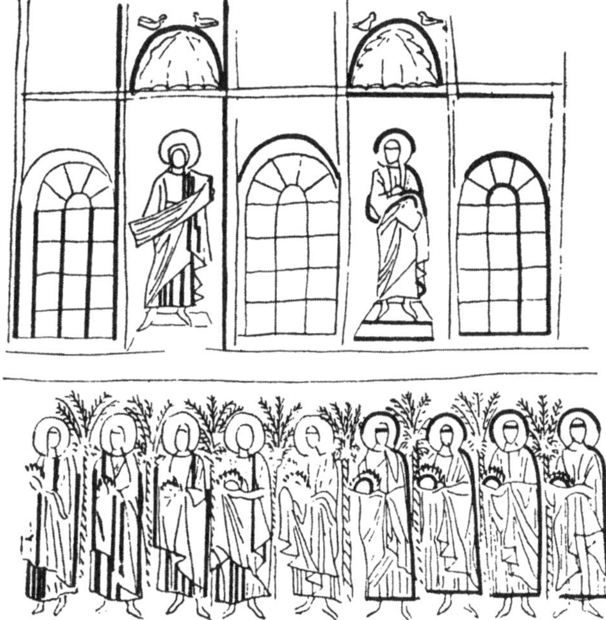

113
Mosaic,
Ravenna,
sixth c.

The art of the Byzantine model prevailed in southern Italy, owing to frequent contacts with Byzantium, while in central and northern Europe there was a transition to an art whose sole means of expression was the line. There was a retreat to silhouette art and sometimes even to contour art.

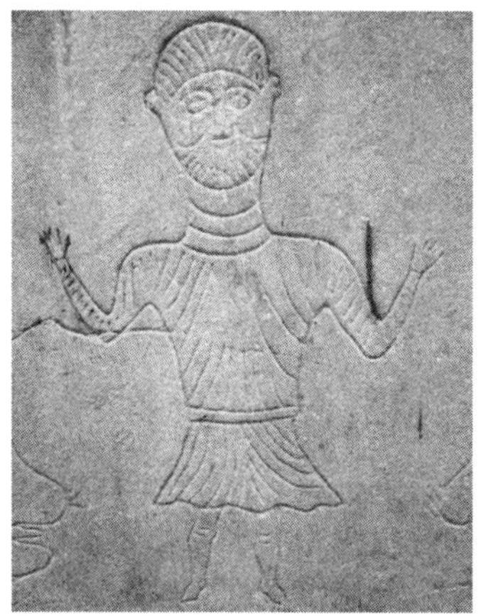

114
From a sarcophagus,
Charenton-du-Cher,
seventh c.

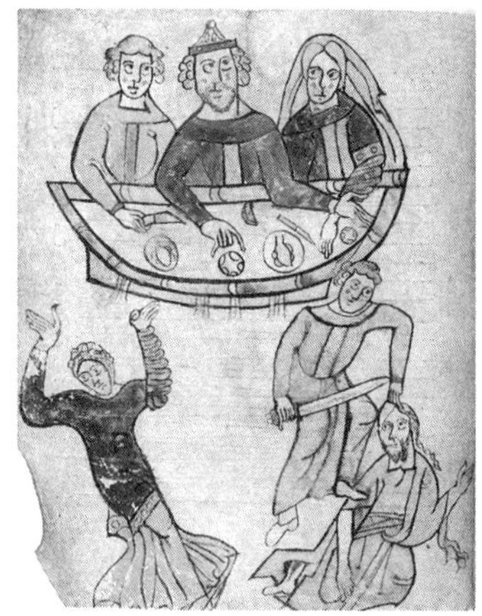

115
Miniature,
Chartres,
ninth c.

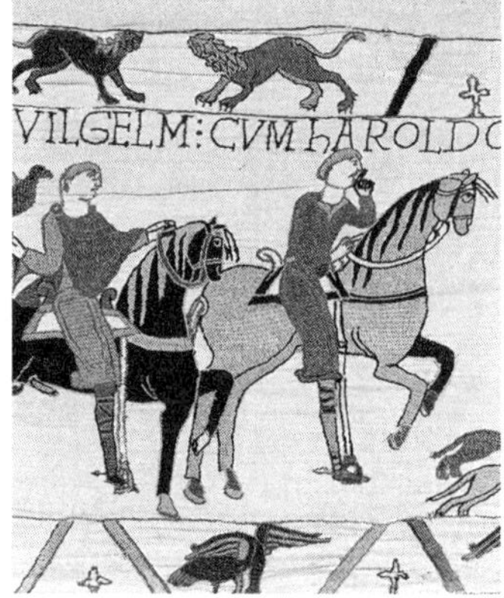

116
Tapestry,
Bayeux,
eleventh c.

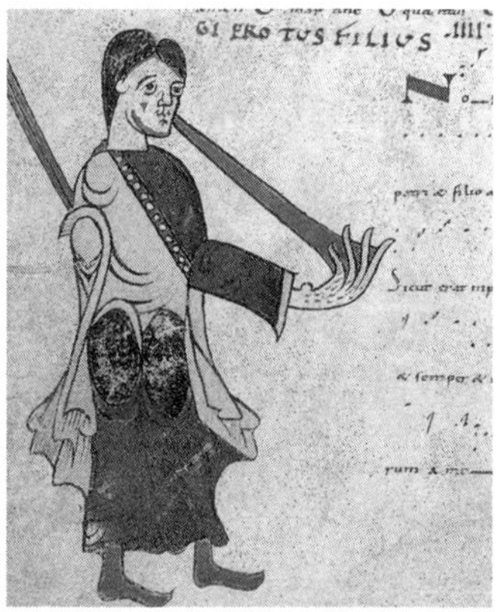

117
Miniature,
Auch,
tenth–eleventh c.

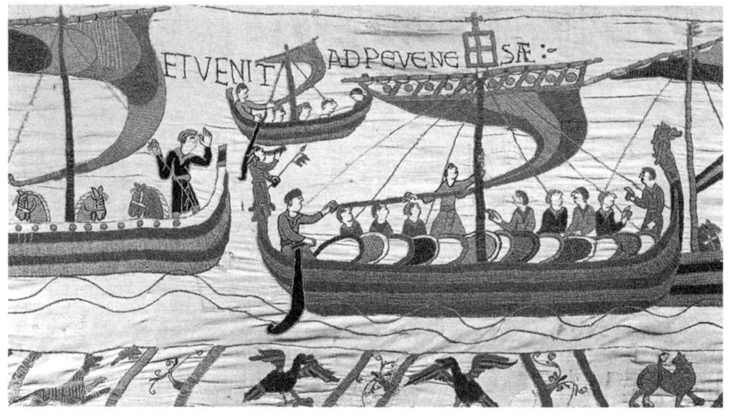

118
Tapestry,
Bayeux,
eleventh c.

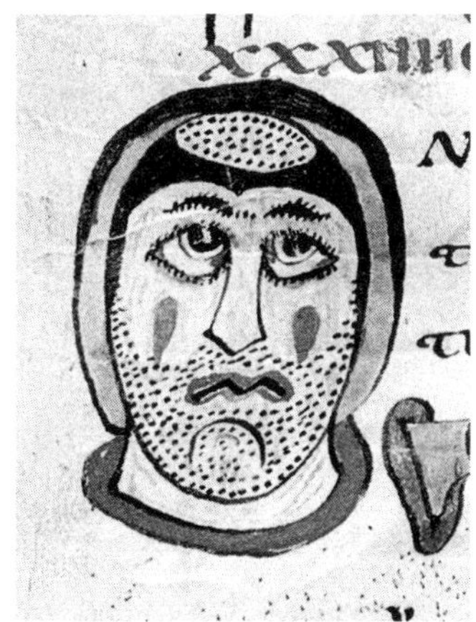

119
Miniature,
Meaux or Cambrai,
seventh–ninth c.

A model of seeing more or less corresponding to the early phases in Egypt prevailed in central and northern Europe. The measure of all the years separating Romanesque art from the original Egyptian art is the chronological measure of decline.

The common designation Romanesque art encompassed different categories of phenomena in the visual arts, incommensurable phenomena: from the primitive stages of visual consciousness of the silhouette and the contour — to early stages of the solid. Byzantine and southern Italian painting represented a very different model from the primitive painting of northern and central Europe. If, however, we apply a common designation to Romanesque art of the whole period, this is because of architecture, whose uniform character was the common link of the art of the period.

When we analyse Romanesque and early mediaeval art we obtain a particularly muddled and opaque picture. Formal analysis only discloses the chaos that results from the overlaying of components that are utterly foreign to one another, coming from a variety of periods and territories, but cannot explain the social determination and inevitability of these forms. By defining their so-called "origins," formal analysis cannot explain why the means of expression corresponding to the conditions of existence in one territory were **taken up** by another. Nor can it explain the **particularity** of these forms — the specific variations in which they occur within a given territory, the difference that exists between the imitated and the imitating form.

Still taking formal analysis as a basis (i.e. qualifying formal elements alone) we can state that in both Egyptian and Romanesque art, one finds works of art in which a range of different dimensions is used to represent figures depending on their place in the social hierarchy.

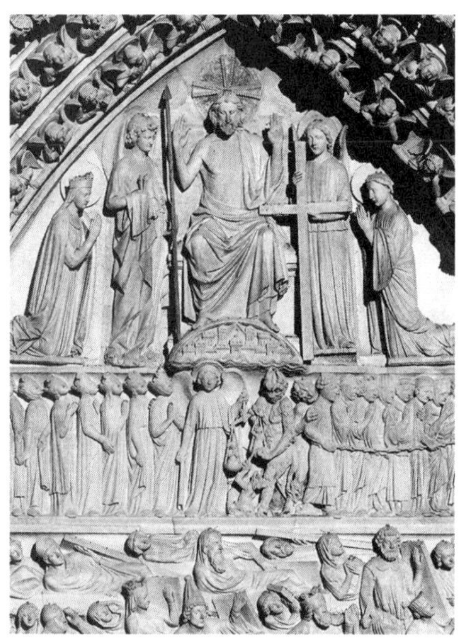

120
Sculpture, Notre-Dame, Paris, thirteenth c.

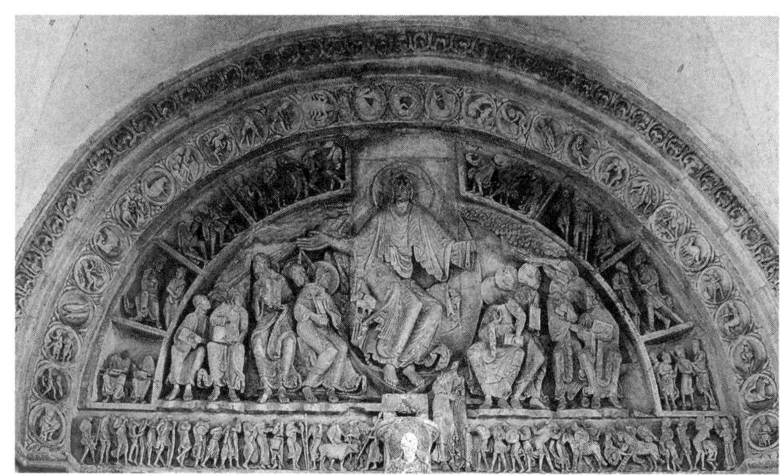

121
Sculpture, Sainte-Marie-Madeleine, Vézelay, twelfth c.

However, it is unclear to which **practical** relationship in the real world this formal analysis corresponds and of which stage in social development it is the result. In other words, what is its historically determined **realism**?

In order to explain this, we have to go beyond formal analysis and move on to defining the model of visual consciousness. What is visual consciousness? It is a measure (one measure) of the reflection of the real world that a particular society has achieved at a particular stage in its historic development. Formal elements are none other than the means used to express a certain visual consciousness. The development of realism is infinite – extending as far as a complete reflection of reality – but each concrete stage in its development is historically determined and, necessarily, historically limited. The visual consciousness expressed by a contour inside a contour and by the resulting **intentional perspective** is one such limited, historically determined stage in visual consciousness, one in which the size of figures is not defined according to commensurate relationships but according to the emotional attitude towards the figures.

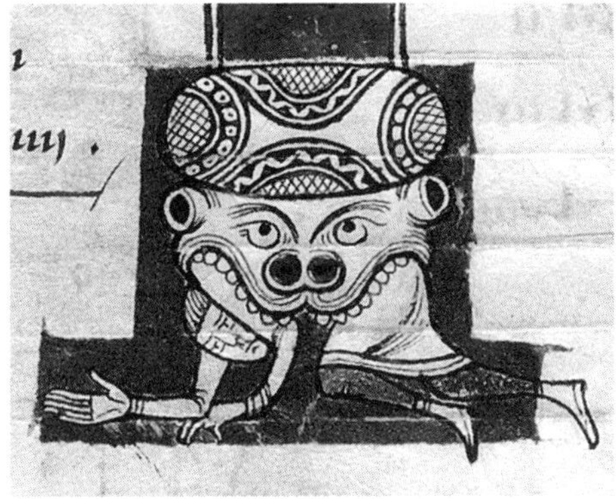

122
Miniature,
France,
eleventh c.

In order to explain why it was necessary for early mediaeval societies to adopt intentional perspective as a practical expression of their ideological superstructure, we need to consider not just **seeing** but also its **social conditioning**. Intentional perspective – being one component of Romanesque art – was the ideological equivalent of the material supremacy of the priests in the early Middle Ages.

Romanesque art is not Heliolithic art. History is not a mechanical repetition of what has gone before. However, the fact that the same, known past components returned to prominence is evidence of certain analogies in the structure of the historic system itself. Intentional perspective would thus be a form of ideological pressure exerted by the priestly caste on early mediaeval society, its acceptance by society (in itself evidenced by the use of this perspective in numerous art works) would be proof of society's ideological surrender to these influences.

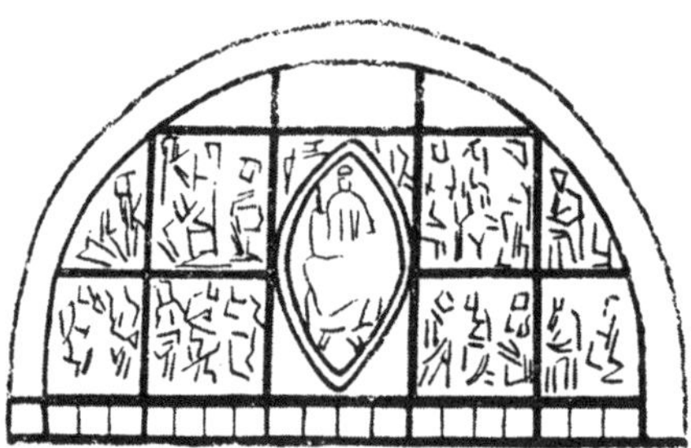

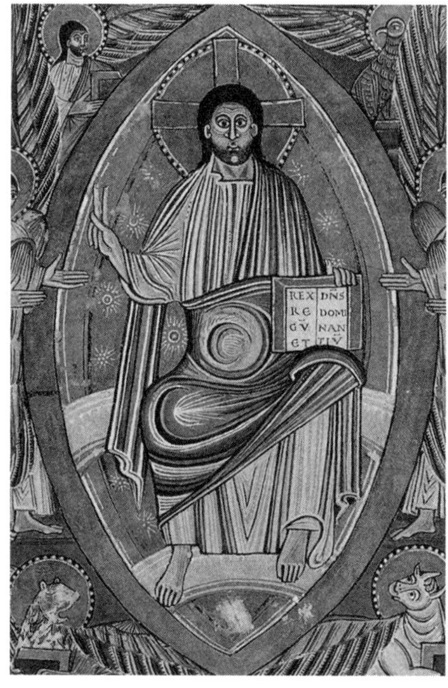

123
Miniature,
Tyniec,
eleventh c.

From the point of view of formalist critique, it is impossible to explain how the same model of painting could have found its application in both the context of Eastern European Byzantine and in Western European Romanesque architecture. From a formalist perspective, operating with the notion of **style** and the distinct complexes of form composing the style, there is no way to explain how the same model of painting was used not simply in various, different styles of architecture, but also that it appeared to be fitting in both cases, fully in accordance with both forms of architecture – the architecture of Byzantine domes and the Romanesque architecture of groin vaulting.

Moving from form to seeing, we will need to define which practical, real components of seeing make this model of painting conform both to the one model of architecture and also to the other.

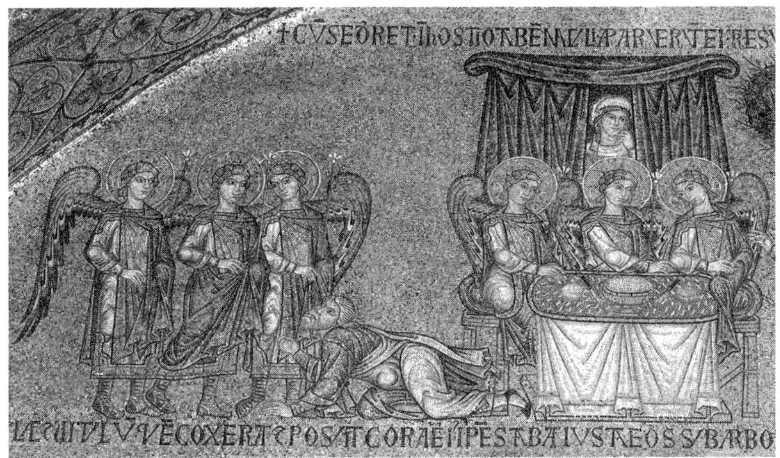

124
Mosaic,
Venice,
thirteenth c.

A connection between painting and architecture is achieved by way of the **architectonisation** of painting, by saturating it with formal elements transferred from architecture. This transfer is based on afterimage phenomena. The stimulation of the retina of the eye produced by looking at a shape does not cease after transferring the gaze to another shape. It still lingers for a while, gradually weakening, as the processes of retinal regeneration take place. During this time, the newly observed shape is overlaid by the trace of the shape that was being looked at previously. It is this conformity of architectural harmony with the genuine, true nature of our seeing that we perceive as beauty.

Thus, if early mediaeval painting could be equally easily connected to Byzantine and Romanesque architecture, this means that the same formal component – connected with painting – existed in both models of architecture. In this case, the square dome and the square base of the groin vault, reflected in painting as a square grid of dimensions and proportions.

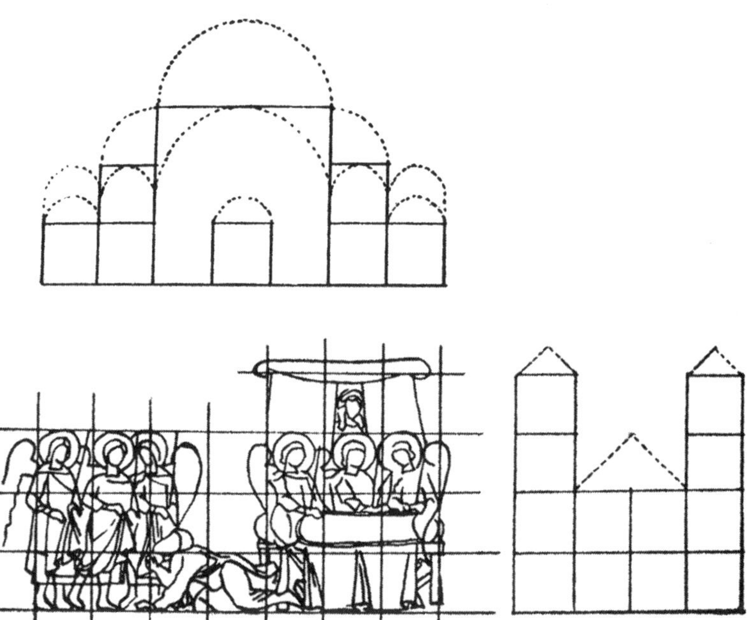

We are only able to explain such issues after considering the problem on the basis of visual analysis; they cannot be explained from the position of formalist critique.

This also demonstrates, however, that the early mediaeval period was not in complete and consistent decline, as is usually supposed. The construction of Romanesque architecture was not regressive in relation to Roman architecture but rather disseminated and consolidated vault construction, in spite of its Heliolithic components. The continuity of development in building construction remained unbroken and progressed without interruptions – if not in quantity then at least in terms of quality. Moreover, progressive architecture (even in comparison with Antiquity) precipitated the development of visual art as a whole. The architectonisation of visual art was carried out with reference to vaulting construction.

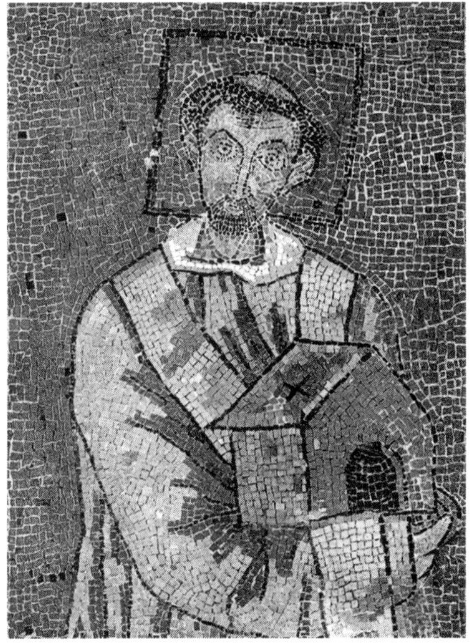

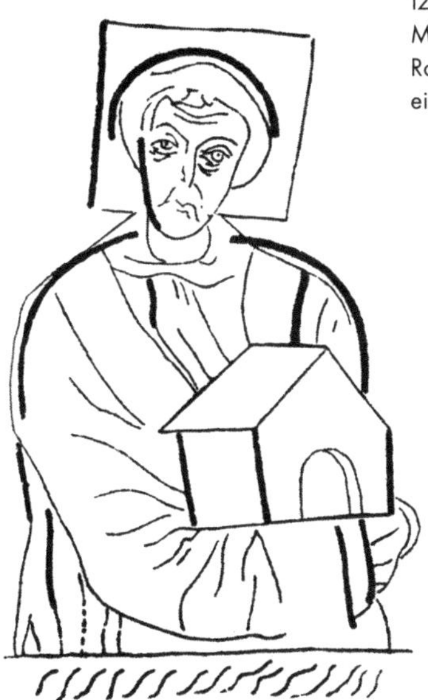

125
Mosaic,
Rome,
eighth c.

In the ancient world, the process of architectonisation referred to columnar architecture. Linear components of this architecture permeated art, consolidating and preserving its linearism. Architectonisation to a flat silhouette on the smooth surface of a wall and to the linear play of entablature, columns, etc. inevitably led to the increased linearism of this same visual art.

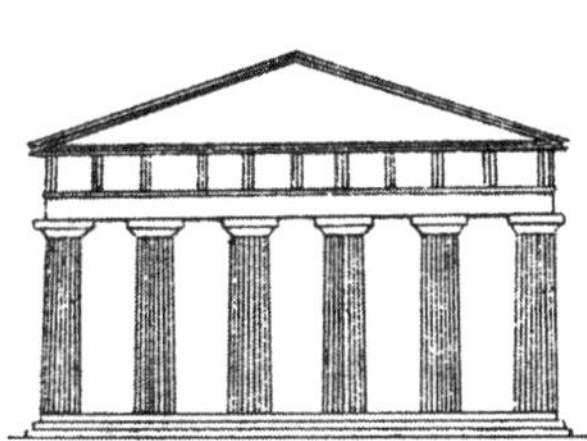

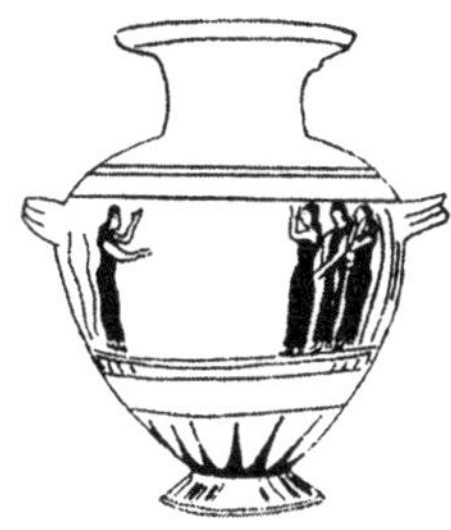

Whereas references to **three-dimensional**, spatial vaulting naturally suggests the scrutiny of three-dimensional elements, naturally introduces components of solids and space — even when visual art itself still follows the model of contour or silhouette-seeing. In ancient art, architectonisation consolidated the existing model of silhouette-seeing. To pass to three-dimensional visual consciousness, Hellenistic painting had to overcome its reliance on architectonisation. Hellenistic painting is non-architectonic, however; it is counter-architectonic.

In a new, changed situation, the same method of architectonisation becomes the method leading to the acceleration of the development of visual consciousness and its transformation into a consciousness of three-dimensional forms.

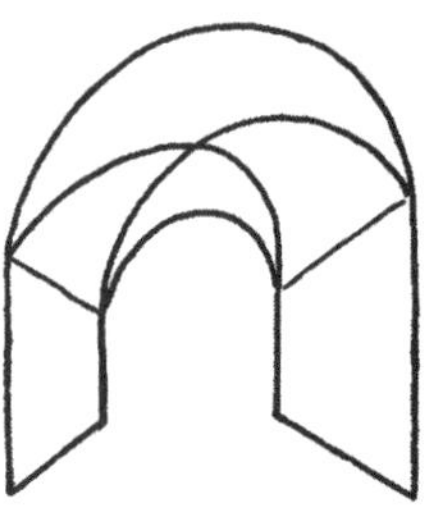

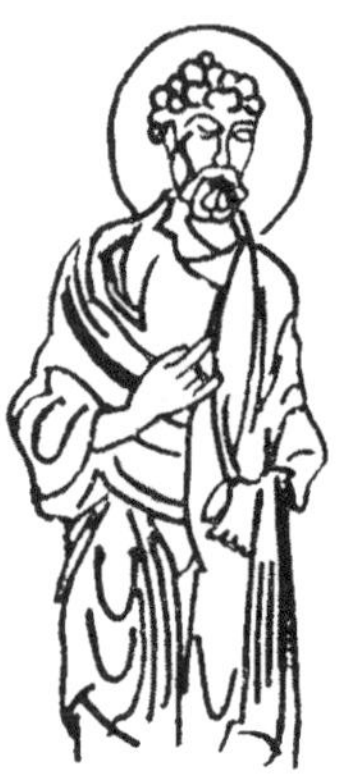

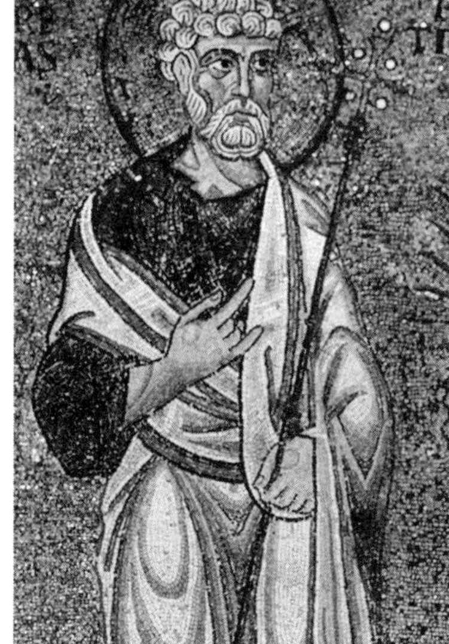

126
Mosaic,
Trieste,
twelfth c.

Subjected to architectonic influence, even the Heliolithic components of Romanesque art succumbed to an accelerated transformation. They absorbed components of three-dimensional forms and space from architecture and transformed themselves into solids.

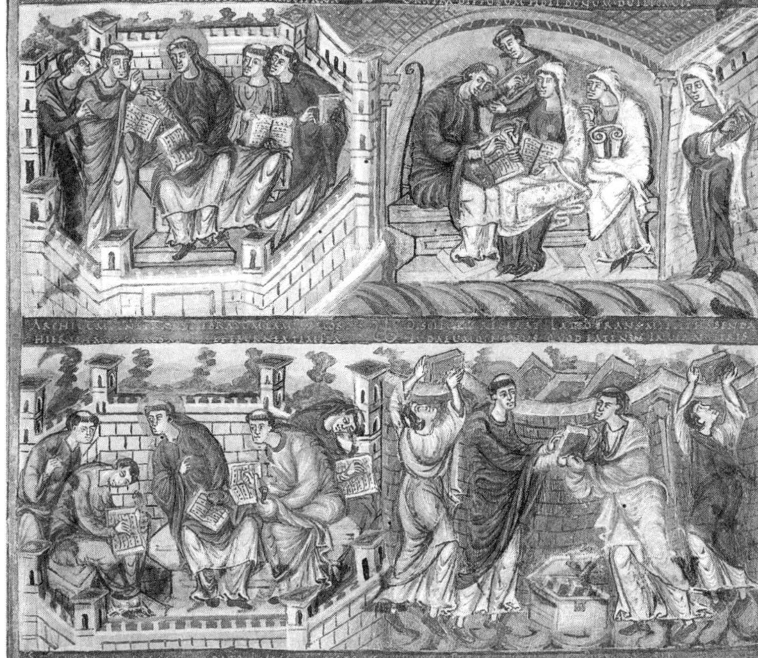

127
Miniature,
Carolingian art,
ninth c.

128
Mosaic,
Italy,
tenth c.

129
Mosaic,
Monreale,
twelfth c.

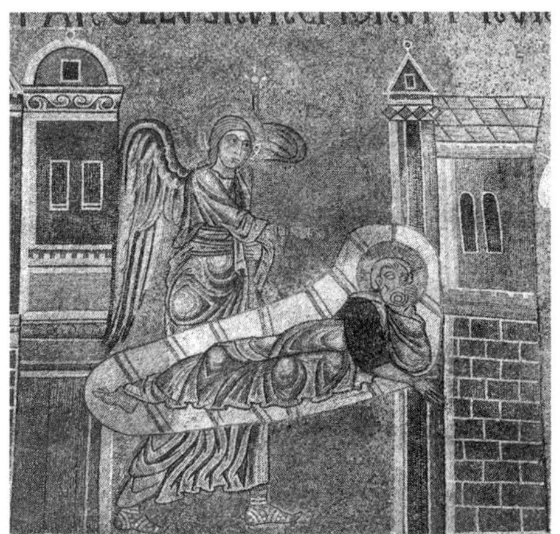

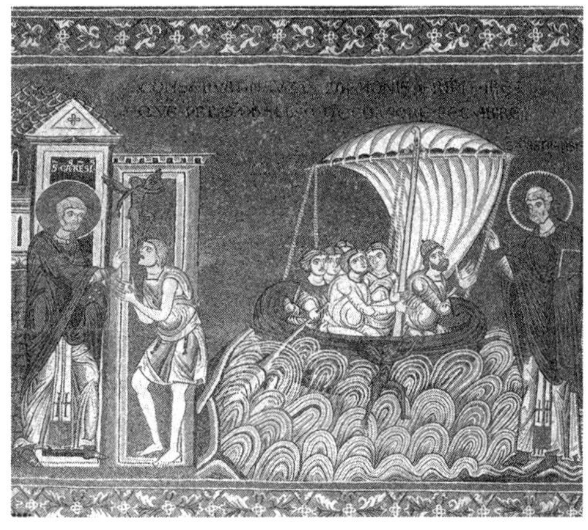

They transformed **directly** into components of solid-form-seeing from contour within contour (bypassing the silhouette stage). It was possible to pass directly to Renaissance painting from the Romanesque (in its Byzantine interpretation), as did Cimabue and Giotto.

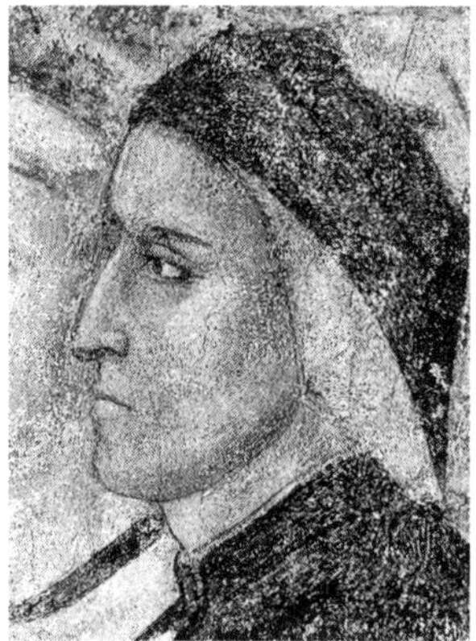

130
Giotto (school of), Portrait of Dante, wall painting, fourteenth c.

Formalist aesthetics fails to take note of the specific qualities of the development of mediaeval art – its accelerated dynamics, its leaps across entire periods of development and the co-existence, in a single work of art, of different themes with different social and ideological significance, different degrees of historically attained realism, different levels of visual consciousness.

The form of the work of art should be derived from the model of seeing, determining which range of visual reality it corresponds to, what sort of visual consciousness should be applied in order that the form deployed should be its true expression. In other words, we bring form down to the ground of a realism that changes throughout the course of history and develops throughout successive social systems. We consider the question of form to be a consequence of the historical process (in the realm of seeing). Only then are we able to grasp both form and content as a dialectic unity, as two reflections of the same process. Historical change, the development of the forces of production, and the transformation of class structure in society can be seen to explain both the changes in content and the practical, empirically verifiable development of visual consciousness.

The basic model of seeing generally prevailing in early Mediaeval Europe (with the exception of the Mediterranean seacoast) is the contour model.

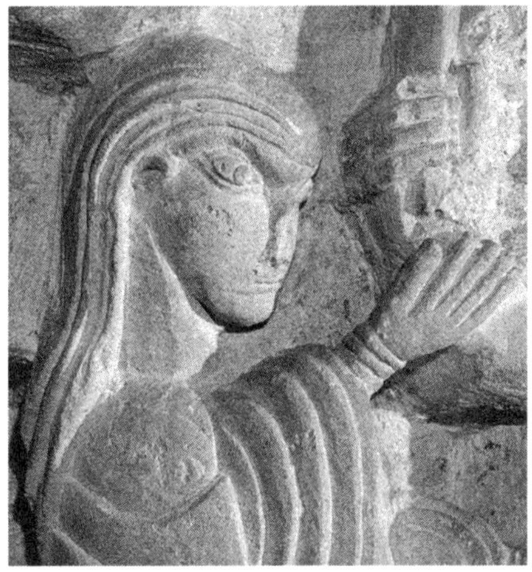

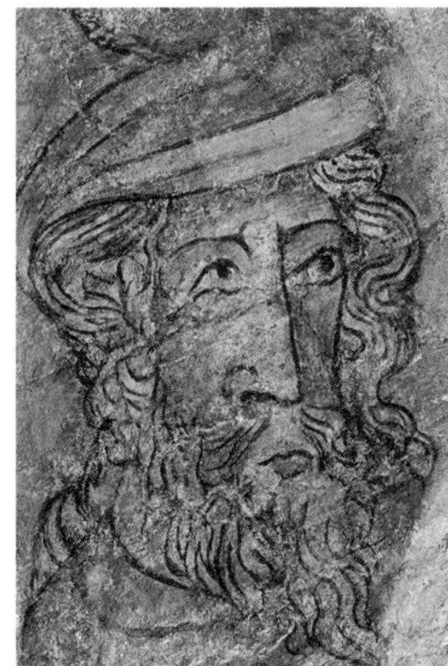

131
Sculpture,
Poitiers,
eleventh–twelfth c.

132
Wall painting,
Gniezno,
fourteenth c.

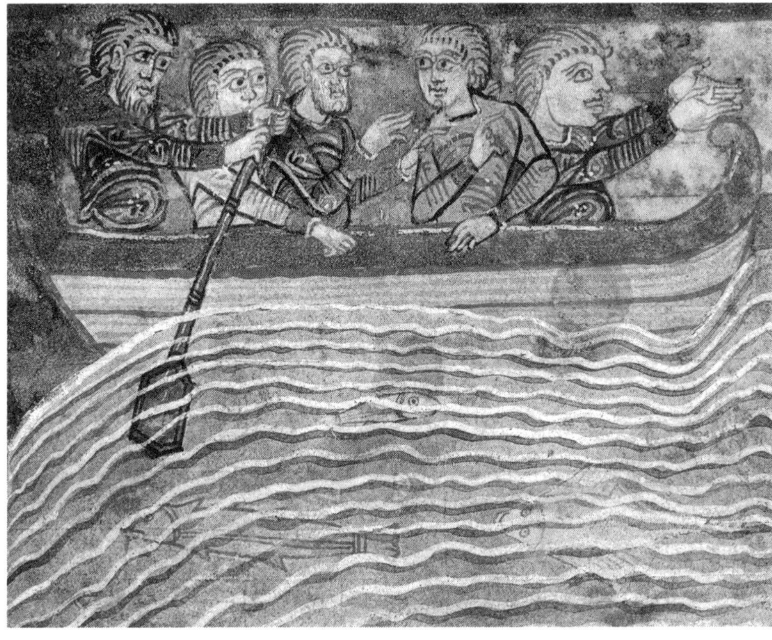

133
Miniature,
Poitiers,
eleventh c.

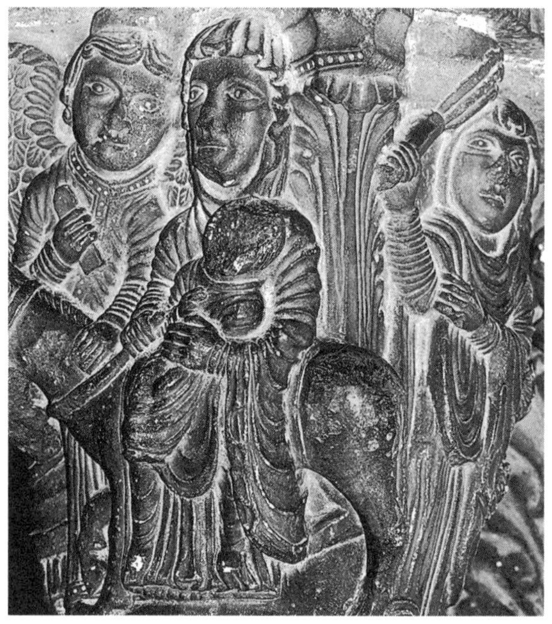

134
Sculpture,
Arles,
twelfth c.

As a result, perspective is intentional, the size of figures expresses the author's attitude towards them — a religious-hierarchic attitude. The question of rhythm and of the composition of parallel rows only appears in around the tenth century.

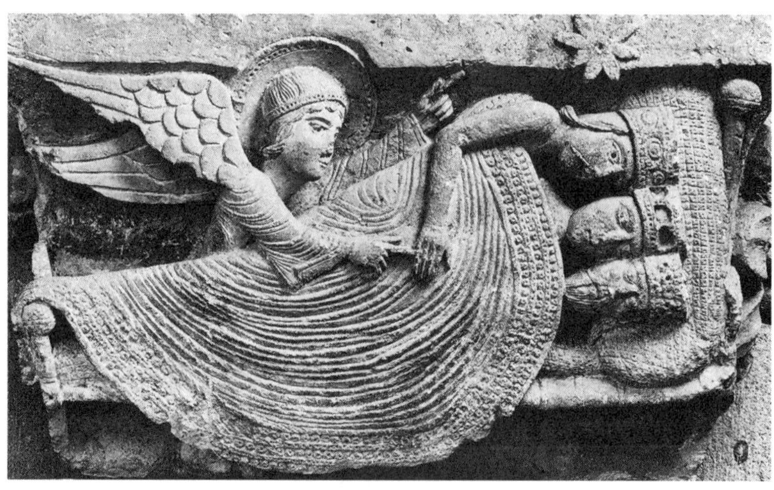

135
Sculpture,
Autun,
twelfth c.

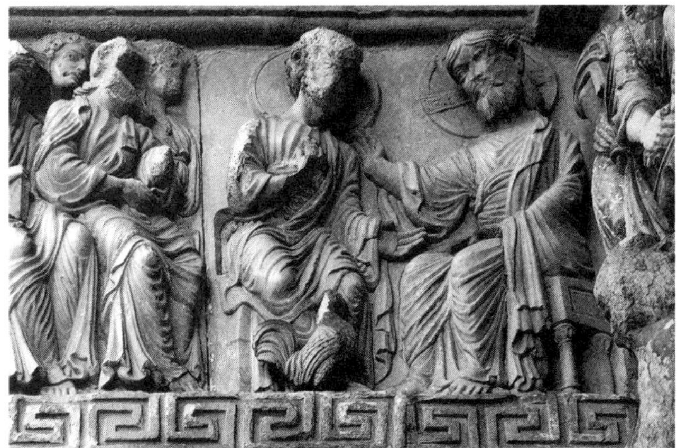

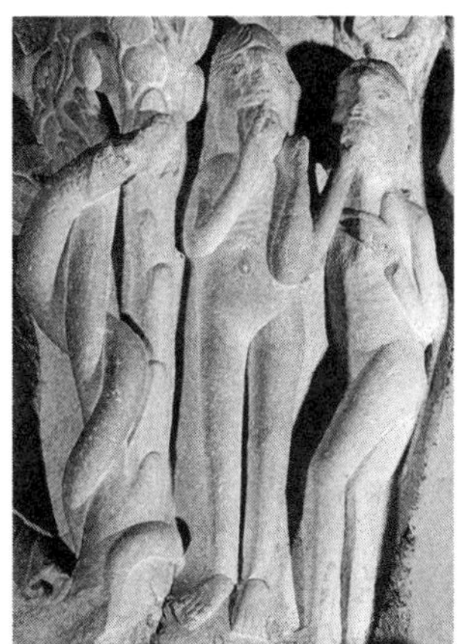

136
Sculpture,
St-Gilles-du-Gard,
twelfth c.

137
Sculpture,
Cluny,
twelfth c.

In Greece, this arrangement originated on the basis of silhouette-seeing. In Romanesque art, the architectonisation of rhythmic rows appears before the pure model of silhouette-seeing – before the model of seeing that corresponds to it. But let us not forget that the mediaeval period was not an era of creating culture anew but an era of the **reconstruction** of culture based on a new social system. Development was accelerated. External cultural impulses were involved. Models transmitted from more cultured states were influential (Byzantium, Islam), as were the monuments of Roman art that remained in these territories.

The main reason, however, was that the process of cultural reconstruction was taking place against the backdrop of a different social system. Feudal society develops in place of slavery, founded not on the personally disinterested slave-commodity, but on a partly free, taxed peasant-serf, whose participation in social revenue is greater, and whose social position is consequently higher. This explains the increased dynamics of social processes and the unevenness of development, leaps across entire periods of evolution and the coexistence in the same period of different, chronologically unrelated forms of social systems. The Middle Ages were not a dead period of history. Quite the contrary: it was one of the eras with the most accelerated social transformation based on a new historic system. This is why problems were taken up on the basis of contour seeing, characteristic of a later period. In the Gothic era, visual art passes over into the silhouette model of visual consciousness. The sequence of developmental stages is repeated in the same way as it was in antiquity. As then, contour seeing passes into silhouette seeing. And as then, the line drawing appears in pure silhouette seeing, supplementing the silhouette. In this way, we can connect the model of seeing and its formal elements in the Gothic era with the art of the Phidian era. This connection and unity result, in both cases, from the same model of visual consciousness. The same problems are characteristic for Gothic as for Greek art in the Phidian era. The same architectonic form, the same rhythm of parallel rows, the same linearism as the principal formal means, expressing the Gothic model of seeing. The differences between them can be brought down to differences in architecture. As we know, the process of architectonisation relies on saturating visual art with formal elements carried over from architecture. The character of architecture determined which formal elements appeared in the work of art: whether the groups of pointed arches appropriated from the Gothic, or colonnaded schemes, softened by curving spirals, seen by the artist in Greek architecture. Alongside the common method of carrying over forms from architecture to sculpture and painting, there were concrete differences, resulting from the variety of the formal groupings characteristic of each of these chronologically distant periods.

Passing from the Gothic to the Renaissance, we see again the recurrence of the same stages in the development that succeeded one another in another historical sequence: in the developmental line of Greco-Hellenistic-Roman culture. Silhouette-seeing transforms into solid-form-seeing. Developing out of Gothic premises, the Renaissance moves to seeing solids in three-dimensional space. The same process is repeated in both cases: the flat silhouette of Greek painting passes into three-dimensional, convex Hellenistic-Roman painting. The same flat silhouette of the early Gothic passes into the convex solid form and the perspectival space of Renaissance painting.

That the same course of development took place in both cases, some fifteen centuries apart, testifies to the existence of a causal relationship. Solid-form-seeing follows silhouette-seeing in both cases. The premises of silhouette-seeing inevitably lead to seeing the solid form located in three-dimensional, converging space. In both cases, the development of seeing leads to the formation of **the same** three-dimensional visual consciousness.

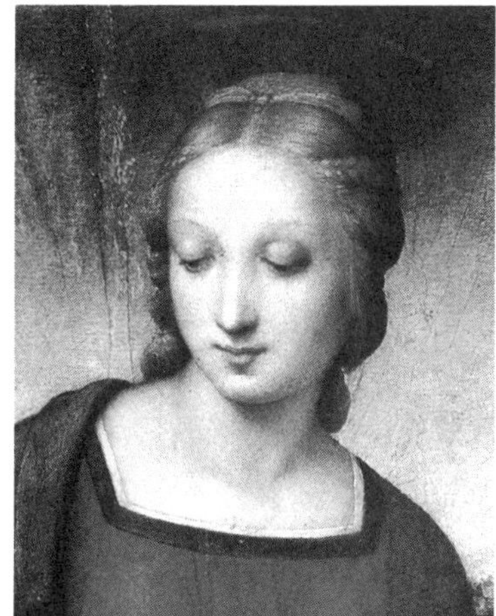

138
Rafael,
Madonna of the Goldfinch,
detail,
sixteenth c.

Development in antiquity lasted several thousand years and took the form of a slow, gradual progression of small changes. In the Middle Ages, however, development was accelerated, uneven, and particular models of seeing, already attained in the previous course of history, co-existed, were overlaid within the framework of the same work of art. And so, besides similarities between developmental processes that led to the same goal – to attaining three-dimensional visual consciousness – there were differences in the way these processes occurred .

In both cases, both in antiquity and the Middle Ages, the development of the forces of production led to the **production of commodities** and to **commodity exchange**. These were reflected in three-dimensional seeing and the visual consciousness of the solid, which best expressed the commodity essence of objects. The most important characteristics of the object as commodity are its mass (size) and its weight (scale). It was to this very commodity-seeing of nature, to noting within it those qualities that characterise it **as commodity** that the transformation of visual consciousness was directed in both cases.

The differences were the result of the fact that the commodity economy in Antiquity developed on the basis of the slave system. In the Middle Ages, however, this same economy emerged from the development of feudal society. History sometimes runs its course in similar ways, but never identically. One should to be able to see differences as well as similarities.

In the Hellenistic period, as in the Renaissance, the artist focuses on the scrutiny of the solid form and on three-dimensional space. However, the Renaissance artist does this more accurately and better. His observations are more precise, while the means with which he expresses spatial depth have been formulated in the scientifically worked out system of linear perspective.

The **scientific** system of Hellenistic perspective was the perspective of parallel oblique projection, originating from Euclid's stereometry. This perspective made it possible to express the convexity and three-dimensionality of a single object, but not to express the spatial recession or the gradual diminishing of objects with increased distance. The Hellenistic artist expressed spatial recession in a purely **intuitive** manner, diminishing objects that were further away in a free manner and applying foreshortening as a result of instinct rather than of calculation.

Only the discovery in the Renaissance of three-dimensional **convergent** perspective allowed for the removal of the hitherto existing contradiction between the convex representation of a particular object and the placing of several objects in parallel within a space. Only then did the third dimension of space become an active component, drawing in the eye of the spectator and defining the degree of distance in spatial recession.[7]

The full theory of convergent perspective appeared as the mathematical working-through of the long-standing, intuitive, and imprecise observations made by artists — it was the theoretical universalisation of their extensive painterly practice. It thus contributed to an unquestionable **expansion** of realism. Three-dimensional consciousness thereby acquired the exact and precise means of expression it had previously lacked.

But in order to accomplish the **mathematical** universalisation of the visual observations of hundreds of painters, the no less considerable work of hundreds of mathematicians on mathematics itself was required. Mathematics had to reach a higher level.

The general development of the forces of production called for urgent mathematical solutions to practical problems arising from the developing commodity economy:

7 Translator's footnote: Strzemiński uses the term "three-dimensional converging perspective." Because, in Polish, the terms for "converging perspective" and "linear perspective" are synonymous, we have chosen to use the English term "linear perspective" in place of translating literally Strzemiński's discussion of Renaissance perspective as "converging perspective" for greater clarity and consistency.

1. **clocks** (reducing the measurement of **time** to the spatial dimensions of cog wheels),
2. **mills** (the same issue of expressing the measurement of time through the spatial dimensions of wheels),
3. **navigation** – the compass technique of and calculations of geographic latitude and longitude (relating spatial dimensions and the inclination of the sun to the precise measurement of time)

The development of the forces of production confronted mathematicians with a number of challenges, arising from the nature of the commodity economy itself. Solving these tasks demanded a thorough method of mathematical abstraction (algebra). Thus, the following remained inextricably linked:

1. the developing forces of production emerging from the commodity economy,
2. the practical tasks imposed on mathematicians by the commodity economy,
3. the development of mathematics and the further development of the method of abstraction,
4. three-dimensional **convergent** perspective as a mathematical abstraction of the understanding of the means of expression of three-dimensional visual consciousness.

The commodity economy required that commodities be **uniform**. Its characteristic qualities were to be measuring, weighing, and counting. Renaissance visual consciousness is a reflection of these commodity qualities transferred to the realm of seeing. In the age of the developing commodity exchange, man sought those qualities in the natural world surrounding him that had the characteristics of the commodity. If the Renaissance artist could more fully express three-dimensional space, the convexity of the mass of a solid, then this was because in the framework of the feudal system, commodity exchange liberated a greater supply of forces of production than the Hellenistic system, based on slavery, had been able to.

Another difference may also be noted: with the transition to the commodity exchange in antiquity and the three-dimensional commodity form-seeing associated with it, architectonics disappears completely. The commodity seeing of the Hellenistic era sees individual objects but does not note their unity; it fails to link them by transferring the afterimages of forms. The eye observes each object separately and evaluates each individual object as a commodity. Hellenistic painting was not only non-architectonic, but counter-architectonic.

The Renaissance is different. Long after achieving visual consciousness of three-dimensional form, the work of art at this time continues to be united by way of a common architectonic rhythm.

139
Melozzo da Forlì, *Sixtus IV Appoints Bartolomeo Platina Prefect of the Vatican Library*, wall painting, Rome, fifteenth c.

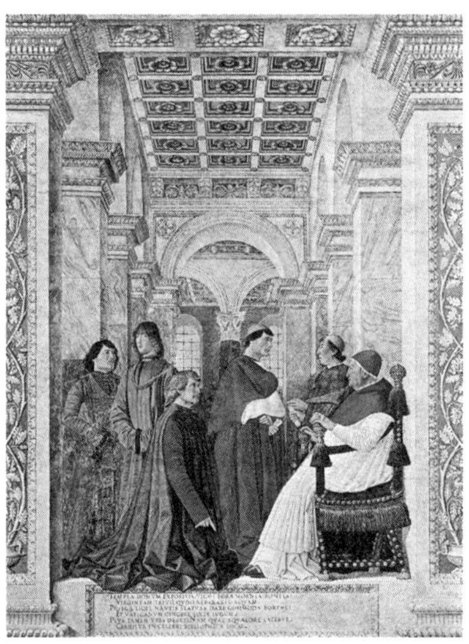

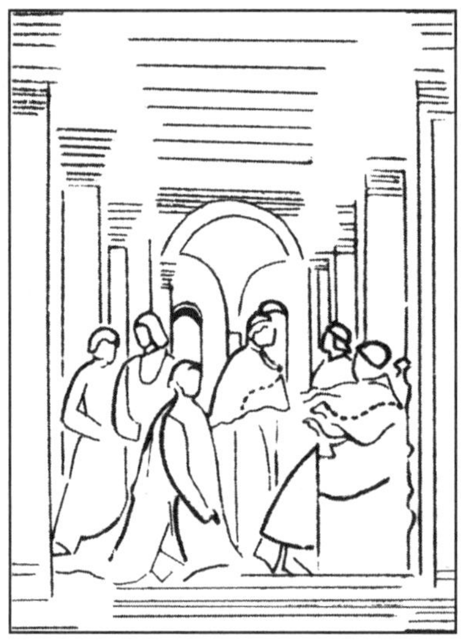

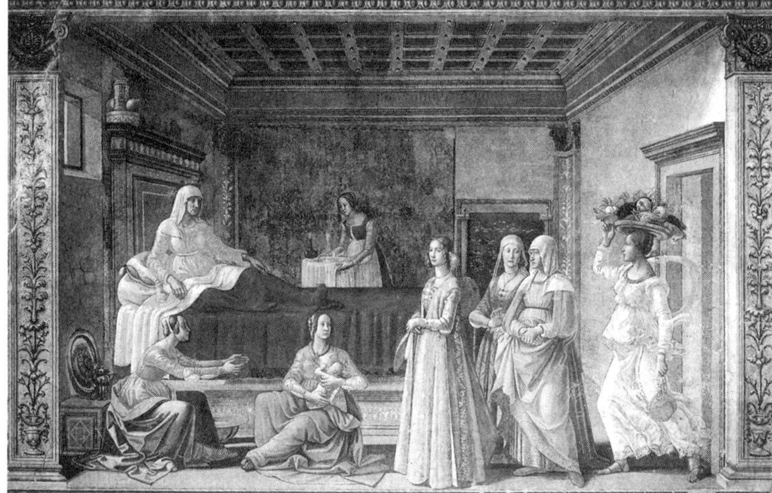

140
Ghirlandaio,
The Birth of St. John the Baptist,
wall painting,
fifteenth c.

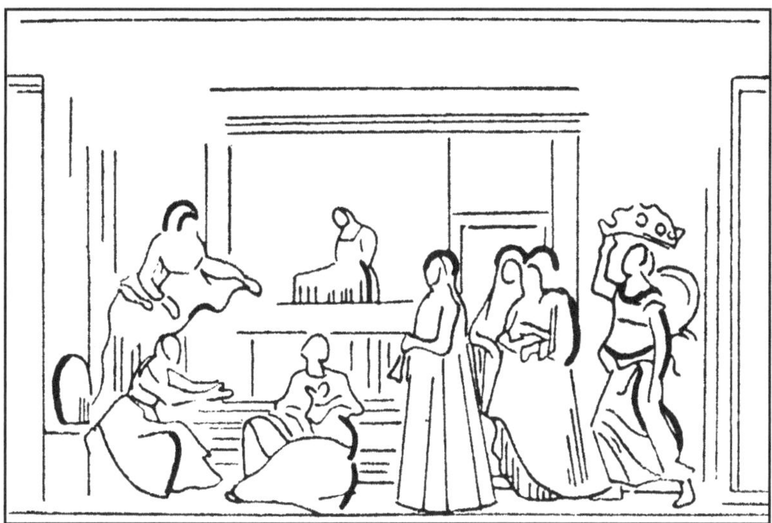

The architectonics of the work of art that develops on the basis of free craftsmen's towns (the ancient **polis** and the mediaeval free urban commune) and emerges in the context of **silhouette** visual-consciousness and the silhouette form (as, standing out from the background, the silhouette offers the most **easily** observed afterimages) — this architectonics does not disappear in the Renaissance, but continues to exist, to co-exist with the visual consciousness of solids. Gothic architectonics continues to exist, no longer seeing the world through silhouettes but spatially.

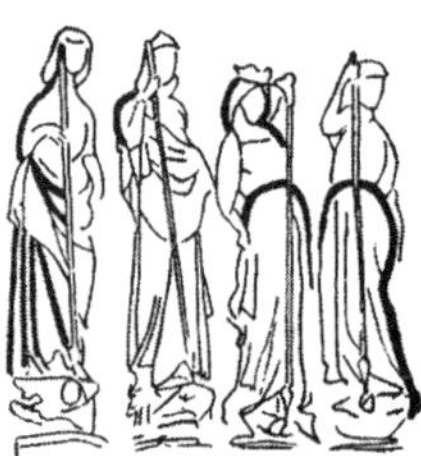
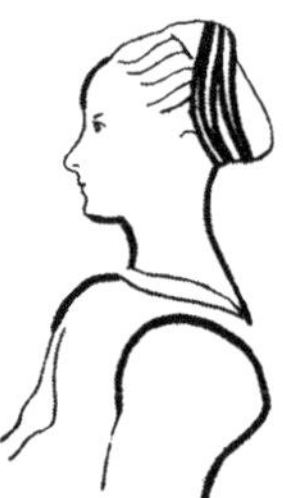

141
Gothic order, thirteenth c. and Domenico Veneziano, *Portrait of a Young Woman*, 1460–1465

The Renaissance paints the object with sharply drawn boundaries, convex and modelled, with colour corresponding to the object's colour in nature. This is a manner of seeing directed at perceiving all the components of shape, convexity, and colour that characterise the object and make it distinct. It is like the pure seeing of the **commodity** qualities of the object, characterizing its objective, verifiable properties and identifying the object from among other objects. It is a manner of seeing the object as such, fully independent from other objects.

If, in spite of this, a form of composition growing out of commodity consciousness failed to develop, if composition **expressing** the commodity character of social relations failed to arise, this is because there were restraints within society. The representation of the world as a harmonious and united whole was expressed through harmony and the architectonic conformity of the work of art. Architecture seemed to claim that the world is capable of indefinite development, that there were no significant obstacles that could stand in the way of the free human spirit. The eloquence of this architecture was the universal eloquence of Renaissance humanity as a whole. The free spirit of man, his inquiring mind, the welfare produced by his personal energy – these were the purport of this humanism. The restraints that prevented drawing the final conclusions of commodity-seeing, that did not allow for the full, unimpeded expression of the commodity, the already **capitalist** essence of this society, such was the unfinished historical role of the urban middle class in the late Middle Ages and early Renaissance.

Mobilizing the masses against feudalism, it did not carry the same burden of slavery that had weighed down democracy in antiquity and• weakened its strength. The middle class of the Renaissance was able, for a considerable time, to mobilise **all** people under the banner of freedom to investigate the branches of life, the laws of the infinite development of the human mind, the right to shape one's life in accordance with freedom of conscience. The middle class took all the lower segments of the society along with it in a series of civil wars:

1. Cola di Rienzo's uprising as leader of a republican revolt by the people of Rome;
2. The Peasants' Revolt (Tyler's Rebellion) in England,
3. The Jacquerie (peasants' revolt) in France;
4. The Hussite wars in the Czech lands;
5. The rising of Pomeranian towns against the Order of Teutonic Knights (in alliance with Casimir IV Jagiellon);
6. Revolt of the Comuneros (War of the Communities of Castile) in Spain (against Charles V);
7. The Peasants' Wars in Germany.

The ultimate consequences of solid-form-seeing for commodities do not emerge so long as there is a hegemony of urban democracy over the **entire** people. The humanistic purport, introduced by Renaissance democracy, finds its expression in an architectonic, harmonious vision of the world in which contradictions are resolved and the common interests of the whole population are architectonically linked. The **political** practice of linking and uniting the widest masses of people, of mobilizing them for revolts and civil wars, finds its reflection in the **artistic** practice of uniting all components of the work of art, their mutual transfer and overlaying and creating a harmony of architectonic rhythms. Architectonics appeared only as a cover – masking the forces of nascent capitalism and the developing commodity economy – on behalf of **all** the people.

The popular revolts failed to overthrow feudalism and failed to create a republic of traders, craftsmen, and peasants, but they did weaken

• During the second Peloponnesian war, twenty thousand Athenian slaves escaped to Sparta, weakening the Athenian democracy's forces of resistance. For the slave, "his own" democracy was a worse enemy than a remote aristocracy.

it to such a degree that a new force emerged alongside feudalism – the primitive accumulation of nascent capitalism, now out in the open. Architectonic rhythms disappear from art at that time, while commodity-seeing, the seeing of **commodity mass production** – develops in full.

The development of the forces of production in the Renaissance attained a level superior to that of the Hellenistic era. This explains the attainment of a superior, fuller realism in the Renaissance, a fuller development of the visual consciousness of three-dimensional space and of discovering the means to express three-dimensional forms.

However, the same development of the forces of production led to a particular class situation in which the middle class organised the struggle of the masses under its leadership. This leading role in politics, as the link among all anti-feudal forces, found its artistic reflection in the harmonious architectonics of the work of art. This was the formalism of the early Renaissance.

Commodity-seeing could only emerge in full when the obstacles standing in the way of the development of commodity exchange were removed.

A system of evaluation and aesthetic criteria proper to and based on commodity-seeing develops as a result. Aesthetics are defined by the model of visual consciousness – they are its causal result.

The solidity of the Renaissance object is connected with the idea, the sensation of a certain weight that is proper to it. The problem of distributing forms in space, the appropriate correspondence with their weight, becomes the fundamental problem of Renaissance aesthetics. The problem of the equilibrium among forms and the harmonious relationship among them – these were the principal formal-compositional problems according to which Renaissance aesthetics were shaped. A typical example of the composition of balanced solid forms is the triangular composition.

What is remarkable is that the composition of three-dimensional forms, balanced as if on a pair of scales, corresponds to the aesthetics of the matter-of-fact, objective, commodity-seeing of nature as a collection of three-dimensional forms. **A commodity model of composition corresponded to commodity-seeing.** Triangular composition is a typically Renaissance solution. The merchant's scales became the scales on which the perfection of beauty achieved was weighed, and the measure of beauty became the measure of the tradesman's honesty.

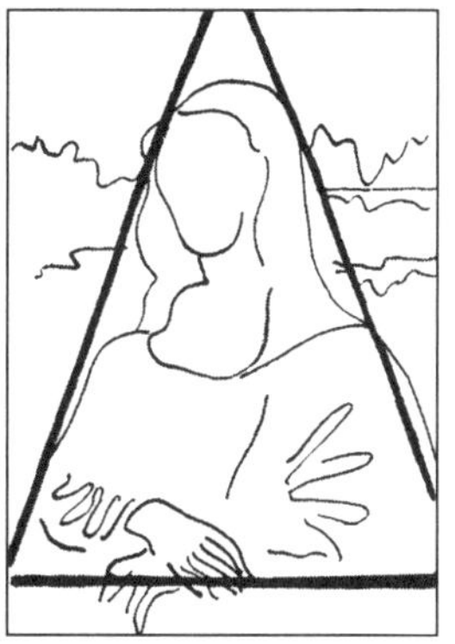

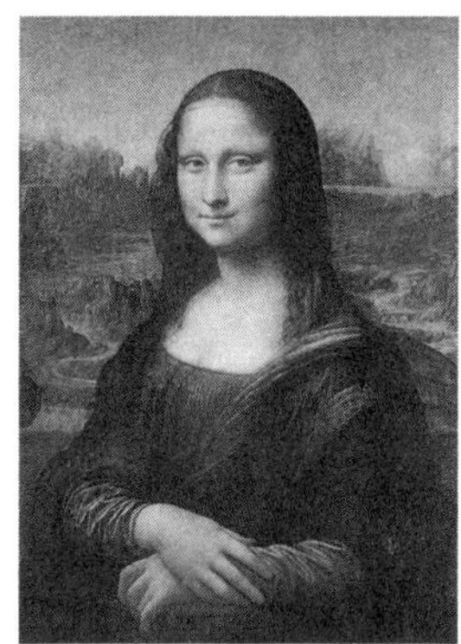

142
Leonardo da Vinci,
Mona Lisa,
sixteenth c.

Wealth, abundance, and lavishness of quantities of commodities arranged in perfect equilibrium – this was the ideal that the wealthy middle class of the late Renaissance imposed upon society. The composition of equilibrium and moderation – this was the formalism of the late Renaissance. A formalism that measured the perfection of artistic achievement with scales and cubits. A formalism whose achievement lay in the new discoveries of realism and was determined by these.

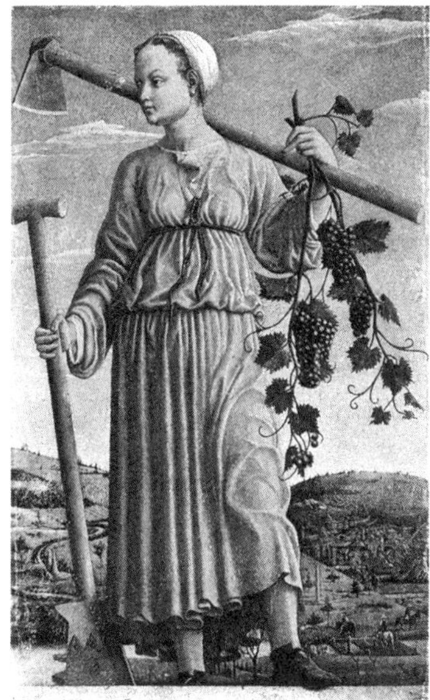

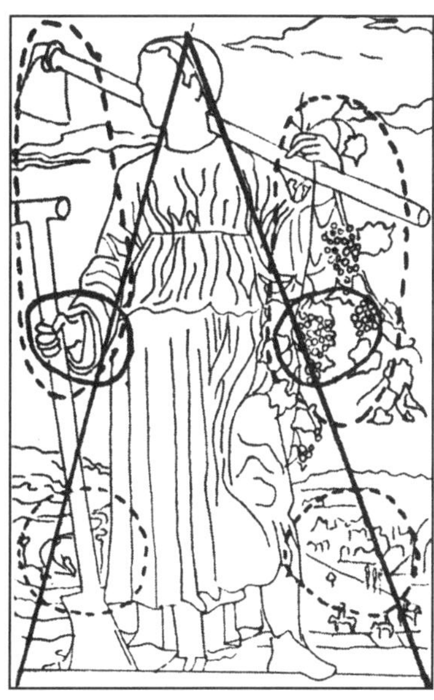

143
Cossa,
Autumn,
fifteenth c.

chiaroscuro-seeing

The object painted by the Renaissance painter has all the objective qualities characteristic of the commodity. It is an object that is drawn properly in all perspectival foreshortenings, modelled with shading to appear solid, and coloured with its own local colour, distinct from the colours of other objects. Three-dimensional seeing is, in essence, commodity seeing. The Renaissance, with its orientation towards commodity seeing, could see all the components of seeing characteristic of the objective, commodity, non-human nature of the object, but rejected as irrelevant those aspects that were not characteristic — which it saw as marginal.

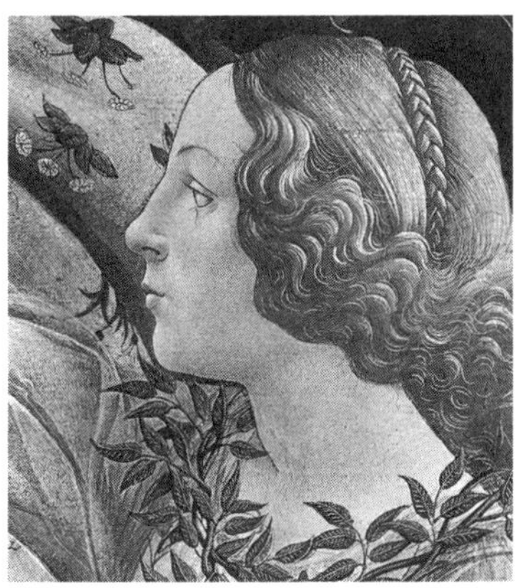

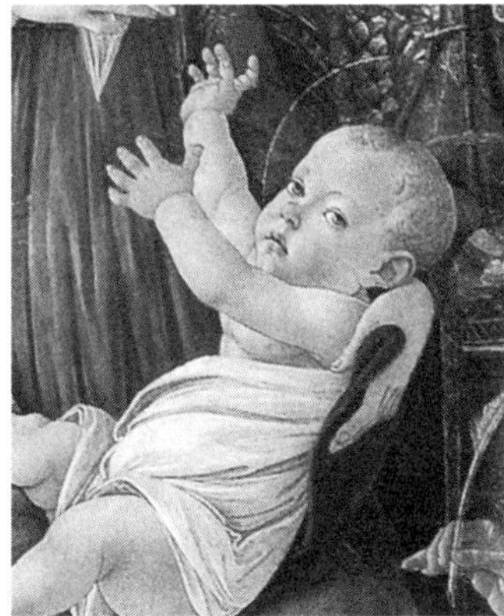

144
Botticelli,
The Birth of Venus,
detail,
fifteenth c.

145
Botticelli,
Enthroned Maria with Child with John the Baptist and John the Evangelist,
detail,
fifteenth c.

146
Botticelli,
Coronation of the Virgin,
detail,
fifteenth c.

147
Rafael,
St. Catherine of Alexandria,
detail,
sixteenth c.

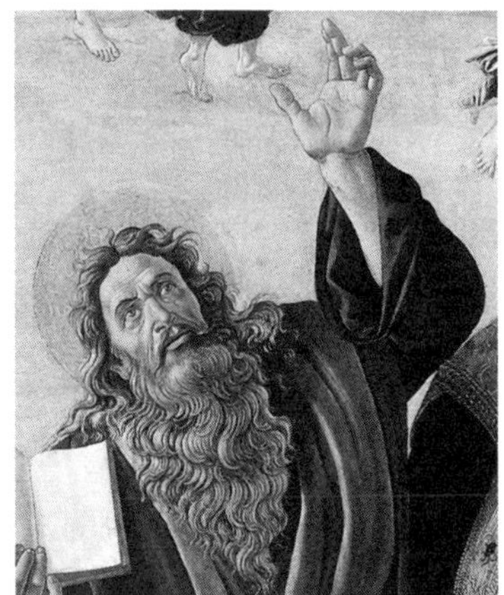

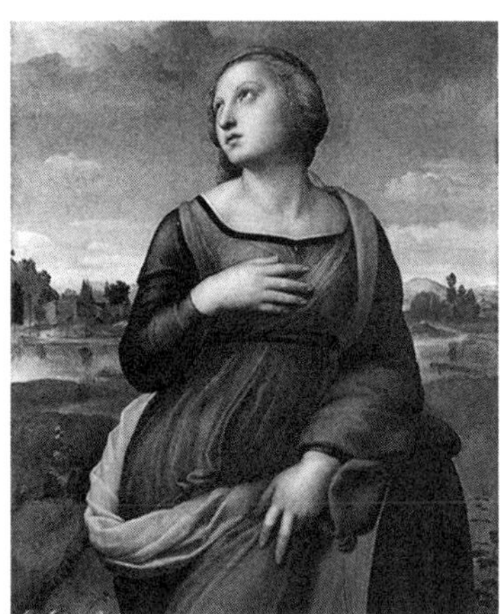

The Renaissance did not take cast shadows into account, for its realism was the realism of the object "as such." Shadows interfered with seeing the actual reality of nature. Shadows were, for the Renaissance painter, a kind of subjective illusion, not connected with the object. Shadows blurred natural forms and, at times, even concealed them. Shadows were inessential, unreal. Shadows could be moved arbitrarily or their direction changed, but they had no capacity to change the actual convex **shape** of a solid. For Renaissance painters, three-dimensional form was reality, while shadows were an illusion, something subjective, interfering with clear seeing. The history of the transition from the Renaissance to the Baroque was that of the gradual increase in the consciousness of shadows and their real existence. A new visual consciousness increases by way of the accumulation of small observations, small quantitative differences, until a new model of visual consciousness arises as a result. The accumulated, small, quantitative differences introduce a new quality. Taking care to preserve the distinct local colour of the object, the Renaissance painter painted the whole object with one colour, shading it with the same colour. He also applied the same colour for shading and rendering the convexity of the three-dimensional form. In effect, he rendered the local colour of the object. The local colour of the painted object could be verified and compared with the local colour of its model in nature. It was enough to place one next to the other. The tester fully matched the original.

In seeking to draw out a greater convexity of the three-dimensional form, a later painter increased the shading nearer the edges of the object. Bringing out its three-dimensionality, he intensified the light and shade effects that could be achieved by way of the same colour that was on the object. Another painter introduced darker colours and in this way achieved a still more pronounced convexity. This is in the first years of the sixteenth century. This gradual evolution leads to a manner of painting in which a local colour remains only in bright parts of the object, while in areas in shadow, there are only darker hues of a colour common to all objects.

Hitherto, every object had had its distinctly local colour. Shadow was emphasized solely by the intensification of the same local colour. The visual consciousness of chiaroscuro, which is to say, a consciousness taking into account the objective existence of shadows, shatters the hitherto cohesive Renaissance colour-system. In place of a system of distinct local colours of objects, a new colour system appeared whose purpose was not the distinctness of objects but connecting them through the common hue of the shadow. Dark colouring (the colour of shadows) enters into the composition of all the colours of nature and becomes the unifying colouristic bond of the painting. This is how the Baroque begins, the art of the second half of the sixteenth century and the entire seventeenth century.

In deep shadow, the object merges with the background. There is no continuity of contour. Contours fade away in the shadows.

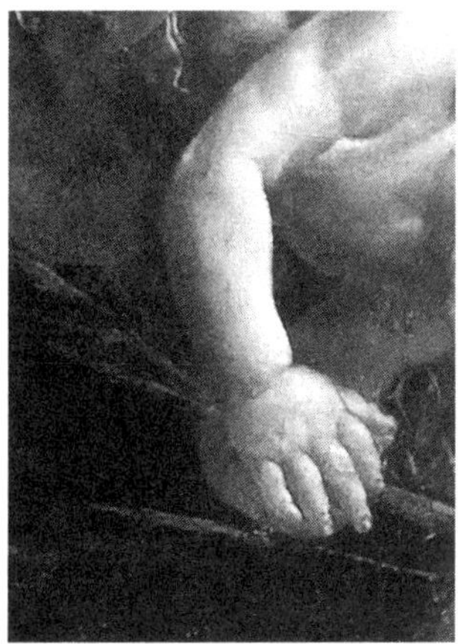

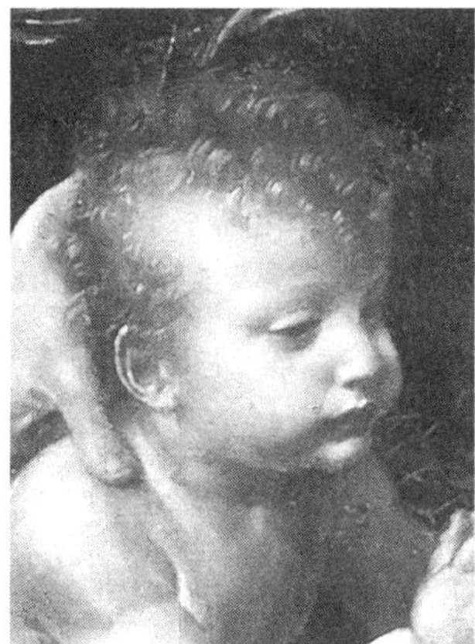

148
Leonardo da Vinci,
The Virgin of the Rocks,
detail,
fifteenth c.

149
Leonardo da Vinci,
The Virgin of the Rocks,
detail,
fifteenth c.

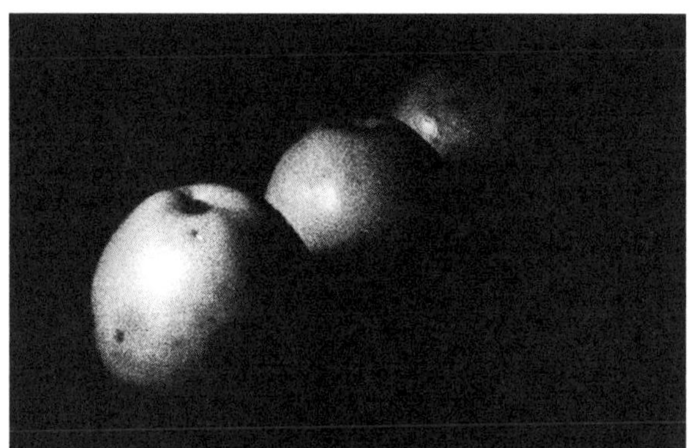

150
Nature photography

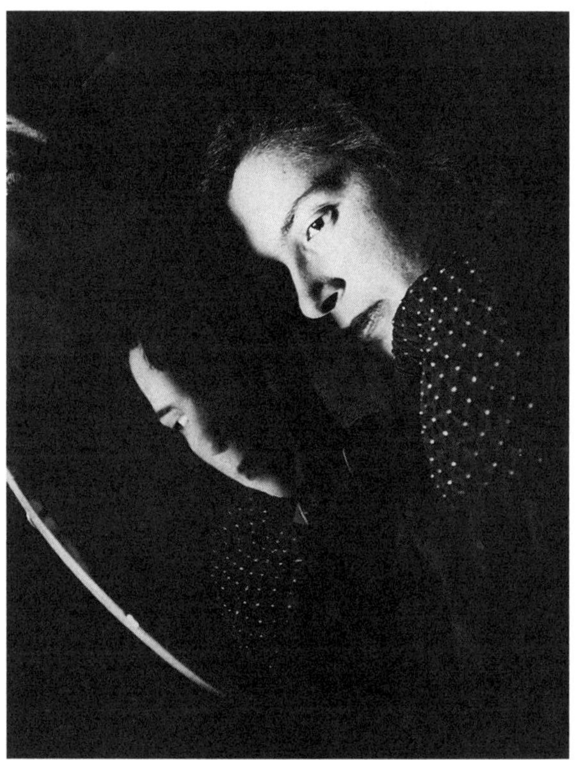

151
Krzywobłocki,
Portrait of Ms. Halina Hornung,
twentieth c.

Contour line not only fades away in the shadows. It also fades away in the passage from shadow to light; it is subject to being broken in several places. The object no longer has a single, continuous contour line.

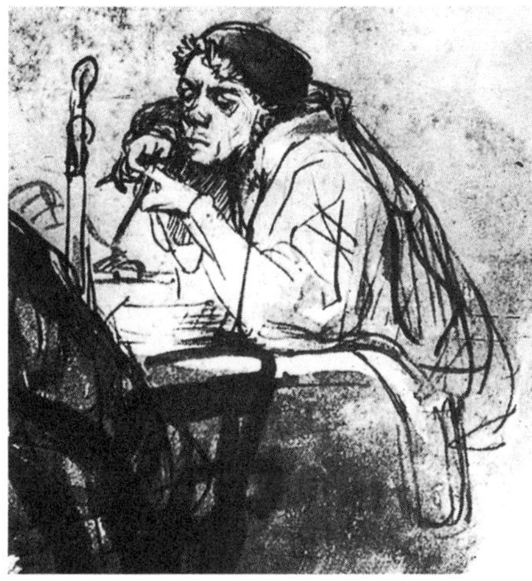

152
Rembrandt,
Scribe Sharpening His Quill by Candlelight,
drawing,
seventeenth c.

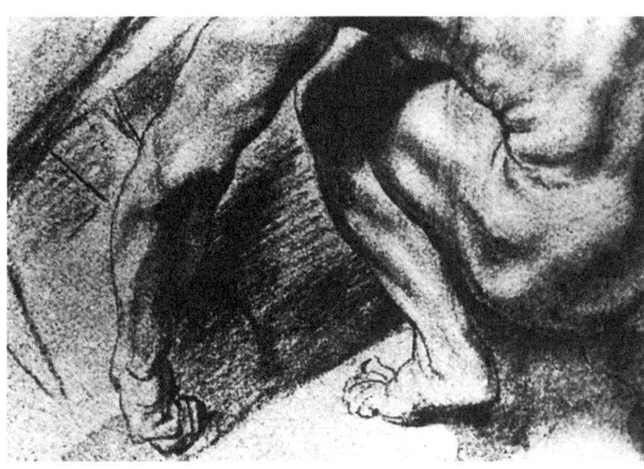

153
Rubens,
Miraculous Draught of Fishes,
detail,
seventeenth c.

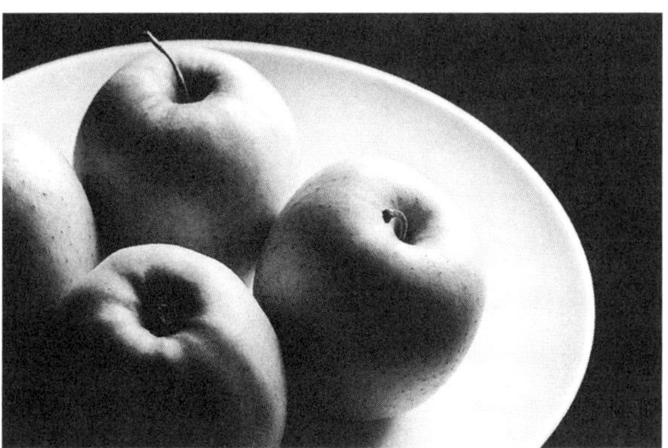

154
Nature photography

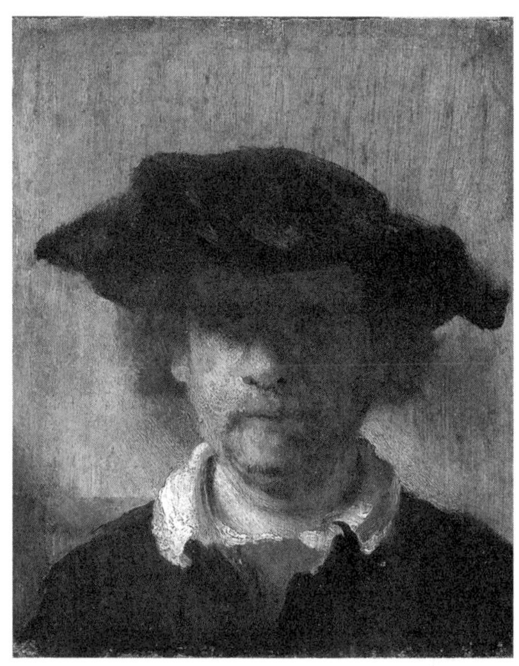

155
Rembrandt (studio of),
Self-portrait,
seventeenth c.

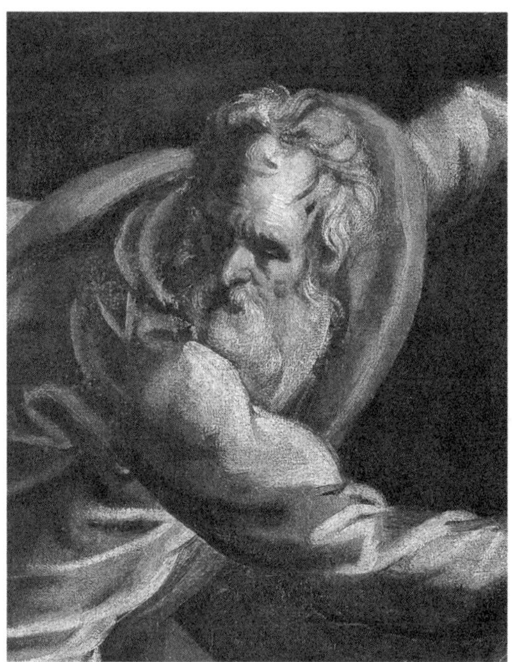

156
Tintoretto,
St. Mark Rescuing a Saracen,
detail,
sixteenth c.

A regard for the play of light and shade (hitherto rejected as elements immaterial to and uncharacteristic of the material nature of the object) shatters the entire extant system of Renaissance form. The object is no longer Renaissance paintings' object, isolated from its background. As an effect of the play of light and shade, it partially melts into the background. The object is in sharp focus in some places, while, in others, contours melt into the background.

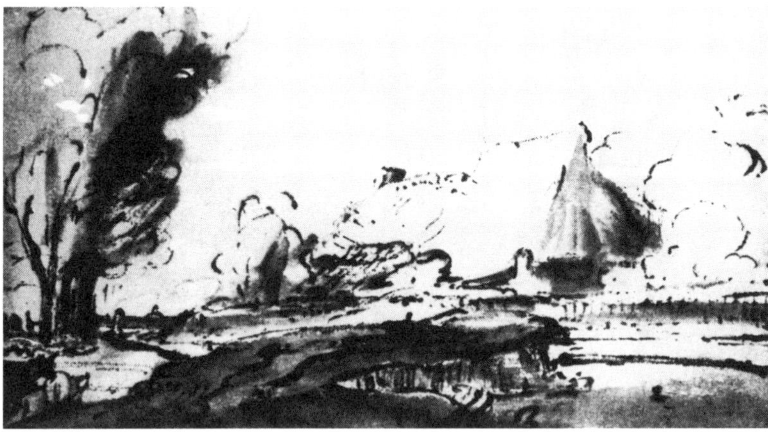

157
Rembrandt,
Path over a Bridge,
drawing,
seventeenth c.

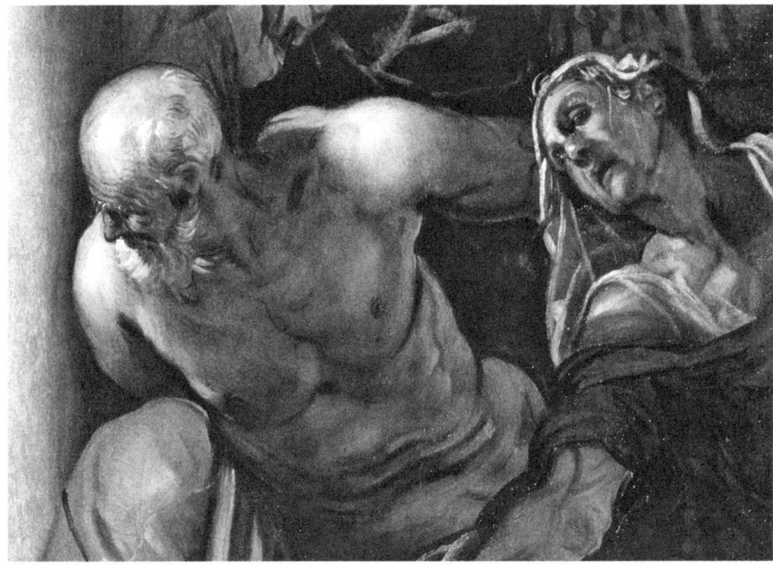

158
Tintoretto,
The Probatic Pool,
detail,
sixteenth c.

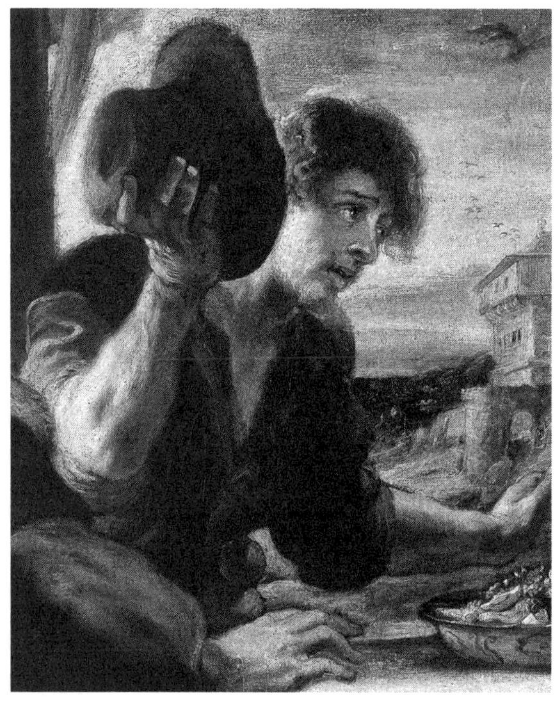

159
Rubens,
Supper at Emmaus,
detail,
seventeenth c.

The system of distinct colours authentic to the object was reduced to the basic colour of shadow – a dark colour. This colour enters into the composition of all colours authentic to the object, tinting them to a greater or lesser extent, in accordance with the intensity of light. The addition of a shadow of darker colour lends the picture a unity of hue. Its intensification, the submerging of colours in shadow or, alternatively, their emergence from it to appear either more or less clearly – this is the basis of Baroque form.

The rhythm of the intensity of chiaroscuro, the rhythm of the casting of light and engulfment by shadow – these are the foundations of the Baroque aesthetic.

The picture no longer consists of isolated objects. The changeability of objects in light and shade dissolves forms into their background in some places, while displaying them sharply in others. The shadow of the background passes into the shadow of the object. The object melts into the background. Shapes that are clearly defined in certain places fade away in others.

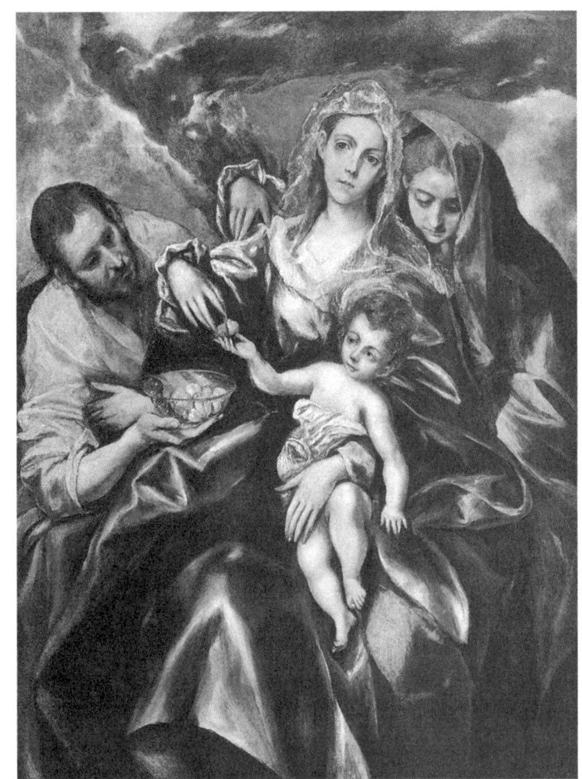

160
El Greco,
The Holy Family,
sixteenth c.

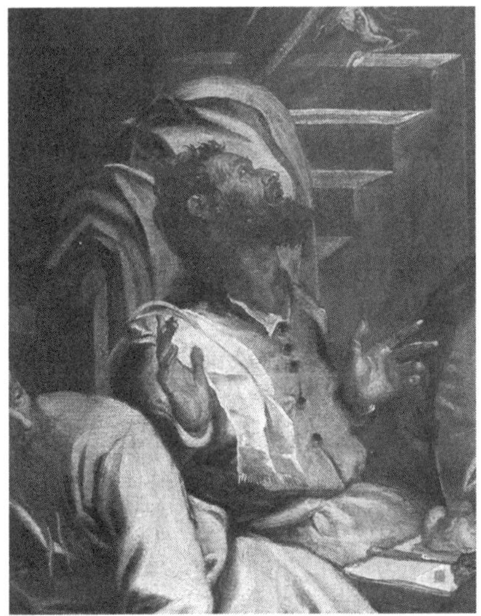

161
Tintoretto,
The Last Supper,
detail,
sixteenth c.

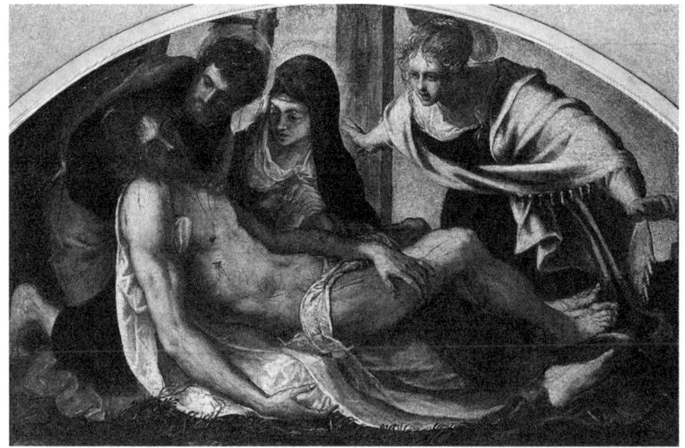

162
Tintoretto,
Pietà,
sixteenth c.

This is how the commodity object came to be broken up for the first time. The visual consciousness of light and shade effects blurred the contours of objects and introduced into them shadow colour (from the background) breaking up the unity of a colour specific to the object that had hitherto existed. The distinctness of the object, the distinctness of its character as a sample of a commodity, was made to give way to seeing the whole — to the process of seeing.

The change that occurred in the manner of painting nature — in the very **approach** to the observed object — coincides with wider shifts taking place at that time in leading philosophical and scientific thought. We see a convergence between the changes taking place in both cases.

The Renaissance painter did not observe the object (visually), but **studied** it, drawing out its essence and shape, constructing the object according to his knowledge of mathematics and perspective. Thus, he over-painted the draughted object with a single specific, "true" colour (which could be compared by placing it up against the object) — the colour of the object as such, isolated from the influence of arbitrary factors existing in the real world. He shaded the object in such a way as to emphasise all the curves of three-dimensional form, to show the object in full relief. If the actual arrangement of light and shade made it impossible to show the full relief, if the object's contours faded away, dissolved in shadow, then he painted these parts of objects in a different chiaroscuro, conditioned by light falling from another side.

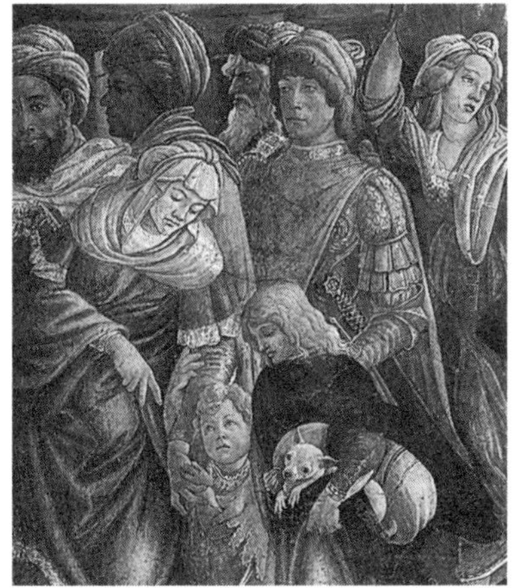

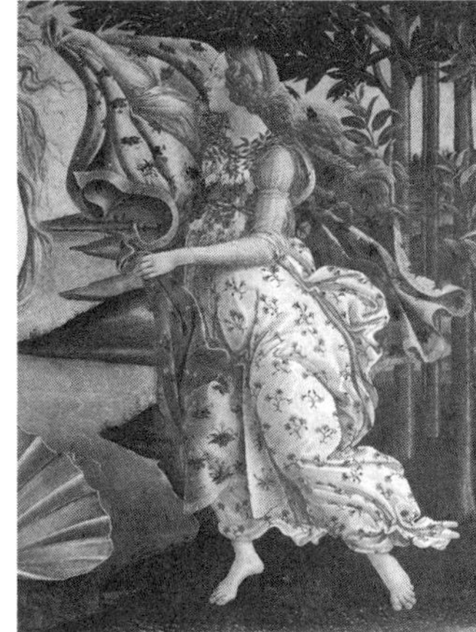

163
Botticelli,
The Youth of Moses,
mural,
detail,
fifteenth c.

164
Botticelli,
The Birth of Venus,
detail,
fifteenth c.

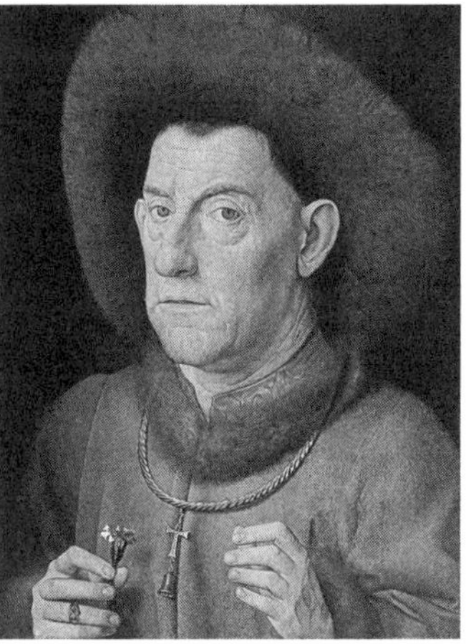

165
Jan van Eyck (follower),
Man with Carnation,
sixteenth c.

In this way, an image was created of the object that expressed its "essence," but was not commensurate with observation. The object was derived not from accumulated, concrete, experimental observations but from speculative, logical **reasoning** concerning the nature of the object and its form. This reasoning was expressed with the aid of mathematically and logically inferred means. The drawing of the object was a drawing of a logically determined three-dimensional form, drawn with all the required perspectival foreshortening, but it did not account for the actual course of thoughts prompted by the observation of the three-dimensional form — emerging, sketching out the object in some places and fading away in others.

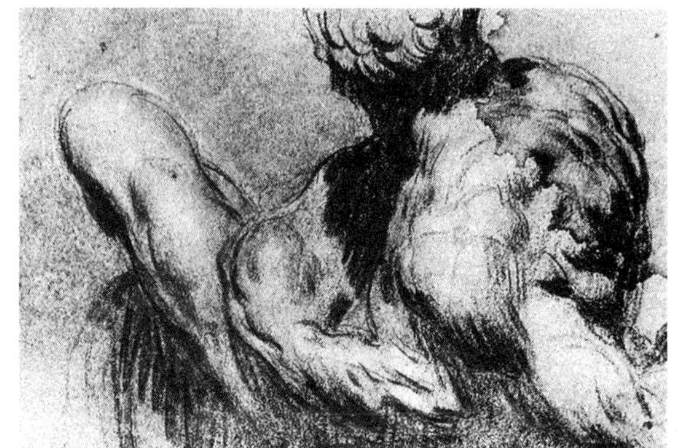

166
Tintoretto,
Study for a sculpture,
drawing,
sixteenth c.

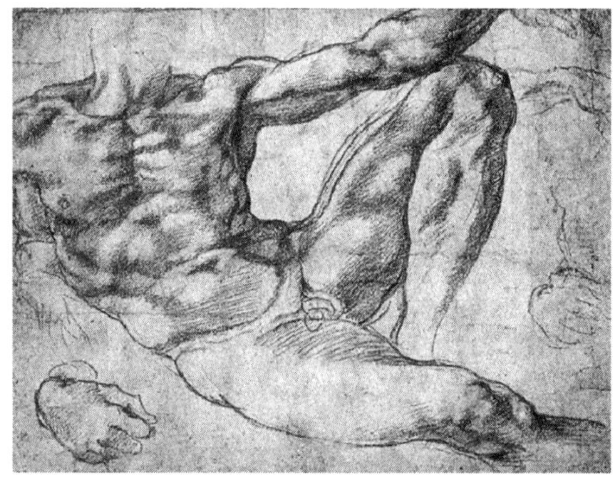

167
Michelangelo,
The Birth of Adam,
sketch,
sixteenth c.

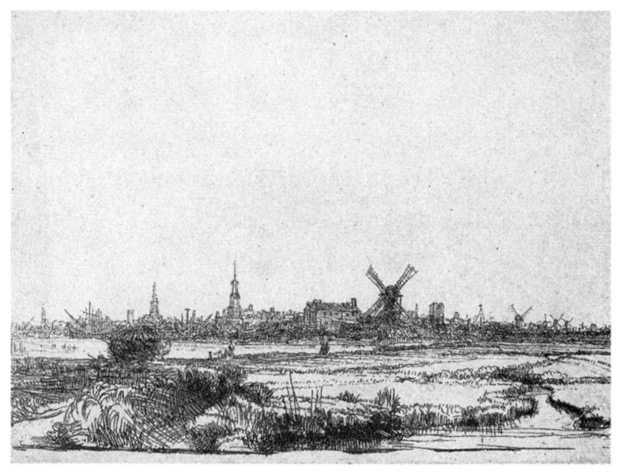

168
Rembrandt,
View of Amsterdam from the Northwest,
seventeenth c.

Rather than deriving his drawing from empiricism and the accumulation of **observations,** the Renaissance painter offered a drawing that was a logically inferred construction of the object. Not the reality of observation, but the unity of the object inferred by reasoning concerning what it is like, how it "should" be, if it is to be itself.

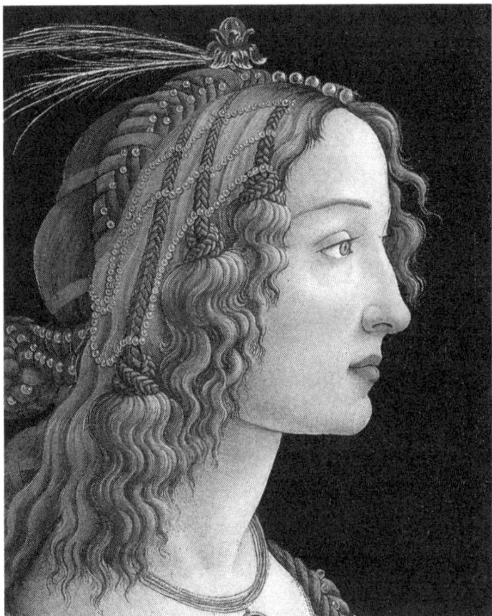

169
Botticelli,
Portrait of a Young Woman (Simonetta Vespucci),
fifteenth c.

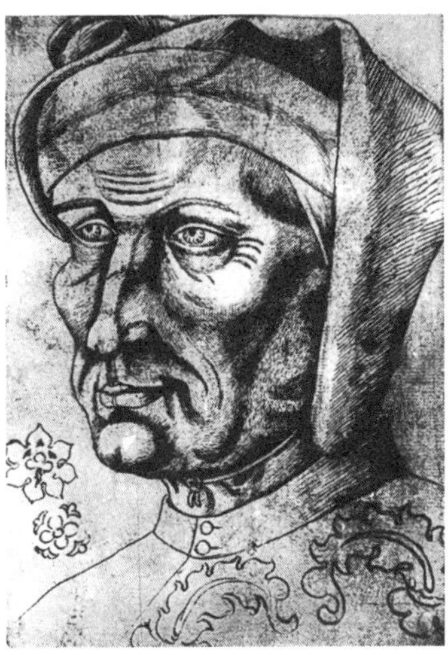

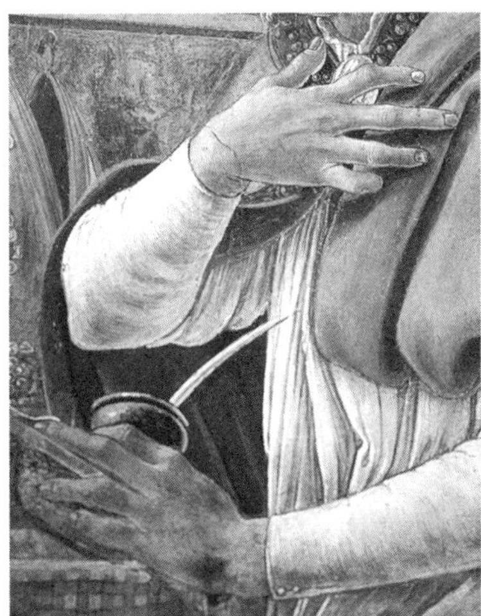

170
Pisanello,
Study of a Head,
fifteenth c.

171
Botticelli,
St. Augustine,
detail,
fifteenth c.

Sixteenth- and seventeenth-century painting developed by passing from logical reasoning concerning how an object looked, to concrete **observation**, to accumulating observations, to empiricism. It was an empiricism that was limited to issues of light and shade. That the object had its own distinct borders, dividing it from the surrounding space, was known through practical experience. Using this experience, the object was painted in such a way as to clearly delimit it from its surrounding background. This was a construction of the image of the object on the basis of logical reasoning and inference. The object was painted in the manner in which it **should** look, logically speaking, and not in the manner in which it **looked in practice.**

This contradiction between earlier and later visual consciousness — the contradiction between the logical inference of the image of the object and its real image — became evident on the occasion of Rembrandt's painting *The Night Guard.*

Rembrandt's clients, members of craftsmen's guilds, people of commodity-seeing, demanded to have their **whole** faces painted (like a whole **commodity** and a whole **sample** of a manufactured product).

They considered it a slight to their human dignity that Rembrandt painted them only in part (brought by light out of the shadow); part of their faces ("how can one paint half a face instead of a whole?").

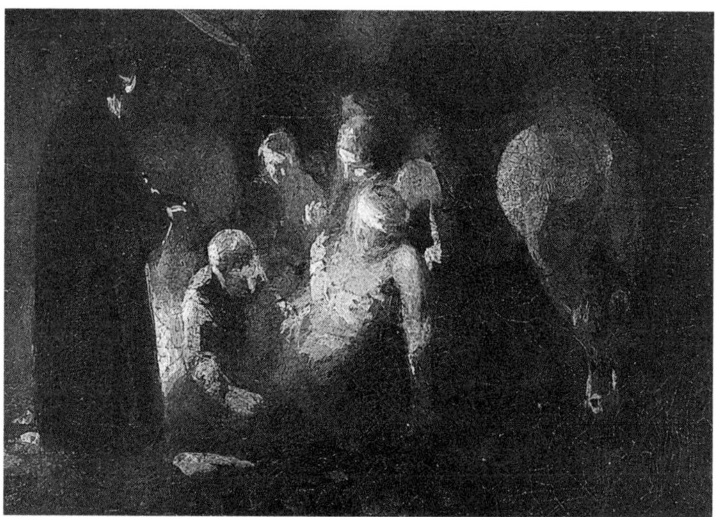

172
Rembrandt (follower), *The Good Samaritan,* seventeenth c.

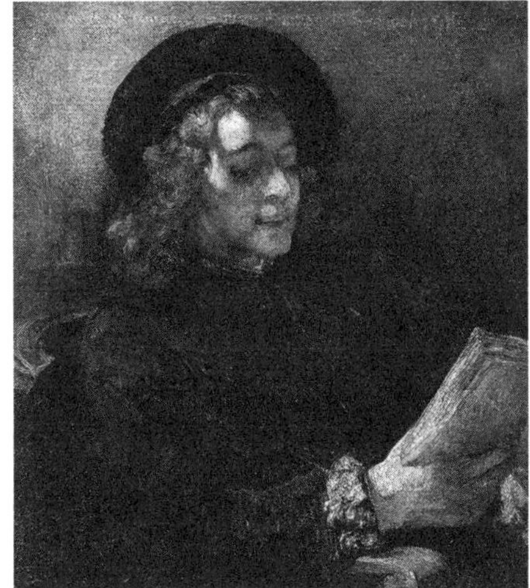

173
Rembrandt,
Titus Reading,
seventeenth c.

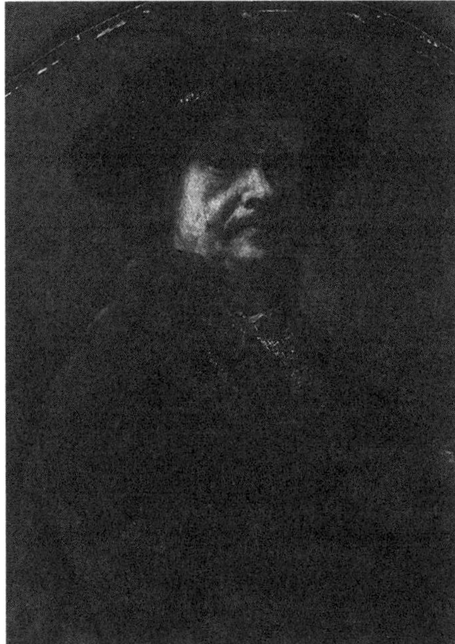

174
Rembrandt,
Self-portrait,
seventeenth c.

Besides the conflict of commodity-seeing with empirical seeing, there was another conflict here – between the feudal mentality of craftsmen and Rembrandt's progressive, burgher's thinking.

But this was also the path upon which philosophy had entered, moving away from its scholastic past. The transition of painting from the speculative construction of the object to the empiricism of real human seeing, the claim that a mathematical and logical definition of the three-dimensional object is something other than its definition on the basis of visual observation, corresponded to the transition of philosophy in the sixteenth and seventeenth centuries to empiricism. Instead of creating systems explaining the nature of the world based on logical **reasoning** and drawing conclusions from a number of arbitrarily accepted basic concepts (often taken from theology), philosophy moves to the position of investigating and understanding reality. Not an abstract and detached reasoning concerning the nature of the world, but **understanding** by way of observation, experience, and the gradual universalisation of sensory data — this was how leading philosophers defined the working method in the sciences at the time. Philosophy becomes the methodology of empiricism — an experiential science enhancing society's forces of production. Philosophy grows out of its contemporary empirical science as the universalisation of its methods.

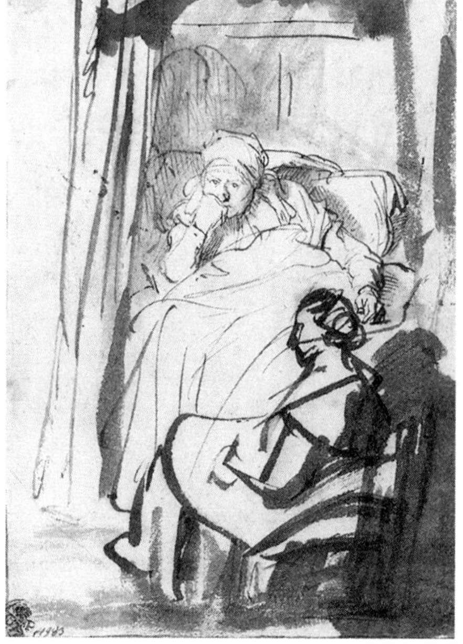

175
Rembrandt,
Saskia in Bed,
drawing,
seventeenth c.

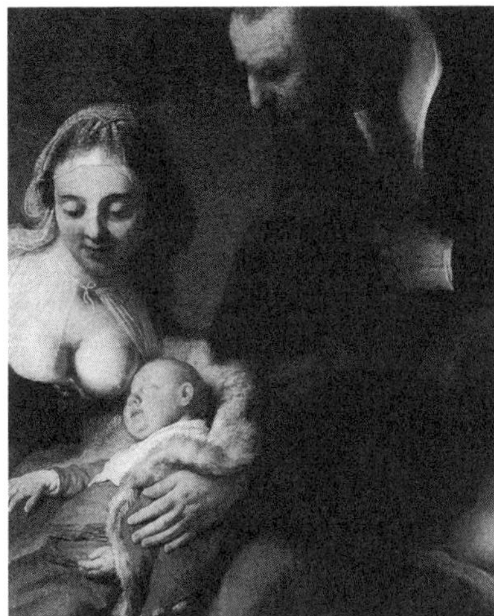

176
Rembrandt,
The Holy Family,
detail,
seventeenth c.

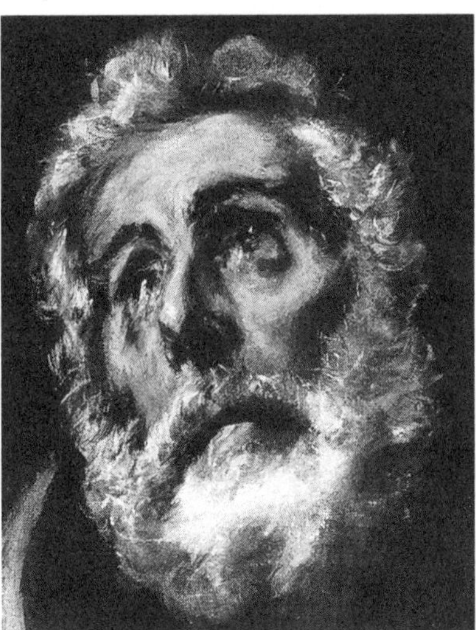

177
El Greco,
The Repentant St. Peter,
detail,
seventeenth c.

The method of the visual, experiential investigation of the phenomena of light and shade and of their influence on the visibility and shape of the object was the same empirical method, the experiential investigation of facts, the determination of causal relationships between phenomena and their universalisation by way of precise mathematical rules, introduced in their philosophy (as theory) and in their science (as practice) by the empiricist and materialist philosophers:

- F. Bacon (1561 – 1626),
- Galileo (1564 – 1642),
- Hobbes (1588 – 1679), and
- Newton (1642 – 1727),

who was a philosopher in so as far as he universalised his study of natural science.[8]

The philosophy of this period takes the form of generalizing the methods applied in many branches of science, formulating the methods relating to the understanding of the world deployed in practical science not as concrete methods of any particular science, but as a method "in general," devoid of anything particular or concrete. Abstracting from what is particular and concrete, specific to the given science – philosophy takes what is general, what lies at the foundation of science (as a whole) and constructs out of this the rules of scientific investigation. In this way, philosophy organises and systematises general laws defining the newly founded empirical scientific method.•

The application of these same empirical methods in the realm of visual phenomena leads to a fuller, more precise realism and contributes

8 See I. Newton, *Philosophiae naturalis principia mathematica* (*The Mathematical Principles of Natural Philosophy*, trans. A. Motte, to which are added *The Laws of the Moon's Motion According to Gravity* by John Machin, vols. I, II [London: B. Motte, 1729]).

• "For in our speculating we either seek to penetrate the true and internal essence of natural substances, or content ourselves with a knowledge of some of their properties." Galileo Galilei, "History and Demonstrations concerning Sunspots and Their Phenomena," in *Discoveries and Opinions of Galileo*, trans. Stillman Drake (New York: Doubleday, 1957), p. 97, reproduced in K. Park and L. Daston, *The Cambridge History of Science: Volume 3, Early Modern Science* (Cambridge: Cambridge University Press, 2006), p.744.

"...he tried, now with logical arguments, now with magical adjurations, to tear down and argue the new planets out of heaven." Letter from Galileo to Kepler, 19 August 1610, in Karl von Gebler, *Galileo Galilei and the Roman Curia*, trans. Jane Sturge (London: C. Kegan Paul & Co., 1879), p. 26.

"Everything that does not result from phenomena, is a hypothesis, and hypothesis [...] should not be admitted..." (Newton). [I. Newton, *Philosophiae Naturalis Principia Mathematica*, 1687, a fragment of text after the famous statement: *Hypotheses non fingo* ("I feign no hypotheses," "I frame no hypotheses," or "I contrive no hypotheses") *General Scholium*, 1713 edition of the *Principia*). ▸

to a new, superior model of visual consciousness – **chiaroscuro visual consciousness**, derived from the empirical, from observation.

Despite the previous position of scholastic philosophy, detached from practical knowledge, sixteenth- and seventeenth-century philosophy becomes the generalization of rules and methods applied in the practical sciences.

The development of the forces of production at that time had attained a level on which it became necessary to connect practice with scientific theory. In order to develop further, the labour of the craftsman and the labour of manufacturing needed to be supplemented by the labour of the theoretical scientist, by the systematic investigation of nature, its laws and phenomena. The sixteenth and seventeenth centuries saw the emergence of not only philosophies that universalised the methods of empiricism but also the appearance of sciences investigating (using the empirical method) a series of branches of nature that were the foundation for the development of philosophy. This investigation of nature practised by the newly emerging practical sciences required a method and a system. This method was **empiricism**.

In place of **reasoning** about the world and its essence, there comes **investigation** and the description of phenomena. In place of logical definition, the **description of properties** characterizing the phenomenon or the object. This is how empiricists defined the tasks and methods

‣ I. Newton, "Mathematical Principles of Natural Philosophy," *Book III. Proposition XLII. Scholium general*, p. 694: "...I would not like to invent hypotheses. Whatever is not deduced from phenomena has to be called hypothesis, but, on the other hand, there is no place for hypotheses."].

"I do not want to believe anything that has been proscribed over and above the circumstances of the human experience. I want to rely on my eyes; I want to see the circumstances of events and to believe only in what I saw. I advise my pupils not to take my word for it." (Bacon)

"I want to know each and every circumstance. That is why first of all I shall make a few experiments, since it is my intention that experiment speak out... such is the course which should be taken when examining natural phenomena." (Leonardo da Vinci)

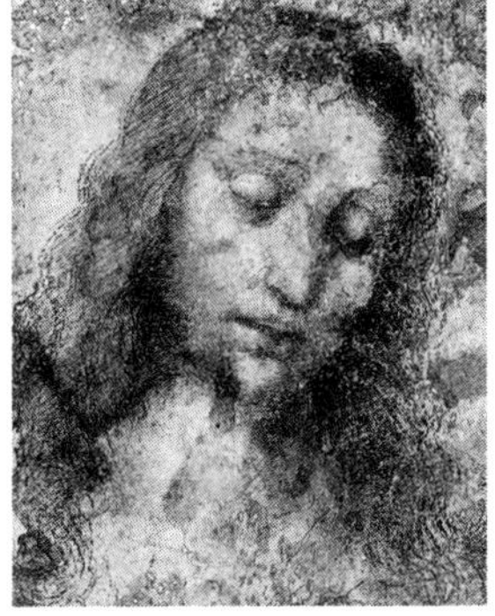

178
Leonardo da Vinci, *Head of Christ*, drawing, 15th c.

of the newly developing science, whose purpose, they thought, was to investigate phenomena that could not be deduced from general ideas, phenomena demanding observation and instruments.

Ordinary observation ceases to suffice. The more penetrating grasp of the properties of a phenomenon or object demands the creation of instruments facilitating observation. In parallel with the development of the technical sciences, instruments facilitating their development appeared:

- The thermometer — Galileo (1597),
- The refracting telescope — Lippershey (1608),
- The telescope — Kepler (1611),
- The barometer — Torricelli (1643),
- The pneumatic pump — von Guericke (1650),
- The microscope (observation of microorganisms) — Leeuwenhoek (1675),
- Greenwich Observatory — (1675).

Thanks to these instruments, the discovery of the following natural phenomena and their generalization into theory becomes possible:

- The earth's magnetism and electricity — Gilbert (1600),
- Systemic blood circulation — Harvey (1628),
- The wave theory of light — Huygens (1678),
- The law of gravity — Newton (1684).

The empirical method becomes an expression of the developing forces of production of the period.

This same empirical method, transferred to visual observation, leads to the production of a new visual consciousness — **chiaroscuro** consciousness. This new visual consciousness arises in direct relation with the production activity of the period, with its forces of production, consolidating the achievements of thinking — of man's cognitive work, emerging from the struggle for production of essential material goods — in the model of seeing attained.

Development in the realism of seeing is thus a reflection of the development of forces of production. The transition to the empirical method and to the development of the technical sciences accelerated this developing realism in all fields of human activity.

However, the development of the forces of production is linked to changes in the social system. Having ownership of the developing forces of production, the bourgeoisie no longer struggles for the right to exist within the feudal system but for the full realization of its objectives. Revolutions follow (1598 – Holland, 1642 – England).

This newly acquired, superior visual consciousness is used as the means of ideological pressure. The aims imposed by bourgeois culture in the original period of the accumulation of capital were: to rationalise the class interests of developing capitalism with the help of chiaroscuro seeing, and in conformity with nature to have its class-conditioned purport imposed on other classes as the absolute truth, binding for everyone. Hence, alongside **chiaroscuro realism**, **chiaroscuro formalism** emerges and develops – no longer reflecting the forces of production but the class system and relations of production of the period. One is conditioned by the other. One is inherent in the other. The contradiction between the realism of the sixteenth and seventeenth centuries (empirical chiaroscuro-seeing) and formalism in the same period (imposing the class interest of emerging capitalism as absolute truth) is not a simple contradiction but a dialectical opposition, a unity of opposites.

This formalism relies on making full use of the realism of the period, but in simultaneously using it in such a way that the image of the world received conforms with the interests of the bourgeoisie struggling to seize power, that it serves as its argument in the political struggle. The essence of formalism should therefore be sought within, rather than outside the realism of the given period – in the manner of **exploiting** this realism.

Taking as a point of departure the realism of a given period, it was used in such a way as to make the received image of the world represent the bourgeois struggle for its class interests as being universally valid and in accordance with the natural order. The empirically verifiable conformity of the components of seeing with nature was to prove that not only seeing but the significance of the work of art as a whole was in accordance with nature and therefore true. Conformity with nature was thus the necessary condition of formalism's class-determined purport, imposed on other classes.

This conformity with nature – as a shroud for the emerging capitalist purport – was not confined to the visual arts. The progressive thinking of the period used the argument of accordance with nature, with the natural order of things, contrasting the natural order of the world to the existing, imposed, feudal order. Natural cultural systems arise in the following way:

1. Natural law as the foundation of **rational** social systems (Grotius);
2. The theory of the state of nature as the agreement of the **natural interests** governing every man (Hobbes);
3. Natural system of ethics (Hobbes);
4. Natural religion recognizing only what is common to all denominations and corresponding to the common views of all people (Herbert of Cherbury);
5. Natural system of social economy (physiocrats)•

And, finally, chronologically the last:

6. The natural law of exploitation (*On causes of perfecting the forces of production of labour and on the order by which products are divided in a natural way between various classes of people* — A. Smith[9]).

("An activity in accordance with nature is free and right" — Spinoza.[10])

The empirical method showed that an investigation of the objective world, existing outside ourselves, leads to a gradual discovery of the truth. The more our investigation is in accordance with nature, the closer we are to the truth. Nature became the affirmation and measure of the truth. This was one face of naturalism (as a cultural movement) related to the progress of the empirical method in science.

But besides this investigative relationship to nature, there was another face of naturalism — a worldview that concealed the subsequent consequences of the battle cries of the bourgeoisie preparing for its decisive battles. In this naturalism (a worldview that was philosophical, not scientific, exploratory, or technical), the criterion of nature was not used as a shroud for objectively scientific interests but for class

9 See. A. Smith, *An Inquiry into the Nature and Causes of the Wealth of Nations*, 1776.

10 The exact quotation is: "Spinoza maintained — like the stoics — that such conduct, natural and free, is just; acting in accordance with nature, free and just: these are three names of one thing." W. Tatarkiewicz, *Historia filozofii*, p. 100.

• The offshoot of these natural systems is also the so called "natural seeing," that is, conceived in the abstract, the model of seeing of an average individual. It was a mistake of natural systems that they understood man outside history, as an unchanged being (at most — tainted in the course of history). The notion of natural seeing is tainted with the same mistake. Seeing is not unchanged, but, like man, it is shaped by the material conditions of existence throughout history and develops with the development of forces of production created.

interests. The word "nature" is in both cases identical, but in one case it designates an investigative territory in which objective truth can be attained, while in the other, "nature" is used in order that its authority (as a criterion of truth) shroud the class purport of natural systems (law, religion, social systems, etc.), the class purport of bourgeois philosophy.

These two very different faces of a seemingly uniform return to nature should be clearly distinguished – the empirical method vs. the worldview, the political argument. They were two dialectically opposed manifestations of the same historical current. But just as the consolidation of the empirical method would have been impossible without the universal worldview's turn towards nature, so too, achieving the trust enjoyed by "natural" systems would not have been possible without the verifiable authority of the empirical method, without its achievements and discoveries.

The general position of philosophical naturalism is to make of nature the criterion for truth. For this reason, the formalism of the sixteenth century could not have developed without the achievements of chiaroscuro-seeing. Conversely, the significance of realist-seeing – its class conditioned deformation of nature – could only be justified by a full exploitation of its resources. To have a natural foundation in nature, to intensify the realism with which it was seen, but to use this seeing in such a way as to obtain an image of the world that was in accordance with the class interests of the developing bourgeoisie – this was the developmental path taken by seventeenth-century formalism: to show the world in such a way that made the historical role of the bourgeoisie look significant and positive.

This deformation of the image of reality was thus not contradictory to the new achievements of visual consciousness. It was simply deformed in accordance with its own assumptions. By way of this deformation, the protagonists of the primitive accumulation of capital swelled with spiritual eloquence, dramatic struggle, the dynamism of great deeds, and the radiant light of genius. More than that: the same eloquence was accorded to landscape and still-life (so called "earthly goods," or, plainly speaking – riches). This was made possible by the skilful deployment of **compositional clues**, their disposition, and the use of light and shade effects. In this way, the chiaroscuro realism that was achieved contained within itself the **chiaroscuro formalism** with which it was dialectically connected. Similarity to and reference to nature was necessary to lend credence to suggestions in line with the class interest of the bourgeoisie as it undertook its decisive battle for rule over the people. In order to present the class interest of the bourgeoisie as being in accordance with the truth of nature, the meaning of the work of art had to be conveyed though forms that avoided provoking any doubt that they were nature itself — and nothing more. Hence, conformity with the most superior attainments in the realist-seeing of nature was a necessary condition for the spectator not to notice that besides the realism of seeing nature itself, it was the class purport of bourgeois painting.

Sixteenth- and seventeenth-century painting developed on the basis of empiricism. Observation of nature showed that not all shapes are lit with the same intensity. Some are the focus of more light, others — less. The background can also be darker or lighter, depending on light. As a result, there are juxtapositions of light and shade of different strengths in the picture (as in nature). This can be a very strong juxtaposition of full light (on the object) and full shadow (in the background behind the object). It can also be a very weak juxtaposition, where the light of the object is the same as the light of the background.

The greater the contrast between light and shade, the more obvious it becomes. Even the same image, if we present it in a less contrasting photograph, attracts less attention than a photograph with strong

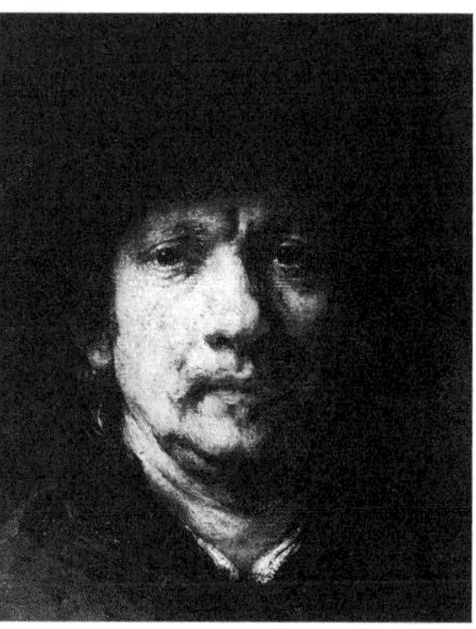

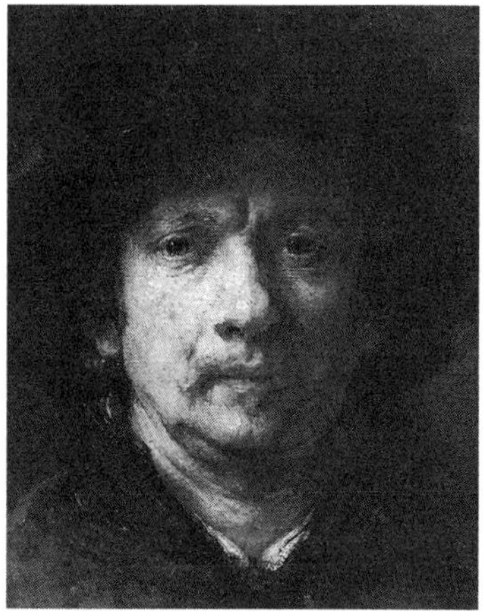

179
Rembrandt,
Self-portrait,
seventeenth c.

contrasting light and shade. A contrasting image attracts attention while a uniform image diffuses it.

In the (contrasting) photograph on the left, the image acquires a focused expression and attracts more attention than the diffused one on the right. Hence, having both prints side by side, our gaze settles on the contrasting one.

Observation proves that points with strong contrasts of light and shade attract the eye of the spectator — in nature as well as in the picture. The point in the picture where there is the strongest contrast of dark and light attracts the most glances.

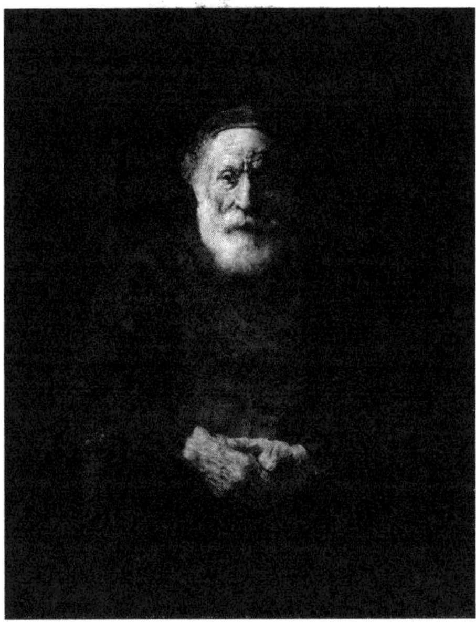

180
Rembrandt, *Portrait of An Old Man in Red,* seventeenth c.

The stronger the contrast of light and shade at a particular point, the more it attracts the gaze, and the longer the eye rests on it. These things can be tested empirically, noting the number of gazes that within a given time, we level at particular points of the picture. Marking on the picture the points that attract the gaze most, we find that their distribution is neither uniform nor random, but that they are grouped according to the strength of contrasts of light and shade — the stronger the contrast, the more it attracts the gaze.

Thus, we are able to identify the particular points in the picture that attract attention. Depending on the number of gazes cast, we are able to determine their meaning and the force with which they catch our eye.

181
Rembrandt,
The Return of the Prodigal Son,
seventeenth c.

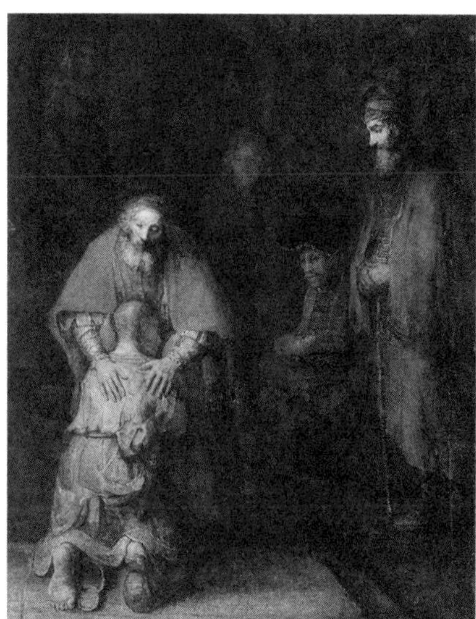

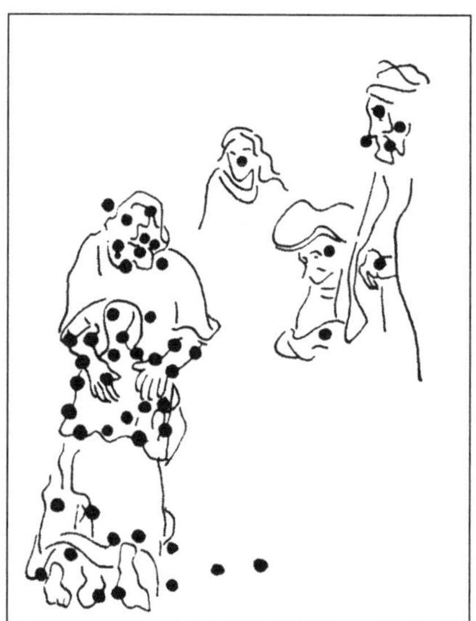

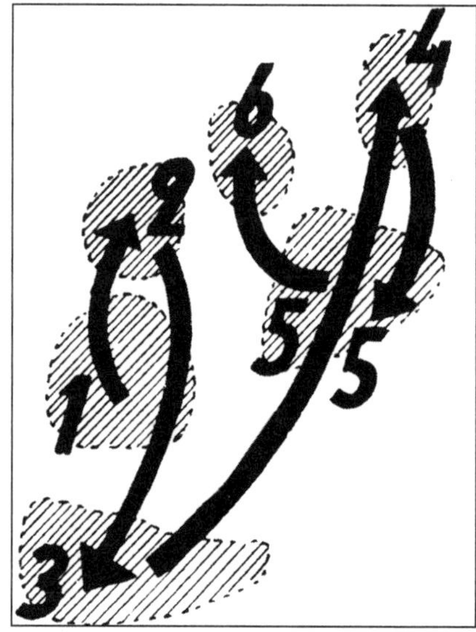

Looking at the picture, we see the strongest compositional clue best, i.e. the first, which attracts most gazes. The number of gazes attracted by each successive point in the painting will depend on how strongly it stands out. The result is that the eye does not look at the painting by wandering at random over its surface, but passes, in turn, from one compositional clue to another until all there is to see in the picture has been exhausted.

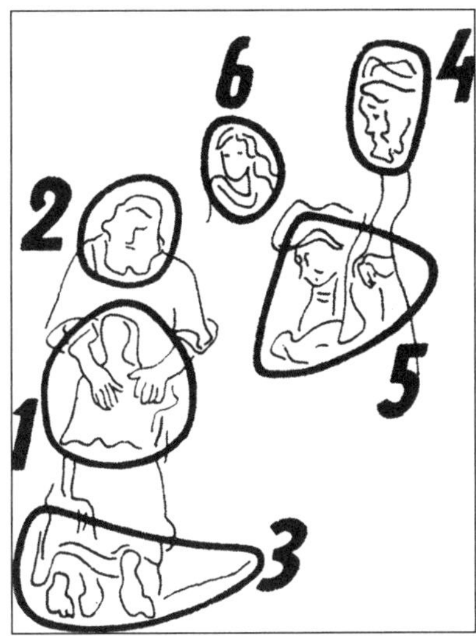

This imposed, organised order of viewing emphasising what the artist suggests as being **most important** in the picture (the content of the compositional clues) — gives a clear expression of the picture's content. The various forms in the picture do not speak all at once but in order, as organised and appointed by the artist. This is why the main content of the picture (found in the main compositional clues) is perceived before secondary content. Expressed by means of chiaroscuro-seeing, nature is elaborated by way of compositional clues. Some points are emphasised (we see these foremost), while others are weakened (and hardly penetrate our consciousness as we barely perceive them). The use of compositional clues simplifies the decoding of the picture's intentions.

Analysing Rembrandt's *Self-portrait with Saskia*, we will define its compositional clues. These are found in areas of contrasting light and shade, and their ordering depends of the strength of these contrasts.

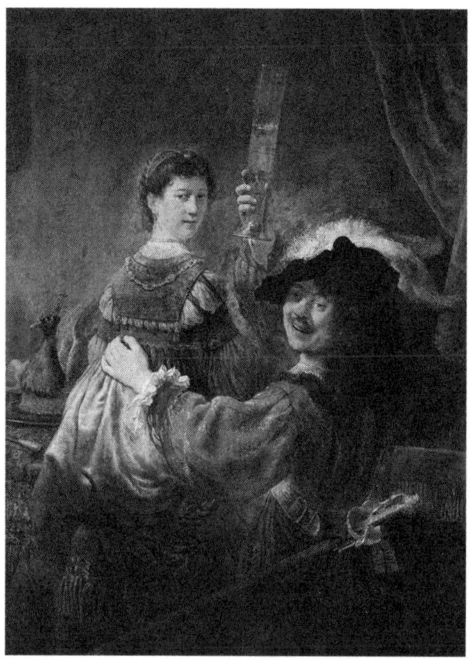

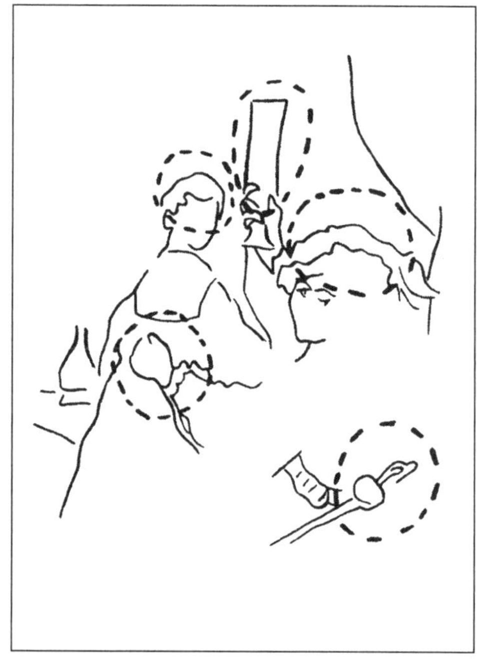

182
Rembrandt,
Self-portrait with Saskia,
seventeenth c.

As we can see, the compositional clues are placed:

1. At the meeting point of the white ostrich plume and the black hat;
2. at the hilt of the sword;
3. on the hand embracing his wife;
4. on the hand holding the glass;
5. on his wife's face.

What is the meaning of this placement of compositional clues? It means that the significance of particular objects in the painting should be noted in the order dictated by the sequence of gradation of the compositional clues. This means that:

1. Rembrandt considers the most important fact, worthy of universal emphasis, to be his possession of the expensive ostrich plume from overseas on his black hat;
2. he regards having a sword with a precious hilt to be the next important fact. Both these objects testify to Rembrandt's position in the hierarchy of bourgeois society, acquired by way of possessing the appropriate riches;

3. the fact of possessing a wife (more accurately — her body) comes after the possession of wealth in terms of importance. Indeed, this conforms with the bourgeois rule — first wealth, then wife;
4. the precious glass with wine (also from overseas) indicates another aspect of the joys flowing from consumption, guaranteed by an adequately large fortune — joys of consumption being the highest purpose in life, attained by accumulating as much wealth as possible;
5. the face (the human face) of his beloved wife comes only fifth in this scale of values.

This was the significance that the period's primitive accumulation of capital gave to the painting, and this is how it appealed to the mentality of the society of the time. These were the ideals (consumption and accumulation of wealth) and ideas that the bourgeoisie, as the leading class, imposed on the masses. In the era of the primitive accumulation of capital, this was formalism's method of presenting the goals of the bourgeoisie as accessible to all and attractive to all so as to make bourgeois ideals the general norm for all.

Presenting the joys of consumption as the most essential, genuine goal of every man, to replace feudal consumption — class-based, closed, and determined by origins and birth — with a democratic, bourgeois-consumption model accessible to anyone who acquires wealth — this was the platform for the struggle with feudalism over the "natural" right to bourgeois consumption unlimited by anything (other than wealth).

The "natural" right to consumption, accessible to every man, was the slogan that drove the masses to struggle against feudalism and to realise the class interests of the bourgeoisie. The "natural" right to consumption is expressed via the "natural" representation of consumer goods, made particularly attractive by their appropriate rendering in the picture and the use of compositional clues. The praise of consumer goods and their joys is concealed in the majority of paintings of the period. Their subject matter is not labour but the delights of consumption. We see games of dice, drunken brawls, dancing, scenes of gluttony and merry-making in scenes of the lives of the lower classes. Even the poor and beggars are depicted in the act of eating. The objective realism of seeing as a tool to understand the world was used to deform the image of reality in accordance with the class interests of the increasingly powerful bourgeoisie.

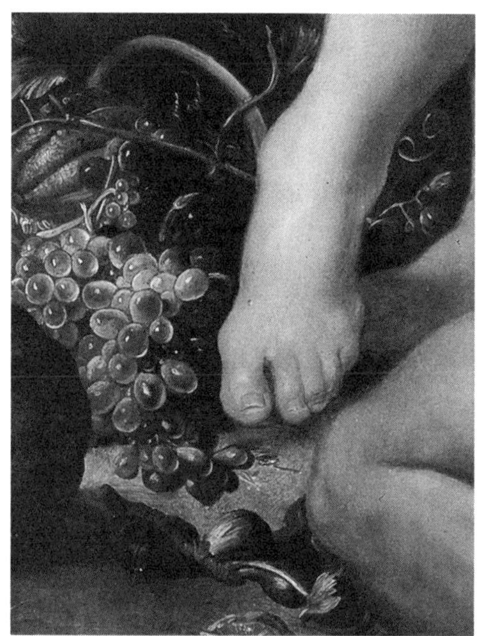

183
Rubens,
Crowning of the Hero,
detail,
seventeenth c.

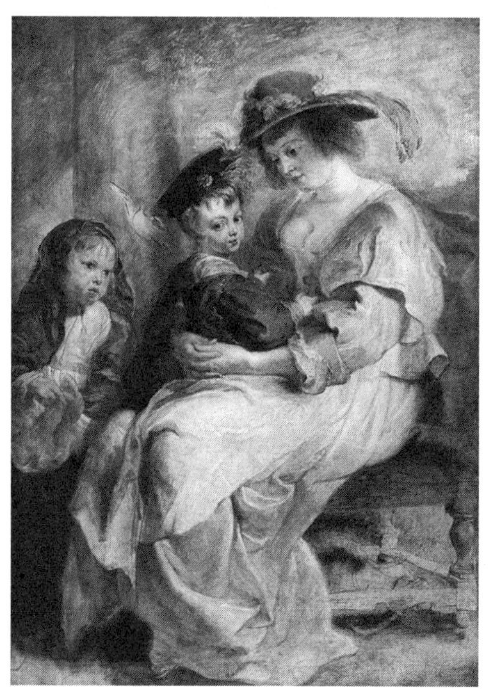

184
Rubens,
Helena Fourment
with Children,
seventeenth c.

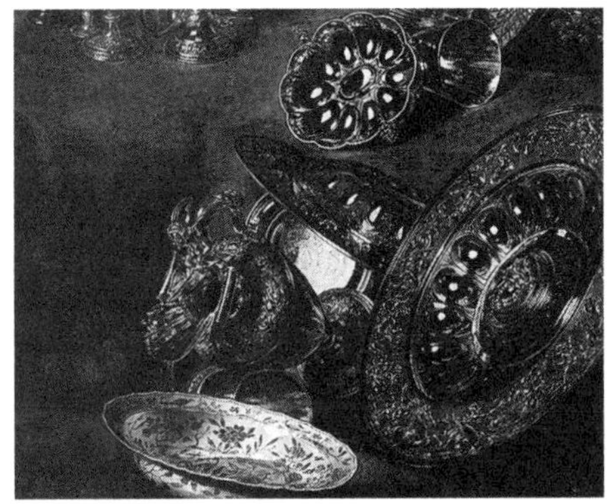

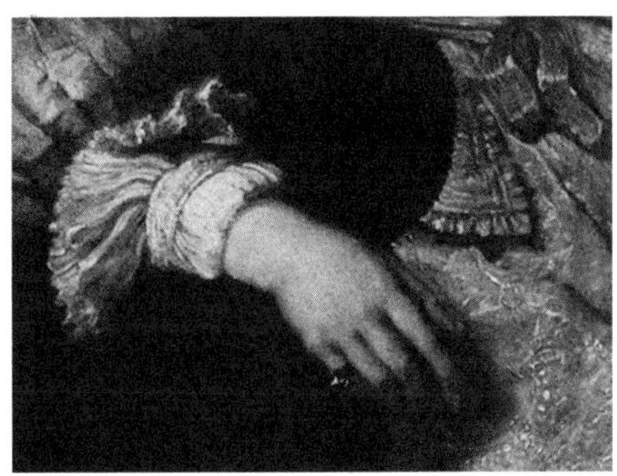

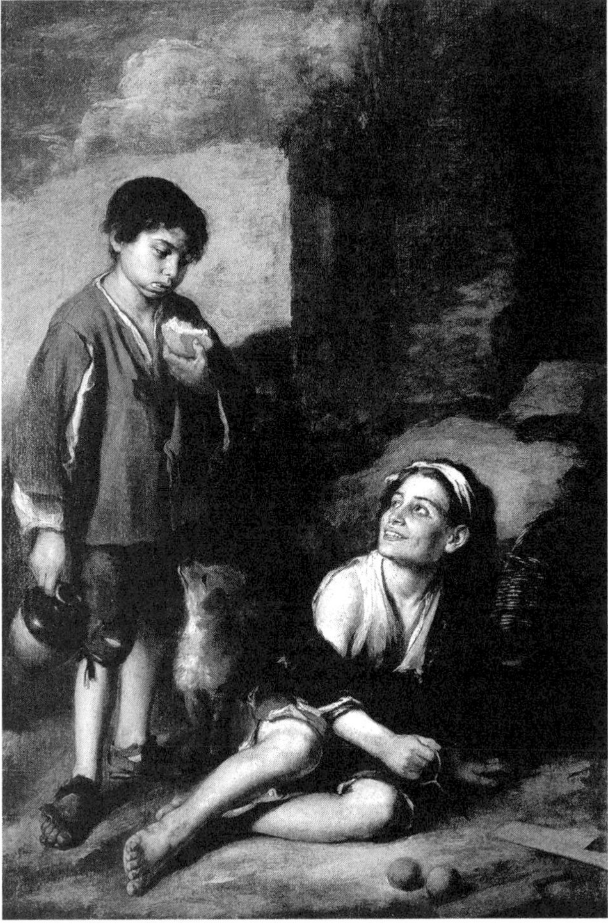

185
Rubens,
Helena Fourment in her Wedding Dress,
detail,
seventeenth c.

186
Rubens and workshop,
Bacchanal,
detail,
seventeenth c.

187
Murillo,
Two Peasant Boys,
seventeenth c.

That it was better to feed the masses was made more than clear by the age of bourgeois revolutions – in Holland and England. In replacing the feudal system with a bourgeois-capitalist system, it changed all the relations that existed among people. The notion of man itself took on a purport other than the scholastic, feudal one it had had previously.

With time, the emphasis to be found on objects begins to fade away from Rembrandt's paintings. The compositional clues increasingly emphasise only man – his face, hands, chest. The focus of attention comes to centre on **man** himself.

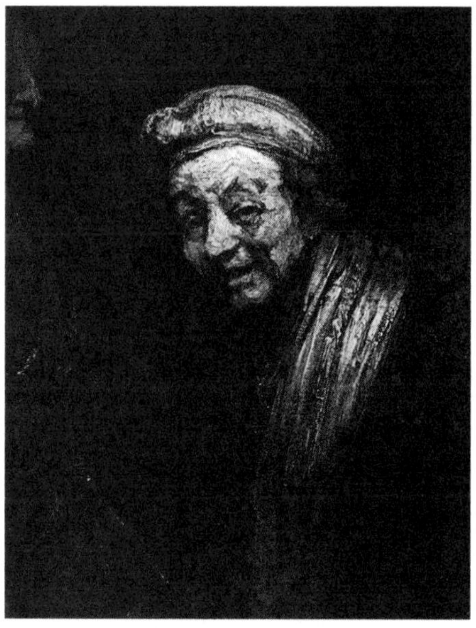

188
Rembrandt,
Self-portrait,
seventeenth c.

The compositional clue emphasises only his thinking forehead – not even his entire face. The attention is focused on thinking. "I think, therefore I am." (Descartes[11]) The thinking individual can and must

11 "I think, therefore I am" (1637) in the French original, "Je pense, donc je suis" (1637), R. Descartes, *Discours de la methode*, 1637, English trans., *Discourse on the Method*, [Part Four], trans. R. Stoothoff in *The Philosophical Writings of Descartes*, Vol. 1, trans. J. Cottingham, R. Stoothhoff, D. Murdoch (Cambridge: Cambridge University Press, 1985), p. 128.

be the judge of truth and justice, without awaiting supernatural assistance. Man possesses reason, which rules alone and independently. This reason has its foundation in human nature as constant and unchanging.

This is an expression of **bourgeois humanism** – identical in Descartes and in Rembrandt – that takes the personal truth of the individual ("natural" man), his personal dignity, the courage of his individual thinking, and his heroic struggle for the righteousness of his own convictions to oppose the imposed "supernatural" truths of feudal scholasticism.•

We have to realise with all clarity this specificity of sixteenth- and seventeenth-century humanism, its line of development, which united the heroes and martyrs of thinking, who emerged from the contemporary historically progressive role of their class. We have to realise the **class** character of this humanism and the relation between the slogan of **individual** enrichment and the slogan of individual heroism in the struggle for the **personal truth** of "natural" man. We also have to see the mobilizing mottos of nascent capitalism.

These ideas, however, could not have been expressed had the realism of chiaroscuro visual-consciousness not been discovered in the course of extensive empirical investigations. The expression of the **activity** of thinking, the expression of the activity of the human face, the expression of the **humanistic** purport of nascent capitalism (still progressive, in its struggle with feudalism) was only possible using

• This was not a case of Rembrandt restricting himself to the confines of the strictly professional, narrow concerns of a guild, or to purely "expert" painterly problems. An awareness of the use of compositional clues emerged from natural systems as a whole.

This same reality is expressed by Descartes, as though responding to Rembrandt: "Now a painter cannot represent all the different sides of a solid body equally well on his flat canvas, and so he chooses one of the principal ones, sets it facing the light, and shades the others so as to make them stand out only when viewed from the perspective of the chosen side." R. Descartes: *Discourse on the Method,* Part Five, trans. R. Stoothoff in *The Philosophical Writings of Descartes,* Vol. 1, p. 132

This is how the rationalist Descartes, whose "reason," capable of independent cognition of the world, which later became the foundation of the development of materialism, replies to the painter Rembrandt.

the method of compositional clues. And compositional clues developed from the observation of the effects of light and shade on the object. In order to express man as a thinking and feeling being, it was necessary to focus the whole attention on his thinking forehead, to position this forehead within the principal compositional clue, and to oppose the light of the thinking forehead to the heavy darkness of the surrounding background. The individualist purport of bourgeois humanism could not have been expressed in any way other than by way of chiaroscuro-realism. The components of formalism, i.e. the class-conditioned deformation of the objective image of the world, are dialectically connected with the consciousness of chiaroscuro-seeing itself.

The development of visual consciousness was the result of the growth of the forces of production. The development of the realism of seeing, like the development of speech, occurred in response to the needs posed by the development of production, which acquired increasingly perfect and complex forms.

But the growth of the forces of production over the course of history contributed to a succession of antagonistic systems. The successive ruling and exploiting classes attempted to subject the newly acquired principles of seeing to their own interests and to transform them into a tool of ideological influence. One has to be able to distinguish clearly a component of objectively developing seeing from the exploitation of this seeing for the purposes of the class struggle taking place in the given period. In other words: the new, empirically verifiable, development of seeing and the class-conditioned purport, contributed by one of the classes engaged in the struggle. We have to remember that it is not only the warring classes that change over the course of history, but also the ideological arguments by way of which they consolidate their existence. This is why the same visual resources may be deployed by both warring classes. In the sixteenth and seventeenth centuries, the reactionary feudal-catholic class developed chiaroscuro-seeing in order to lend credence to and to render more real (to represent as truthfully as in nature) its purport of opposing bourgeois revolution.

What was the nature of the opposition between these claims? It was the **political** struggle of the bourgeoisie to establish its own form of state and its own social system, translated into the realm of general ideas. The main conflict was played out in relation to the question of what was to be the source of all laws and social systems: "natural" man and the "natural" law of nature? Or the necessary and eternal truths of religious revelation? In the realm of ideas, this was a conflict between empirical science and a philosophy based on revelation. "Finite existence has its source in eternal existence," claimed the Jesuits (Suárez).[12]

To justify these claims — to show that the temporal world had its source in the eternal world, to express an opposition between the begotten and the made and to show it in such a way that no one would have any doubts — this could only be done by using all the resources of the newly acquired chiaroscuro seeing. The task that we encounter frequently in Spanish and Italian art of the sixteenth and seventeenth centuries was to show the infinite universe in its cooperation with the temporal world, to represent it so realistically that this realism could serve as visible proof. Proof by reason, used in philosophical treatises, debates, and enunciations, was to be replaced by a visible proof of **realistic interpretation** ("as true as life"). Heavenly grace, the light from above shining on the people on the earth, had to be shown using all the empirical achievements of chiaroscuro-seeing. It was only possible to express this by way of the appropriate placing of compositional clues, intensified or muted as required.

Two compositional clues were distinguished and opposed to one another: light falling from above and the figures of people below. This was how theological purport was expressed. The light of grace from above shines onto the activities of the people on earth.

The same realism of chiaroscuro-seeing was used to render concrete two different messages. To express the courage of individual thinking in Rembrandt, and, in Murillo, to embody a philosophical message, subordinate to theology. Deformation of the image of reality was inherent in the very components of realist-seeing, facilitated and derived from the specificity of chiaroscuro-seeing itself.

12 Francisco Suárez, *Disputationes metaphysicae*, 1597. See also F. Copleston, *A History of Philosophy*, Vol. 3, *From Ockham to Suárez* (Westminster, Md: Newman Press, 1950), Chapter XXII, "Francisco Suárez (1)."

189
Murillo,
St. Roderick,
seventeenth c.

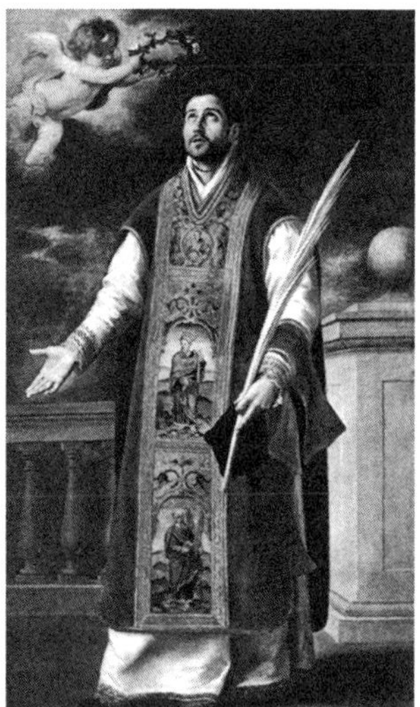

190
Murillo,
La Toilette Domestique,
seventeenth c.

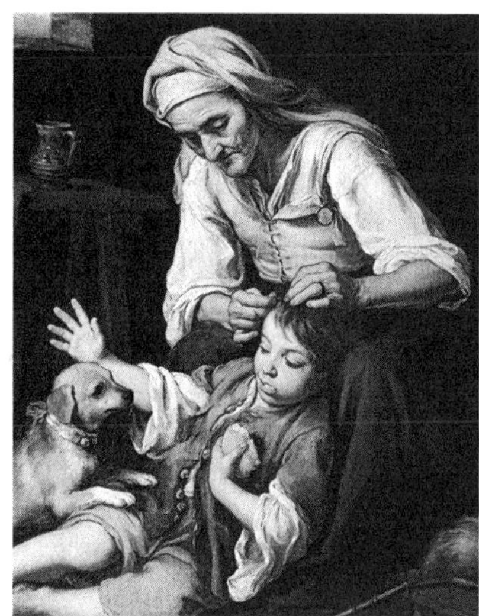

191
Murillo,
The Virgin Mary and St. Felix of Cantalice Holding the Infant Jesus,
detail,
seventeenth c.

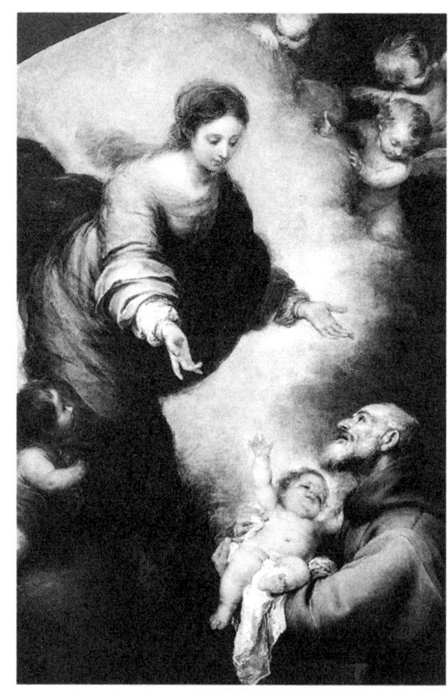

The light falling from the upper compositional clue, lighting up the human figure and drawing it out from the darkness of the background, gives it an inspired expression and the radiance of inspired thought, radiating from heaven. In this way a feudal lord — an owner of hundreds or thousands of serfs, an exploiter and looter — is transfigured into a person of lofty inspirations and wisdom, sent by divine grace from heaven — he is lifted above ordinary human dimensions and transposed into the world of superhuman beings.

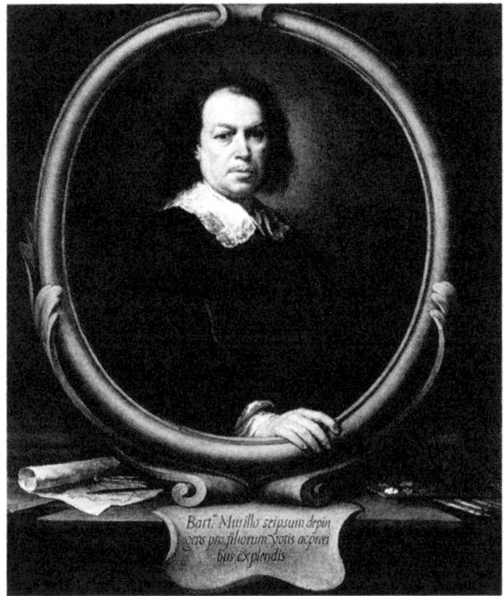

192
Murillo,
Self-portrait,
seventeenth c.

The suggestiveness of compositional clues drew out heroic purport and facilitated the mobilization of the forces gathering on both sides in the tumultuous period of the bourgeois revolutions and the primitive accumulation of capital. The heroic purport that was drawn out was both bourgeois — seeking its rationale in man himself, empirical man, his thoughts and nature — and religious and feudal — presenting the power of man as dependent on inspiration and grace sent from heaven.

Even landscape comes to be composed according to the method of compositional clues.

As a result of the intensification of contrasts between light and shade, the dramatic suggestiveness of landscape becomes several degrees more intense. This landscape acquires the character of a heroic landscape. This is entirely comprehensible in view of the considerations above. But what were the philosophical, social, and other claims in whose name this mobilization of heroism was undertaken?

193
Ruisdael,
Landscape,
seventeenth c.

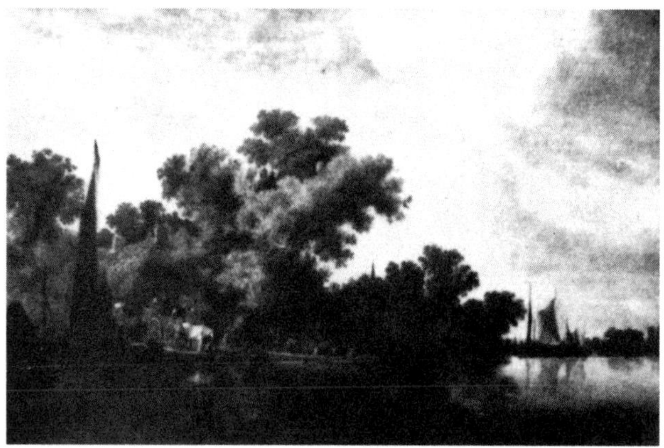

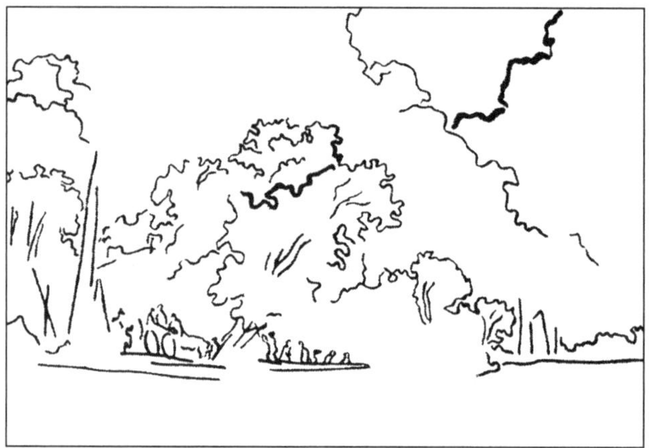

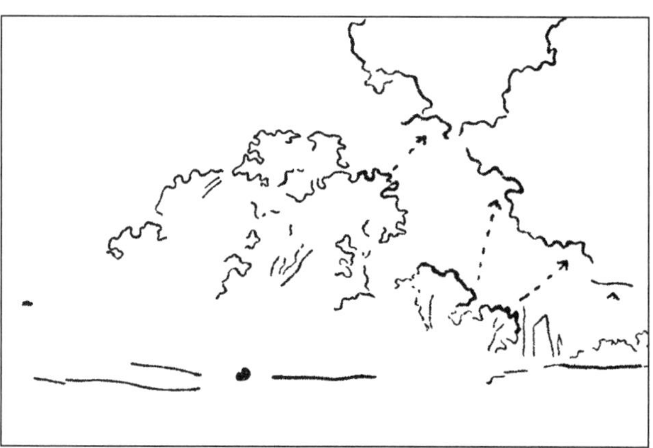

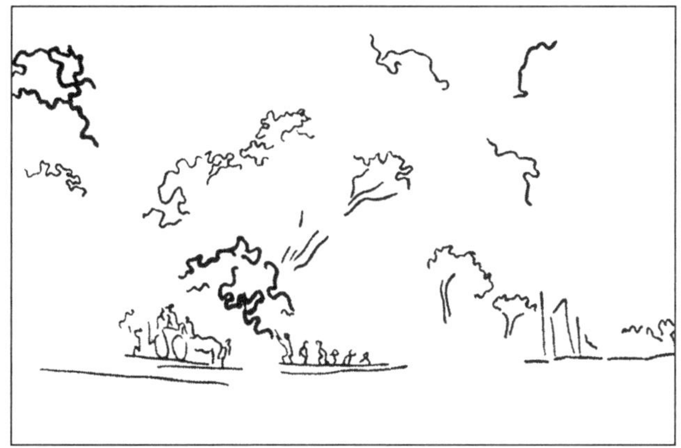

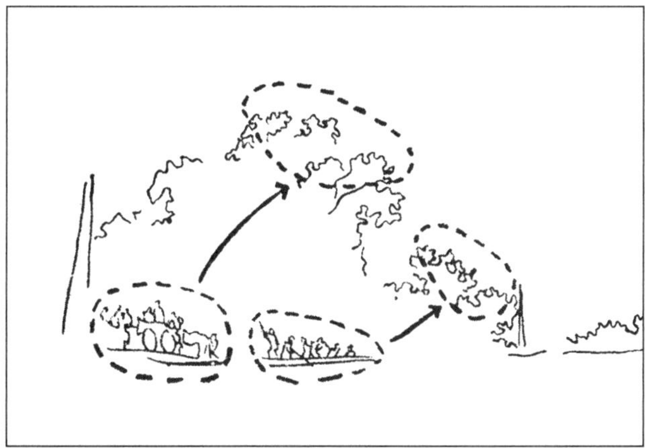

In order to read these claims, we will define the compositional clues.

As the analysis shows, the main compositional clues have been positioned in pairs. The compositional clue located in the trees (or on the ground) responds to the compositional clue in the clouds. The forms in each of the pairs have been rendered in a similar manner. An architectonisation of trees into clouds has taken place. As a result, the **entire landscape** has been imbued with elements of the clouds and the storm. The turbulent history of the Dutch and English revolutions, the Thirty Years' War, the overseas trade expeditions, and the colonial trade by sea have made their way into the painting and permeated it with their dynamics.

At a deeper level, there was a clear philosophical foundation for this mutual "seeping through" of natural elements, of likening trees to clouds, people to trees, and clouds to earth and trees, lending a uniform shape to nature as a whole (rather than treating each object differently). The ideological foundation of the picture contains Giordano Bruno's precepts:

1. on the unity of matter in the world;
2. that matter is living, and therefore free,[13]

as well as Spinoza's teachings on overcoming the dualism of body and spirit in favour of the uniform substance of reality: "The order and relation of substance is the same as the order and relation of ideas."[14] Negating the dualism of the universe, he proclaimed the universal determinism of nature understood as a mechanism. Nature has no purposeful order; it is not governed by the supernatural; there is only the chain of cause and effect. It is pantheism in which God is nature while nature, devoid of the supernatural, is governed by the determinist laws of cause and effect.

The thought that in order to express the unity of nature, to show it **visually**, in a manner accessible to our sight, could only have been formulated by way of its close connection with the general development of philosophical thought. What philosophy expressed with speech, words, and general notions, Ruisdael expressed in a way that could be seen: nature — not theological but secular, developing in and of itself without the assistance and patronage of supernatural factors — this is the nature of Bruno and Spinoza. It was with these "heretics" — the first burned, the other censured — that Ruisdael shared his ideas.

Thus the formalist deformation of the image of reality, made possible by the use of the method of compositional clues, turns into its opposite, developing on the platform of the progressive intellectual movements of the period. In the course of its development, formalism changes into its dialectical opposite, into a historical realism of a higher order. The bourgeois revolutions fought for the claims of this realism — social, political, and cultural.

13 Giordano Bruno, *De la causa, principio, et uno* (*Concerning Cause, Principle, and Unity*, 1584) especially "Dialogue Five," pp. 273 – 289.

14 B. Spinoza, *Ethics, Demonstrated in Geometrical Order* (*Ethica ordine geometrico demonstrata*), 1677, Part 2, Proposition 7, proof, see W. Tatarkiewicz, *Historia filozofii*, p. 99.

full empirical seeing (full development of the bourgeoisie)

Both solid-form seeing (Renaissance) and chiaroscuro-seeing (Baroque) were based on the schema of three-dimensional **convergent** perspective.

This perspective was able to express all the degrees of distance (the diminishing size of objects) and all the foreshortenings in which we see lines moving away from us at an angle in depth. In order to accurately define these dimensions, it was agreed that there was a point positioned facing us, in our line of vision, level with our eyes, i.e. on the horizon. This point, corresponding with the direction of our gaze, was the vanishing point for all the lines parallel with our gaze.

Thanks to the geometric construction achieved in this way, it became possible to define the location and dimensions of every possible direction and every possible section of a chosen line.

Three-dimensional convergent perspectival constructions enabled painters to define every object located at any distance precisely. Three-dimensional **convergent** perspective made it possible to measure and draw every object in a mathematically correct way. The spatial effects of the fifteenth, sixteenth, seventeenth, eighteenth, and the first half of the nineteenth century were based on this perspective: effects – it would seem – founded on the infallible laws of mathematical calculation.

In reality, however, this seemingly mathematically infallible convergent perspective is inadequate to the reality of our seeing. Its seeming infallibility was based on a purely conventional assumption that we embrace the reality before us with a single gaze, at the end of which lies the vanishing point. If we accept this assumption, we inevitably accept all its further consequences, all the consequences of this perspective. But we never look at nature with a single fixed gaze. Our eyes wander from object to object. Resting on some, omitting others, wandering in different directions, our seeing is not an immobile mathematical diagram, but a mobile physiological **activity**.

Convergent perspective assumes that we embrace the whole field of view with a single, fixed gaze. We look at the vanishing point, and then we see the image of the world. This may accord with mathematics, but it does not accord with the reality of our seeing. We never look at the world with a single fixed gaze. Our seeing consists of mobile gazes. We look at various objects in turn, we level gazes in different directions and a uniform image of visible reality only arises from consciously summing these up. Hence, the image of the visible world emerges not in a single, fixed gaze but through integrative thinking.

A single gaze — reasoned logically and outlined mathematically that embraces the whole field of view — is a fiction that is contrary to the experience of the common process of looking at the world before us.

If we try to consistently implement this fiction and construct an image in accordance with it, its contradictions become apparent.

In order to keep the whole image within the field of view (looking with a fixed gaze) we have to place the central viewing point somewhere in the middle of the picture and to place all objects at an appropriate distance from this point (according to their significance in the painting).

This central point (marked by converging perspectival lines) is in the middle, between the heads of mother and child. The cradle (bottom left) and the table with the candle and jug are at the same distance from this point. To see the whole picture **simultaneously,** embracing it with a single fixed gaze, we have to fix it on this central point. Is this what happens in reality?

Let us move to practice. Looking at figure 194, we realise that we are **unable** to fix the eyes on this logically construed central point. Involuntarily, our eyes wander off to look at the child or the mother. We look at the picture with roving eyes — lingering on the compositional clues.

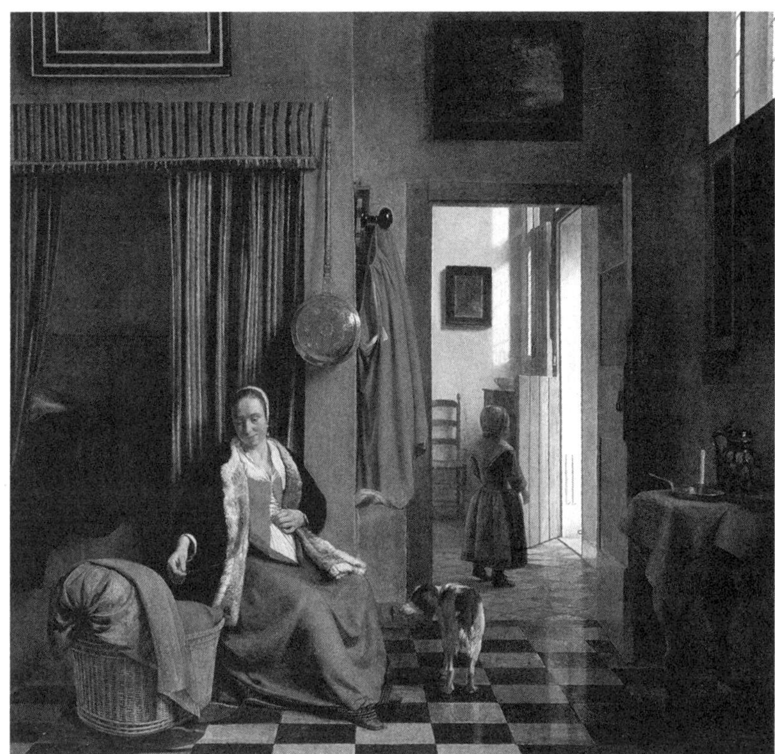

194
P. de Hooch,
Woman Lacing Her Bodice Beside a Cradle,
seventeenth c.

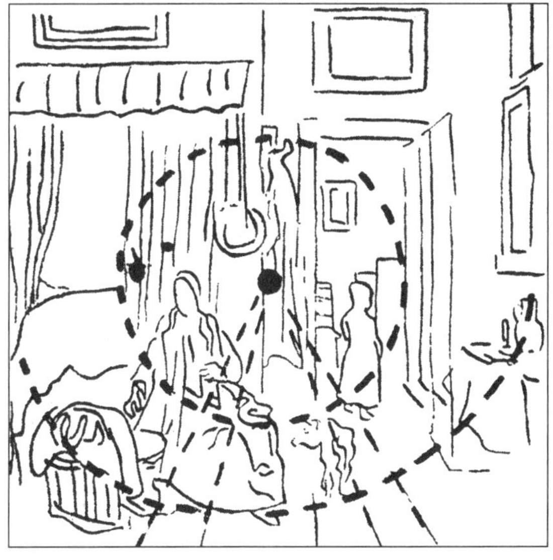

Fixing the gaze on one, single, artificially construed, central point of the picture makes seeing the whole picture impossible.

Bearing in mind how we look at the picture, experiments persuade us that, **in reality**, we view it with a mobile gaze, lingering on the compositional clues.

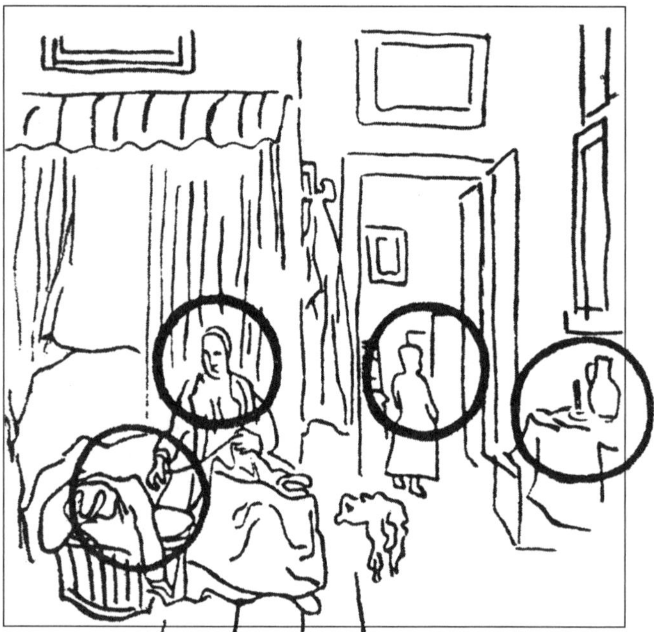

We see in Vermeer a similar case.

The central point of the picture, which is to be looked at if we are to see the whole, has been placed at the woman's elbow and marked as the vanishing point of the perspectival lines.

If we were to be able to keep our gaze fixed on this point, all the objects would be arranged around the circumferences of concentric circles. However, looking at the reproduction, we find ourselves unable to keep the gaze fixed on this artificially construed point. In practice we have to look at the painting with a shifting gaze if we want to be able to see it. Not even the fact that a painter like Vermeer has placed the main compositional clue here (the strongest contrast of light and shade) can arrest our gaze.

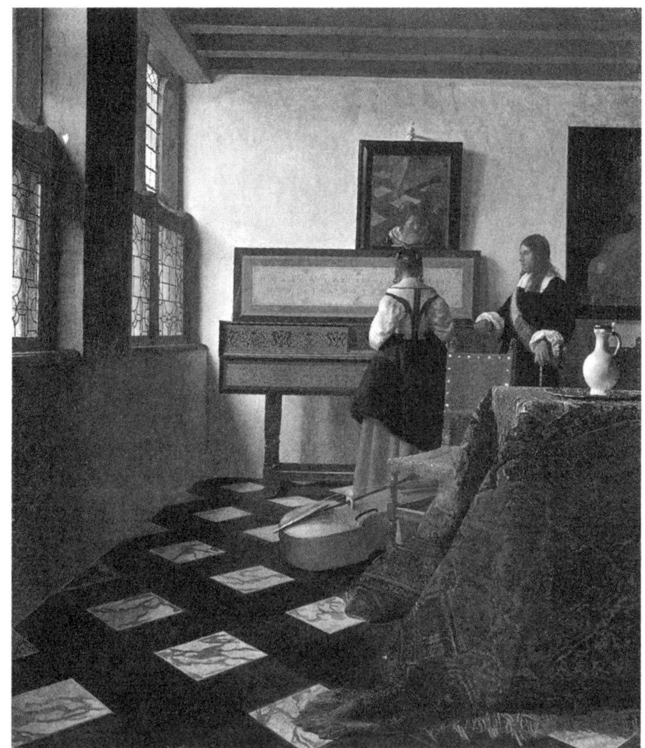

195
Vermeer,
The Music Lesson,
seventeenth c.

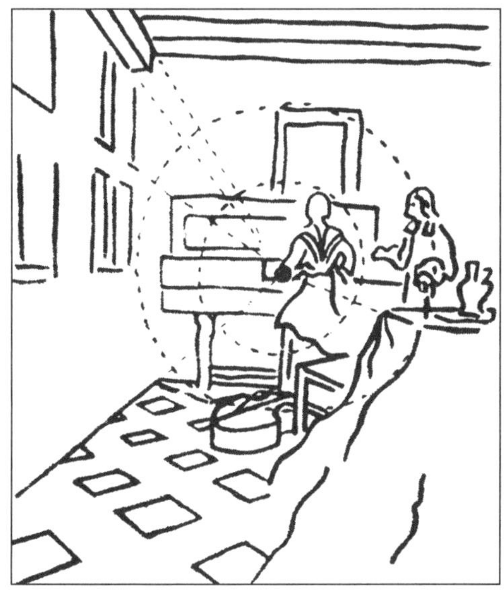

Even this contrast cannot arrest the gaze. The artificial concept of a single fixed gaze, contrary to our everyday experience of seeing, is the cause of the evident formalism of the picture. The compositional clue emphasizing the least interesting point in the picture (in so far as its subject matter is concerned) is in contradiction with its subject matter.

For this reason, over the course of further evolution, three-dimensional **convergent** perspective – born of mathematical calculations – came to be opposed by the real, physiological truth of our seeing, a mobile seeing. This was how a new visual consciousness developed – the consciousness of mobile seeing, not mathematically, but physiologically construed.

The consequences of this model of seeing were the easiest to note – they found their expression, above all, in the domain of colour. Previously, in Baroque seeing, colour always remained itself. What changed was its saturation: the admixture of darker colour for shadow. But the basis of the colour remained unchanged. Red always remained the same red, shaded to a greater or lesser degree, tinged with a darker shade of colour.

With mobile seeing and shifting the gaze from one point to another we have to take into account the reaction of the optic nerves. Our eyes do not only see colour. This seeing is not an abstract, ideal process of seeing occurring outside the material components of the human being. Seeing is a reaction of the optic nerves. When we look at a given colour, it acts on our optic nerves. The photochemical processes that occur as a result affect the reaction of the nerves, exhausting their sensitivity to seeing the given colour. When we shift the gaze to the next object, we see the opposite colour. Slowly, the optic nerves become sensitive again and we are able to see the correct colour of the object. If we shift our gaze again, we see the opposite colour of the next object. This process of the emergence of opposite colours was decisive in the development of the Impressionist colour system. Painting became colourful not because it suited the subjective predilection of a few painters, but because painters saw the world in mobile seeing and realized that in mobile seeing the world is colourful and that after each colour we look at we see its opposite colour. This is why, instead of the grey and chiaroscuro colours, they saw the many-sided and intensely colourful character of nature. The foundations of the Impressionist colour system are visual — the real, empirically verifiable process of mobile seeing.

The realism of Impressionism is the realism of mobile seeing — the practical physiological process of looking at the world with a mobile gaze. The colour of each object ceases to be unequivocal when the gaze is mobile. It depends on the colour previously seen. We transfer the opposite colour from each previously seen object, e.g. from red we transfer green, which appears in the eye as a result of looking at red. After looking at the colour yellow, we transfer blue. In this way, every object will absorb all the opposite colours of the surrounding objects' colours. Colour ceases to be uniform. It has flickers and colour variations, conditioned by the impact of the colours seen previously. With a mobile gaze, colour is not **a single** reaction of the optic nerves, but a result of the **multiple**, overlapping **relations** entailed in the process of viewing, the result of multiple gazes levelled at surrounding objects — and, at the same time, the result of actual, verifiable photochemical processes occurring in the eye in reaction to the colours of the objects seen.

As we have seen, Impressionist colour arose from the realisation that our seeing is not the single act of an immobile eye but a multiple activity and a process in time — and not out of any desire to brighten up the picture or out of some indefinable aesthetic reason. The new visual consciousness achieves mobile seeing, which spans over a duration of time. A new painterly form arises on the foundation of this new visual consciousness and consists of different, overlapping relations, independent of one another and expressed by separate, rather than merging, brush strokes. Each brush stroke introduces a new colour situation and expresses new visual relations — a new moment of seeing.

There are thus two messages contained in the philosophical premises underpinning the singularity and novelty of Impressionism:

1. The observed phenomenon or object should not be considered in mechanical detachment from the observer. There exists a mutual relation between the observer and the phenomenon observed. One influences the other, one becomes the other, as things are never distinct and independent from one another.
2. The purely mechanical Newtonian division between space and time also collapses. From the position of Newtonian mechanics there is

empty space, in which there may (or may not) be matter. Time — in which empty space or the matter within it may persist (so long as it appears at a particular point in space) — exists in isolation from space.

From the position of dialectical materialism, both space and time are only forms through which we see the movement of matter. Their existence is mutually dependent.

Let us recapitulate the entire course of mobile seeing once more. We discovered, experientially, that we do not look at the reality before us with a single, logically deduced gaze, but with a seeing that is mobile, wandering from one object to another. We look at an object. We see its colour. But this seeing does not take place in a sphere from which the properties of the senses are detached (from matter). This is not outside the material reception of spiritual, subjective sensations. We see the object because its matter acts upon the matter of our eyes. This is the verifiable, quantifiable action of one matter upon another. We see colour because the object acts on our eyes by way of radiation. What is this action? The production of photochemical reactions in the nerves of the retina of the eye. As a result of the **chemical** changes that occur in the nerves of the retina, the nerves lose their sensitivity to seeing the viewed colour. As a result of this exhaustion of the ability to see colour, when the gaze shifts to another place — to another object — we see it in the opposite colour to the one previously seen. If, for example, we previously saw a green object, after transferring the gaze to a new object, we see it first as red, irrespective of its actual colour. It is only after a (short) period of time, when the regenerative process of the nerves has taken place, that we will see the object in its actual colour.

The phenomenon of the emergence of succeeding colours is explained by that fact that the process of seeing does not occur in the ideal world of ideas and minds alone, but is a result of the **material** action of the given object viewed on the **matter** of the retina of the eye. The object, external to man, and man's optic nerves both participate in this process.

After the nineteenth century, after the study of the physiology of vision, it became impossible to speak of the "true" colour of the object — independent of our receiving apparatus — of colour eliminated from the material process of seeing. The influence of the material components of seeing is most forceful in mobile seeing — and such is our actual seeing of nature. It is expressed by the emergence and fading out of succeeding colours.

The sequence of visual activities and reactions occurring in the eye is as follows:

1. Looking at the (first) object and seeing its local colour;
2. a dulling of the sensitivity of the optic nerves to this colour and its fading away;
3. the transfer of the gaze to the second object;
4. looking at the second object without seeing its local colour. Instead, our eye contains the opposite colour to the colour of the first object;
5. the fading away of the succeeding colour and the seeing of the local colour of the second object;
6. a dulling in the sensitivity of the retina to the local colour of the second object and its fading away;
7. the transfer of the gaze to a third object.

When looking at nature with a uniformly mobile gaze, we see both the local and the succeeding colour of every object. We see every object in two colours that follow one another — in an opposite, succeeding colour of the previously seen object, and in a local colour, characteristic of the given object. The first colour is the eye's reaction to the preceding object, the second colour — to the object currently being viewed. We could only not see succeeding colours on the condition that we eliminate the material, physiological components of the eye, conditioning seeing — we could only see in such a way if we were incorporeal spirits, seeing without the eyes taking part. To speak of seeing in isolation from the material apparatus of the eye, to speak of "true," "non-subjective" colour, independent of the biochemical processes occurring in the eye — is the purest idealism.

We are the same matter as the matter outside us — and no artificial, separating, or dividing line can be drawn. Matter is continuous and each of its parts acts on the other ones. Action by external matter causes quite particular changes in our body matter, and this is the reception of sensations.

Negating material changes that occur in us in the process of receiving sensations is actually based on the assumption that we receive sensations not through the body (the eye, etc.) but the spirit, whose substance does not change in contact with matter.

Only then would it be right to paint the objective world of external objects as real – and to eliminate the inner world as spiritual, subjective, and not real.

But if we recognise that we are the body, we must base our visual consciousness on all observed facts of a material process of seeing.

The movement of the mobile gaze in relation to the pictorial plane would take the following course – stopping at viewing points and passing from one to another:

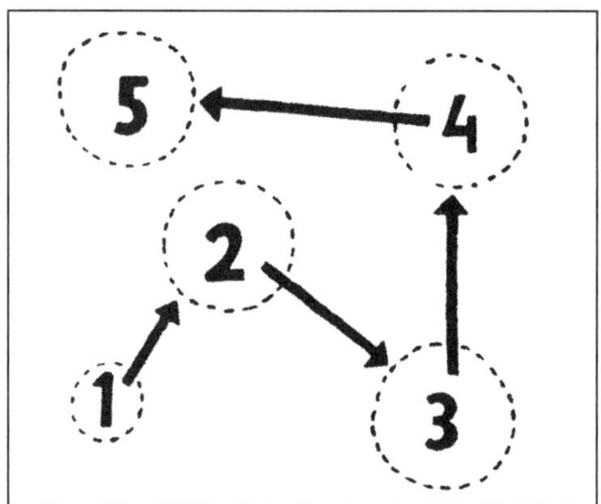

What colours will the attentive observer see at each of these points?

At entry point 1 – the gaze falls directly on its local colour (l_1) which will be seen.

At point 2 – the gaze, transferred from point 1, will not immediately see its local colour (l_2), but under the influence of the colour seen previously at point 1 (l_1) it will see its succeeding colour (n_1). Only after the colour (n_1) fades away, will the local colour of the particular point be seen (l_2). And so, at point 2, the order of the colours seen will be (n_1) – (l_2).

In the same way, at point 3 there will first be colour (n_2), the opposite colour (l_2) to the one seen previously. Only after its fading away will we see the local colour of point 3, i.e. (l_3).

At each of these points, we first see a succeeding colour (n), related to looking at the previous point, and only later, the local colour.

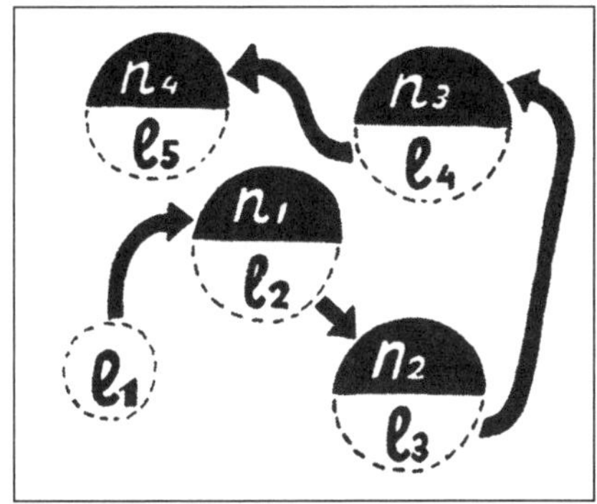

The general sequence of colours, which we would successively see in each of these points, would be as follows:

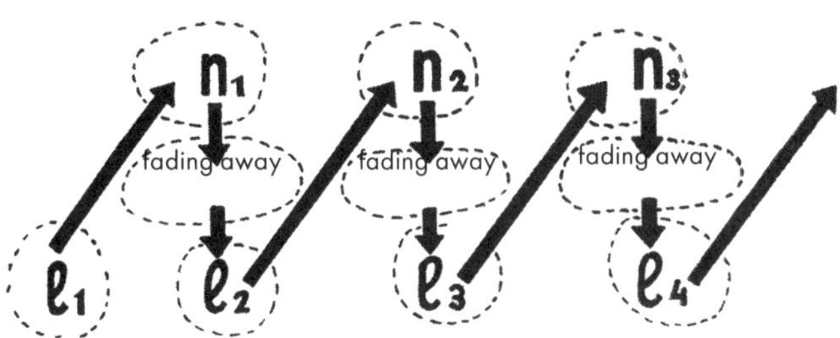

The transition to the empirical method, which began in the sixteenth century, led to the formation of chiaroscuro visual consciousness. The object constructed in the picture "as it should look" was replaced by the object painted "as it looks in reality" (in terms of light and shade).

The transition to mobile seeing is not something fundamentally new. It results from the further development of visual empiricism. A newly observed fact of visual consciousness is that we see the world with the help of many gazes levelled in different directions, that we see it with a mobile gaze — that the postulation of an immobile gaze is a fiction that has been logically inferred by reason, but is incompatible with our experience. In this way, following an empirical path, the realism of mobile seeing develops as a reflection of the real **physiological** process of seeing. The development of the empirical method makes it possible to capture the real, verifiable phenomena that occur in the physiological, material process of seeing. In the course of its development, the empirical method leads to a general change of criteria and evaluation. In examining the relationships between the objective world of objects and their receiver (the spectator), it cannot stop short at the old abstract schema that claims that the observer (undefined, general, abstract) receives sensations (immaterial and abstract) and, thanks to these, perceives (sees) the world of objects.

This schema was closely connected with a specific stage of development; it was the culmination of the historical experiences that had been accumulated and made possible the construction of an image of the world in accordance with the knowledge at the time. This was in the period of the formation of the principles of **three-dimensional convergent perspective**. Only isolating the perceiver from the perceived, opposing the observer and the observed world, made the logical construction of perspectival schemes possible. The fundamental opposition, on which three-dimensional **convergent** perspective was constructed, was on isolating the perceiver, placing him in at one point in space, opposing him to the rest of the world — as the subject and the object of perception had been opposed.

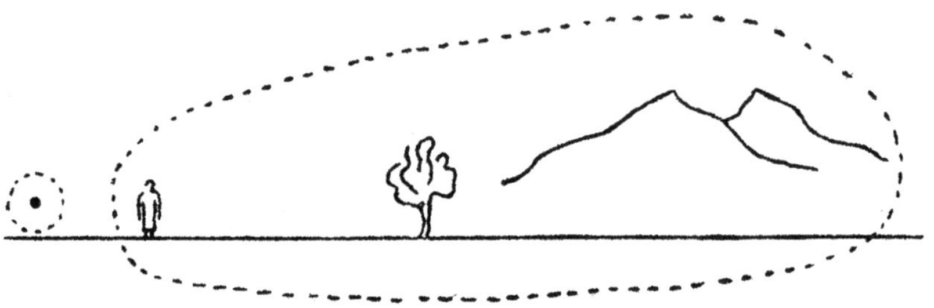

Only once it had been accepted, as the basis of reasoning that the observer occupied a single fixed point in space, did it become possible to draw a cluster of lines radiating from this point and connecting it with all more significant points on surrounding objects – this allowed for the construction of space independent of the observer.

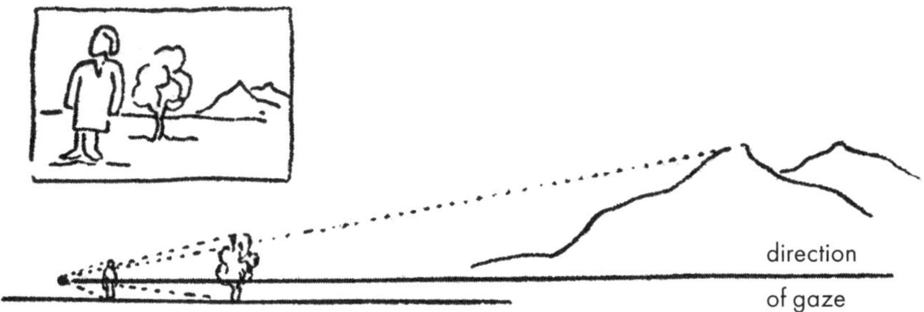

It was the distinction between the seeing individual and the world seen, opposing **who** does the seeing to **what** is being seen, that made possible the mathematical measurement of the angles from which we look at every object, the definition of the direction of the gaze and its vanishing point – in short, the entire perspectival scaffolding within which the image of seen reality is inscribed. The construction of convergent perspective is therefore transferred from philosophy to seeing the principal opposition between the perceiver and the perceived world, between the subject and the object; it confirms their opposition and distinctness.

But this same isolation of the individual can be found in other, parallel tendencies of the period:

1. **individual truth** and the heroism of the individual, fighting for Renaissance humanist values;
2. **the individual interests** of every individual as the natural foundation of rational social systems (Hobbes[15]);

15 See T. Hobbes, *Leviathan or The Matter, Forme and Power of a Common Wealth Ecclesiasticall and Civil, 1651*; in the Introduction Hobbes writes about the state as the perfect artificial man – Leviathan, in whom "the *wealth* and *riches* of all the particular members, are the *strength*;" *Leviathan* ed. with Introduction and Notes by J.C.A. Gaskin (Oxford: Oxford University Press, 2008), p. 7.

3. **individual enrichment**, the individual appropriation of the forces of production as principal tools of the bourgeoisie for coming to power, positioning itself for future battles decisive in the struggle to rule over society.

It was only possible to sketch out a convergent perspectival construction by distinguishing the observer's eye from the remainder of the surrounding space, by bringing all lines to this central point — the eye. The only path to the differentiation of the bourgeoisie as a class was by way of the material emancipation of the "free" bourgeois individual from feudal-scholastic bonds, and by enrichment.

Each in its own field and with its own notions, the new formulations achieved by philosophy, mathematics, and spatial seeing reflect the reality of the contemporary historical situation. The split between subject and object, the formulation of the principles of convergent perspective, are none other than articulations, by way of a different terminology, of the basic purport of the historical process — the construction of scientific and other models on the basis of the model taken from the essence of the social process. The class struggle made it possible to reach for new scientific formulas rising to a superior level of development, modelled on the struggle of the middle class with feudalism. These new formulas were possible thanks to the transference of historical social experiences, achieved at a new stage of class struggle and their translation into the language of scientific thought. It was by extrapolating from the experiences of the historical situation of the middle class of the fifteenth century, fighting for its rights in the feudal system, that insight into the essence of three-dimensional convergent mathematical perspective, the deduction of its principles, became possible.

The isolation of the subject, the isolation of the observing individual — being the expression of the development of bourgeois-capitalist forces as a result of the development of commodity exchange — was the basis for the deductive method. The last philosopher who used this method to logically deduce his thesis — on the ability of human reason to independently understand the world — was Descartes. Thereafter, the deductive method serves only ends that are contrary to the scientific propositions attained, confirming the impassable boundary dividing the subject from the object and justifying an idealistic conception of the world.

•

After having already written this section, I came across a similar schema, cited by M. Cornforth[16] from L. Wittgenstein's work *Tractatus Logico-Philosophicus.* Wittgenstein writes:

"The subject does not belong to the world, but it is the world's boundary. Where, **inside** the world, is a metaphysical object? You say that it is the same with the eye and the field of view. But in reality – you do **not** see the eye. And nothing exists in the field of view from which one can infer that it is seen from the direction of the eye. Since the field of view has no form as such."[17]

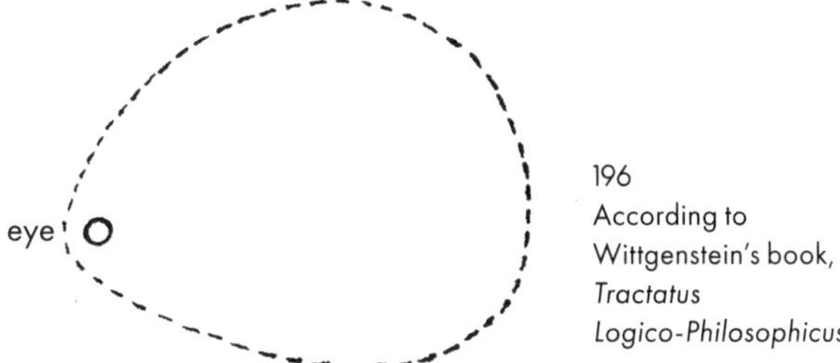

196
According to Wittgenstein's book, *Tractatus Logico-Philosophicus*

16 M. Cornforth, *Science versus Idealism: In Defence of Philosophy against Positivism and Pragmatism* (Westport, CT: Greenwood Press, Publishers, 1975).

17 L. Wittgenstein, *Tractatus Logico-Philosophicus*, 5. 631, 63, trans. D.F. Pears and B.F. McGuinness with introduction by Bertrand Russell, revised edition (London: Routledge & Kegan Paul, 2014), p. 69.

"5.632 The subject does not belong to the world: rather, it is a limit of the world.

5.633 Where *in* the world is a metaphysical subject to be found? You say that this is exactly like the case of the eye and visual field. But really you do *not* see the eye. And nothing *in the visual field* allows you to infer that it is seen by an eye.

5.6331 For the form of the visual field is surely not like this.

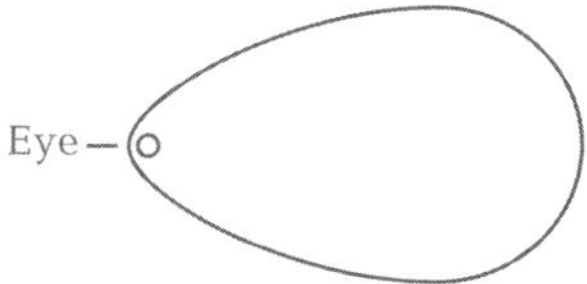

Like all logically deduced systems, this schema develops all the consequences that follow from a basic assumption that has been arbitrarily postulated by the author (or rather, based on the nature of his experience as a whole). Further consequences that follow logically from the assumption of an **unsurpassable** boundary, dividing the subject from the observed object:

1. the absence of the subject in the observed world;
2. an opposition between the perceiving subject and the perceived world;
3. a qualitative difference between the perceiver (spirit, idea) and the perceived world (soulless matter);
4. the objectivity of the **external** world as verifiable and palpable matter – and the un-verifiability of the subjective inner world;
5. the inscrutability of "things in themselves"[18] – existing in the material world – by the qualitatively different, spiritual, perceiving being.

In all logical systems one should analyse not the course of logical reasoning but the fundamental, empirically verifiable, starting point. In this case – the thesis concerning the absence of the subject in the perceived world.

On the basis of what state of knowledge could such an assertion have been formulated?

1. On the basis of not knowing about the material components of the nervous system that determine the reception of sensation. On the basis of an assumption that the reception of sensation occurs in an abstract way, impossible to define more closely and more precisely, and that sensations are not an empirically verifiable reaction of the nerves to verifiable effects of matter.
2. On the basis of an assumption that there exists a complete physical separation between the external world and the human body, which not only do not meet and unite (at most by touching) since they are separated by an impassable dividing line, emptiness (not air). On the basis of a state of knowledge that recognized as the only existing forms of a substance the solid and liquid state (but not gas) and knew

18 Wittgenstein, *Tractatus logico-philosophicus*
"3.221 Objects can only be *named*. Signs are their representatives. I can only speak *about* them: I cannot *put them into words*. Propositions can only say *how* things are, not *what* they are."

nothing about the radiation of various forms of energy, and did not know this because both the object and the subject of knowledge are in continuous **physical** contact through the surrounding air and through all the forms of the radiation of energy.

This assertion could thus have been formulated as a universalization of the knowledge of the period preceding the development of physics, chemistry, and physiology. Further reasoning is only the logical (very logical) development of this state of knowledge.

This model of the world once made it possible to formulate the principles of three-dimensional **convergent** perspective and to make logically inferred drawings (in all foreshortenings, distances, and inclines) of each of the objects that expressed the commodity seeing of the fifteenth-century middle class. The logical **separation** of these objects was determined by the nascent empirical, materialist knowledge of the world. But when L. Wittgenstein claimed that "the world is divided into atomised facts, completely loose and independent..., between which we can observe no link"[19] — this means no more nor less than returning again to fifteenth-century commodity-seeing — the seeing of completely disparate products, independent of one another — to a model of science that does not investigate, but only classifies and describes the world. His principal model of reasoning is based on erroneous, now non-scientific foundations.

19 Strzemiński quotes freely from Wittgenstein's *Tractatus logico-philosophicus* after: M. Cornforth, *Science Versus Idealism: An Examination of "Pure Empiricism" and Modern Logic* (1946); L. Wittgenstein, *Tractatus logico-philosophicus* (thesis 2.04 – 2.062): "What is the state of affairs, a fact — is the existence of atom fact. The totality — the sum of existing atom facts — is the world. Atom facts are independent of one another. On the basis of the existence or non-existence of one atom fact we cannot infer the existence or non-existence of another atom fact".

"2.04 The totality of existing states of affairs is the world.

2.05 The totality of states of affairs also determines which states of affairs do not exist.

2.06 The existence and non-existence of states of affairs is reality. (We also call the existence of states of affairs a positive fact, and their non-existence a negative fact.)

2.061 States of affairs are independent of one another.

2.062 From the existence or non-existence of one state of affairs it is impossible to infer the existence or non-existence of another."

Actually we cannot assume that the subject is completely separate from the perceived world, since we know that:

1. matter is continuous and one part interrelates with another;
2. sensation can be brought down to material changes, verifiable and measurable. In this way the "subject" matter is in continuous connection and exchange with the matter of the perceived world. This connection can be seen in practice. Contrary to L. Wittgenstein's assertion that we do not see the eye, it exists in the field of view and can be observed in the process of mobile-seeing (as well as in others, but more on this later). Summarizing the progress of models of seeing we would have to express it according to the following schematic:

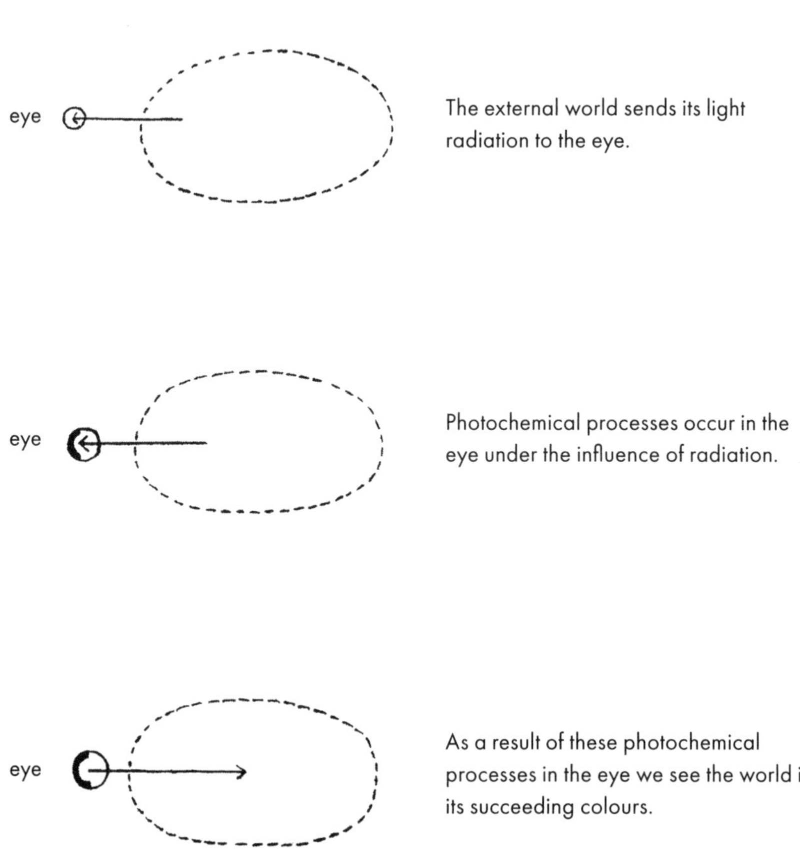

It is this appearance and disappearance of the succeeding colour that reveals how we see the eye in the field of view. This is an empirically verifiable fact and in accordance with autonomous findings achieved in physics, chemistry, and physiology. The mobile-seeing of the Impressionists in painting produces the same results as objective knowledge of matter in the sciences. This is why the resulting general theoretical schematic is one and the same.

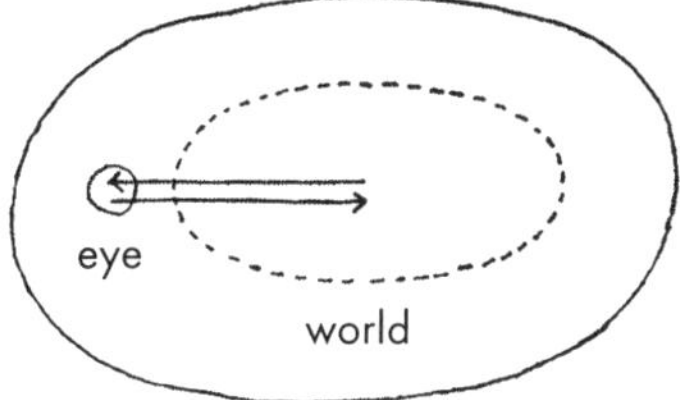

The matter of the external world and the matter of the human body are in a state of continuous mutual interrelation; this interrelation can be measured and verified.

By bringing Impressionism down in this way to the actual basis of seeing and defining the foundation of its visual consciousness, we discover that these were formed by way of the influence of the objective interrelation of external matter and the material components of the eye. The facts observed in the course of mobile-seeing abolish the abstract and idealistic model of "the received sensation," resolving seeing into a verifiable interrelation of matter and changes of matter.

If, despite this, the Impressionists deployed a theory that contradicted their practice, if (in theory) they reduced their art to pure direct sensation — to subjective sensation ("nature seen through the artist's **temperament**"[20]), if they explained the objective truth of developing seeing as the private property of the personal impressions of a particular artist — we see in this a typical example of consciousness lagging behind practice. Practice testified to Impressionist seeing's being limited to the material changes occurring in the eye. Whereas the theory

20 Paraphrase of Émile Zola's famous claim "The definition of the work of art cannot be other than this one: the **work of art is a fragment of the world seen through the temperament**." [author's emphasis] after E. Zola, *My Salon* (1866), in his "Mon Salon" (1866), Emile Zola, *Le bon combat, de Courbet aux impressionistes,* eds. G. Picon and J.P. Bouillon, (Paris: Hermann, 1974). Zola ended the fifth article, "Realists in the Salon," dated 11 May 1866, with this sentence.

tried to justify the changes with arguments taken from subjective and idealist movements in philosophy.

This discrepancy explains the mistake made by many critics. Instead of examining the Impressionists' **work**, instead of explaining their painting as resulting from changes in visual consciousness, instead of disclosing the realistic foundations that determined the transition to Impressionist form — they repeated the Impressionists' **words**. They made the same mistake as those who would think, on the basis of the **declarations** of the English revolutionaries (1642), that they were building the biblical state of Hebrew judges and prophets, overlooking the basic fact that the outcome of the English revolution was the emergence of a colonial state of bankers, navigators, and merchants.

It is easier to repeat words than to examine the facts.

Instead of repeating the Impressionists' theories and using these to explain their practice, they should have defined the conditions in which Impressionist seeing was formed and read their form as deriving not from theory, but from seeing itself. By explaining the change of form through the discovery of the newly acquired components of visual consciousness, we will bring the Impressionist phenomenon back to a Realist basis, we will be able to define Impressionism as a historically determined increment in the realism of seeing.

We will be persuaded that the Impressionists' works are the effect of new, objective, and precisely definable components of visual consciousness, that the same phenomena were discovered by the physiology of eyesight at the same time, that these phenomena have their foundations in the material eye. We will also be persuaded that the Impressionists' theory does not express the realistic, empirical essence of their painting but only the ideas of Wundt, Mach, Avenarius, and others who were popular at that time in bourgeois society. But just as this knowledge developed **in spite of** these views, Impressionism also developed as a result of the development of visual empiricism, **in spite of** its theory. This development of seeing in Impressionism was in line with the general process of the development of the forces of production and was its reflection. However, the theory was the class-determined deformation of this process, it was one of the attempts at ideological disarmament and disorientation, carried out in the interests of the bourgeoisie. The historical limitation of Impressionism lies not in its break from the preceding "realism" — since in reality it constitutes only the further development and deepening of this realism. The historical limitation of Impressionism is the limit of the empirical method as a fundamental cognitive method of the bourgeoisie.

●

The empirical method, by its very nature capable of considering and examining only **already existing and consolidated** facts, becomes a cognitive tool of the **bourgeoisie consolidating itself**, spreading its rule over society as a whole, through the Dutch, English, and French revolutions. Only when concrete facts took place in historical reality testifying to the actual existence of bourgeois components was the empirical method universally adopted by the bourgeoisie consolidating itself.

The empirical method uncovers and establishes — by observing and gathering them — facts of our seeing that cannot be inferred by reason. Instead of an image of the world deduced from the precepts of three-dimensional perspective and the mental inference of the convexity of solid forms, it produces an image akin to the one that appears via our actual seeing. Visual consciousness rises to a superior stage of development thanks to the empirical method: rather than a three-dimensional consciousness of the world as a collection of solid forms inferred by reason (the consciousness of the age of nascent commodity exchange) a visual consciousness based on the physiological process of seeing appears and develops. The empirical method, applied to visual consciousness, transforms it into a consciousness of **physiological seeing**. Reducing the subject as well as the object to matter, to material components of seeing, it does away with the division between what is "subjective" and "objective," hitherto idealistically inferred by reason. The image of the world seen though physiological seeing contains components derived from external matter and from the matter that forms the spectator, in equal measure.

When referring to impressions, one should emphasise their essence. On the one hand, they may be defined subjectively, as being impressions existing solely within us, impossible to verify by any reality — in which case their truth is reliant upon our inner, irrational confirmation. Following this line, we come to a point at which realism is "what I regard as true" — which is to say, to pure solipsism.

On the other hand, by contrast, impressions may be conceived of as being the result of the material cause that evokes them. Following this objectivist line, we arrive at materialism (impressions are the image of bodies in the material world). But then we have to realise the nature of the effect of these material bodies and the essence of the impressions they evoke. We will then see that we do not become conscious of all the impressions we receive at once, and that we do not immediately come to know the world in full. We will see that this takes place continuously, over the course of the historical process as a whole, that our penetration of the essence of the known world is a progressive movement, that we define realism not according to the irrational "inner conviction" of "what I consider real," but historically, by defining the range of knowledge achieved at a given stage of history and by realizing **what and how much** our impressions discover in the objective, natural world at this stage in development.

Irrational realism explains nothing — we should be very clear about this. By posing the problem in purely subjective terms ("because I consider it realism") it renders the scientific examination of realism as the historical, progressive process of developing visual consciousness impossible. Instead, it renders absolute and preserves one or another of the periods of development arbitrarily selected.

The empirical method developed over the course of a long period (the sixteenth, seventeenth, eighteenth, and nineteenth centuries). Its development was generally parallel with the development of bourgeois society. Every empirically discovered fact of seeing influenced the transformation of visual consciousness. This was how the chiaroscuro visual consciousness (sixteenth and seventeenth centuries) expressed in Baroque painting came into being. Later, in the nineteenth century, the mobile visual consciousness expressed in Impressionist painting developed. Impressionism is none other than the **realism of mobile-seeing**. This is its strength and weakness: its realism — which represents the period with a precision that only mobile seeing can offer; and its formalism — as a result of which this image of the period was incomplete and falsified in class terms. Mobile-seeing is more complete than preceding models of seeing — it reflects the process of seeing more accurately, but the sources of a formalism that deforms are to be found in the specificity of this seeing itself.

The realism of mobile-seeing arose as a result of a long preparatory evolution, lasting the entire eighteenth and the first half of the nineteenth century. Step by step, minor observations accumulated. Step by step, it was noted that the local colour used in Baroque painting does not always remain the same (in practical empirical seeing) – unchanging and independent of the influence of the surrounding colours – but changes as a result of movements of the eye.

Over the course of the eighteenth century, the idea of natural law seeks an ever smaller degree of justification in the metaphysical conception of abstract "reason" and increasingly relies upon experience. Transferred into the realm of visual laws, this experience discovers the variability of colour. One and the same local colour (e.g. red) appears in various hues. This was a consequence of the incomplete, as yet unconscious observation of the variability of colours taking place in mobile-seeing. Reduced to its realistic basis and categorised as a model of visual consciousness, Rococo painting is an unconscious and incomplete mobile-seeing. The line of development ran as follows: Watteau, Boucher, Tiepolo, Fragonard, Goya – a line moving away from a single unchanging local colour (coated in Baroque shading) and passing into its great variability (within certain general limits). Local colour appears as a group of many different hues of the same colour. This was conditioned by the impact of the succeeding colours that arise when looking at other, adjacent colours.

Painting developed in this way throughout the entire eighteenth century, extracting a greater variability of local colour and an ever-greater variety of hues of that colour.

Over the course of the few short years of the French Revolution, this kind of painting ceased to exist. By 1792, David has come to dominate, completely and unquestionably. What does he represent? Critical writing about him, past and present, is an ideal illustration of the powerlessness of the idealistic method.

Those writing about David usually approach him from two positions. They either focus on their personal impressions and feelings in response to David's painting, or they focus on historical matters. But even the best, dialectical, materialist approach to history can never be associated with the subjective impressions of the writer – or **the unanalysed** David.

David's painting needs to be brought down to a practical, verifiable, realistic basis in visual consciousness – and the class purport expressed by way of this visual consciousness. There is no absolute, timeless realism of seeing — only **historical** realism, developing in line with the development of the forces of production.

What was David's realism? What were the components of observed reality of which it consisted?•

David did not see the variability of colours in mobile-seeing. David did not see the play of light and shade floating over objects and making their contours appear and fade away. The "sculptural" quality — that he was accused of — was, in fact, a visual consciousness of solid-form and commodity-seeing, analogous to the model of seeing of the second half of the fifteenth century. The range of his observations did not exceed the simple rendering of solid form, logically inferred. The realism and tactility of his figures was the reality of commodity-seeing. David's seeing, deduced by reason, was three hundred years behind, in comparison with empirical, chiaroscuro-seeing (of the sixteenth and seventeenth centuries) and in relation to the empirical seeing of the variability of colour in mobile-seeing (eighteenth century).

If David's seeing came to prevail as the predominant model of seeing in the era of the Revolution and Napoleon, despite this backwards shift, then this was because his visual consciousness corresponded with the visual consciousness of the majority of his audience — the new social class that came to rule in the new system. The three hundred years by which seeing was set back are a measure of the visual underdevelopment that was a measure of the social oppression prevailing before the revolution.

Only by reducing the realism of seeing to its historically achieved degree of development can one discover its real purport — to establish the components that formed it and the observations it was based on. We are then able to understand that the realism of seeing expressed in the works of Fragonard and Goya was related to the developing forces of production of the eighteenth century, appropriated by the ruling class of the time to express its class purport just as it appropriated the material goods produced as a result of the development of these forces.

• In the social and political life of this same period, we see a shift away from the consistent empiricism of the Encyclopaedists, with their mechanistically understood materialism, to natural law, deduced by way of abstraction. The idea of a cult of "absolute Reason," the "highest Being," etc. emerges from Jacobin spheres. This is an analogous regression in the sphere of world-views.

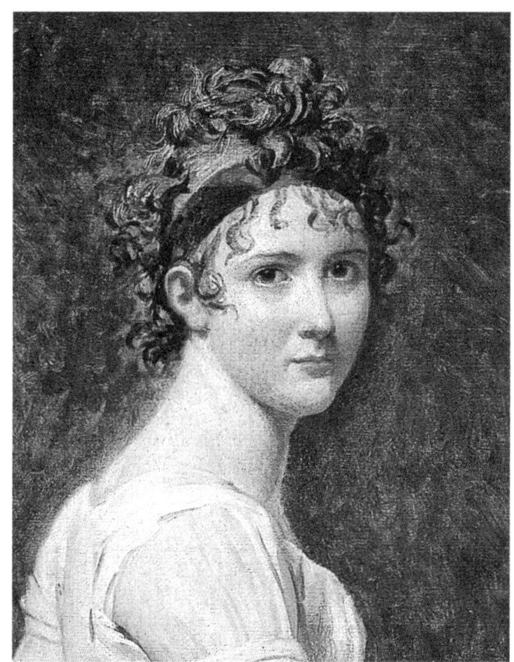

197
David,
Portrait of Madame Récamier,
detail,
eighteenth c.

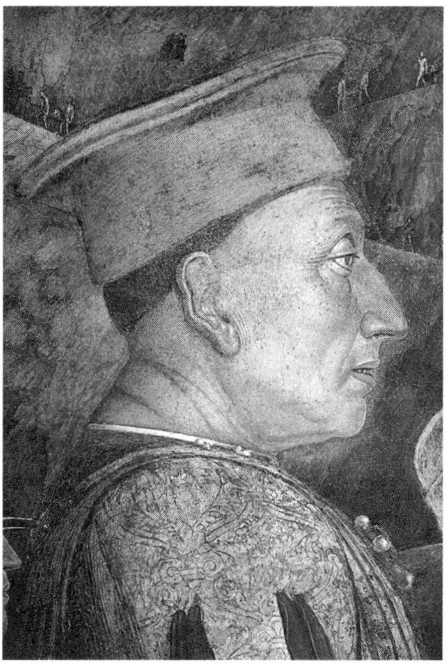

198
Mantegna,
Lodovico II Gonzaga,
mural painting,
detail,
fifteenth c.

Things might all fall into place very neatly if we were to relate the "effeminate" painting of the Rococo painters to an effeminate, declining feudal class, and the "healthy," robust painting of David to the dynamic, rising bourgeoisie. But what are we to do when an analysis of the components of David's seeing uncovers his backwardness, in contrast to Rococo painting's greater progressiveness and its broader scope of historically progressive class purport? In such a case, artistic backwardness would be linked to a historically progressive class — and the whole idealistic model would lose its seemingly beautifully designed symmetry.

Contradictions that cannot be understood by way of arbitrarily applied idealistic models can be explained with ease when transferred onto the solid basis of the class struggle.

We then find that Rococo painting developed on the social basis of the feudal-monarchist elites, constituting one of the branches of the Enlightenment movement in general — developing and deepening the empirical method originating in the sixteenth and seventeenth centuries. The objective progress of seeing (being a reflection of the general growth of the forces of production in this period), expressed itself by way of the observation of changes of colour occurring in mobile-seeing. Hitherto uniform local colour turns into colour broken into a series of related hues.

However, this development of seeing took place amid the narrow social base of the declining class — and, appropriated by the feudal-monarchist elites, was used to articulate their class purport. The refined way of life of feudal groups, expressed in paintings by means of the most sensitive seeing of the era, was to serve as proof of the enduring cultural mission of these classes, their natural right to govern.

This clash between a parasitic, artificial subject-matter and its expression by means of the highest possible visual consciousness of the times was one manifestation of the more widespread, fundamental contradiction between the mature forces of production in France at the end of the eighteenth century and their appropriation by the feudal-state system.

It goes without saying that this type of painting collapsed with the decline of its social base. The subject matter of Versailles's pastoral games did not correspond to the class purport of the bourgeoisie. Moreover, neither did the visual consciousness that it encountered as it rose to power.

In class societies, both the material base and the cultural superstructure are in the hands of the ruling class. The visual consciousness that had formed during the eighteenth century had been appropriated by the feudal classes and used by them to express their own class purport. It is a measure of the class oppression prevailing prior to the French Revolution that the visual consciousness that was formulated after the Revolution marked a turning back by three hundred years. David expresses the new purport of bourgeois society in formation by way of forms corresponding to the visual consciousness of solid forms. The realism of mobile-seeing, the realism of visual empiricism, was replaced by the realism of solid form inferred by way of reason, by the realism of commodity-seeing. This was a verifiable measure of social oppression and class exploitation.

It is wrong to oppose David the "realist" to the "unrealistic" painting of, for example, Fragonard. Only someone with an ahistorical view of realism – for whom the realism of three-dimensional commodity-seeing is the only possible, absolute model of realism could do so. The question should be posed in another way: Not "which of them is a realist?" but "on the basis of what visual consciousness, what visual observations, does his art evolve and what is the social purport, falsified in class terms, that he expresses by way of this seeing?" Then we will receive the answer: Fragonard, by means of an incomplete mobile-seeing, attempts to evoke suggestions of lasting progress and the leading role of those social groups realising the goals of the Enlightenment (the feudal-monarchic classes supported by the wealthiest members of the bourgeoisie). David, meanwhile, deploying solid-form seeing (in correspondence with the general model of seeing of this class) expresses a purport that facilitates the historical deception undertaken by the bourgeoisie – the exploitation of the revolution of the people in order to establish its own class rule. Such a purport presented the bourgeoisie as the heir of the great consuls and Caesars, presented civil servants of the Directorate and Empire as heirs of the magnificent Catos and Ciceros. As a whole, they imposed a classicizing screen, behind which were concealed the invisible shifts and political manoeuvres of the bourgeoisie as it rose to power.

One should closely and precisely define the basis of David's realism and classicism. The confusion of these concepts is especially frequent in relation to David. In which respects is he realist, and in which classicist? The advocates of simple and univocal definitions are unable to decide: if David is a the realist then he could not have been a classicist. If, however, he was a classicist he could not have been a realist. For some, that same sharply defined form and those carefully chiselled solids of his are a manifestation of the truest, most palpable realism, while for others, they are the truest qualities of classicism ("which always had a clearly drawn contour line"). Is his precise drawing of solid forms an indication of classicism or realism? If we judge realism subjectively, then nothing save our personal predilection can determine if a work of art is realist. In this case, we are not operating with measurable and verifiable objective criteria, we are not defining **what and how much** the artist saw, what quantity of observations contributed to his whole model of seeing, but resorting to a purely irrational evaluation of realism, on inner, subjective convictions, uncontrolled by reason. Seeking a touchstone in the individual and in his convictions, thus, in ourselves, we fail to perceive the historical process of the development of realism. Understood subjectively, eternal and unchangeable realism is in reality a borderline anti-historicism[21] and a negation of collective progress.

It is thus difficult to define, from the point of view of this subjective realism, what the sharply drawn and precisely rendered solid forms in David's painting may be: palpable realism or the infallible perfection of classicism. A subjective realism makes it impossible to differentiate between these phenomena. It abandons evaluation to personal tastes and predilections.

Only when the problem of realism is seen in historical context, when we define the stages of the growth of realism over the course of history, when we define consecutive models of visual consciousness — will it become possible to position David on the line marking the progress of historic development. We will then define his visual consciousness as that of three-dimensional solid forms (which was attained at the end of the fifteenth century). David's realism was a realism developed on a par with this consciousness. His sharp, precise drawing of solid forms is an expression of the realist visual consciousness at a particular stage of historical development.

21 Strzemiński uses the term "antyhistoryzm" (anti-historicism) to mean anachronism.

David's classicism does not lie in this drawing but in purely thematic sensations. His drawing of solids is not related to antiquity but to the late renaissance. It is not an imitation of the flat silhouettes on antique vases, nor of the primitive relief-painting of Roman frescoes; rather, its perfect mastery of solid form and space resembles the works of Mantegna, Ghirlandaio, and Signorelli. The subject matter of his paintings, however, relates to the history of republican and imperial Rome. The opposition of the classicist and the realist, impossible to resolve on the grounds of subjectivism and irrationalism, is easily explained from the vantage point of a historical background. David was a realist in solid-form seeing and a classicist in subject matter.

By removing the obstacles that had restrained the development of the forces of production, the Revolution constructed culture on an expanded social base. The increased dynamism of the new, emergent culture of the victorious class yields results in a relatively short period of time. Géricault and Delacroix exhibit their paintings in around 1825.

Upon analysis, the visual base upon which the form of these paintings developed has to be defined as the visual consciousness of chiaroscuro-seeing.

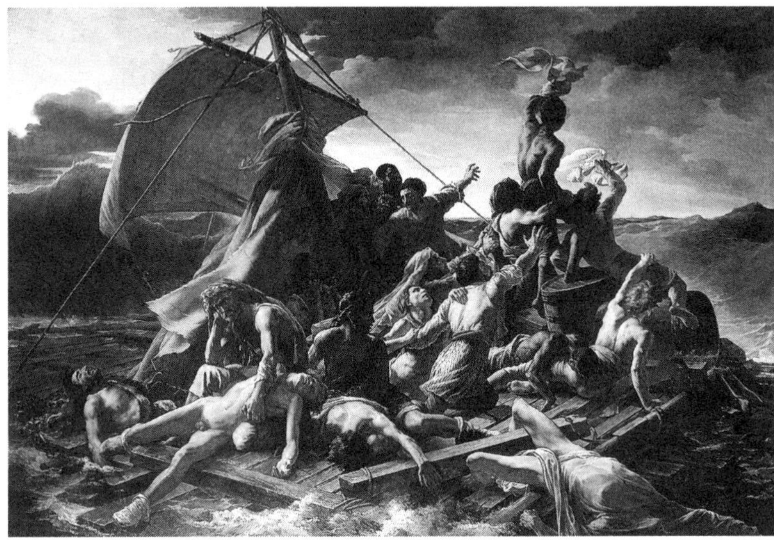

199
Géricault,
The Raft of the Medusa,
nineteenth c.

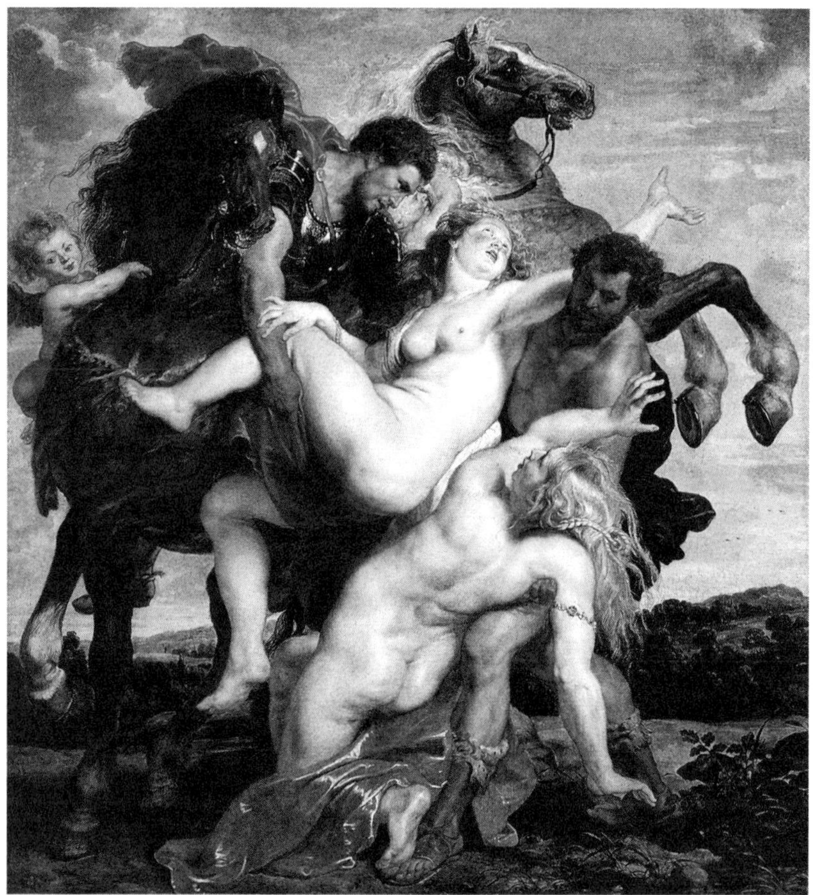

200
Rubens,
The Rape of the Daughters of Leucippus,
seventeenth c.

Over the course of the thirty years that followed the Revolution, French painting followed a path leading from Mantegna (end of the fifteenth century) to Rubens (beginning of the seventeenth century). In 1825, French painting faced the same questions that painting had faced in 1625. It owed this rapid development to the intensified dynamics of the post-revolutionary age.

Nevertheless, development continues. France is the leading country in Europe in which the contemporary bourgeoisie is realizing its most progressive régime. Visual consciousness continues to develop. Around 1848, Corot, Millet, and Courbet appear. Delacroix exhibits his later works.

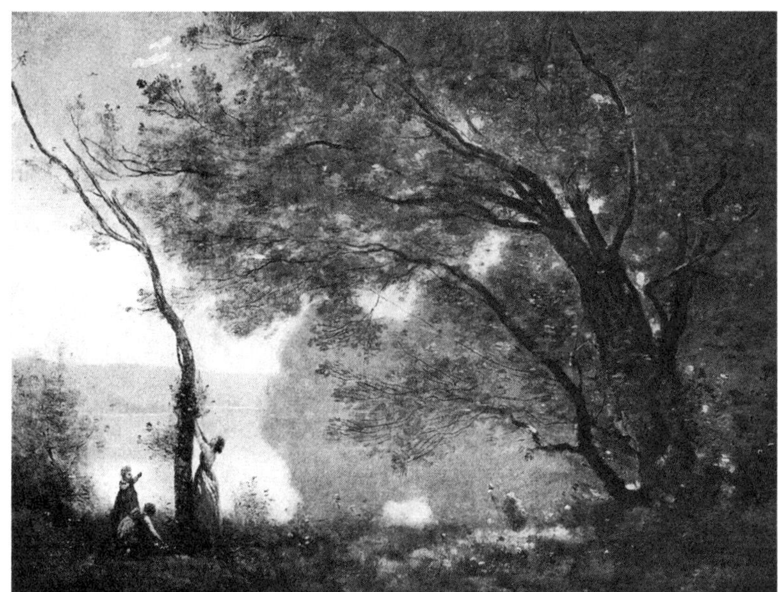

201
Corot,
Recollection of Mortefontaine,
nineteenth c.

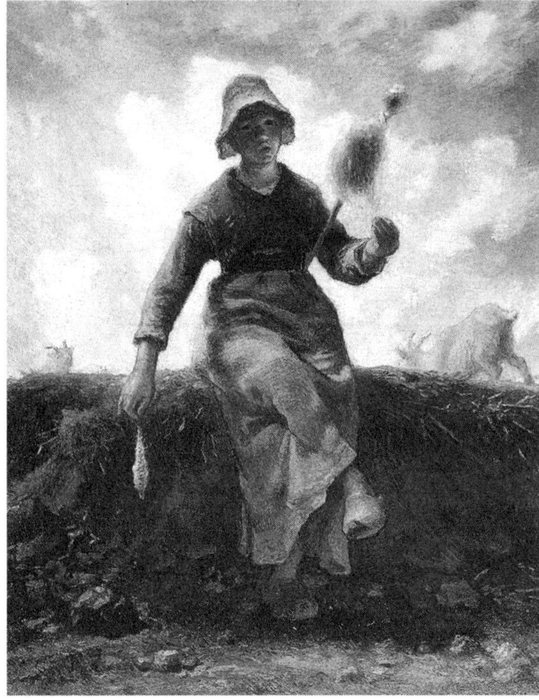

202
Millet,
The Spinner,
nineteenth c.

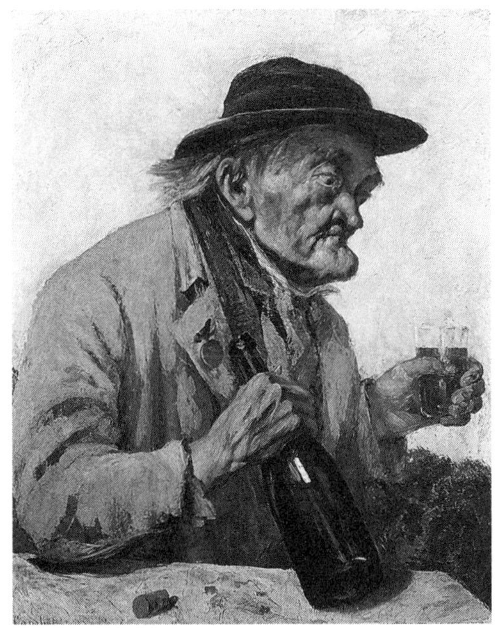

203
Courbet,
Old Man with a Glass of Wine,
nineteenth c.

This period passes into history under the heading **bourgeois realism**. Sometimes, it is simply called realism.

In a sense, this heading makes it absolute, as though imposing the view that it was the only and the highest achievable end of realism, after which realism no longer develops, but regresses and declines. Was that the case in reality? Let us consider the successive components of this realism so that we can understand why this period has been recorded as being so exceptional, why it was received as the most genuine, unforced expression of its era, and, in the eyes of many people, as the most true expression of reality in general, as the most true, most timeless realism for all times.

Looking at pictures by the main painters of the period, we note their soft modelling and the thoroughly worked light and shade in its many gradations and passages — analogous to that of the Dutch school. This was testimony to a well-formed observation of light and shade phenomena, to the existence of a profound visual consciousness in the domain of chiaroscuro. Contributing to this was the work of preceding generations (Géricault, Delacroix), who had consolidated this consciousness on the basis of the work of Dutch and Flemish painters.

On closer observation, however, we see that this chiaroscuro is not only expressed by the simple shading or lightening of particular parts of objects. To every darkening or lightening, there is a corresponding and simultaneous change of **colour**. Every shadow and every degree of light contains not only darker or lighter colour but also an admixture of a colour **other** than the local one. Within the framework of a certain generally adopted schema, colour changes and takes on the hues of other colours. It is thus a use of colour that is derived from an underdeveloped and unconscious mobile-seeing. The increased dynamism of the bourgeoisie, founding its culture on a wider social base than pre-revolutionary and feudal France, covered in the course of sixty years (1788 – 1848) the road that it had taken history three hundred years to cover (the sixteenth, seventeenth, and eighteenth centuries). The incomplete mobile-seeing that characterised the Rococo became the property of the developing bourgeoisie as it began its rule. It expressed the purport of the class system being consolidated by way of this seeing. With this progressive seeing, the most superior model of visual consciousness of its time, it expressed its progressive right to life – the right of the class that has not yet reached the limits of its development sketched out by history.•

Such were the newly acquired rights of the bourgeoisie, expressed in the painting of the period:

1. **the right** to universal, democratic-bourgeois **leisure** and to the consumption of the fruits of one's labour – expressed in the development of landscape painting (through the lyricism of the landscape observed on Sunday outings);
2. **the right to cultural heritage**, to history seen through the eyes of the bourgeoisie and to the great masterpieces of the literary tradition – expressed through the development of historical painting and painting with themes based on literature;
3. **the right to consolidate the bourgeois way of life as the universal social norm** – expressed through the development of genre painting;
4. the democratic-bourgeois **right to participate in political life**, to criticise and reform reality – expressed in works of critical realism (the universal right to vote).

• In those years, for instance, Saint-Simon regarded bankers and manufacturers as the natural leaders of the working class.

This criticism of existing reality, showing the poverty of the people – their underdevelopment, the social injustice they suffered – was conducted from the position of the consolidating bourgeoisie, from its democratic-republican standpoints. This criticism showed the wrongs the people suffered, showed the dark sides of their life, but showed them as remnants of feudal times, remnants that would disappear with the consolidation of the democratic, universal education of the people and their increasingly bourgeois wellbeing.

There were attempts to make critical realism absolute, to detach it from its class base. In speaking of critical realism, it should be clearly defined precisely which socio-economic systems and which of the antagonistic relations originating from these we have in mind. It should thus be noted that the purport of the process of the formation of this critical realism was defined by the democratic bourgeois left, striving for a democratic, bourgeois republic and attempting to mobilize, under its leadership, the broadest masses of people, promising the reform of all existing deficiencies. This is why works of critical realism depicted only those conflicts that had been inherited from feudalism, those conflicts that could be solved by the victory of the bourgeoisie – but did not depict conflicts within the bourgeoisie as it consolidated its rule and the nascent working class. The class-deformed and falsified image of reality was perhaps nowhere so clear in the painting of the period as it was in critical realism.•

The hitherto uncommon variety of subjects produced the illusion that everything, the entire world, was reflected and expressed in the painting of the times, that there were no framing historic limits or obstacles. This was a result of the progressive role of the bourgeoisie at that time, taking possession of the world, making itself at home in it, and getting to know it. It had not yet reached its limit points, at which battles with the antagonistic class awaited it. That is how it was able to limit its field of view and introduce a tendentious deformation into the image of reality seen. This deformation occurred only in a small section of critical realism.

• The only exception that I know of is the Russian painter Nikolay Kasatkin, who, in his paintings of miners, shows the developing resistance of the nascent working class. But that was already in the 1890s.

The dynamics of the post-revolutionary development of the bourgeoisie was so strong that, as we have seen, it was able to travel in only sixty years the road for which world painting required three hundred years. From David, with his constructed, three-dimensional commodity-seeing, through the empiricism of Delacroix and Géricault, to the incomplete mobile-seeing of Corot and Millet. This development of seeing went together with a widening of the range of themes. It seemed that the ever fuller and more precise seeing embraced all sides of life increasingly fully, that there is no contradiction between the progress in seeing and the subject matter expressed by it. The general development of the forces of production, which demanded increasingly more precise and fuller seeing, still does not encounter restraints from the relations of production. Therefore, a conflict between the development of seeing and the subject matter expressed through it still did not arise.

This seemingly unlimited and full realism was, in reality, the very limited realism of a single moment in history.

In strengthening the forces of production, the further development of history formed the working class. The forces of production develop, and their development is the objective factor that increases the power of the working class. The further development of the class struggle does not follow the line of the progressive liquidation of the remains of feudalism by the bourgeoisie. The purport of the struggle becomes the safeguarding of the positions attained against the developing pressure of the working class. One of the ways of ideologically disarming the opponent was the class-conditioned deformation of the image of visual reality. As soon as the working class entered history, bourgeois realism collapsed. This happens at different times in different countries, depending on its stage of development, but it is a constant phenomenon. The hitherto parallel development of seeing itself and the expansion of the range of the subject matter it covers comes to an end.

Under the pressure of the developing forces of production, the contents of visual consciousness continue to develop. But we see an increasing deformation of the image of visual reality at the same time in the themes expressed by way of this model of seeing as it developed. The development of seeing entered into conflict with the actual, full seeing of processes occurring in life. We have to be fully aware of the twofold nature of this subsequent development, differentiating between a development in visual consciousness and a class-conditioned limitation of the field of view of the world. Both the one and the other derive from the fundamental cognitive method formed out of the empirical method by the bourgeoisie over the course of its historic development. This method is both the source of bourgeois realism and of its historically determined limitations. The limitations of the empirical method, which were, in essence, the limitations of the class that developed it over the course of the sixteenth to the nineteenth centuries as its own principal cognitive method — made it possible to capture **phenomena** that had already been accepted and could be observed, but were not a sufficient cognitive tool to discover nascent and emerging **processes**. The empirical method offers a faithful and full image of what **is**, but cannot capture what is in the process of formation and change. Herein lie its limitations, determined by history and defined by class. Variability is discovered by activity and not by observation. The inadequacies and limitations of Impressionist realism are not the result of Impressionism's departure from any genuine realism that preceded it. This preceding realism was not an absolute realism but simply bourgeois realism — seeing reality though the eyes of the class that was in the process of setting about ruling. Its objectivism and its ability to increase and expand the range of observation were the result of the fact that the bourgeoisie of that period had not yet reach the historically determined limits of its development — it was able to see and to observe without putting its class position at risk.

As we have seen and shall see in due course, Impressionism did not depart from realism, but, on the contrary, developed the empiricism of its seeing, discovering a whole series of physiological phenomena within our seeing. If, despite this, it took on an incomplete, falsified image of its contemporary reality, then this was because it was let down by the method of visual empiricism itself, which, as a method, was inadequate to fully capture the world and the processes taking place within it.

This method — formulated by the bourgeoisie in the course of its historical development — this specific cognitive method of the bourgeois class underwent various changes. It began as an incomplete and fragmented method — at first studying only light and shade phenomena (sixteenth and seventeenth centuries). Over the course of its development, it encompassed an ever-wider range of phenomena, noticing almost everything concerning the physiology of our seeing, breaking with all conventional norms in favour of the full empiricism of physiological seeing. If this full truth of physiological seeing failed to deliver a full image of reality, this is an indication of the limitations of this method as a cognitive tool — and of the limitations of the class that created this tool in its own image and likeness.

The gradually developing empirical method revealed the inadequacy of previous methods of reflecting reality; it proved that the image of the world, constructed logically by reason at the end of the fifteenth century in accordance with all the principles of three-dimensional **convergent** perspective, drawn in all foreshortenings, inclines, and diminishments, with the shading of objects to render them convex — the reality of commodity-seeing — does not correspond with our real, empirically verifiable model of seeing. The "natural" and physiological seeing resulting from observation was in opposition to the image of reality constructed by reason.

In logical terms, every object **has** its own clearly distinct boundaries. However, observation reveals that we do not always **see** these boundaries, and that sometimes they fade away and disappear.

In logical terms, every object has its own distinct colour. However, observation confirmed that we **do not see** the pure, distinct colour of the object, that the colour that we see — that appears on our retina — is a material and verifiable effect of the matter of the external world acting on the material components of our visual apparatus — that in mobile-seeing (and such is our real seeing) the phenomenon of variable and multiform colour appears.

But the acceptance of the mobile gaze entails further consequences, this time not only as regards colours but also in the field of drawing and shape. The mobile gaze not only charges the relations between colours, but also the mutual relations between the shapes seen in nature. Shifts in the gaze are accompanied by shifts in perspective. Instead of one vanishing point, as had hitherto existed in perspective, as many of these appear as there are gazes cast into space. **At the end of each gaze, a vanishing point appears.** A series of shifts occurs in these same lines, relative to their position in relation to each single vanishing point.

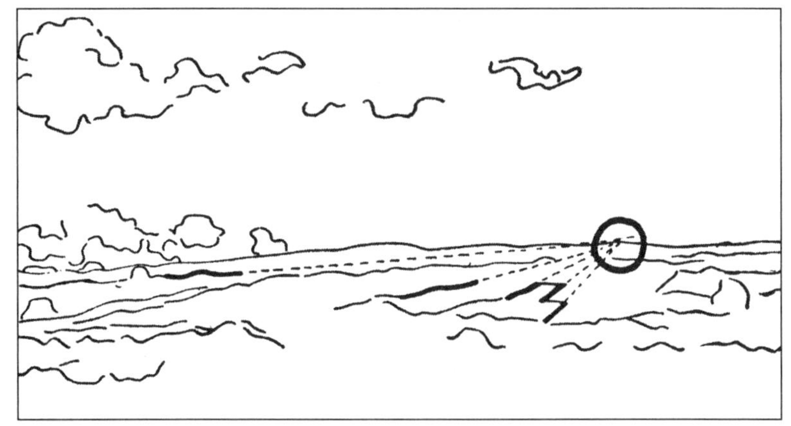

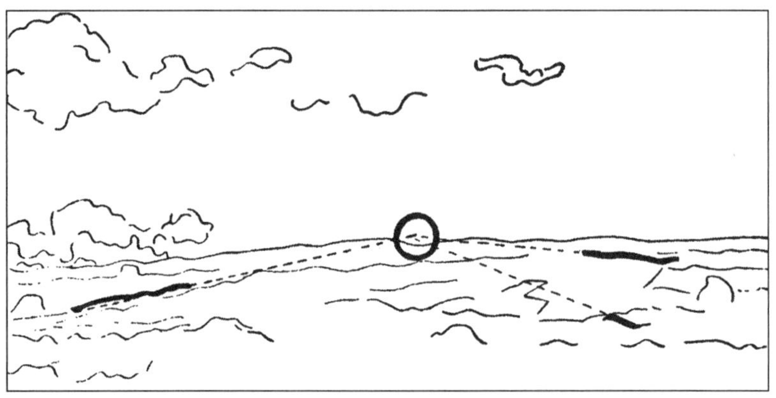

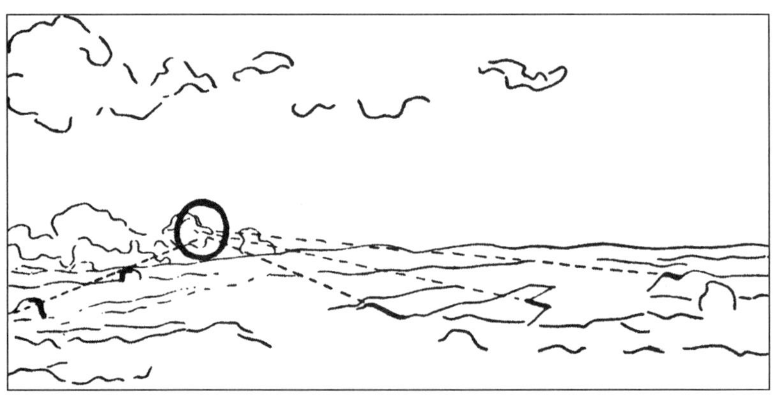

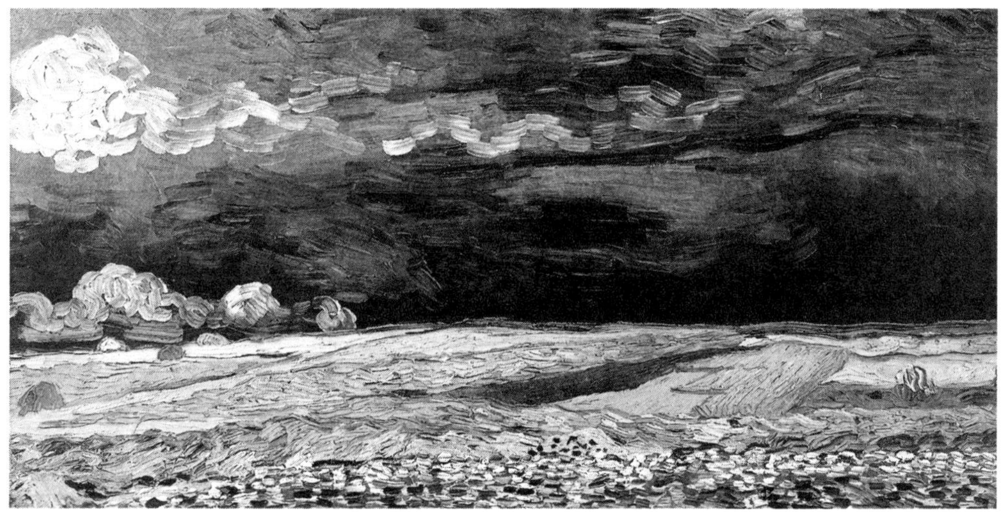

204
Van Gogh,
Wheat Field with Crows,
nineteenth c.

Indeed, such a wide landscape can only be seen — its whole expanse taken in by the eyes — by panning the gaze across the horizon. We can only see the expanse of a wide plain if we look at it with a number of gazes. A single, immobile, fixed, theoretical gaze is unable to take in such a wide space. To see this landscape, we cast several gazes. This is what we do in life. Transferring everyday experience from our lived practice into the sphere of perspective abolished the hitherto existing principle of a **single** vanishing point in the picture — the basic principle of classical, convergent, three-dimensional perspective. This perspective can exist in logically inferred theory but does not exist in the empiricism of our actual, physiological viewing of the world. We look at the world not with a single, fixed gaze, but with a number of gazes cast in different directions — and each gaze has, at the end of it, its own vanishing point. The placement of the gazes cast, is, in essence, a reconstruction of the process of looking at nature, following the process of seeing — such as it has been in reality and not according to some idealistically inferred and centralised single gaze. This is why nature itself decides at which points we will level our gaze and where vanishing points will be placed.

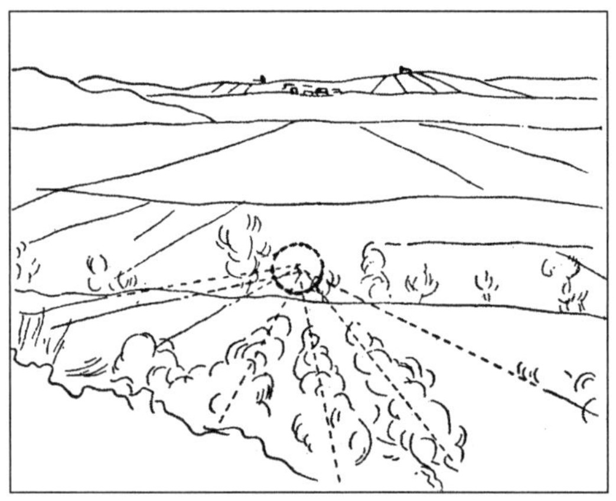

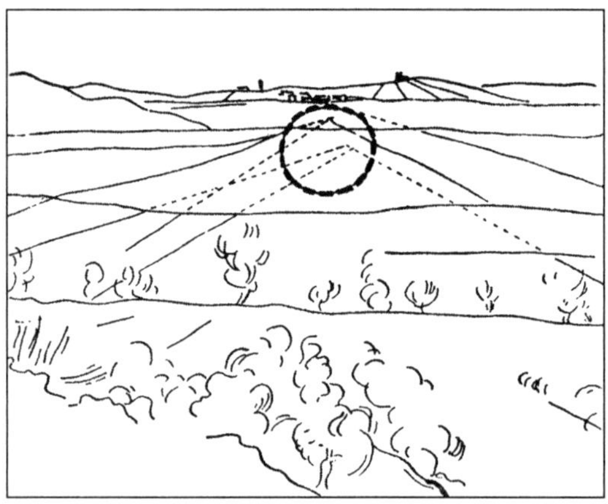

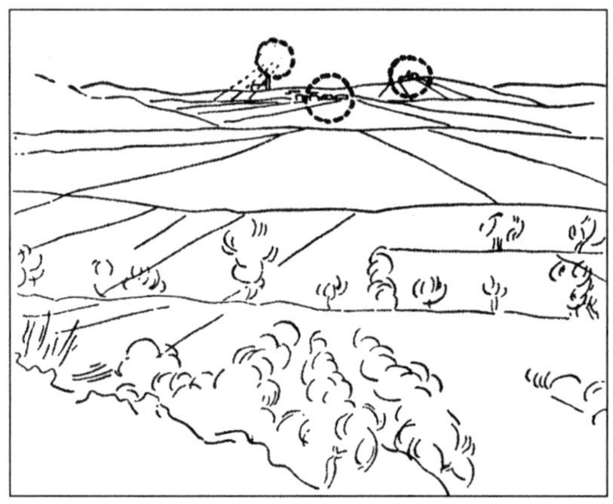

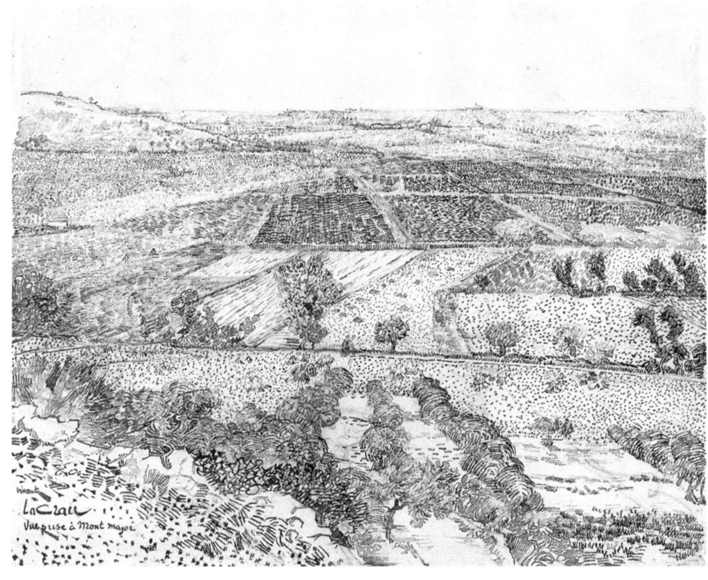

205
Van Gogh,
Harvest at La Crau with Montmajour in the Background,
nineteenth c.

The depth of the landscape determined the placement of vanishing points. Gazes receded from the closer planes of depth to ever more distant ones. And vanishing points positioned themselves in accordance with these gazes — from the nearest to the ever more distant. The spectator's gaze, penetrating ever further planes of depth, repeated the process with which we look at the landscape in everyday life. Since seeing — as we should be well aware — is not a one-off, undefined, abstract **act** of seeing, but an activity, a **process** of looking over a certain duration in time. Nature has its "points of interest," which attract more attention (and gazes). We see it by passing from one point of interest to the next — and at each of these a separate perspectival vanishing point is produced, marked to a greater or lesser degree.

We see every reality little by little, casting gazes at particular "points of interest."

Only as a result of all of these gazes will the image of nature emerge, such as we saw it in the course of the **real**, physiological process of viewing it. Not the image of objects, inferred by reason, logically deduced, but the empirically captured reflection of this process, whereby we look at nature.

The image received in this way is in reality a complex of several images, derived from several different gazes overlaid on top of each another. For every reality we look at, we see not one, but several images.

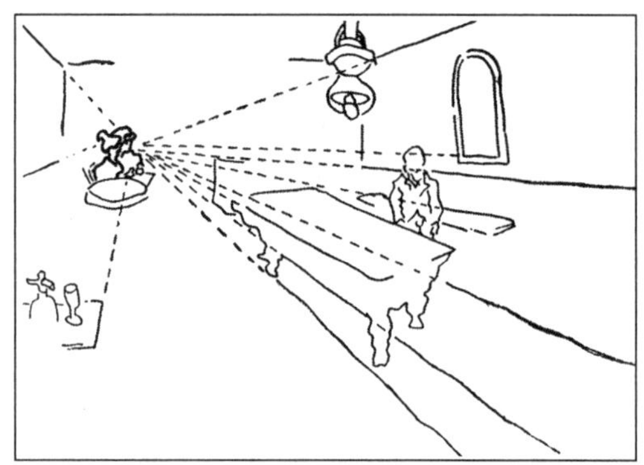

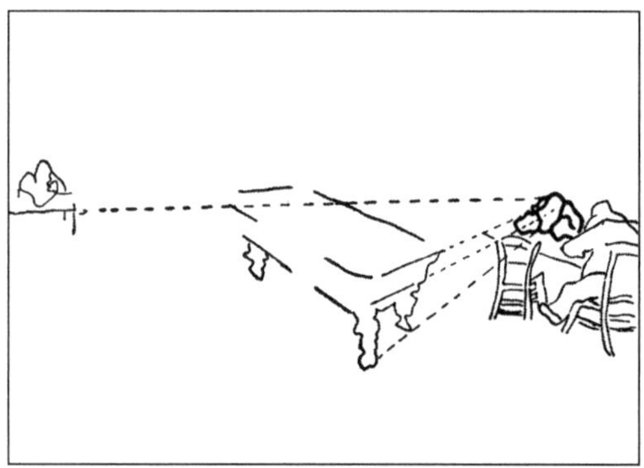

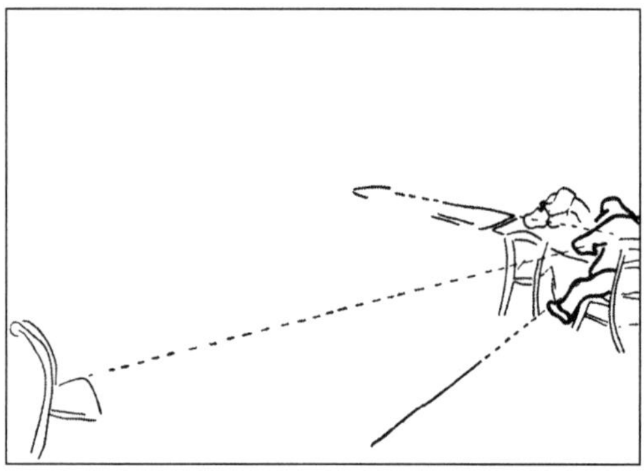

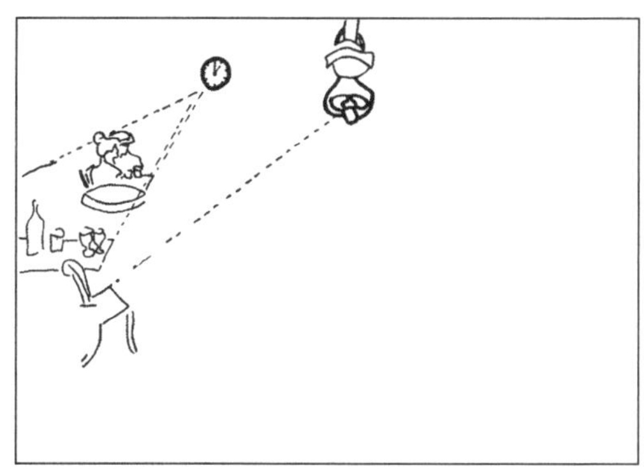

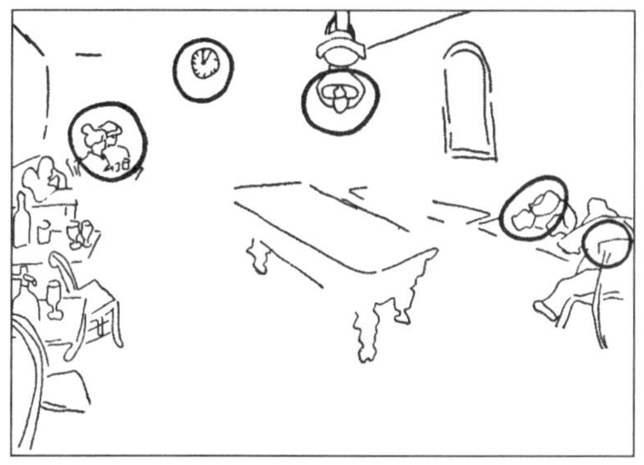

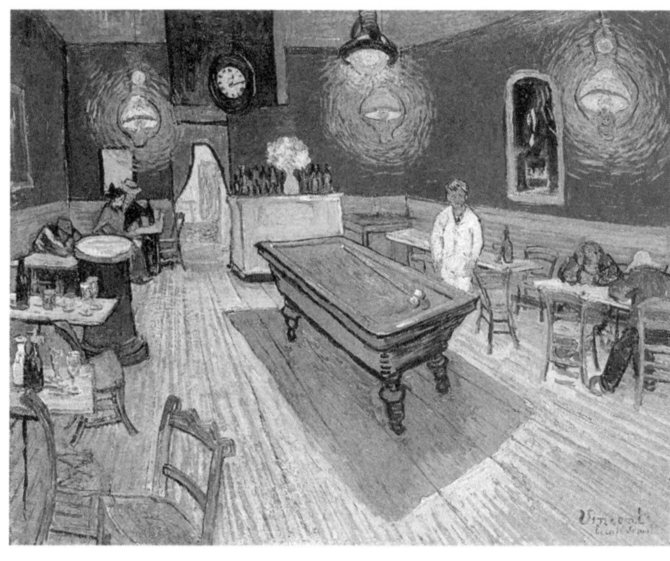

206
Van Gogh,
The Night Cafe in Arles,
nineteenth c.

What essentially distinguishes Impressionism from the preceding era is that Impressionism makes the purport of seeing dependent both on external objects looked at and on **seeing** man. The whole issue comes down to whether it is admissible to introduce into the scope of seeing the visual sensations that derive from the properties of our receiving apparatus and not solely from external objects. Should the seeing man be related to the subjective and unverifiable world (and therefore regard Impressionism as a departure from the historically developing line of the increase in realism) or, should we acknowledge this **seeing** man as a material being, capable of being scientifically investigated and tested (and by this accept that Impressionism enriched the hitherto existing realism with phenomena related to the physiology of seeing)?

In other words — the issue comes down to whether man's organism, with its sensory experience and reception of impressions, is as verifiable as the world of external objects, or whether we have to deem it unknowable and its sensations and impressions purely subjective and arbitrary.

The opposition of the "objective," scientifically investigable world of external objects, and the unknowable, "subjective" world of man, could arise at a particular stage of knowledge, at which the external world was accessible to scientific investigation, whilst the knowledge of man and his receiving apparatus was non-existent.

The state of science in the first half of the nineteenth century was such that the physical and chemical sciences existed but not the science of physiology. At this stage of development, in accordance with the state of knowledge achieved, one could speak of the objective reality of the external world, open to knowledge, whilst regarding as subjective and unknowable what concerned man and his functions.

In those times, one would speak of "sensations," without analysing them or specifying, that is to say — without reducing them to measurable and material changes in the human organism. One would speak of the "reception" of these sensations, without analysing which components of the material human body were responsible for the fact that by acting on the senses, external objects reached the brain, where they were processed into consciousness and knowledge. Seeing was understood one-sidedly as a passive reflection in the eye. The eye reflected the abstract sensations of objects seen, like an inanimate mirror.

These sensations were processed, in an undefined, abstract way, into consciousness. Both sensations and their reception were sensations "in general," "in the abstract," sensations that could not be concretely specified. At this stage in development, it had to be deemed that only those things are objective in seeing that originate from a mirror image of known and scientifically investigated objects in the external world. Whereas the entire range of seeing conditioned by the human receiving apparatus had to be deemed unreal, subjective, and arbitrary. The introduction of these unknowable (or rather unknown) phenomena, had to be regarded as a departure from realism – arbitrary, subjective, philosophical idealism. At this stage in development, it was historically determined and correct to treat Impressionism as one of the expressions of philosophical idealism, as a subjective and arbitrary tendency.

But every new scientific discovery changes the existing form of materialism. Now we should subject Impressionism to a realistic analysis and relate its practice to scientific physiology, rejecting the idealistic theory that has accrued over the course of history. We need to bring out that realism of Impressionism that is its **physiological seeing**. Even the vocabulary that we use when speaking of seeing needs to be changed. Instead of abstract sensations and abstract pathways to their reception, we need to define by way of which knowable and measurable changes in our visual apparatus it became possible for light falling from external objects to process itself into an image and thought and reach our consciousness. Not undefined, visual "sensations" but concrete, photochemical changes in the endings of optical nerves, i.e. where the light falls, reflected from external objects. Not an abstract "reception" of visual sensations by an abstract human being, but the functioning of nerve impulses, i.e. short, electrical changes transmitted along the network of nerve cell chains, carrying the sensations from the eye to the appropriate centres of the cerebral cortex.

We do not see the objects of external reality by way of the penetration of their immaterial reflection into our consciousness, but through a series of material changes in our receiving apparatus. This is why what gets through, as a result of all this, includes both the external objects and the changes that occurred in the receiving apparatus. And all this is the truth of seeing as a physiological function. Impressionist seeing — the true, empirical seeing of real man, physiological seeing — should be investigated with the aid of physiological criteria. Then we will be able to define which aspects of it are empirical, physiological seeing — its realism — and which have historically accrued through the influence of idealist theory — which are due to anti-realist arbitrariness. The practise of Impressionism was based on expanding the scope of observation and on the inclusion of experiences from the physiology of seeing. It was thus precise and verifiable. Its theory, however, was not able to locate the scope of this observation accurately and defined it as "temperament," "the artist's inner world" — as subjective and arbitrary.

This divergence between idealistic and unscientific theory and materialist practice always existed in Impressionism, leading to formalist deviations and to the collapse of numerous, usually weaker, painters.

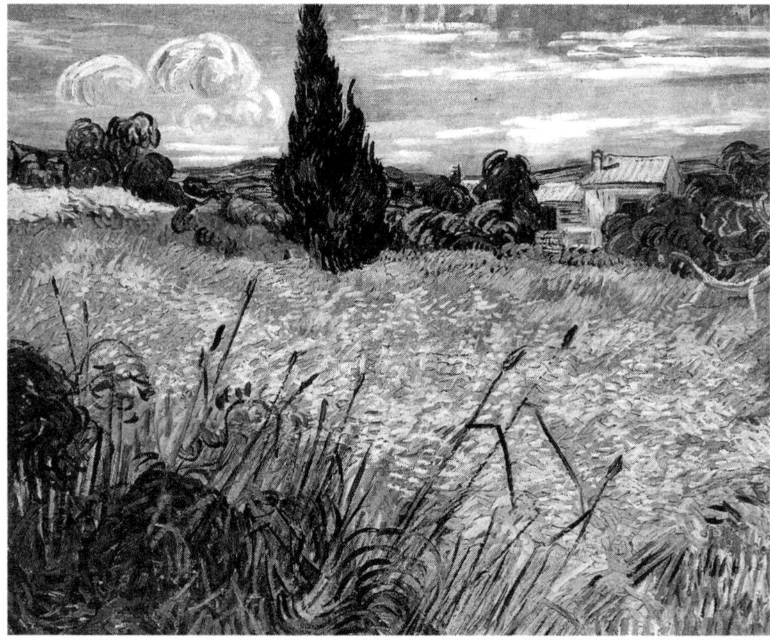

207
Van Gogh, *Wheat Fields with Cypresses*, nineteenth c.

A measure of realism in Impressionism is the compatibility of its model of seeing with physiological data — and this is the only way it ought to be tested. Analysing an Impressionist painting, we have to define which of the data of physiological seeing lie behind it, conditioning it. There is no other explanation.

As a result of the transition to full physiological seeing, visual content is enriched by components derived from the reaction of the organism, from its functions, from the process of receiving visual sensations. The very **manner** of seeing itself, the manner of **looking at nature** becomes an essential component of seeing as a whole.

Looking at Van Gogh's painting, for instance, we see that it clearly contains identical, recurrent divisions.

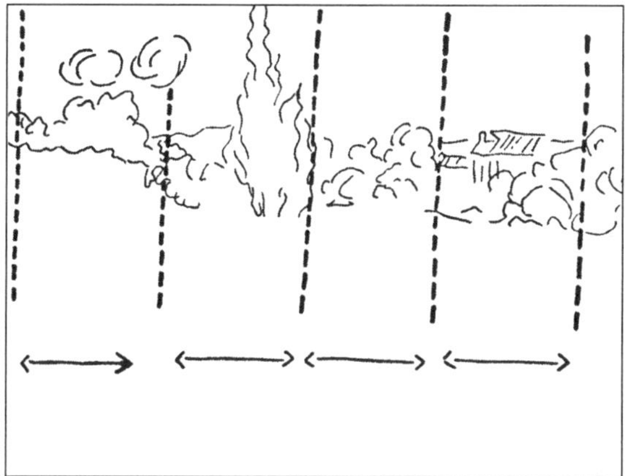

One could simply stop right at this observation, without trying to explain its causes. But that would be a purely formal analysis — superficial, and not explaining the essence of Van Gogh's realism. We can only reveal this realism when we are able to explain the given form by way of the physiological properties of seeing, if we can define those characteristics of the **process of seeing** that have conditioned and imposed the identical, recurrent divisions. In other words — how should we be looking at nature, in order to see it as painted by Van Gogh (with the same divisions)? And is the gaze with which he looked at it the same, normal, natural physiological gaze with which we look at it?

We will find the answer by sketching out the centres of interest of the gazes levelled at this landscape.

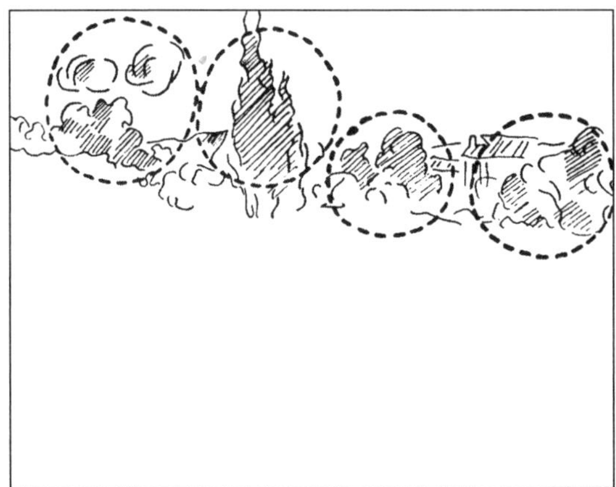

Four gazes, spanning across the horizon and each focusing on a different point of interest. Since each gaze has the same field of view, these four gazes are placed along the horizon outline of four identical, recurrent fields.

Recurrent, identical divisions in the painting did not appear because the "formalist" Van Gogh chose to do this for unknown, subjective reasons, but because he reproduced precisely the process of viewing the landscape in four parallel gazes directed in succession. And our eye, as we know, has its specific anatomical construction and the scope of its field of view is more or less constant.

The following schema represents the course of the process of looking:

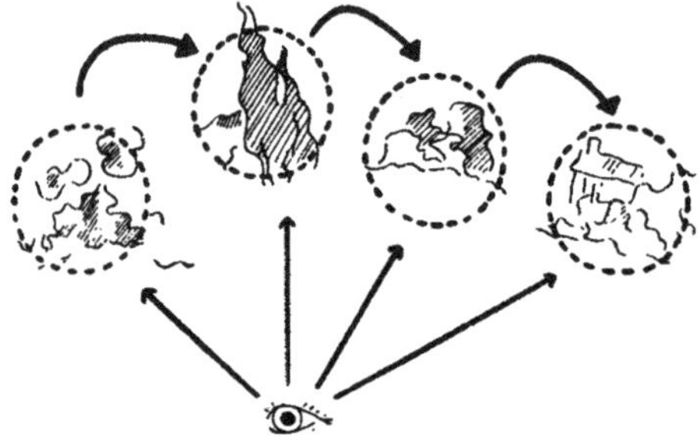

1. the position of the spectator in relation to the landscape (the eye),
2. the directions of the four gazes levelled at the landscape (straight arrows),

3. the (field of) view seen in each gaze,
4. the direction of the eye's meandering's while passing from one centre of interest to the next (rounded arrows).

The same process of distinguishing successive gazes can be observed in another painting.

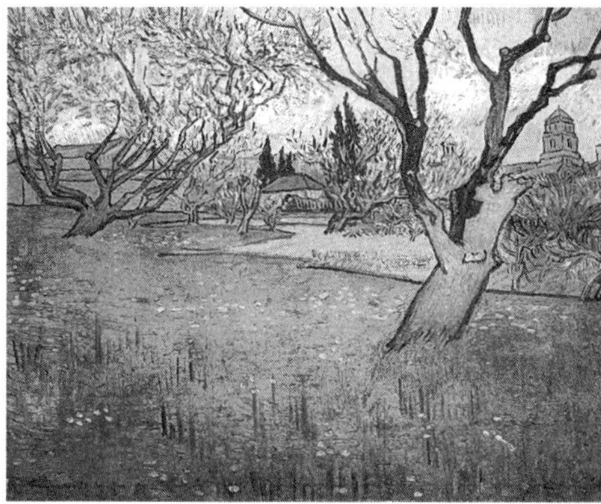

208
Van Gogh,
View of Arles with Trees in Blossom,
nineteenth c.

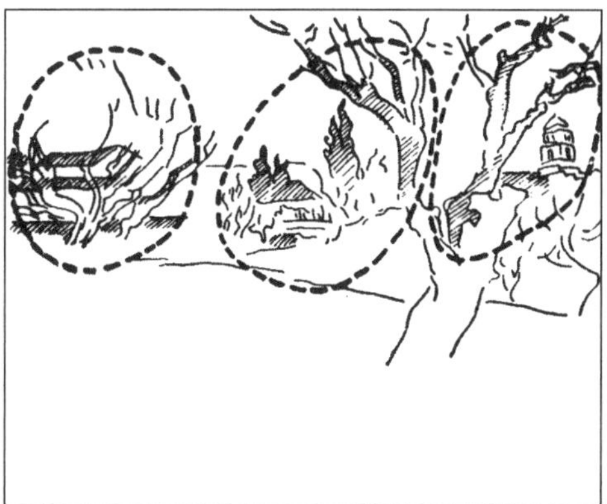

Here we can distinguish three gazes levelled at the landscape.

The entire visible purport of the landscape has been contained in these three gazes. If we try to remove these three fields of view from it, we are left with an almost complete void, seen peripherally (seeing sideways, beyond the field of view).

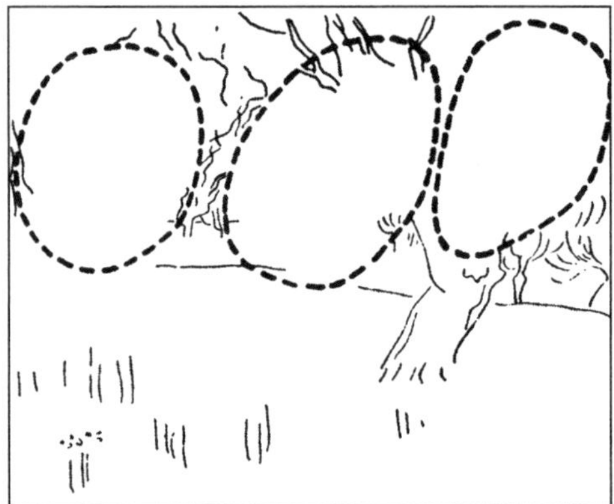

These three gazes have captured the whole essence of the landscape, extracting all that there was to be seen. Only non-essential fragments remain outside them, painted (i.e. seen) in a blurred and hazy manner — this is how our peripheral vision sees.

If one wishes to reproduce the entire course of the process of looking, one has to find an answer to the question of what determines the number of gazes and why they were directed at these (and not other) points.

Our everyday experience of seeing provides the answer. Our gazes are not cast at random. Their placement is not regular and continuous.

The reality that we see before us contains certain defined points that attract our attention. These points are located where the accumulation of visual stimulants is at its most dense. They impose themselves on our sight and attract our gaze because they have the greatest number of tensions (line, light and shade, colour, movement, etc.). The presence of these visual stimulants automatically attracts and arrests our eyes. In the real physiological process of seeing nature, we do not see in a continuous and uniform way, looking at every point in it, but intermittently, with separate gazes, automatically attracted by nature's visual stimulants. It is in these places that the greatest number of gazes is cast. Where there are no stimulants, however — we see with **peripheral** vision, seeing nature located beyond the our field of view.

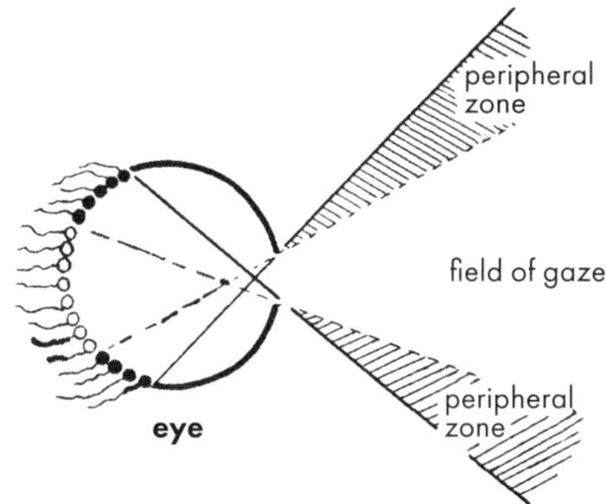

Peripheral vision is determined by the anatomical properties of the eye. The retina's optical nerve endings are not identical. The nerves sensitive to colour are located at the centre of the retina. Outside these, near the edges, nerve endings are located that are insensitive to colour, reacting only to light. That is why with the centre of the retina we see colour and with its edges — only light, and light-and-shade effects.

Thus, the field of view is not uniform, but consists of two concentric zones: the central field of the gaze, where we see clearly and colourfully, and the peripheral zones, in which colour fades away and we see only light and shade (in a specific grey, **peripheral** colour), and in which the forms of objects are blurred.

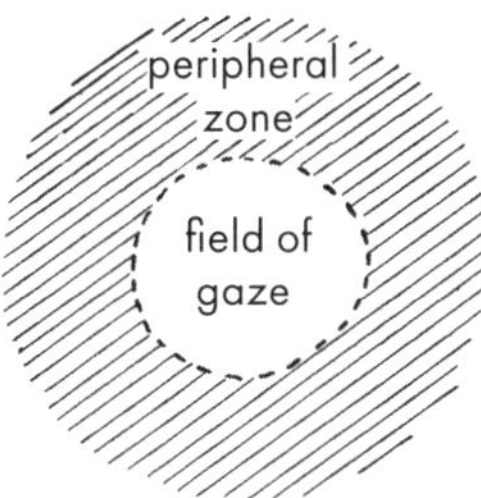

The difference has come about over the course of the evolution of the species, e.g. nocturnal animals and birds only have nerves reacting to light, but do not see colours. The hen has only nerves reacting to colour and so can see nothing at night.

Investigating the essence of our physiological process of seeing we must understand that the gazes with which we look at nature are not all of the same sort, that they consist of two areas: the central, colourful, clear field of view, and the peripheral zones, in which colour as well as the distinctness of objects fade away.

We do not look at nature with several gazes of the same kind, in which it appears with the same distinctness, but with gazes that each has its own peripheral zone.

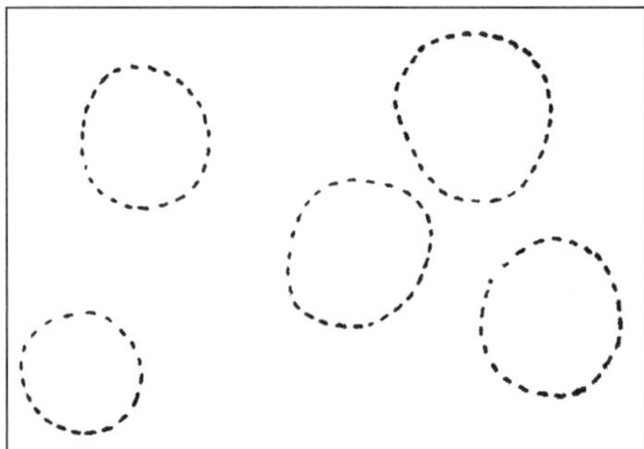

This is the zone of transition from seeing in full to seeing nothing, and so the distinctness of shapes and colours of the nature that we see is not constant, unchangeable, but depends on whether we see it in the centre of the field of our gaze or in a peripheral zone. In the centre of the field of view we see clearly and in focus; in the peripheral-vision zone, a blurred and unclear image.

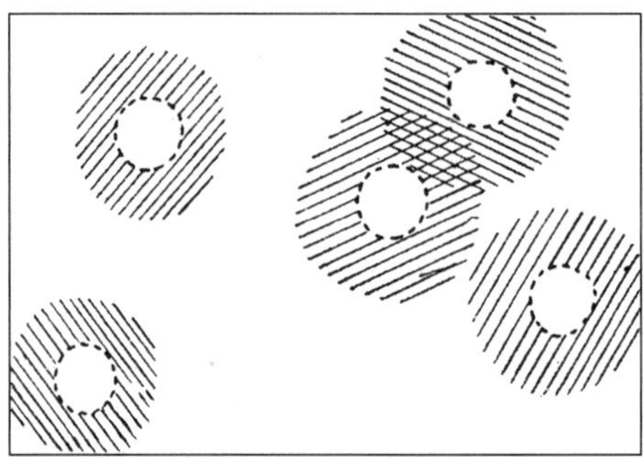

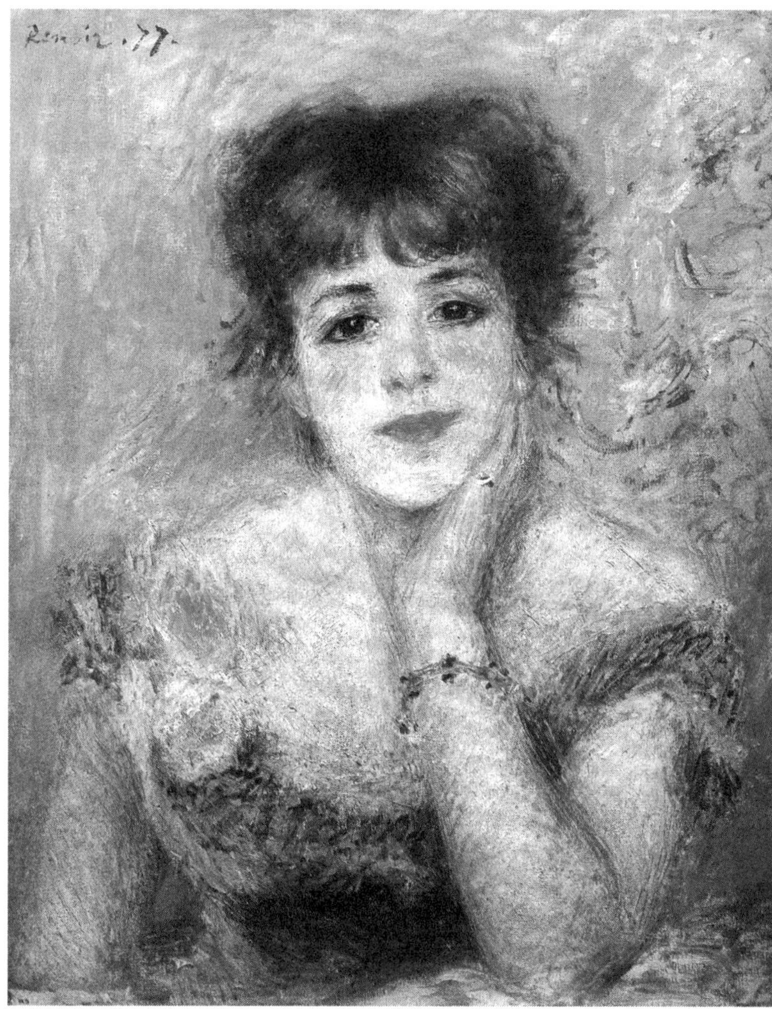

209
Renoir,
Portrait of Jeanne Samary,
nineteenth c.

The field of view is the face; the background is in the peripheral zone. Even the chin is seen in less focus than the forehead, since the passage from one to the other falls here. The centre of the field of the gaze is on the forehead. Visibility weakens from the forehead in all directions and passes into the background in the blurred zone of peripheral vision.

But the blurring of seeing does not occur only in peripheral vision. It also occurs in seeing at a distance.

As a result of the anatomical properties of the eye we only see clearly by accommodating the eye to a particular distance. We see as blurred and unclear anything that is closer or further away. If we want to see something that is at another distance, then we have to accommodate the eye to seeing at a different distance, to accommodate the eye's lens.•

In our practical, day-to-day seeing, we constantly transfer the eyes from one object to another, constantly changing the convexity of the eye by transferring the gaze from one distance to another. We transfer the gaze from objects that are closer to objects that are very far away, and from these to those that are in the middle-distance. The eye is constantly on the move, not only changing the direction of its gaze, but also the distance it is looking at. **Muscle movements** are constantly occurring in the eye, accommodating it to seeing at a particular distance. Thanks to these accommodating movements, we are able to see the spatial depth. During the era when visual consciousness did not go beyond noticing only those observations that contributed to seeing the logically constructed solid form of the object (e.g. in Hellenistic, late Gothic, and early Renaissance painting), all objects were shown equally clearly at a distance. Images were constructed of objects as such, as they "should look," irrespective of practical seeing.

The phenomenon of the blurring and sharpness of objects was observed in the period of chiaroscuro-seeing (sixteenth and seventeenth centuries) — at first in its simplest form — as objects further away were blurred by an increasingly thick layer of air. This was the first observation on the path to the departure from objects as such (excluding **seeing** man), towards objects rendered as we see them.

However, aerial perspective did not in itself yet incorporate visual practice as a whole, did not incorporate the living man who undertakes the empirically verifiable **activity** of seeing, who sees actively and whose aims this seeing serves.

Accommodative seeing, seeing into the distance or as far into the distance as we set, adjust the eye to see — is an anatomical fact that

• The same phenomenon occurs in the camera, which gives a clear picture only at the depth of field to which the lens is adjusted. To transfer the focus to a different depth of field, we adjust the lens. There is a similarity in the structure of the eye and the camera.

accords with the everyday practice of seeing and, as such, has to be included within the scope of visual consciousness.

Consequently, we see clearly only in the direction and at the distance to which we accommodate the eye. To simplify, let us assume that we have, before us, three depths of field, one behind another (in reality, there will be significantly more, depending on the configuration of the topography).

If we accommodate the eye to the closest depth of field, we see it distinctly, while the two further planes will be indistinct. We will see the first plane clearly against the background of the other two, merged into one another.

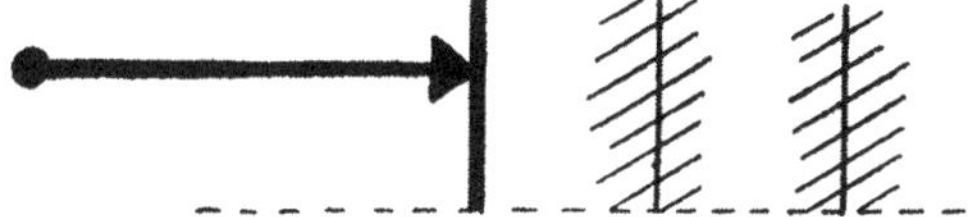

In a plan view (in perspective) this would look as follows:

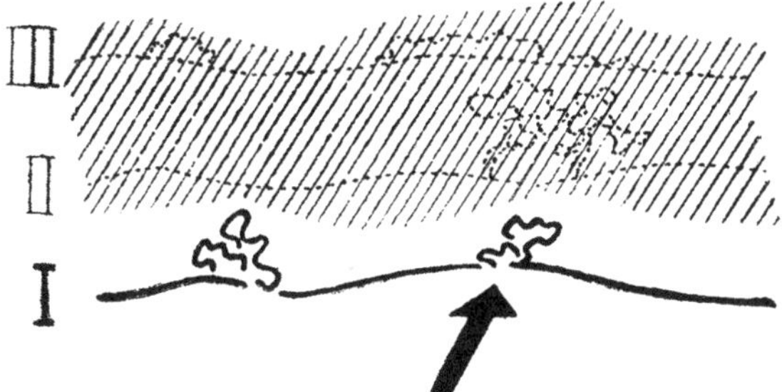

Accommodating the eye to the distance of the second spatial field, we see it delineated sharply, while both the first and the third will appear blurred and merged into one another.

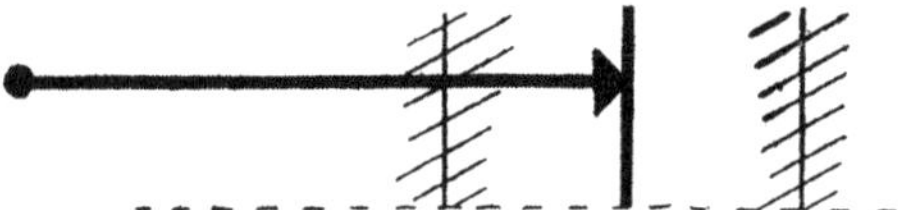

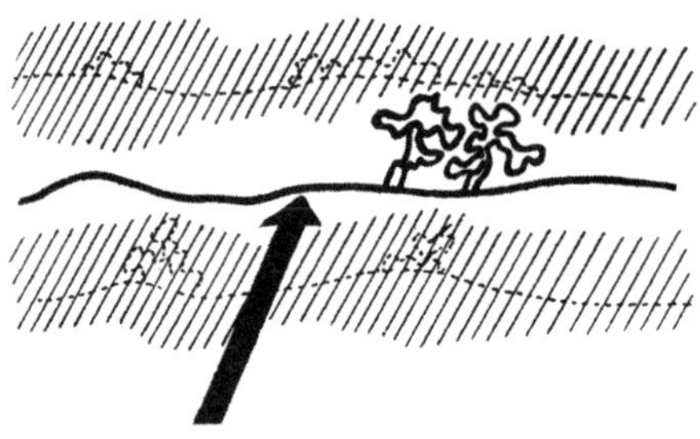

Looking at the distance of the third plane of depth we see it clearly against the first two merged spatial planes.

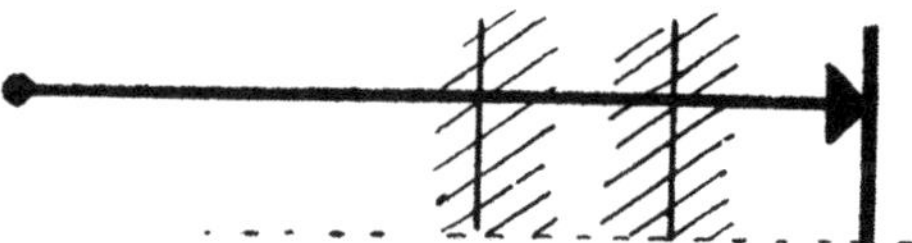

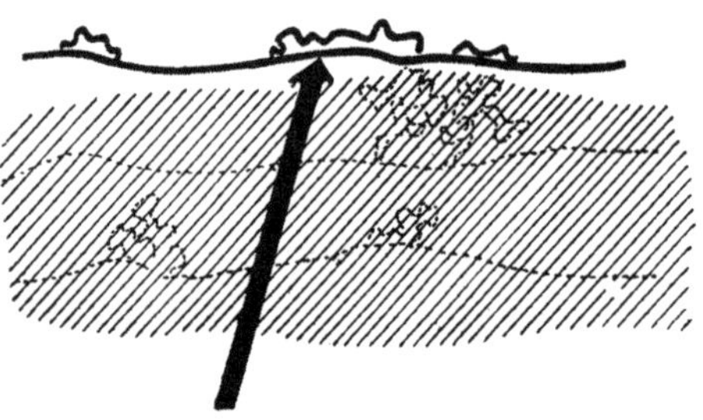

We achieve the same results by means of photography. As a result of the similarity between the construction of the eye and the photographic camera, only those planes to which we set the camera lens appear in focus, while others will merge into one another.

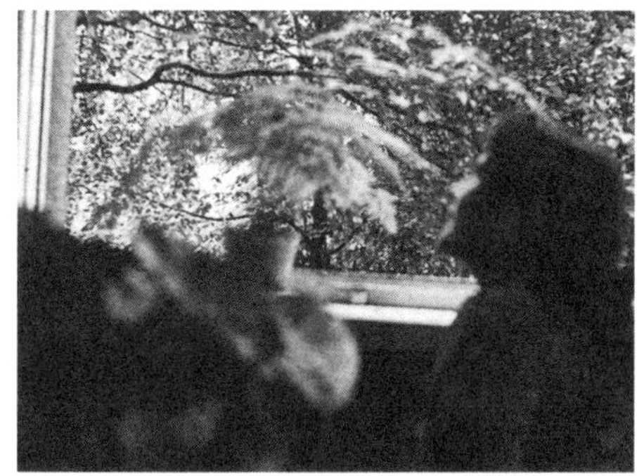

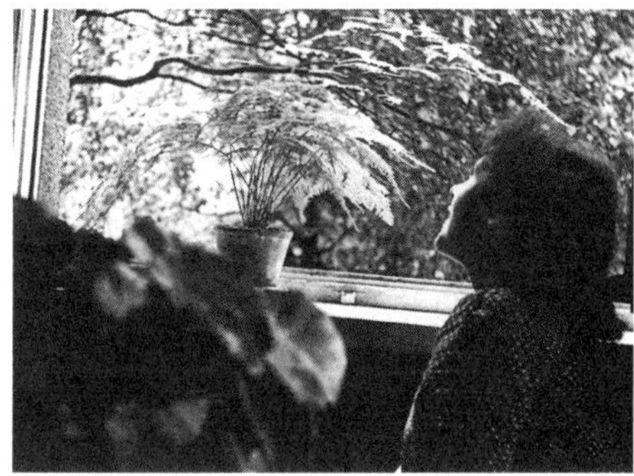

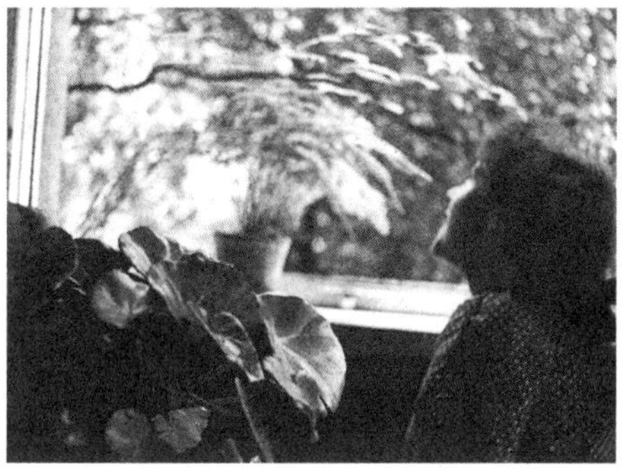

210
Nature photography

Only from the position of an accommodative seeing is it possible to refute Berkeley's claim• that "we do not actually see space and forms

• See G. Berkeley, *An Essay Towards a New Theory of Vision*, 2nd edition (Dublin: Jeremy Pepyat, 1709).

at all; we only see light and colours, only through correlating sight with touch do we perceive depth and physical objects."•

Accommodative seeing supplies the evidence that we **see** space and can be tested in practice. We see it by contracting the eyes to adjust to a distance, and we see it through the blurring of the planes to which we have not accommodated the distance of the gaze — we see it with the *activity* of our human, physiological vision, we see directly.

But in order to arrive at this argument, the passive image of objects seen has to be correlated with human activity, the **activity of physiological seeing.**

It is characteristic that the assertion of Wittgenstein, the logical analyst, concerning the material absence of the object in the observed world ("there are no proofs that we see the eye"[22]) can be refuted only on condition of including the observer, the matter of his body and his physiological seeing, in the external, material world of objects. For, it should be understood that distinguishing the spectator from the seen world, recognising only external objects as being exclusively verifiable, material, and objective, dematerialises the observer, who receives abstract, immaterial "sensations" from material objects of the external world in an abstract and immaterial way.

The assumption that we perceive (see) not by way of the empirically verifiable activity (seeing) of a material human organism, but by way of the abstract "mind," "senses," "sensations," "ideas," etc.,[23] lies at the basis of both the one and the other claim.•• Attempting to construct an image of the world while eliminating the perceiving (seeing) man, forces us to accept a method defined by idealist philosophy rather than the material method whereby this image is received by way of the action of matter on matter.

Herein lies the idealism of those who accuse Impressionism of departing from realism, of subjectivism and idealism, for replacing the

• Cited in W. Tatarkiewicz, *Historia filozofii*, Vol. 2. [p. 148].

•• I.e. both Berkeley's and Wittgenstein's.

22 L. Wittgenstein, *Tractatus logico-philosophicus*, "5.633... But the eye you do *not* see in fact." See footnote 18.

23 See M. Cornforth, *Science versus Idealism: An Examination of "Pure Empiricism" and Modern Logic* (London: Lawrence & Wishart, 1946), pp. 156—159, esp. Chapter 9, "The Philosophy of Wittgenstein," "6. Where has Wittgenstein led us?"

observation of external objects — external to the observer — with the observation of the **action** of the matter of these objects on the **matter** of the human body and the physiology of seeing arising from it.

But the sensations that we receive by way of seeing have to be justified, have to have their material foundation — they cannot remain unverifiable sensations in the abstract. If we exclude the objective, physiological basis of these sensations, how are they grounded in the reality outside them? In such a case only sensations remain — sensations in the abstract, sensations detached from reality — unverifiable sensations.

The assertion that the only objective world is the world of external objects aims in fact to remove the material and physiological basis of these human sensations that is the verifiable, knowable human body, reacting to the material, verifiable, and measurable action of external objects. It thus detaches sensations from their material basis, it is their rejection into an incorporeal world.

We see the world with the aid of our receiving apparatus — and we see it as our eye sees it, i.e. in accordance with the physiology of seeing.

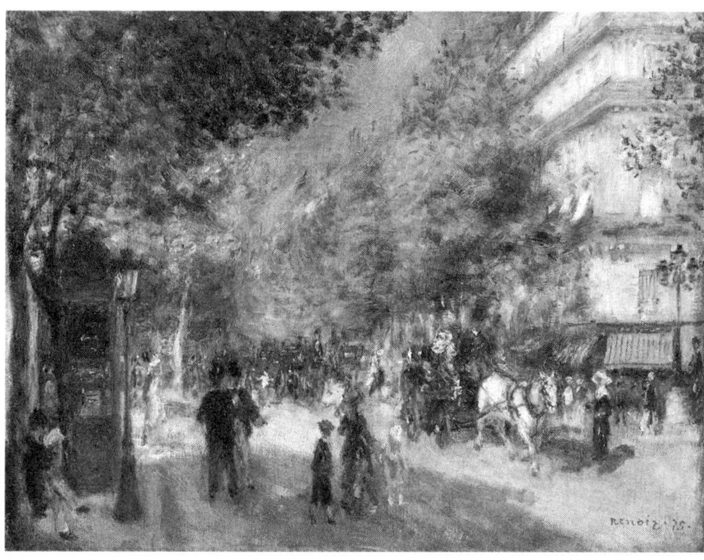

211
Renoir,
The Grands Boulevards,
nineteenth c.

Analysing Renoir's painting, we find a number of gazes cast. For example, in the foreground, at the bottom, the gazes have been levelled at two groups of people.

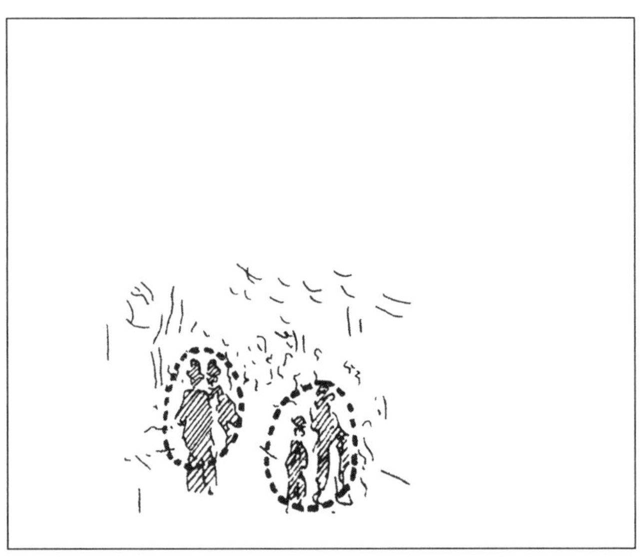

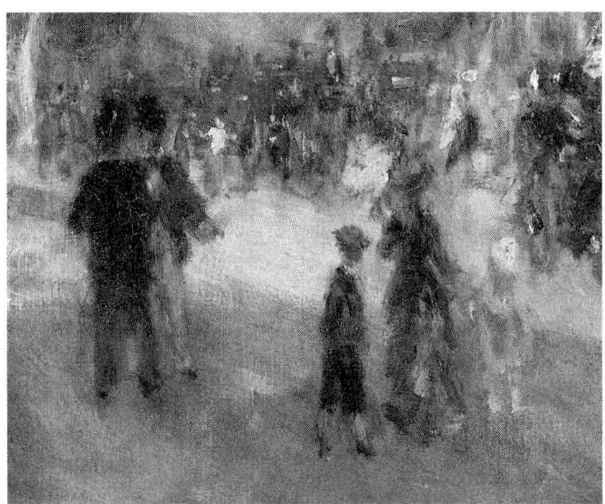

These figures, seen in direct gaze, appear distinctly, while everything on a different spatial plane (in the distance), which cannot be seen in direct gaze, appears in a blurred field by accommodation. Everything that was in the same plane of depth, but beyond the reach of the direct gaze (e.g. the figure on the right in the group on the right) appears in the blurred, peripheral field. The combination of direct seeing, peripheral seeing, and accommodative seeing comes to form the two gazes as a whole.

The two gazes levelled at the right side of the picture were directed at two different spatial planes at varied depths.

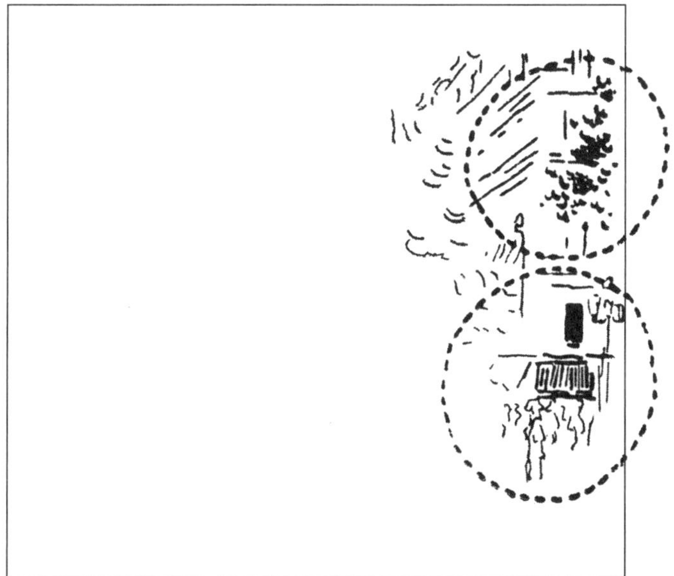

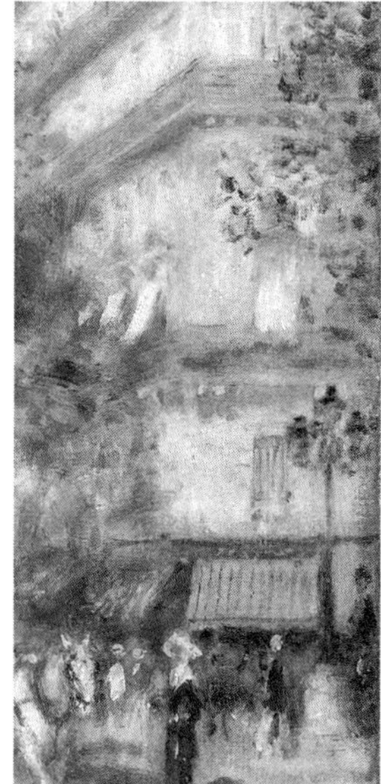

In the lower gaze, the eye reaches into the distance, as far as the wall of the house. This is why a sharp direct gaze hits only the window and the awning hanging beneath it. What is nearer (the crowd, the street lamp) or further away (the shady side wall of the house) in this case were relegated to the sphere of accommodative seeing and subject to blurring and haziness.

The upper gaze pauses closer-by, at the branches and leaves growing **in front of** the house. This is why the leaves are in focus, while the depth of field that was in sharp focus in the lower gaze (the house) found itself in the accommodative zone, blurred and hazy.

In this way, each of the gazes came to rest on a different spatial plane, attracted by the fragment of nature that contrasted more strongly with the rest. We see here a property of physiological seeing – the gaze automatically rests on the clearest, most strongly emphasized fragment of nature.

The same phenomenon occurs in the upper part of the picture.

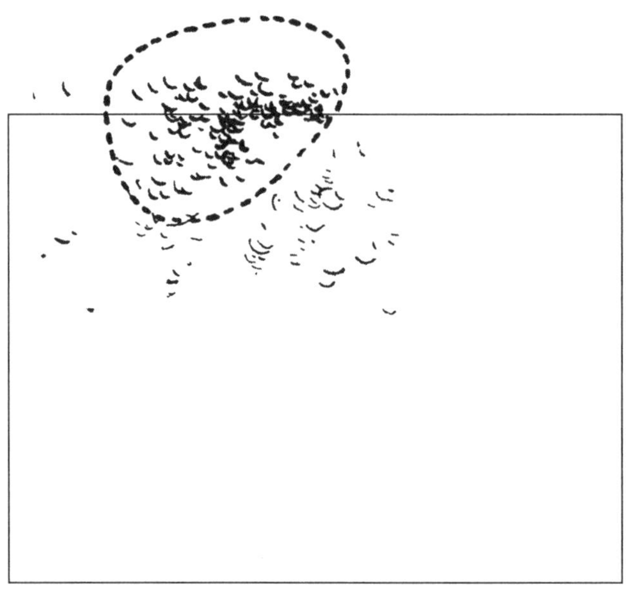

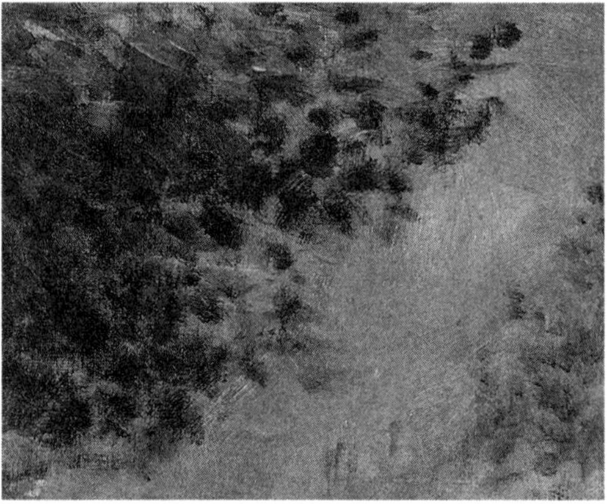

The direct gaze draws out the sharp upper leaves and branches of the tree on the left. Whereas the other trees, further away, and the parts of the same tree positioned nearer, are relegated to the accommodative and peripheral field. Whatever is closer and whatever is further away than the distance to which the sight has been accommodated has been blurred, as it lies in the accommodative field.

The same phenomenon is even more pronounced in the gaze levelled at the horse and carriage. The horse is quite sharp (especially its head), the coachman is slightly blurred, the couple seated in the carriage have almost completely faded away.

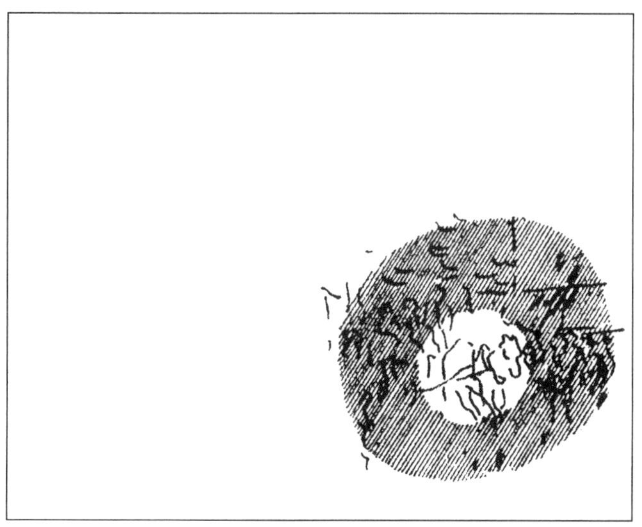

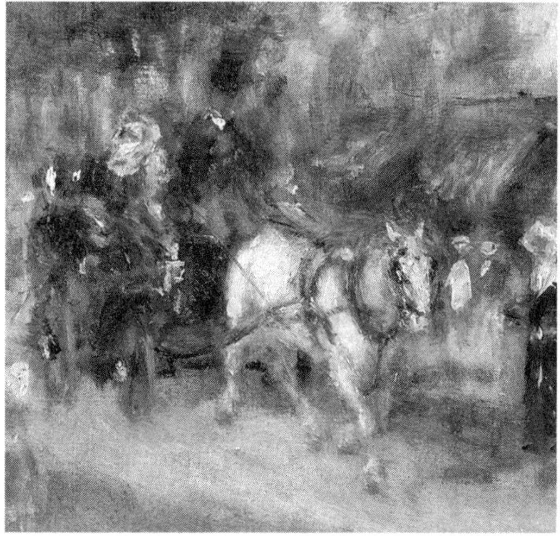

We see the reason for this if we take into account that being the most mobile, the horse attracted the most attention. The coachman's movements were weaker, while the figures sitting in the carriage did not move at all. It is the automatism of physiological seeing that has resulted in the places where the greatest number of visual stimulants attracts the gaze. The horse attracted the most attention (the greatest intensity of movement), and so the gaze rested on the horse.

The rest, i.e. the coachman and the couple riding in the carriage, were found in the accommodative field, the further away from the horse, the more blurred.

But we have to distinguish the haziness occurring in the peripheral field from accommodative haziness. In both cases, we encounter an unclear and hazy seeing, although the physiological causes of this blurring are entirely different.

In peripheral vision, we see the world with a sidelong gaze, we see it with the nerve endings that do not see colour. This is not simply hazy but also **colourless** seeing; it is more or less like a colourless and out-of-focus photograph.

In accommodative seeing, blurring occurs in the central gaze and includes the spatial planes on which the eyes are not focused. This we do not see through the peripheral parts of the retina but through its centre, i.e. through the nerve endings capable of receiving colour sensations. We see in colour, but blurring occurs as a result of the merging of the spatial planes that we do not see in focus and clearly. There follows a mutual exchange, and the colours combine. The colour emerging in this way combines all the colours within the accommodative field and is an intermediary of these.

Hence, the particular colour of the accommodative field – close to grey but also containing all the surrounding colours. We have to know how to see this colour in nature, to discover it with the eyes of the scientist and realist. For instance, there were many who attempted to imitate the famous blue of Cézanne, without understanding that it was not a formal, arbitrary "beautiful" colour, but the accommodative colour, seen and studied in nature – the colour in which all the local colours of Provence combined with the colour of the sky. This one colour, characteristic of this particular place alone, was impossible to imitate. It had to be seen where it actually existed. The attempts to apply "Cézanne's blue" in paintings painted in other places, were shallow formalism and cosmopolitism.

The accommodative colour is the resultant of all the surrounding colours – the colour of all refracted reflexes, reflections of the sky and the atmosphere. One has to know how to see it in the real nature before us – to see it with a gaze that can observe and see not only the object to which it is adjusted, but also the space in the accommodative field – the space that surrounds all the objects seen. Physiological seeing is the full realization of visual practice, its only gauge is the reality of our seeing.

Analysing the process of seeing and distinguishing its components, we find:

1. mobile-seeing as the real physiological seeing with which we look at the world;
2. succeeding colours arising through mobile-seeing as a result of photochemical changes in the optic nerve endings;
3. the division of the field of view into concrete-seeing (where the gaze is cast), the peripheral field (which we see with a sidelong gaze), and the field of accommodative seeing (at the centre of the gaze but not at the depth of field in focus);
4. the existence of several vanishing points corresponding to each gaze levelled. Each turn of the gaze marks out its own vanishing point.

In three-dimensional **convergent** perspective, there was a convention of assuming (contrary to the actual process of seeing) that we perceive the world with a single, immobile gaze, fixed in a single direction (the vanishing point). The location of all the lines existing in reality was defined in relation to this single vanishing point and to a single gazing point. But with a change in the direction of the gaze, its vanishing point shifts. The line viewed previously now lies at a different angle in relation to a new direction of the gaze and, as a consequence, the perspectival foreshortening, in which it should be drawn, will be different. It should be represented as receding rapidly into the distance.

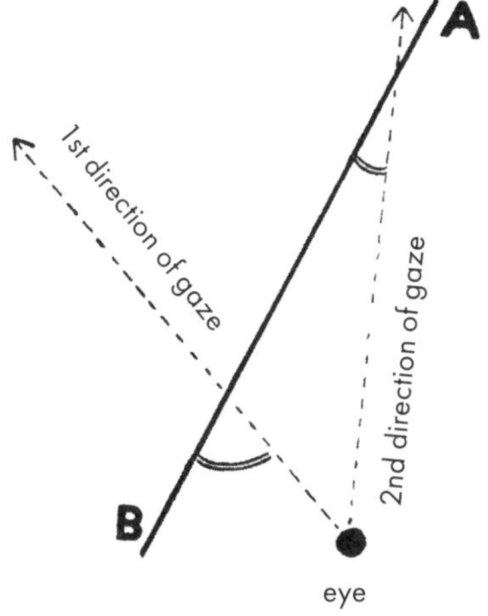

In the second gaze, it is almost perpendicular to the direction of the gaze, and so it would have to be drawn as almost parallel to the person looking.

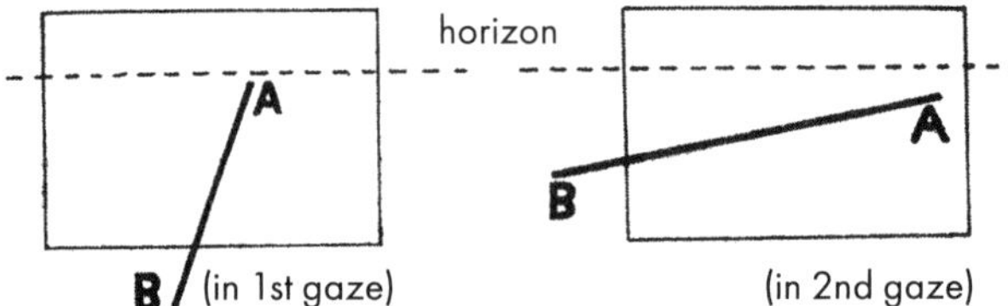

With the change in the direction of the gaze, the angle at which we view the line changes, and this changes its angle of incline in relation to the horizon, changes its position in relation to the direction of sight, and changes its perspectival shortening.

If we look with a mobile gaze, then there is no immobile object and no single stable line. Immobile and stable lines exist only in relation to a **single** gaze, but with the change of the direction of the gaze, all lines wander, shift, change their location and direction.

Let us take an example:

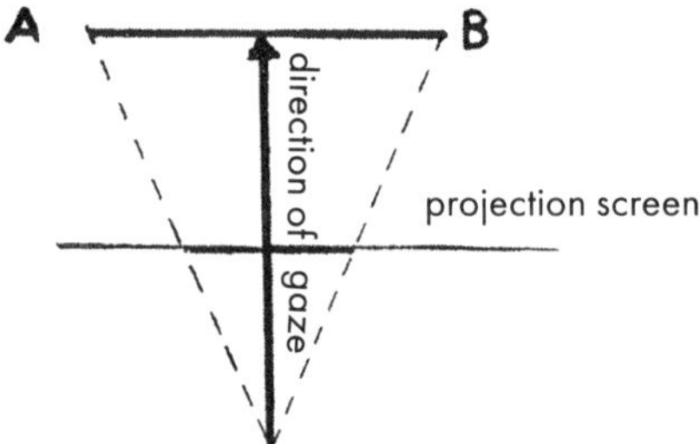

We have a horizontal line AB. We look at its centre. Projected on to the screen of the picture, it would look like this:

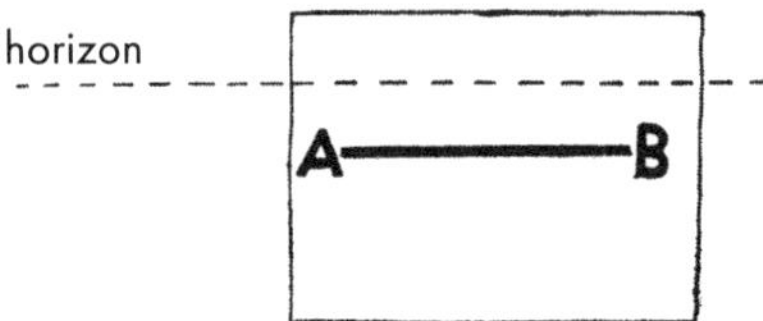

Line AB looks like a horizontal line, parallel to the horizon. Its position is wholly in accordance with principles of three-dimensional **convergent** perspective. A line parallel to us always appears as a horizontal line in the picture. But when our gaze is satisfied with this view and when, in accordance with mobile perspective, we try to see what the line looks like with the gaze levelled at point B, we receive a very different and unexpected view.

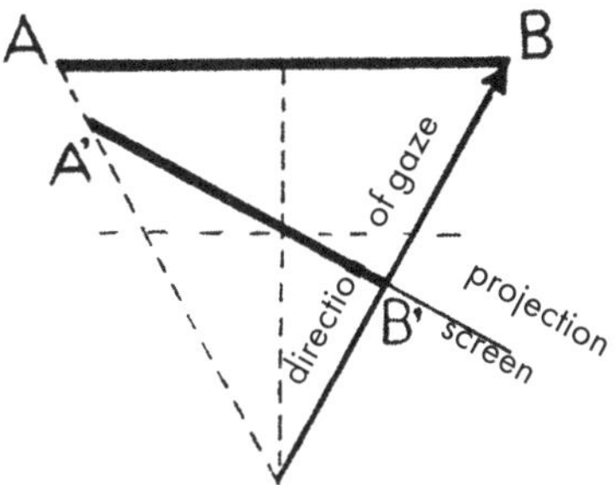

The projection screen (always perpendicular to the direction of the gaze) will be in an oblique position in relation to line AB. In effect, point A lies closer to the projection screen and point B further away. Line AB ceases to be parallel to us. It becomes an oblique line, receding into the distance.

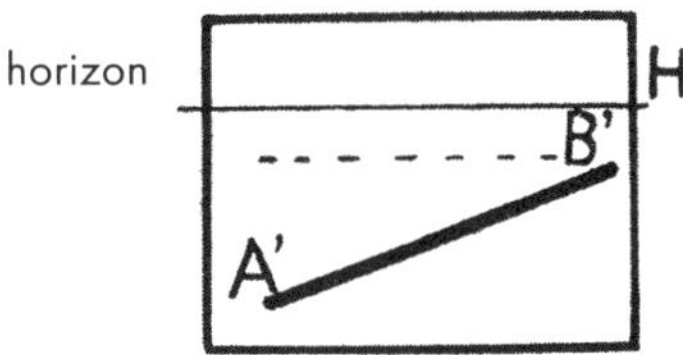

An analogous phenomenon occurs if we level our gaze at point A.

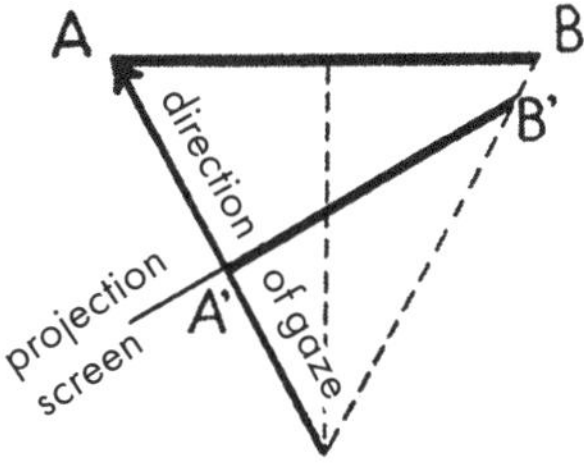

Then the projection screen (perpendicular to the direction of the gaze) passes line AB obliquely. The end of the line on the right finds itself closer to the screen than the one on the left. Line AB, receding from us, will appear in the picture as follows:

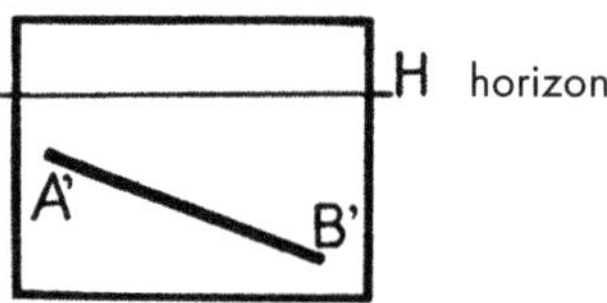

The fundamental truth of three-dimensional **convergent** perspective was the claim that nature (viewed from a single, defined point) always offers the same image, that its image will only change if we change the **observation point**, if our position in relation to it **shifts**. However, as we see in mobile-seeing perspective, nature changes even when we do not change position in relation to it, and we remain in the same point of observation. It changes with the changing **direction** of the gaze. For every gaze, a new configuration of directions, dimensions, and lines arises. Every gaze introduces a new formal situation. The same phenomena occur if we begin to move the gaze in a vertical, rather than a horizontal, direction. The same shifts of lines and changes in proportion occur.

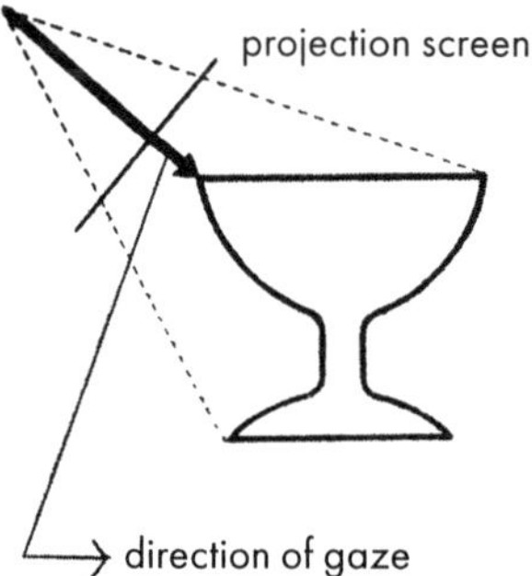

We are looking at the vase with the direction of our gaze focused on its frontal edge. In order to simplify our argumentation, we assume an angle such that the depth of the vase on the projection screen is equal to its height (its angles are equal).

If we direct our gaze at a point above the vase, the projection screen (at right angles to the direction of the gaze) will shift into another position, at a different angle to the vase, and its proportions will alter.

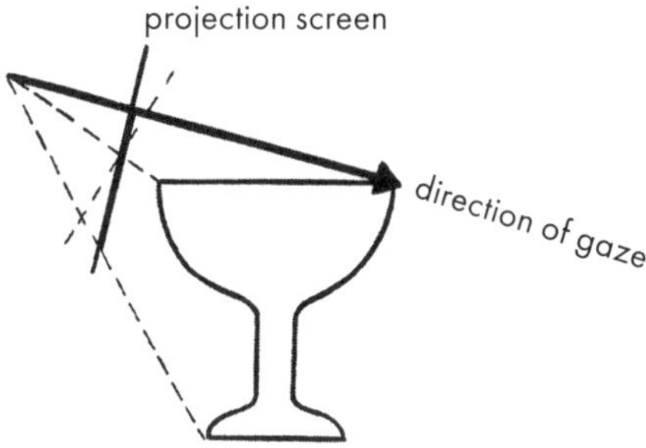

On the projection screen, it will look as though the height of the vase were much greater than its depth. With this altered direction of the gaze, as a result of the change in proportions, the drawing of the vase – as it is projected onto the screen – will look as follows:

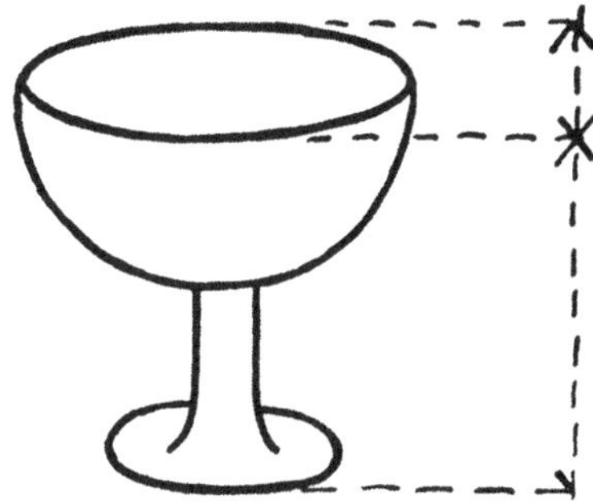

The opening of the vase is less wide and its height is considerably greater, proportionately, than before. If we level our gaze at the point beneath the vase, then we receive yet another account:

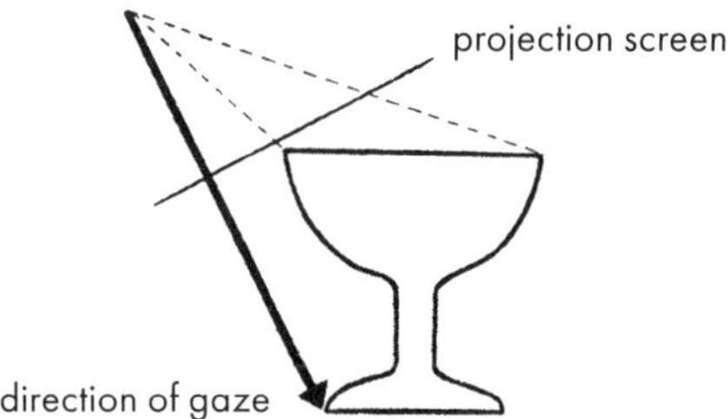

In this account, the projection of the height of the vase is smaller than its depth. As a result, we will obtain the following drawing on the projection screen:

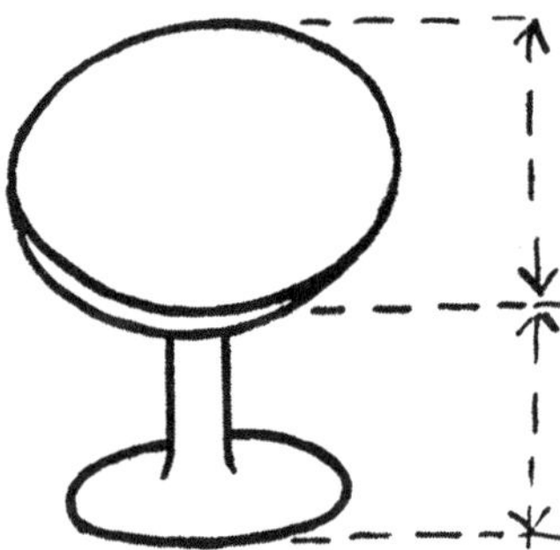

in which the opening of the vase is greater than its height. From the three gazes levelled in different directions, we received as many as three different accounts of the same vase — all equally true and all geometrically verifiable. If the basic thesis of three-dimensional perspective was that from a single point of observation we receive only one image of the object, then the perspective of the mobile gaze, the perspective expressing the reality of the process of seeing nature, results in quite a different thesis: each gaze gives us a different image of the same nature.

The same vase may, for example, appear before us in two images that are both equally true:

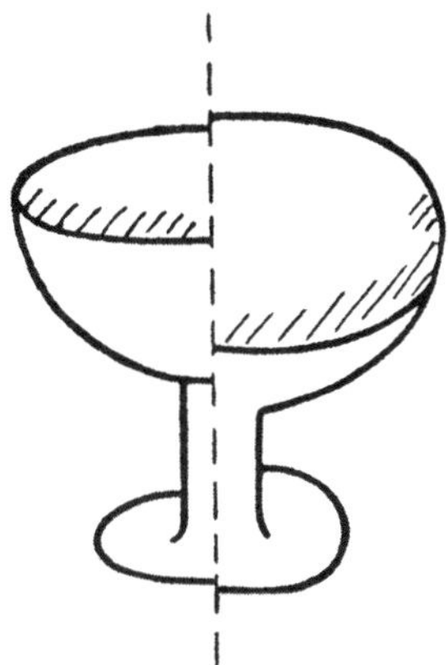

How understandable, in the light of these considerations, Cézanne's observation that "contours escape him" and "all lines shift" becomes! He observed the phenomenon, thanks to the extraordinary sensitivity of his seeing, but could not offer an explanation from the position of the mandatory theory (of three-dimensional **convergent** perspective). He was only able to contradict this apparently infallible theory by way of the truth of his seeing — observing that "contours escape him." And what was an error from the point of view of theory was actually the greatest achievement of his seeing. Thus, if we see in his pictures "deformations" of the following sort:

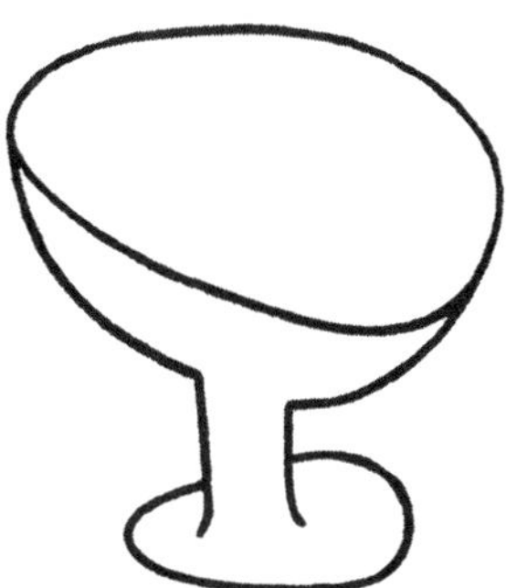

we then have to know that these are no arbitrary "deformations" (distortions of nature) but simply the result of the summing up of two different accounts, deriving from two different gazes levelled in different directions.

These are thus changes, shifts, occurring between two gazes levelled in different directions. To fully grasp the essence of the changes, let us analyse the problem one more time.

The observer's eye is positioned, symmetrically, in front of the cube (the horizontal projection in the drawing). However, in the first instance, the direction of the gaze falls on a protruding front edge of the cube, in the second, on the one on the right, while, in the third, it extends beyond the cube, to the right of it (as a result, the left side of the cube is in the peripheral field of view).

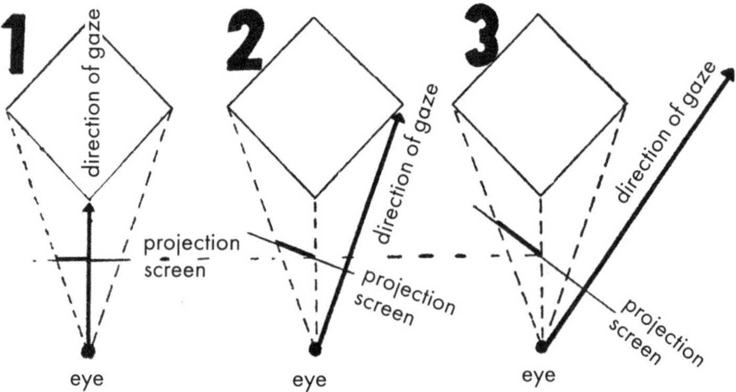

Although the eye of the observer remains in the same place, the cube is no longer the same: in each of the three cases it will be seen differently, in different dimensions and proportions. To confirm this, it is enough to look at the corresponding projection screen (in each case perpendicular to the direction of the gaze) to see how the corresponding views of the cube change. The projection of the face of the cube that lies further away from the direction of the gaze is elongated.

If, on the basis of the projections obtained on the screen, we wish to reconstruct the view of the cube as it would look in each of the gazes, we will find that the further from the direction of the gaze and the nearer the peripheral field, the more the left face of the cube is elongated.

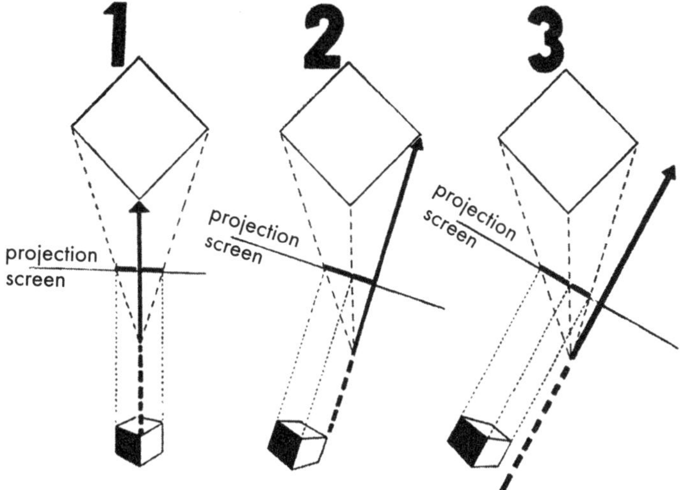

At the same time, however, the position of the cube changes in relation to the eye of the observer. From a symmetrical position (in the first gaze) it becomes increasingly asymmetrical, and the left face of the cube becomes increasingly parallel to the observer. The cube turns around, changing the foreshortening of its perspectival lines. The further we divert our gaze (with the cube thus shifting into peripheral field) the greater and the faster these changes become.

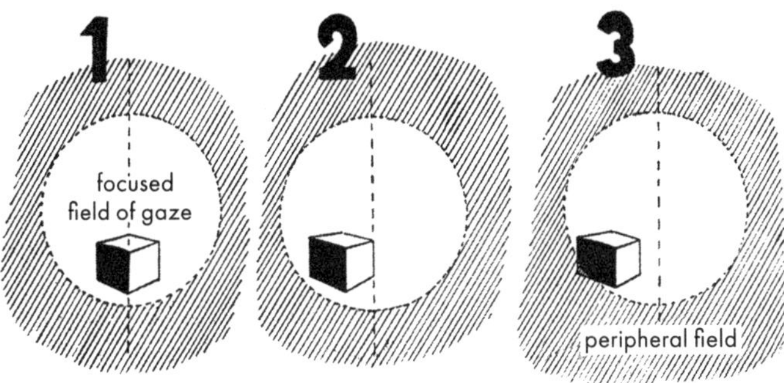

We observe the same shifts in the peripheral field if we replace cubes with cylinders (plane projection).

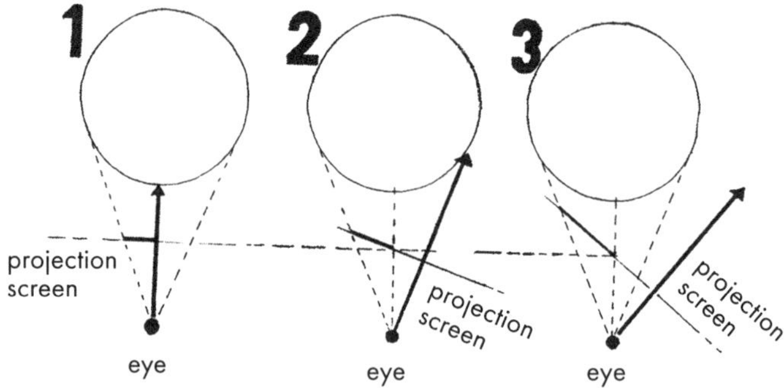

We shift the gaze from the centre of the cylinder (gaze 1) to its right boundary (gaze 2) until the gaze moves beyond the cylinder (gaze 3).

The position of the observer and the size of the cylinder remain unchanged. Despite this, we see a different image in each gaze.

In each successive gaze, the left half of the cylinder is projected in an increasingly elongated form on to the screen. As a result we see it as becoming progressively wider. Its symmetry wavers as the cylinder approaches and enters the peripheral field.

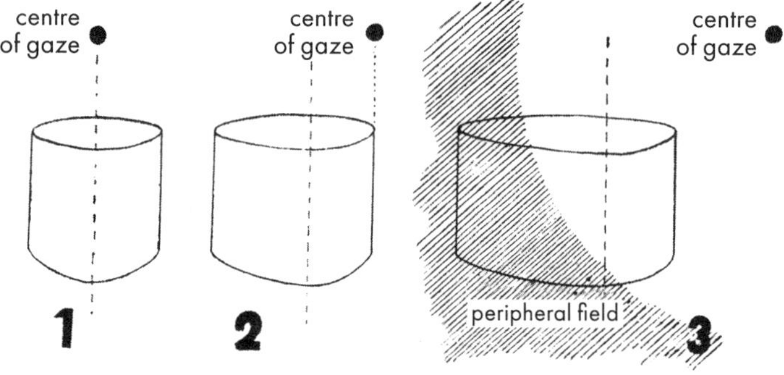

These are thus the phenomena of shifting lines and changing dimensions that occur either on the border of or within the peripheral field.

This is how a new perspective is formed – not the perspective of a single immobile gaze, inferred by reason, but the empirically established perspective of physiological seeing, the seeing that occurs in reality. The basis of this perspective is establishing the mobile nature of our seeing, breaking down the visual process into separate gazes and an analysis of the content of each of these gazes.

We can now state that in comparison with the new physiological perspective, classical three-dimensional **convergent** perspective is limited by its single gaze, which covers only the central field of view. Classical perspective selects, from our physiological perspective as a whole, only those issues relating to a single gaze, and, even then, confines itself to only the central section of the field of view that appears in sharp focus.• Physiological perspective, meanwhile, goes beyond the narrow, conventional limitations of classical perspective. Linear perspective remains binding in the central section of the field of view of each particular gaze, however. We should be aware of this.

The exceptional sensitivity of Cézanne's way of seeing is clearly manifested by the fact that we can explain each of his "deformations" by way of precise geometric diagrams; we can define the points at which his gaze must have been directed in order for the picture to have the divergences of lines that it has.

In each specific case, we have to define:

1. what shifts have occurred in a given object, i.e., what the so-called "deformation" involves;
2. where, at which point, the gaze has to fall in order for it to be possible to see the "deformation" with our practical, empirically verifiable gaze;
3. why the gaze fell upon that particular point and not upon another; what arrested our gaze at this point?

Let us analyse a still-life by Cézanne.

We notice a number of deformations and shifts. Let us analyse these each in turn.

• Hence, for example, the old, nowadays forgotten convention that a picture should be hung in such a way that the spectator be unable to approach it from a distance smaller than twice its longest side, i.e. so as never to be able to view it from an angle greater than 30° — for this is approximately the extent of focus of eyesight. This and similar "rules" prove that classical perspective seeks to limit the fullness of our true seeing by way of convention.

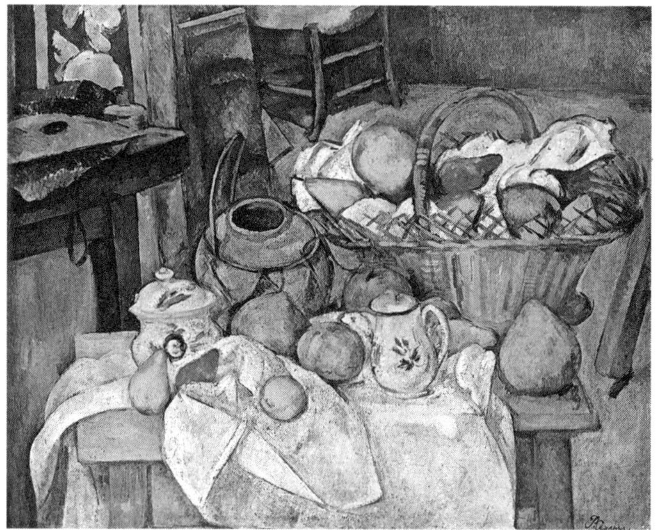

212
Cézanne,
The Kitchen Table,
nineteenth c.

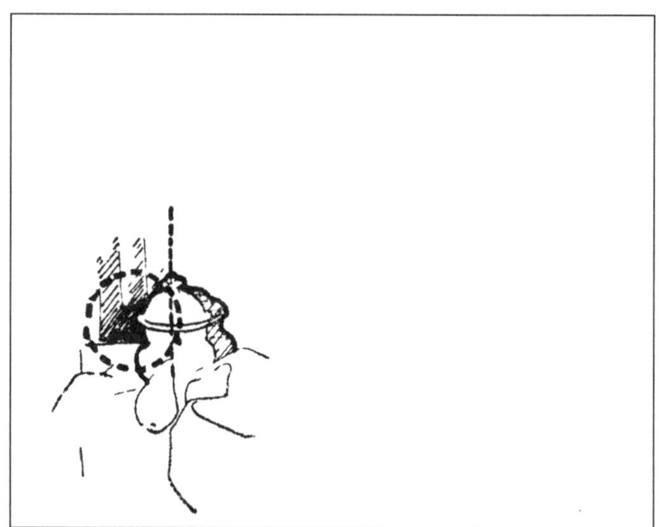

The first "deformation" consists in the fact that the jug has not been drawn symmetrically, and that its right side is wider than its left as a result of the hatched area in the diagram.

We will then see that this is a case of the optical enlargement of that part of the round object that lies in the peripheral field that we have discussed above (as represented in the drawing above). The right side of the jug appears larger to the viewer because it is in the peripheral field. The gaze must therefore have fallen on the left side of the jug, elongating the right side, and pushing it to the peripheries. But why did the gaze settle there and not elsewhere? What was it that made this inevitable?

Looking at the space to the left of the jug, we see that it has the greatest intensity of both linear and light-and-shade contrasts. It was the presence of these visual stimuli that attracted and arrested our gaze. In the centre of the field of view (the dotted circumference), we find the meeting point of table, jug, and background. As we look at nature, our gaze involuntarily comes to rest where visual stimuli attract it. This is why it inevitably fell where it was attracted by the strongest contrasts, i.e., in the place marked in the diagram, and not somewhere else.

Shifts in its contours occurred because the right side of the jug found itself in the peripheral field. Hence, these are not just arbitrary and subjective "deformations," but real shifts in the peripheral field that can be observed empirically (if one's seeing is sufficiently sensitive and developed) and mathematically proven (by way of diagrams and calculation).

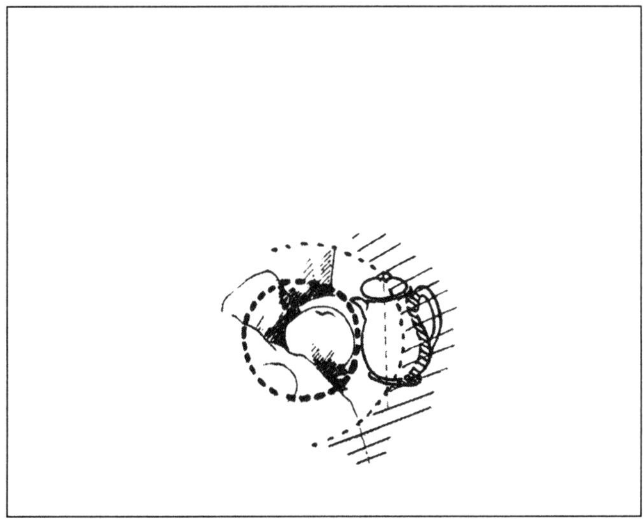

The same reasons explain the second deformation.

The gaze has been arrested in the vicinity of the apple, because this is where there are the greatest variety of forms and intensity of contrasts (linear, light and shade, and colour). As a result, the right side of the jug finds itself in the peripheral field (hatched) and becomes subject to elongation.

The same shift has occurred in the third "deformation."

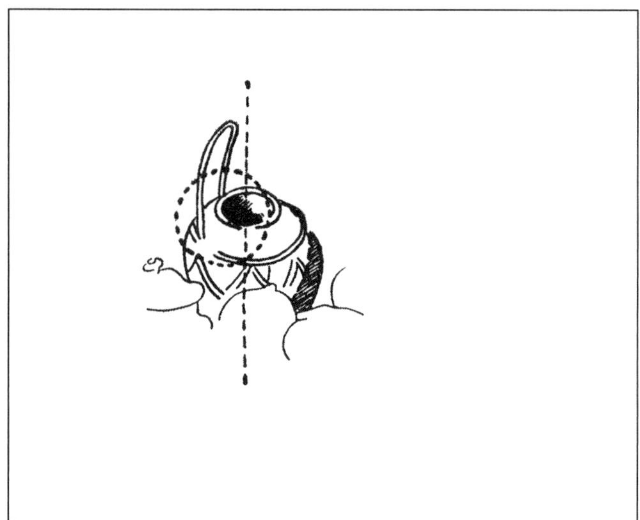

The centre of the gaze was to be found at the left edge of the opening of the pot, the point marked by the greatest intensity of contrasts. This is where there is the greatest contrast between light and shade (the brightness of the external surface of the pot and the darkness of the inside) and between lines (the straight line of the handle and the roundness of the opening). Our gaze does not settle accidentally at undefined and unforeseen points but is subject to the forces of attraction that the stimuli of the surrounding world exert upon our eyes. This is why the gaze fell precisely where it found the strongest stimuli and nowhere else.

The right side of the pot thus found itself in the peripheral field and was enlarged by the amount of the area shown in hatching.

In this case, too, we are concerned with the empirically and mathematically verifiable shifting of contours in the peripheral field, rather than with an arbitrary and subjective "deformation." Any accusation of subjectivism or deformation of nature can only be explained in terms of the ignorance and mental sloth of the person pronouncing it.

The shift of the contour in the peripheral field that we see in the drawing below takes a more complicated form:

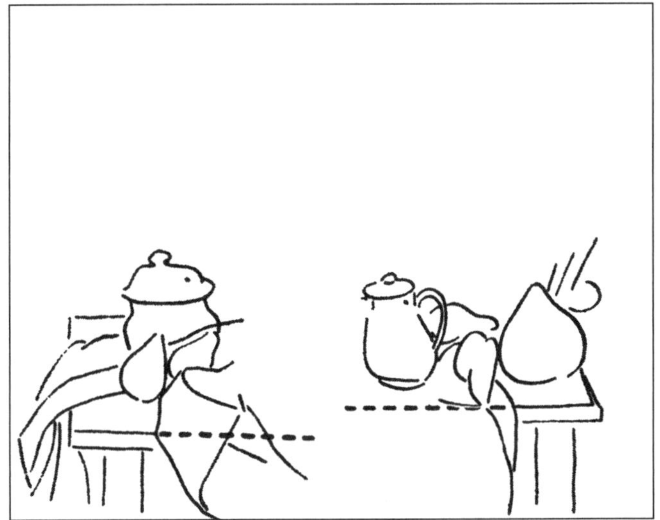

Here the line of the table edge is broken. Its right side lies higher than the left. The same edge appears in two separate parts — in two lines displaced in relation to one another, rather than as a single continuous line. Can this displacement be explained in terms of our seeing? What were the forces directing our eyesight that could have caused this sort of displacement in our practical, physiological seeing?

Let us consider the gazes though which we see this edge. On the right side, our gaze will not settle on the edge itself but will come to rest higher, on the strong contrasts of light and shade among the fruits. We will not be looking at the edge (which we will see in sidelong vision) but at the fruit. This is where the centre of our gaze will fall.

On the left side, our gaze will settle slightly below the edge, attracted by the play of light and shade.

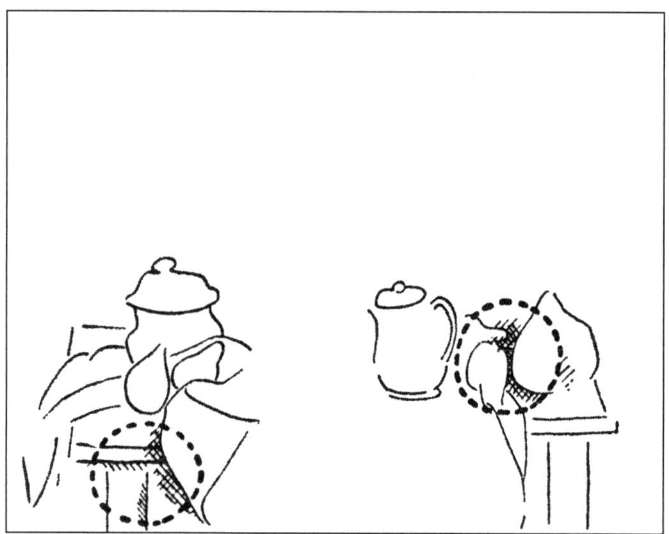

We thus have a model example: those of our gazes that are levelled at the edge are deflected. One falls above the edge, the other below.

Classical perspective did not take these phenomena into account. Only objects existed, in isolation from the person seeing, detached from the visual process. How the object was drawn was determined by distance (the degree of diminution) and the angle of inclination (foreshortening). It was entirely irrelevant how a living, seeing person perceived what he looked at and in what direction he levelled his gazes. Classical perspective was unable to grasp this. Such things were unattainable at this stage in its development. Provided that the position of the spectator in relation to the object remained unchanged, it was assumed that the appearance of the object remained the same.

But let us test this more closely. Does the appearance of the object remain the same in practice if we maintain the same distance and the same position in relation to the object? If all the other factors remain constant, does the direction of the cast gaze not influence the appearance of the object in practice?

The drawing shows two gazes levelled at the table from the same position and from the same distance. One gaze falls upon the table legs, the other passes above the front edge of the table and falls upon the table top.

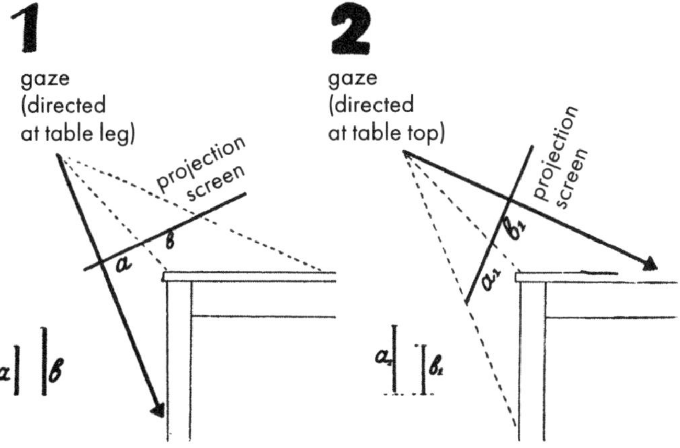

We see in the diagram how the view of the table changes. In the first gaze the view of the table top (b) is greater than the view of its legs (a). In the second gaze, it is the other way round, the view of the legs (a_1) is greater than the view of the top (b_1).

The same thing occurs in Cézanne's picture. In the gaze on the right, levelled at the table top, the view of the table legs is enlarged. In the gaze on the left it is the view of the table top that is enlarged.

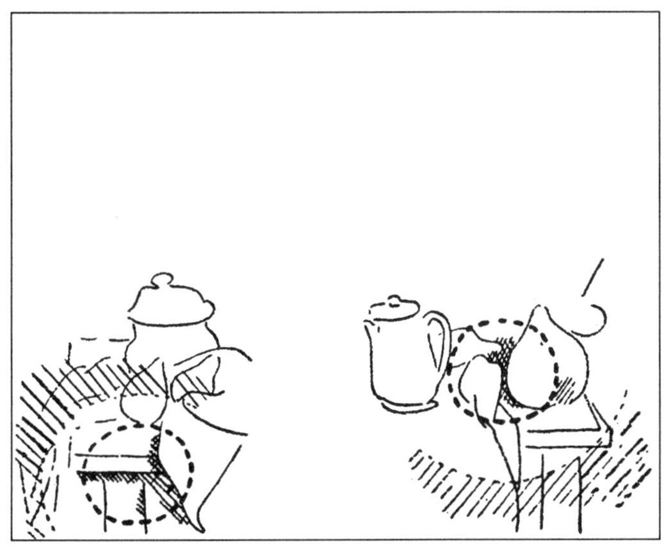

Proportions and dimensions do not depend solely on the position and distance of the object, but also on the direction of gazes with which we view nature. Physiological perspective is more precise than classical perspective. It makes it possible to define not only the size of the object and its distance but also its position in relation to the gazes by way of which we are looking at it.

If it may seem at times too arbitrary and too subjective for the same object in the same place to change its dimensions depending on where we direct our gaze, then let us recall that Plato considered it arbitrary that the same object should have different dimensions depending on its distance. For him objects only existed "in themselves." He therefore thought that since they did not change "in themselves," they should always be drawn the same — the same size, at all distances.

But the aim of perspective is to express all the circumstances of our seeing. The more fully we express these circumstances — the more perfect the perspective.

Thus:

1. not only the absolute size of the object but also its distance;
2. not only the distance of the object but also its position, the angle of inclination at which we are viewing it (foreshortening);
3. not only the specific position of the object in relation to us but also the definition of the gaze with which we look.

In other words — a perspective capable of expressing the practical and physiological course of the process by means of which we look at nature.

How abysmally naïve are those painters with blunt eyesight, who have never observed these phenomena in nature — painters with lazy eyesight, who have never gone beyond the memorised rules of three-dimensional **convergent** perspective imposed upon them, have never observed with fresh eyes that the "infallible" mathematics of this perspective is only a conventional lie when compared with the practical, physiological reality of our seeing — those formalist painters, for whom Cézanne's "deformation" is only a matter of style, deformation (for the sake of form) of what appears as truth to their eyes that see nothing. How easy it is to uncover the falsity of their deformations, not derived from the truth of seeing, but from a "sense of style" and an "inner need of beauty"! It is enough to carry out a geometrical analysis of their deformations to find that the directions of their gazes do not correspond to the painted shifts of the peripheral field. These are the painters for whom three-dimensional **convergent** perspective is their practical truth, who deviate from this perspective solely for formalist and stylistic reasons and not on the basis of the criteria of seeing and observation, who consciously paint untruth and lies in relation to their visual consciousness...

With the perspective of the mobile gaze, we transfer the eyes from one point of nature to the next. Different visual relations occur, partly overlaying one another. Rather than the mechanical, conventional unity of the object, seen with a single fixed gaze, we bring reality down to the process of seeing, such as it is, to physiological activity. The process of seeing consists in a series of gazes and instances of movement (transitions from one gaze to another). The process of our seeing is therefore not continuous, but interrupted — it consists of instances of movement, in which we see nothing, and of gazes, separated from one another by these instances. The fluctuating character of our seeing, the rhythm of pauses following each instance of movement, the mutually altering relations in scale that they produce, are what links pictorial forms with the physiological, material truth of man and his reflexes. The rhythm of the picture is the rhythm of man's reflexes, the rhythm of his psychophysical reactions. It is in this relationship of the rhythm of the work of art to the rhythm of biological, real, psychophysical man, that his humanism lies — the humanism of man that is real, such as he exists, lives, and reacts. Moments of seeing — each of which produces a different account of reality — moments with a different purport, carrying different weight, linked with one another through the irregular rhythm of passing from one gaze to another, moments of movement of different dynamic tension — these are the ultimate schema at which empirical, physiological seeing has arrived.

Rather than the artificial construction of the unity of the object by way of conventional geometric constructions, by way of the conventional, inadequate diagrams of three-dimensional **convergent** perspective, by way of the fictitious, single immobile gaze (with which we never view nature in reality) — the real process of physiological seeing, the reality of mobile-seeing and rhythm, directed by the changing speed of psycho-physical reactions: such is the path to liberation from the mechanistic materialism of objects ruling over man and the transition to humanist realism, defined by the act of the existence of living, acting, reacting, material man, in the mobile, constantly changing, material world of nature. The foundation of this system is changing rhythm, based on the changeability of psychophysical reflexes. It is no longer the object and the commodity, opposed to man, that is the measure of things, but man himself – his muscles, nerves, his psychophysiological system, the real organism of real man.

But the material base of rhythmic phenomena is not contained solely in the eye, in its retina. Rhythm, operating in moments of seeing, as well as in moments of **not seeing** (pauses, passing from one viewpoint to another, the fluctuation from one field of view to another) is produced in those pathways where visual sensations reach our consciousness – through chains of nerve cells, stretching from the retinal nerves to the cerebral cortex.

It is in this way that most rhythmicisation of visual sensations occurs. Man responds to external matter with his whole being, his whole body. The reception and transmission of sensations do not occur in the immaterial world of ideas but in the world of really existing matter and through matter. And man also is matter.

When we speak of receiving sensations, we have to define which parts of the human organism participate in this and what functions take place within these as a result. We will then understand that the transfer of visual sensations from the eye to the brain is not an empty category of abstract logic, nor some reception "in general," but a concrete activity of the nerve chains that stretch from the eye to the cerebral cortex – and that nature in its entirety, as we see it, is also formed under the influence of the processes occurring in these chains.

The nature of this process cannot be explained if treated solely in the abstract categories of logic. On the contrary – this is to tear it from its material base, to blur its concreteness, to take it out of the world of matter, which can be investigated and verified, and to cast it out into the world of "general ideas" and logical "pure concepts."

The victory of the bourgeoisie over feudalism was, among other things, the victory of the superior, empirical, scientific method over the scholastic logical-deductive method. Deploying the logical-deductive method, we can draw conclusions from known, observed facts, but we cannot observe, discover a single new fact that is unknown to us. It is only the empirical method, focused on observation, investigation of nature, discovering **new** facts (and not on reasoning through facts that are known already) that opens up such possibilities. Thanks to this new method, the bourgeoisie as a class was also to achieve its historically determined, scientific materialism and to accelerate the development of the forces of production.

If, therefore, we encounter reflections of the logical-deductive sort, which deploy abstract and universalised concepts, if we hear, for example, that the only truly objective model of seeing nature is one that consists solely in what originates from external objects (i.e., such seeing that is not "deformed" by the participation of man's material, seeing eye), we must be aware that this supposedly logical objectivism of **concepts** is being used to conceal the departure from empirical materialism and the transition to a position of idealist deductive logic.

This supposed objectivism of seeing objects as they are "in themselves," independent of man's visual apparatus, is, in practice, a detachment of seeing from the material base by means of which we see the world. It reduces the **activity** of seeing, which can be investigated, defined, and verified — to the status of a disconnected concept, to an abstraction, to which we assign independent existence. We deprive the processes that occur in **matter** of their material purport, we conceive of these processes as a static and constant idea rather than as processes of material change. The apparent objectivism is, in practice, a scholastic return to idealist logic.

The highest achievement of the bourgeoisie, empirical materialism, should not be opposed with a comparatively backward logical idealism but should be opposed with **dialectical** materialism.

Impressionism should be criticized not from the position of scholastic "entities in themselves," but from the position of historical materialism, defining the historically determined class limitations of the cognition accessible to the bourgeoisie, defining the inadequacy of the empirical method, that cognitive tool of the bourgeoisie, defining the historically determined limits of **bourgeois materialism** — the summit achieved by this class in the course of its development.

Full **physiological seeing** marks the historically determined limit of Impressionism, developed on the basis of the empirical method. This seeing encompassed the whole range of visual sensations, derived from the material nature of the human organism. The historical superiority of the materialist cognition of the bourgeoisie (and thus of its visual consciousness) in relation to the idealist-scholastic systems of the preceding era, is precisely the result of its being based on material, **individual** man. All natural systems took as their point of departure the single, natural, "true" man, empirically verifiable, scientifically investigable, and statistically measurable. The bourgeoisie opposed the idealist, scholastic, feudal conception of man with its materialist understanding of man and was victorious because of the superiority of this understanding. It was a materialism of natural systems, observing "natural," physiological, **individual** man, standing outside the framework of history and society, formed by the everyday practice of the bourgeoisie — a materialism that was limited by class but nevertheless progressive compared to feudal scholasticism. We should acknowledge its relative progressiveness (compared to feudal scholasticism) and its relative truth. We should also be aware of the reasons for the superiority of the physiological understanding of man in relation to idealist understanding.

When speaking of sensations, the idealist will stop short at naming them. The empirical materialist, however, will define the material basis upon which these sensations developed (within the human organism) and as a result of which of the functions of external matter they could have emerged. His definition of sensations will include both elements derived from external matter as well those derived from the matter of the human organism. The idealist's definition will remain purely verbal and incapable of linking these sensations either with external matter or with the matter of man himself (i.e., with his body). All that will be left for him will be to claim that sensations cannot be objectively verified.

Speaking of the **reception** of sensations, the idealist will treat these as though they occur in an immaterial void. He will speak of the true, objective, untainted transmission of sensations into the state of consciousness. The empirical materialist, however, will examine which of the effects of external matter have reached the receptive centres of the nervous system, what reactions have resulted from these effects, by which routes these reactions reached the brain, and what activities influenced them in the process. When we realise that sensations travel along strictly defined, material, pathways of reception, and that while on these pathways they are subject to the effects of the material components of the transmitting apparatus, then we understand the basis of the error of the idealists when they speak of a transmission of sensations untainted (by matter).

In practice, sensations do not travel from the eye to the brain by way of some immaterial void. The nervous system is their conductor. They travel through chains of nerve cells in the form of weak electrical currents from the eye to the brain. Nerves run throughout the organism and are susceptible to all its influences. Visual sensations cannot be separated from the influence of the whole range of physiological phenomena occurring in the organism. These phenomena exert an influence (by way of the brain and perhaps directly) on the sensations transmitted, connecting with them to form a whole. The **rhythmic vibrations** that fill our organism **rhythmicise our visual content**.

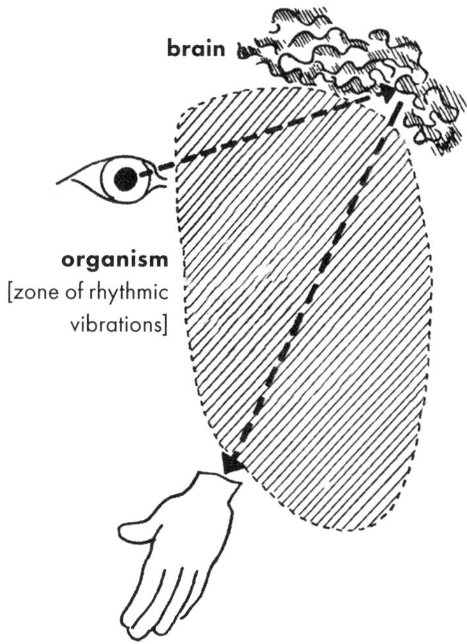

On the path from the eye to the cerebral cortex, visual content is subjected to rhythmic vibrations, to rhythmicisation. (But along with this rhythmicisation of the spectator's visual content, there is a second, additional rhythmicisation within the artist. Motion impulses in the nerves leading from his brain to the hand become subject to further rhythmicisation. It is not only visual sensations themselves that are subjected by the process of further rhythmicisation, but also the means by which they are reproduced, the movements of the artist's hand).

There are two kinds of rhythmic vibration:

1. **mechanical vibrations,** the effect of overcoming the force of weight and the resistance of the organism – the pulse, breathing, body movements dependent on the length of its mobile parts;
2. **bioelectric vibrations,** associated with the functioning of the nervous apparatus and occurring in the form of very weak, alternating, interrupted electrical currents.[24]

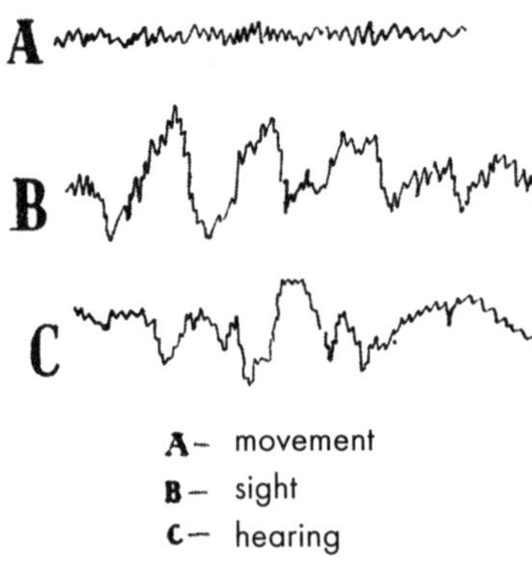

ELECTRO-BIOLOGICAL CURRENTS WITHIN CENTRES OF THE CEREBRAL CORTEX: B.M. Tepłow, „Psychology"

These vibrations are not separate for us. They participate as necessary components in all our sensations, as there are mutual connections among all the individual vertical strands at all levels of the nervous system, especially in the cerebral cortex.[25]

24 Source of diagram: B.M. Tiepłow, *Psychologia*, transl. M. Żebrowska; illustration reproduced from the Russian edition (Warszawa 1950), p. 28, fragment of fig. 7, "Diagram of active electrical currents from different places of the cerebral cortex: A – motion, B – sight, C – hearing."

25 Strzemiński's drawing is based on fig. 2, "Schemat warunkowania na zasadzie teorii zamkniętych łańcuchów neuronów" [Diagram of conditioning on the principle of the theory of closed chains of neurons], p. 223 in J. Konorski, "Podstawy fizjologiczne pamięci [The physiological basis of memory]," *Myśl Współczesna* [Contemporary Thought] no. 5 (1948) pp. 215–232.
It is possible that Strzemiński was referring to the paper given by Konorski on 10 February 1948 at the seminar of the Instytut Biologii Doświadczalnej im. M. Nenckiego [the Nencki Institute of Experimental Biology] in Łódź.

SCHEMA OF THE INTER CELL CONNECTIONS OF THE NERVOUS SYSTEM:
J. Konorski, "The Physiological Basis of Memory"

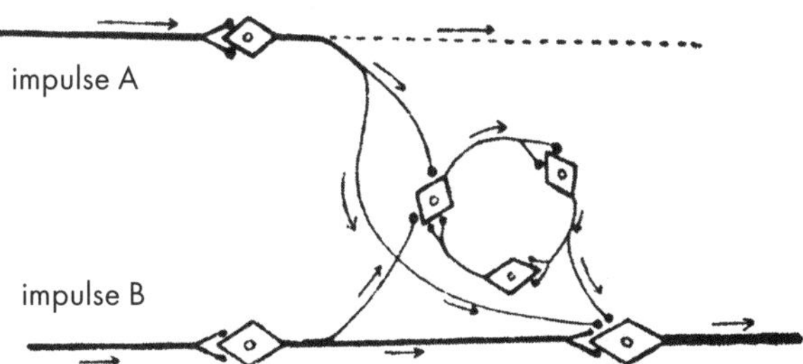

Our visual consciousness is permeated by the components of rhythmic vibrations produced by the rhythmicisation process as a result of the connection of diverse impulses (constituting the basis of conditional reflexes, among other things).

However, we should not universalise these matters. The rhythmicisation of visual content has always existed, determined by anatomical construction. The anatomical basis from which rhythmic phenomena derive are the existence of internal rhythms within the organism, the transmission of impulses from one vertical strand of nerves to another, and the multiple networks of connections among particular centres in the brain.

Though we may not be aware of it, we always see rhythmically. The rhythmicisation of seeing only reaches our consciousness — becomes an aspect of visual consciousness — in certain specific conditions.•

• This explains, for example, the heightened sensitivity of a textile worker testing the quality of manufactured textiles. He does not look at every weave or check every thread but looks at the whole as a rhythm and notices every deviation from it. The same tuning of the rhythm of the body and external matter occurs in the labour process of a metal worker (especially in accelerated precision work), when the attention is focused on a small number of repeated components, and the body rhythm ensures the precision of work only when it is in unity with the resistance of external matter. The average white-collar worker, for instance, never focuses on a small number of repeated elements in his work — his work is spread over a large number of various components. That is why his existence, his practice, does not produce in him the awareness of rhythm. For him it remains "unreal" and subjective.

Rhythmicisation phenomena can usually be observed in those cases where there is a great similarity between the objects being viewed – it is possible to transfer the attention from the objects themselves to the manner in which they are received when there are no unforeseen shapes that might startle the eye. The conditions that enable this sort of merging of the observer with viewed nature, which play a significant role in many processes of production, ought to exist within viewed nature itself.

Let us analyse these problems by way of a concrete painting by Van Gogh.

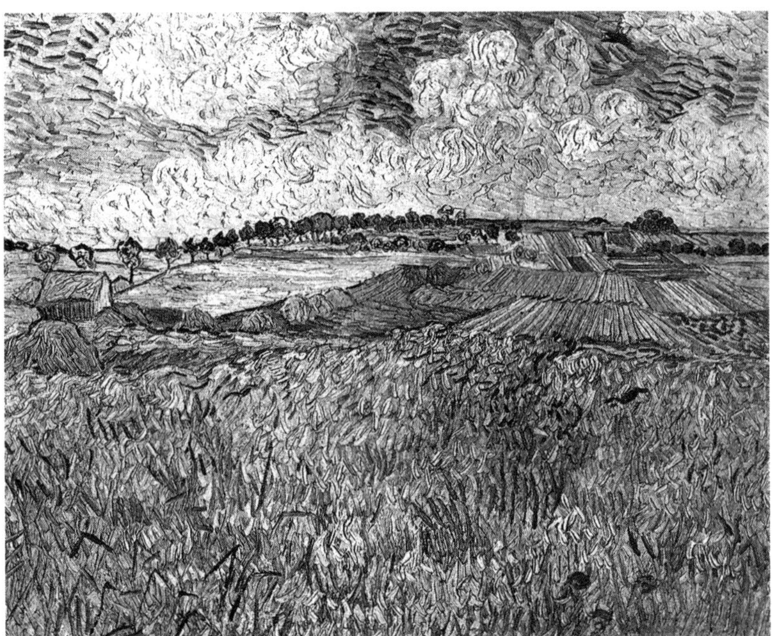

213
Van Gogh,
Wheat Field at Auvers,
nineteenth c.

We see four parallel rows of objects (clouds, trees, haystacks, the border between field and meadow). In each of these rows, there is a significant similarity between the objects comprising the rows (in addition to the differences that exist).

Seeing these rows is subjected to the effects of inner rhythms. Rhythmic rows are created out of the similar rows.

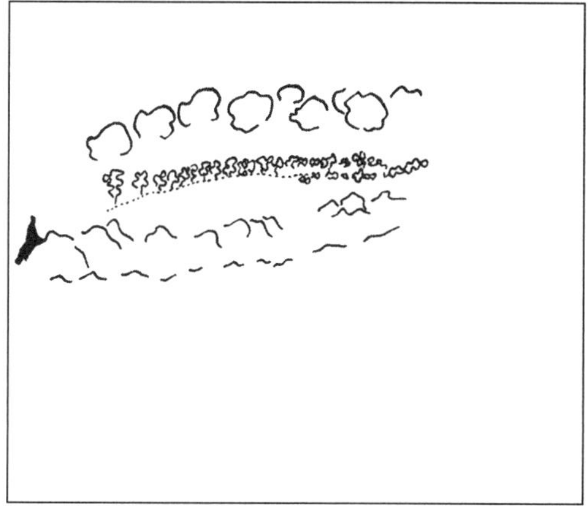

Transferring the gaze from one row to the next, we simultaneously transfer its afterimage, with its already rhythmicised components – overlaying it on each newly viewed row, intensifying its rhythm. Interactions, associations, and interrelations arise among the four rows.

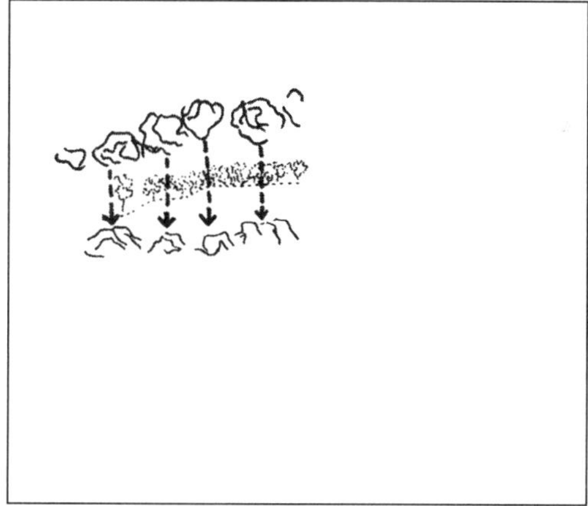

Instead of similar rows, we see four mutually rhythmicised rows, mutually intensifying and increasing their rhythmicisation. The distinctness of the image of individual objects disappears and blurs – instead of these, their rhythmic resemblance appears. Man's rhythms become part of nature. If it is impossible (in physiology) to consider an organism without at the same time considering the environment in which it lives, if the environment should be included in the scientific definition of an organism – then equally, the visual definition of the seen world should be included in the visual definition of man seeing this world. The world exists, but we would not see it without eyes. **Man who sees** is required in order to see the world.

The ease with which it could be perceived as a result of the similarities of the rows being considered was a necessary condition for the development and observation of rhythmicisation. The repetition existing within each of the rows was the necessary condition thanks to which the process of rhythmicisation could be observed.

Thanks to the rhythmicisation, the merging biological rhythms with the image of the seen world, we feel the presence of living, pulsating, breathing, and reacting man in the world being looked at. Not Wittgensteinian scholastically isolated "atomic facts," but the connectivity and interdependency of the whole material of the world – living, material man included.

Speaking of the reception of visual sensations, we could of course express these as pure logical categories. Then they would be sensations in general, sensations in the abstract, something similar to Wittgensteinian "atomic facts," the simplest entities, indivisible and independent of one another. But it is impossible to deduce, by any logical means, that successive sensations are able to influence one another. So long as we remain in the sphere of sensations defined as logical categories, detached from their material base, there is nothing to show that these sensations could influence, transform, or change their content in the process of their reception by our organism. Pure categories of thought, logically inferred, remain alien to one another.

Things look different when we reduce these sensations to their material basis, when we consider them as processes occurring in our receiving apparatus.

Looking once again at the same reproduction of the painting by Van Gogh, we see that all four rhythmic rows are interrupted in one and the same place. This occurs as a result of the intrusion (from below) of the very dynamically striated segment of the field (almost like a vector).

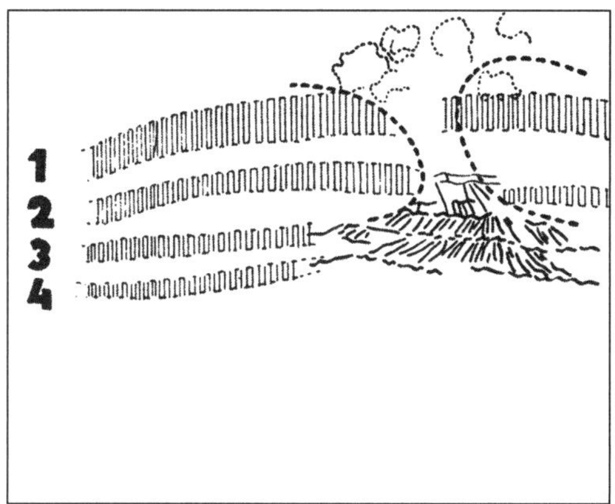

The third and fourth rows are interrupted, in the second a void appears, while the first has shifted upwards — as if by way of a mechanical blow.

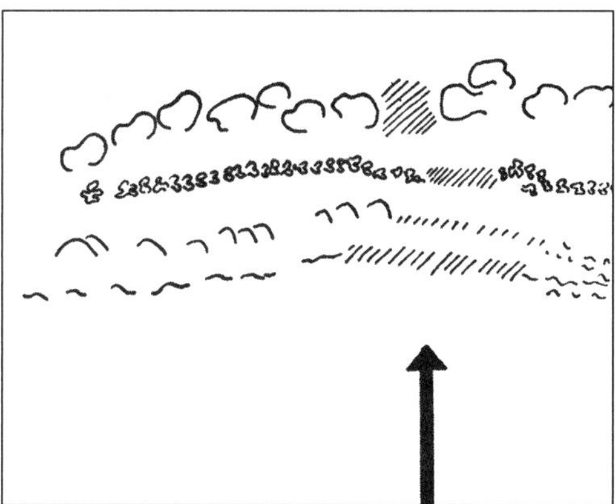

The four rhythmic rows of impulses have been interrupted as a result of the appearance of a new, unexpected, opposing impulse.

The closer the row lies in relation to the field of impact of the impulse, the greater the interruption of its continuity. This is why, for instance, rows 4, 3, and 2 have been completely interrupted, while in row 1, only the clouds have shifted upwards.

After an impulse ceases, the rhythmic rows gradually reconstitute themselves (as we can see on the right).

The schema is thus similar to a schema known in physiology to describe the interruption of a series of reflexes (conditioned and unconditioned) by the unexpected effects of a new stimulus.

The conditioned reflex is the lasting association of two series of impulses, not logically connected to one another, but nevertheless occurring at the same time (e.g. the ringing of a bell and the feeding of a dog). The anatomical foundation of this association is in the structural changes that occur in the nervous system, in chains of neurons (nerve cells).

A conditioned reflex occurs when a stimulus that evokes an innate reaction of the organism is accompanied by another, indifferent, stimulus, and the first of the stimuli initiates a reaction associated with the other stimulus. We can infer from this fact that a functional connection has appeared between the centres of the two stimuli which did not originally exist between them, through the influence of repeated simultaneous stimulation (micro-changes producing a lasting, **anatomical** connection between the nerve cells of one centre and another may have occurred in the nervous system).

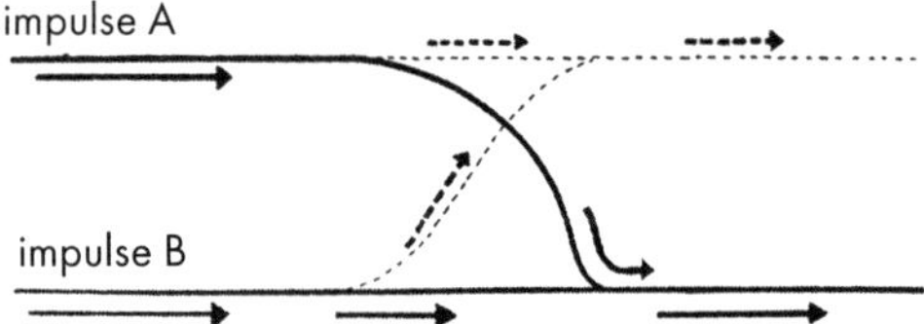

All memorising, or learning, is, in effect, none other than the continuation of the growth processes in the youngest species of pathway in the nervous system, which is the cerebral cortex.

The more groups through which the associations of distant stimuli progresses are formed, the more intense the conditioned reflexes become.

If we compare this schema with the drawing, we see a far-reaching degree of similarity. The differences between the rhythmic rows (on the left side) in Van Gogh's painting are greater and diminish, moving to the right, with the increase in visual associations between the rows. This speaks of the speed of Van Gogh's visual processes. He formed lasting associative connections in the time it took him to observe (and to paint) nature.

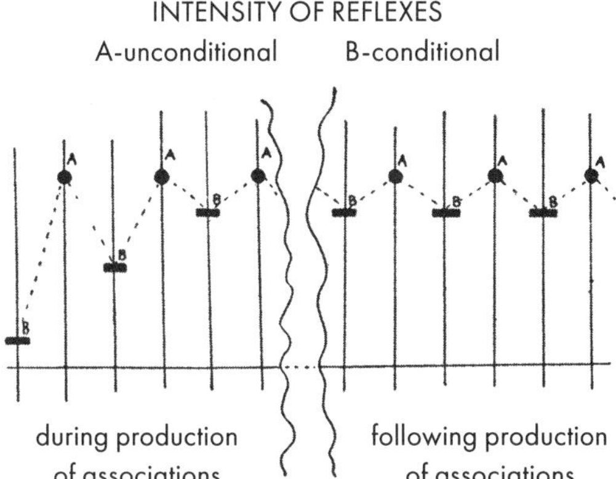

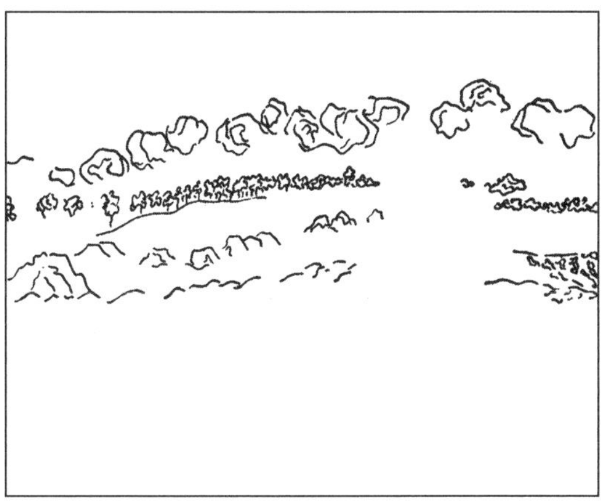

Does this mean that nature, seen by Van Gogh, was rhythmicised and convergent? No. Nature is inexhaustible and possesses an innumerable quantity of visual components. But Van Gogh's seeing of it was in accordance with the physiology of visual reception, resulting from the anatomical construction of the human receiving apparatus. Man sees with the human, material eye and transmits his sensations through his material nervous system, which forms part of the human organism. Awareness of the existence of this organism, its inclusion in the sphere of visual consciousness is the accomplishment of the Impressionists.

But we also know from physiology that the occurrence of a strongly acting, unexpected stimulus interrupts the functioning of the conditioned reflexes acquired.•

The particularly favourable conditions presented by nature (the appearance of four repeated rows), enabled Van Gogh to observe rhythmic associations. The rhythmicisation appeared more clearly than in any of his other paintings.

It was thanks to far-reaching rhythmicisation that it was possible to observe the interfering factor – interrupting the rhythmic rows (not only where they were actually interrupted but in the entire sequence of all four rows).

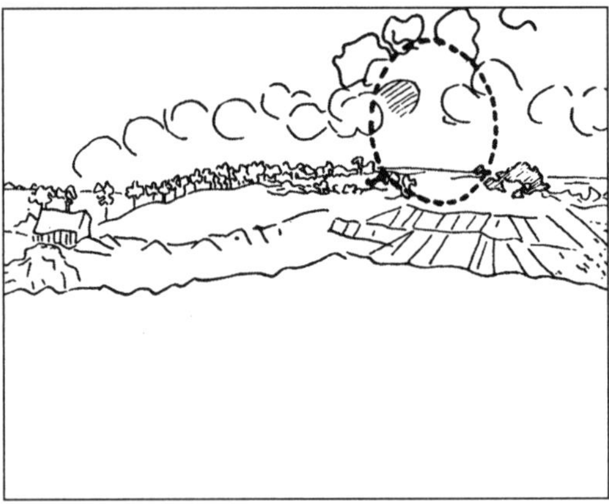

Does that mean that the clouds rose to omit the place where the interfering factor was occurring? No. At the time that Van Gogh was painting his picture, the clouds were moving, not standing still. Many clouds passed by. Some passed higher, some lower. But Van Gogh's eyes, subject to the laws of the physiological reception of sensations, rose and saw the clouds that were passing higher each time they encountered an obstacle.

• E.g. the dogs used in Pavlov's experiments lost most of their conditioned reflexes as a result of the trauma which they experienced during a flood.

E.g. a conditioned reflex (after the ringing of a bell before feeding) fades away if the dog experiences a shock (e.g. electric shock or a wave of air). The reflex returns slowly, after a few repetitions – the dog "remembers" the reflex.

And this is Van Gogh's realism – the realism of living, material man, who sees not in the abstract but through the living, material organism of his physiological body. Not a spiritual, but a physiological reception of sensations.

●

It was only while writing this chapter that I found myself able to position correctly most of the works I produced in the 1930s and 1940s. The idealist and formalist criteria prevailing in inter-war theories of art had made their correct positioning impossible in relation to other phenomena.

Most theoreticians' and artists' thinking assumes the existence of one, **unchanging**, true realism of seeing the world (placed by them somewhere on the cusp of the fifteenth and sixteenth centuries) i.e., corresponding to the transition from a logically constructed solid form to the empiricism of chiaroscuro, as well as the existence of different degrees of departure from this realism: **deformation** (deforming the image of the world) and **abstraction** (a complete non-seeing of the world). Departure from realism was considered to be to the artist's credit.

The fundamental error of this thinking was detaching art (its realism) from the development of the forces of production that determined it – from the historical process. As I have tried to show in this work, the realism of visual consciousness increases over the course of history – and in the course of almost all history the **results** of this development are appropriated by successive ruling social classes and used to express a purport that consolidates their rule. One has to distinguish between what is connected with the development of the forces of production (and develops in a continuous way) and what is superstructure, which is a tool of the class struggle (and develops in leaps and bounds, by way of dialectical negation).

Absolutising **one** model of realism as the true realism was the result of the underdevelopment of the model of seeing of the theoreticians (and most of the artists) whose visual consciousness corresponded to this realism. Instead of working on their inadequate visual consciousness, instead of deepening their realism and widening the scope of the components determining it, they stopped short at an easy, arbitrary

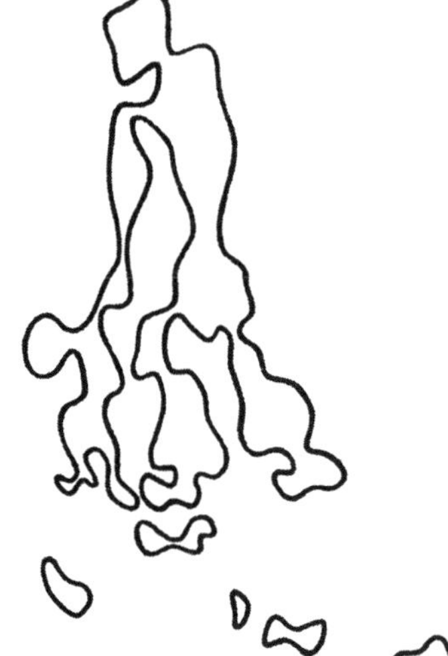

214
Strzemiński,
series: *Deportations*,
twentieth c.

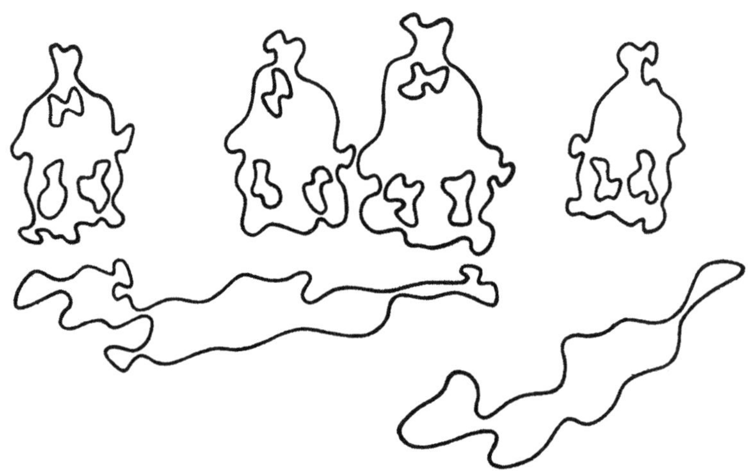

215
Strzemiński,
series: *West Belorussia*,
twentieth c.

"deformation" or "abstraction." The powerlessness of art theorists, incapable of perceiving the **development** of visual consciousness, of noticing the new **realistic** components of seeing that existed in what followed on from the sixteenth century, was in striking contradiction to the practice of the most outstanding artists of the period, who, as we have seen, significantly expanded the limits of the realistic understanding of reality. The realist practice of a few outstanding artists stood in contradiction to the idealist and formalist theory of art prevailing in capitalist society. Theory hindered art and led many artists astray or left them underdeveloped. The art theory created by the capitalist society of the first half of the twentieth century was a reliable and effectively functioning obstacle to the development of art.

However, the small number of theoreticians who tried to deploy the Marxist method associated all manifestations of visual art as a whole directly with the superstructure, not discerning those of its components that, being connected with the development of the forces of production, were subject to the law of gradual accumulation and evolution. They concluded from their thinking that one could cast aside entire periods of history, since there was nothing in them besides the functioning of class. Rather than separating what was connected with the base from what constituted part of the superstructure, rather than separating the historically determined process of the growth of realistic visual consciousness from the (equally historical) process of its application by the superstructure — they consolidated a false perspective in the evaluation of artistic facts, accepting some periods as wholly progressive and rejecting others as entirely backward, and not understanding that one can only treat in this way a superstructure constructed by an alien, antagonistic class. In practice, this position relativised history, depriving it of opportunities for development, and consolidated the same "true," sixteenth-century realism, as propagated by bourgeois art theory.

When I set about making these works (most of which were burned by the Hitlerites during the Occupation) I subjectively experienced them as being realist and empirical, demanding a far greater degree of observation than paintings considered realist.

But I was weighed down by the bias that "realism" is sixteenth century. I was also weighed down by false theories that every departure from this "realism" is a departure towards deformation and abstraction.

From these theories it transpired that anything demanding considerable attention and concentrated and thorough observation was a "deformation," anything resulting from superficial observation was realism.

Only once I began to examine the very purport of the concept of realism did I find that this realism was not always the same, that there was a process of the development of realist-seeing in history, that it is the quantity of observations that determines the model of realism, and that this quantity grows over the course of history. This is how I came to understand that realism is historically determined and historically limited.

Nevertheless, I could not accurately position these works of mine along the line of the development of art. The same formalist bias of theoreticians, that every successive art movement departs ever further from realism — even if this realism was understood to mean the relative, historical realism of the sixteenth century — still weighed down on me. I did not assess them on the basis of their level of visual consciousness but, despite everything, by the degree of their departure from commodity realism.

Only by examining the visual base, by defining the components of visual consciousness, was I able to position them accurately: these are works based on the empirical method, and their aim is to incorporate into visual consciousness the effects of internal physiological rhythms. Thus, this is impressionism (physiological seeing) that differs from historical Impressionism (such as it formed in history) by way of the fact that it allows for a new component of visual consciousness (physiological rhythm, which Impressionism had not usually allowed for). Historical Impressionism developed problems related to the visual content of **gazes** themselves as cast. The **reception** of these gazes, however — the way in which our organism reacts, receives these gazes — generally remained outside the scope of the Impressionists' interests, despite being a component of the physiological process of seeing.

●

impressionist seeing

[First published in *Odrodzenie*, no. 25, 22 June 1947, pp. 4–5]

The same also applies to three-dimensional linear perspective, held in such high regard. Like previous perspectives, it is a creation that is limited to the scope of its time and bears within it the germs of its own decay and conquest. It is in no way an absolute formula for "linear-painterly laws" that enable us to paint space in accordance with the essence of our seeing. The image of nature constructed by linear perspective is a false image.

It is a construction that makes it possible to calculate the dimensions of any shape in relation to its distance and to define the position of any line in its perspectival foreshortening. It would seem that a drawing executed in this way is wholly in accordance with the way we see nature. That this perspective is an absolute perspective, based on immutable mathematical calculations.

But this is not so. Linear perspective accords with geometry, but not with the physiology of our seeing. At the time of its founding, too little was known about the physiology of human seeing. Hence its fundamental error.

The conventional assumption is that the gaze is immobile. Man stands before nature and looks at it with an immobile, lengthy gaze, fixed straight ahead at a single immobile point on the horizon (the vanishing point) and with this single, long, immobile gaze takes in nature as a whole together with all its details. He takes in nature as a whole with one lengthy, immobile gaze.

This is not so. The human eye never sees the **whole** of nature in the course of a single gaze.

1. We never see two spatial planes at a different distance at the same time. We have to adjust our eye especially to each distance. Then we see very sharply and concretely at the given distance: anything closer or further away loses its material structure, dissolving into some sort of neutral spatial mass, defined by colour rather than by any measurable, concrete, three-dimensional phenomenon. (The same can be observed in photographs when using a more precise lens.) And this is where the first falsehood of "normal" perspective appears. Being logically inferred and justified by the "rules" of geometry, it worked on the basis that human eyesight is the passive receiver of everything projected onto its screen by the nature being seen. Whereas our seeing perceives nature in an entirely different way. We see nature in a skipping around way, by way of many gazes, moving into depth and returning to nearer planes. We see nature by shifting, stopping only on the spatial planes that attract our attention, whilst overlooking others. This active character of our seeing is also expressed in the act of selection, as everything essential for our seeing (lying on different spatial planes) is eliminated by our gaze, grasping it for the time being as inessential background — a neutral, undefined area of colour, saturated with space. Every gaze is changeable: an object that, just a moment ago, had been a precisely defined convex solid form becomes part of the undefined background (when looked at from a different spatial plane). Solid forms emerge from the spatial background plane and then merge with it again, and from the sum of these gazes, each with such different content, there arises a complex image of nature, completely unlike the one offered by three-dimensional linear perspective. Not one gaze, but an overlaying of many gazes. Not the passive continuity of one immobile gaze, but skipping around and selective seeing. Not the same definition of all the shapes of nature as three-dimensional solid forms, but the constant variability of the visual content of our every gaze. We can see the same object as a solid form (if we focus our gaze on it). We see the same object as a plane (following its contour line with our eyes). And we cannot see this same object at all if we merge it into the background, focusing our gaze on seeing a different distance.

These are basic visual phenomena. Had art historians wished to admonish painters on the correct representation of space in the picture, they ought first to have familiarised themselves with the essence of our seeing, with the principles governing our seeing, to have asked professionals (such as ophthalmologists, for example), checked whether the canons of "normal" perspective they so praised were in accordance with our seeing – in short: they ought to have properly **grounded** their claims.

2. At the time when three-dimensional linear perspective was being formulated, nothing was known about the reaction of the optical nerves to colour. It was not known that, after gazing for a considerable time at an object, the optical nerves cease to react to its colour. Any student at the academy knows this on the basis of practice, when painting *en plein air* he has tried to capture some colour and the longer he has gazed at it, the more it has lost its original qualities and has become a hard colour, devoid of hue. Colour escaped, vanished. The overtired optical nerves ceased to react.

It is no accident that the period of the greatest flourishing of "normal" perspective saw the greatest withering of colour. Instead of colour, there is only chiaroscuro, slightly tinted. This was the natural consequence of the principle of "a single, immobile" seeing being the basic postulate of so-called "normal" perspective. The proposal of an infallible (because purely mechanical) perspective, and of the way of seeing that it imposed, evidently found its way into the everyday practice of painters, imposing upon them an immobile gaze, fixed upon a perspectival vanishing point. Such was the result of the corset of the immobile gaze, so contrary to the physiological reality of our seeing.

Only mobile seeing, when the image is formed from the overlaying of many gazes, brings with it a renaissance of colour. Every student at the academy knows that he can only capture a colour once he has satisfied his eyesight by seeing other colours and captured the given colour afresh, before it vanishes. That the new seeing of colour is connected to seeing nature by way of multiple gazes, thus with a different type of perspective other than three-dimensional perspective – a perspective whose new component is **time**, determining the overlaying of gazes one upon another, and thus a **space-time**, which is a four-dimensional perspective.

Bonnard's subtlety was not due to an arbitrary desire to paint "with subtlety," while his predecessors (for unknown reasons) did not wish to paint "colour accords, linked in an original and studied way," but due to the fact that capturing colours afresh is a natural consequence of mobile, multiple-gaze seeing. This different model of colour is inseparably connected to the new model of perspective, just as chiaroscuro paintings (whose spatial quality as a whole is exhausted by a scale of passages from dark to light passages, making them very easy to reproduce in black-and-white print) were the inevitable consequence of linear perspective.

The spatial quality of the perspective resulting from the mobile gaze (and Impressionism marks the beginnings of this perspective) is represented by way of a specific colour saturation and a specific quality of colour rather than by way of convex chiaroscuro. To show a black-and-white print of a painting whose spatial quality is determined by the quality of colour rather than by the quality of the dark-light passages, is like positioning a person listening to an orchestra behind a wall of glass and asking him to evaluate the quality of the music on the basis of the musicians' movements, or to guess the melody from the singers' open mouths.

There is thus a fundamental difference between the results achieved by an immobile gaze (defined by three-dimensional linear perspective) and those produced by a mobile, space-time gaze. In the first case, we are given the artificial unity of an **object's** shape, in the second, the **unity of the process of seeing** and the overlaying of contradictory accounts, defining the object in a variety of ways. The unity of the form of the seen object springs from the conventional assumption that we can embrace the entire space before us with a single gaze and see it all, in all its parts, with the same accuracy. The truth of the object has been placed above the truth of real human seeing, because the essential incentives, in this case, were objects — dehumanized things, rather than human matters. Man's significance had, in the same way, been limited within the systems of production, exchange, and consumption in capitalist societies. Man had been demoted to playing the part of the provider of commodities and the profit these commodities could yield for the entrepreneur. A dehumanized system and a dehumanized object were placed above the reality of human seeing and human nature, thanks to conventional assumptions.

Thus the problem does not come down to an opposition between realism and a less faithful painting — a painting in which formalist and aesthetic assumptions deform the hitherto accurate copying of nature. In reality, what we have is an opposition of two realisms. The first is a realism founded on the fiction of a single gaze and the limitation of the visual content associated with it: a realism of incomplete seeing, by way of which we achieve a unified view of the object. The second realism is a realism resulting from the fullness of visual content. In this case, we achieve the realism of the visual process — a multi-faceted, complex, and deeply human phenomenon, rather than the realism of the things and commodities before us.

This process of seeing conveys many contradictory accounts. Each gaze introduces definitions of form that are different from those contained in the previous gaze. A chaos of contradictory, overlaid gazes and contradictory accounts of form emerges for the seeker of the unity of an object (if he has visual sensitivity). In place of the lost unity of the object, he sees only insurmountable complications. The only way out of these is by way of a conscious choice of the form-giving will and a conscious aim towards which one is striving. From the many contradictory definitions, one should choose those that are in line with the intended goal. In this way, painterly seeing frees itself from the imposed, purely conventional canons of three-dimensional linear perspective, from the related demand for an artificial unity of the object — contrary to the essence of our seeing — and makes the transition to a human lyricism, based on real seeing and the will to give form — to lyricism as our reaction to the process of seeing the world. And, at least for the time being, there are no limits to this many-sided and lyrical realism, which is our expression of what we feel and our response to what we see before us. The further development of painting follows the line of an ever-greater enrichment of visual content, an ever-greater contradiction between the received accounts, and the ever-greater significance of the act of conscious choice as man's response to the chaos and contradiction of the seen world. The human unity of the process of seeing and the human unity of lyricism as a response to the seeing of the world. But what can be done if someone does not want to see the subject of eyesight in a painting?

If we want to understand Bonnard's and Matisse's seeing, we have to explain its relationship to reality. It is a seeing that departs both from the seeing typical of the "faded-out" paintings of the seventeenth century and from Monet's smoothly skimming over, colour seeing. Monet's seeing, skimming over, searching for new, brilliant hues, enlivening colour by way of quick transitions from one place to another, did not linger on any one point (the same goes for Pissarro's seeing). This is why the forms of objects are uniformly effaced and we see the image of nature as a sum of colour vibrations. The transition from one place to another (the comparison of colour differences) is so rapid that no contour can be preserved in the eye. There are only the generally marked-out **places** in which objects are to be found — their contours effaced as a result of the overlapping reactions of colours of the object to colours of the background.

Skimming over the surface, this gaze progresses by way of rapid skips (looking closely at colour) of the same speed from one point to another. A rhythm of identical recurring units is created in this way — a rhythm so specifically characteristic of Monet. These equivalent gazes with which he looks at nature, following on one from another — this identical content of the gazes he casts, none longer than any other — are what produce the recurring rhythm of the same units of form. This is why the composition of his pictures consists of the same, recurring divisions, as though inscribed in the uniformly treated and previously divided-up surface of the canvas, uniformly divided into squares and simply filled in with the equivalent meaningful painterly content.

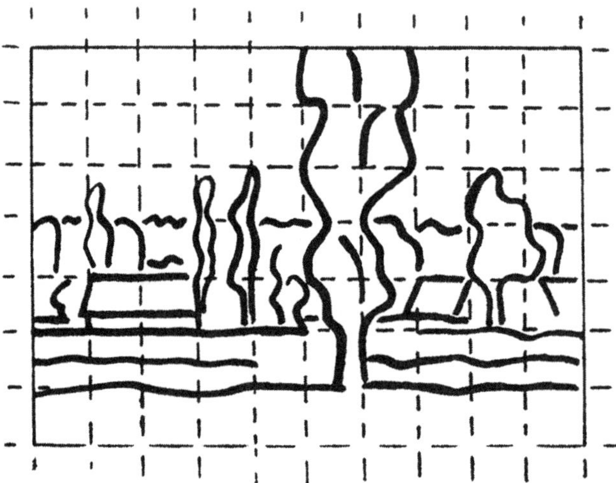

Bonnard's seeing does not skim uniformly over the entire space before him, lending it a uniformly meaningful accent everywhere, but selects specific points lying on different spatial planes. It is thus a seeing that moves into the distance and back again, while simultaneously moving in parallel with the picture plane; settling at any given point on one of the spatial planes, it then moves sideways to another spatial plane, lying closer or further away. This is the origin of the specific properties of his seeing, selecting from nature those points to be looked at and leading from one such point to the next. These points that have been singled out, on which the attention has been focused, are located on different spatial planes, nearer or further away, in different parts of the picture. The spectator's gaze is not left to its own devices, does not wander helplessly all over the breadth and depth of space, but follows the route that the painter had previously marked out when composing the picture.

Thus the questions arise: how do we see space? How are the points interrelated that are singled out by the focus of our attention? The response of painting based on classical perspective was that we embrace the entire space before us with a single gaze, and that we see in a continuous and uniform way without pauses or skipping around. The clarity with which some receding spatial planes appear is defined only by the objective demands of aerial perspective. The further away the spatial plane, the more blurred the shapes of objects, but the passages between them occur in a gradual, imperceptible, and evolutionary manner.

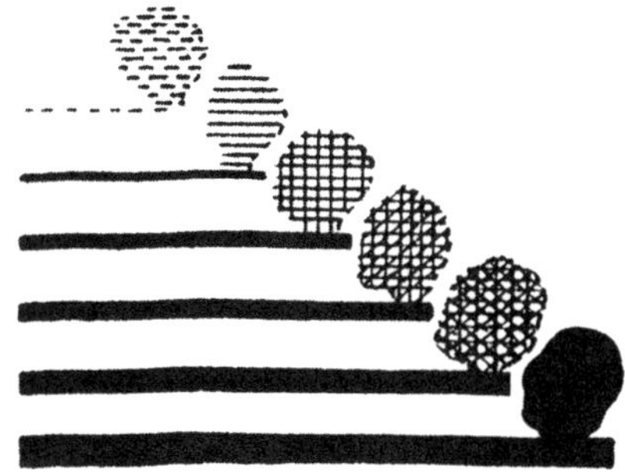

The clarity of the appearance of individual spatial planes diminishes with the increase of their distance.

Impressionist practice contradicts this basic assumption that we are able to embrace space in its entirety with a single gaze. With a single gaze, we see only one specific fragment of space, belonging to a single spatial plane. To pass to another spatial plane, we adjust our gaze to see at that distance, and then we see in sharp focus only at this distance and not at any other. Spatial planes at different distances merge together into a fairly uniform plane of colour, saturated with a space that is the colour of their common denominator. Due to the necessity of adjusting the eyesight to seeing at a specific distance, we cannot see all spatial planes at the same time. We see each spatial plane with a single gaze, skipping around, in a transitional way.

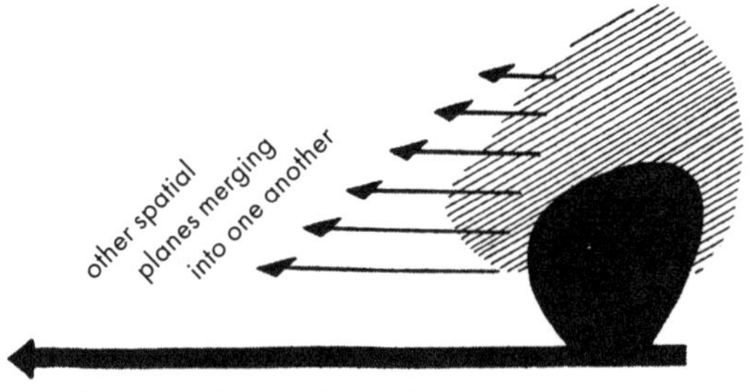

A similar phenomenon occurs if we look at one of the middle spatial planes. The nearer and further planes then merge into a single whole and the middle plane appears clearly.

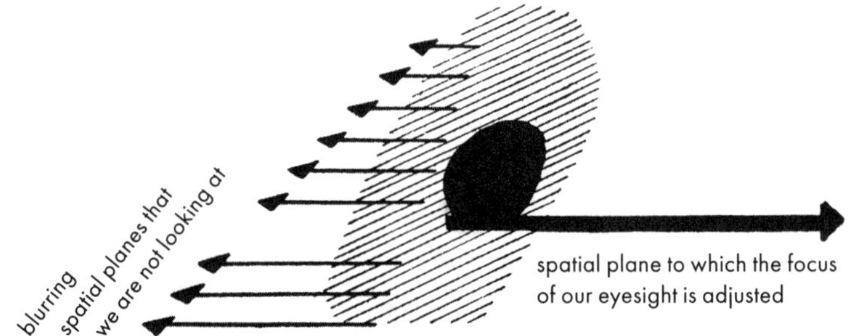

And even if it is the horizon that we are looking at (despite the aerial perspective), it appears clearer than the spatial planes that are nearer and merge into one, because we have not adjusted our eyesight to focus on them.

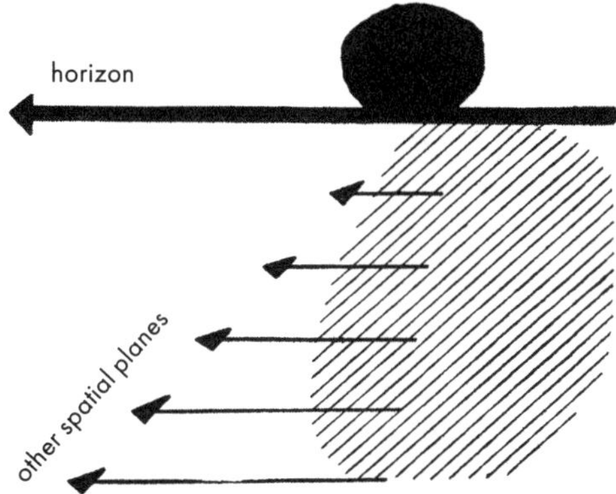

And so the truth of our real, physiological seeing contradicts the logically inferred geometric schemas of three-dimensional linear perspective.

This is why, in Bonnard, whose seeing is not something reasoned out in accordance with the appropriate clauses of perspective but with the reality of physiological processes, we so often see a fragment of the picture against an undifferentiated, almost flat background — the space beyond the object treated like a flat coulisse, positioned vertically. These verticals are typical of Bonnard's paintings and are not the result of his inability to render "normal" spatial qualities, but because the spatial planes lying beyond the field in focus merge into a plane saturated with coloured space. But this same, apparently flat, coulisse appears differently in another part of the picture, becoming a clear and detailed outline of an object, while we now see the coulisse in the spatial plane that was previously in focus. This simply shows that moving the gaze to different parts of the picture has entailed adjusting the gaze to the viewing distance. Thus, a particular spatial plane can become the outline of an object (if we look at it) or a coulisse (if we focus on a different distance), depending on the eye's adjustment. As it moves into the depth of the picture, the gaze pauses at various points, which it sees clearly, and all the other spatial planes, positioned in various parts of the picture in relation to these points, form flat coulisses, saturated with potential space. As a result, the basic principle of convergent perspective — the principle of spatial continuity — falls through. Painterly space is where we see it and is such as we see it. Painterly space is not a function of geometry, but a function of seeing as a physiological process. Bonnard's paintings are not flat, and their spatiality is not the result of their textural facture, achieved by way of tiny spots of colour evoking a specific vibration on the pictorial plane itself, but the result of a general conception of visual space derived from the laws of the physiology of sight. Spatial quality in Bonnard is not the result of technique and its methods but of a general conception of space.

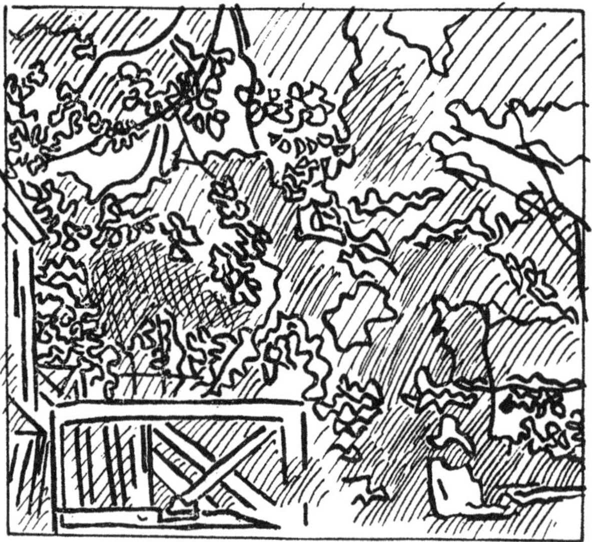

Flatness is always given as a characteristic of Matisse's painting. The objects painted in his pictures are flat in shape and made of colour planes that are clearly distinct at first glance and play with one another in ways that may be significant in aesthetic terms, but do not define the spatial relationships represented. The drawing of the patches is captured in a generalised way, omitting any detail. Two qualities attracted the attention of painters and viewers: the specific, very strong, yet simultaneously toned-down colouring, and the synthetic drawing, enclosing the shape of the picture in a kind of arabesque. Instead of grounding the problem in the only appropriate context – on the grounds of the visual principles determining this kind of seeing – a search for technical methods and prescriptions justifying Matisse's stylistic manner was launched. Formalist criteria were adopted in evaluating Matisse. People whose model of seeing was primitive – for whom the canons of seventeenth-century three-dimensional perspective were an undeniable truth and the most significant of all possible conceptions of visual content – did not notice this degree of realism in his paintings and defined them as non-realist. And since the aesthetic impact of these paintings could not be denied, the conclusion was reached that aesthetic values are created by way of the departure from realism, by way of a formalist observation of the methods used by Matisse to create his aesthetic vision. Instead of realism – formalism; instead of a more profound seeing of nature – its superficial treatment as a "point of departure" to be submitted to a process of stylistic, cosmetic decoration over the course of further painterly work. This was the path to understanding taken by most of Matisse's aestheticizing followers. Painters, for whom seventeenth-century perspective was visual reality, saw Matisse's synthesising form and his marvellous spatial colouring as a departure from visual reality, as an escape into a dreamland. They did not see the flatness of his paintings as overcoming an inferior model of perspective with a superior one, but as a powerless abandonment of the path of acquisitive realism, as an avoidance of an effort that was too demanding. Matisse's painting not as a superior type of realism, but as an abstraction: the wallpaper flatness of his paintings seen as a resignation from a hitherto "correct" spatiality; simplified drawing instead of hitherto perfect drawing – this is how Matisse looked according to the realities of his followers. A painter who was unable to solve the most difficult problems of the previous period and took art back to the level of flat silhouettes.

To avoid this erroneous reasoning, we have to bring the problem down to its visual basis, to the way of seeing that determines and defines Matisse's form, synthetic in shape and colour.

From the point of view of the laws of seventeenth-century perspective, his paintings would have to be defined as entirely non-spatial. As flat paintings. This could be justified both in terms of the lack of relief of the painted objects, as well as in terms of the lack of spatial interrelationships between them, represented by means of this perspective. Assessing their spatial qualities according to the criteria of traditional perspective, we have to consider them as completely flat paintings. And yet, our direct sensations contradict such a definition. Despite the obvious evidence and despite the theory appearing so unshakeable, we sense their spatial quality, we simply cannot define what this consists of.

This flat treatment of objects and the simplified drawing, reducing the painting to some sort of colour arabesque, make it possible to achieve a considerably greater degree of synthesis of form than was possible before, by way of convex shapes and a picture surface shattered by chiaroscuro into a multitude of fragments detached from one another — hence: a painting of visual synthesis.

The question comes down to the following: what sort of seeing makes it possible for us to achieve an optimal visual synthesis?

To view any object, we adjust the gaze to seeing at that distance. We touch the object with our gaze. Such seeing is accurate and complete.

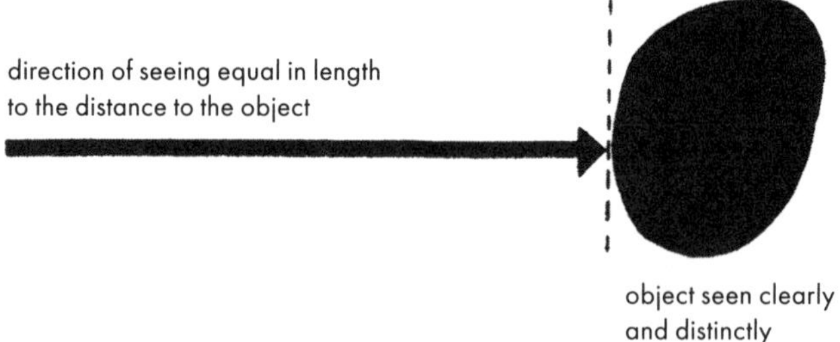

If we stop our gaze a long way in front of the object, then everything that is beyond this looking distance will be merged into one. The outlines of shapes will vanish, partly or wholly (depending on the distance), and their colours will melt into some sort of common hue, forming a colour plane, saturated with space, in which the lightest colour prevails.

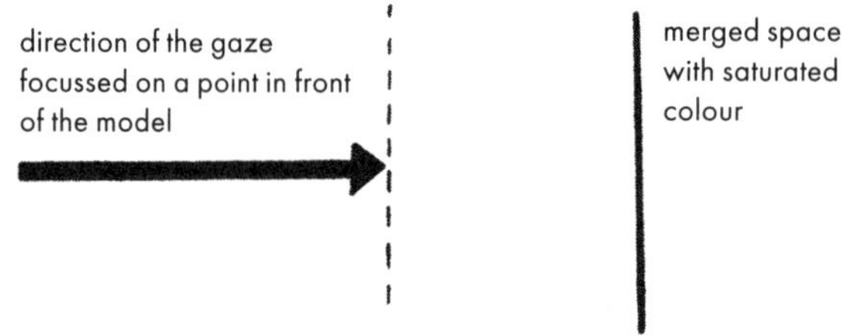

If, however, we adjust our eyesight to a distance not much shorter than the distance to the element of nature being observed, then we see nature in its synthesis. The interfering details of the drawing will disappear — instead of convex shapes we see colour masses of a particular character, resembling a synthetic colour arabesque; local colour will be modified as it absorbs the influence of the adjacent colours.

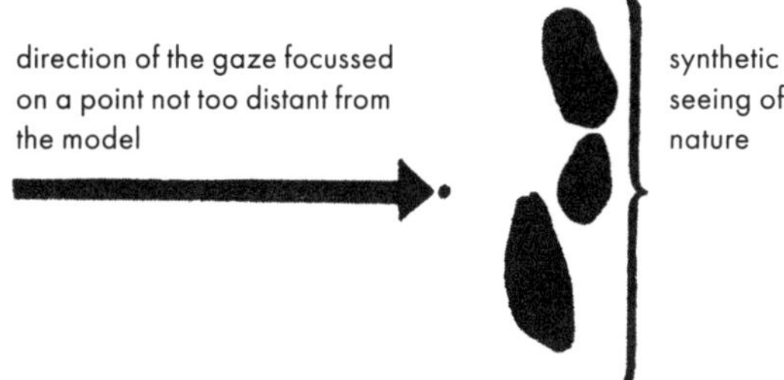

Here, the measure of spatial evaluation is the degree of deviation of colour as compared with the same colour seen "by touch." It is a measure of the evaluation of the space between ourselves, our viewing point, and the different objects in nature. It is space seen without the aid of perspectival diagrams or linear constructions. Space seen directly and expressed by variations of colour.

Matisse's colouring is so hard to copy because, in practice, despite appearances, it serves solely the aim of expressing spatial relationships and the synthetic seeing of nature. This is why someone who understands Matisse "in flat terms" and assesses his colours solely on the basis of its "beautiful" colour arrangements will produce a picture consisting of flat silhouettes lying on a flat picture surface. Its colours may be "beautiful," but they will always remain flat. Herein lies the error of the formalist approach to Matisse. The nature of Matisse's method should be viewed as a method of synthetic seeing.

bibliography

Berkeley, George. *An Essay towards a New Theory of Vision*, 2nd edition. Dublin: Jeremy Pepyat, 1709.

Breton, André. "Le surréalisme et la peinture." *La Révolution surréaliste* 4 (1925).

Bruno, Giordano. *De la causa, principio, et uno* (*Cause, Principle, and Unity*, 1584). Especially "Dialogue Five," pp. 87–101.

Cézanne, Paul. *The Letters of Paul Cézanne*. Trans. and ed. Alex Danchev. Los Angeles: The J. Paul Getty Museum, 2013.

Copleston, Frederick Charles. *From Ockham to Suárez*. Vol. 3, of *A History of Philosophy*. Westminster, Md.: Newman Press, 1950.

Cornforth, Maurice. *Science versus Idealism. An Examination of "Pure Empiricism" and Modern Logic*. London: Lawrence and Wishart, 1946.

Descartes, René. *Discourse on the Method*. Trans. R. Stoothoff. Vol. 1, of *The Philosophical Writings of Descartes*. Cambridge: Cambridge University Press, 1985.

Dilthey, Wilhelm. *Das Verstehen anderer Personen und ihrer Lebensäusserungen*. Berlin: 1910.

Ethics, Demonstrated in Geometrical Order (*Ethica ordine geometrico demonstrata*). First published 1677. Part 2, Proposition 7. Los Angeles: Cavalier Classics, 2015.

Galilei, Galileo. "History and Demonstrations concerning Sunspots and Their Phenomena." In *Discoveries and Opinions of Galileo*, trans. Stillman Drake. New York: Doubleday, 1957.

Galileo Galilei to Johann Kepler, 19 August 1610. In Karl von Gebler, *Galileo Galilei and the Roman Curia*, trans. Jane Sturge. London: C. Kegan Paul & Co., 1879.Gebler, Karl von. *Galileo Galilei and the Roman Curia*. Trans. Jane Sturge. London: C. Kegan Paul & Co., 1879.

Hobbes, Thomas. *Leviathan*. Ed. J.C.A. Gaskin. Oxford: Oxford University Press, 2008.

Kobro, Katarzyna, and Władysław Strzemiński. *Kompozycja przestrzeni. Obliczenia rytmu czasoprzestrzennego*. Łódź: Biblioteka "a.r.", 1931.

Konorski, Jerzy. "Podstawy fizjologiczne pamięci (The Physiological Basis of Memory)." *Myśl Współczesna*, no. 5 (1948), pp. 215–232.

Marx, Karl. "Wage Labour and Capital." *Neue Rheinische Zeitung*, nos. 264–267 and 269 (5–7 and 11 April 1849). Available also: www.marxists.org/archive/marx/works/1847/wage-labour.

Newton, Isaac. *The Mathematical Principles of Natural Philosophy*. Trans. A. Motte. London, 1729.

Pawłow, Iwan [Ivan Pavlov], C. Sherrington, and E. Adrian. *Mózg i jego mechanizm*. Trans. J. Konorski, S. Miller. Warszawa: "Mathesis Polska," 1935.

Plato. *The Republic*. Trans. A.D. Lindsay, London: Everyman's Library, 1992.

Smith, Adam. *An Inquiry into the Nature and Causes of the Wealth of Nations*. London, 1776.

Spinoza, Benedictus de. *The Collected Writings of Spinoza*. 2 vols. Trans. Edwin Curley. Princeton: Princeton University Press, 1985–2016.

Strzemiński, Władysław. "Architektonizm mody." *Architektura i Budownictwo*, nos. 8/9 (1931), pp. 342–343.

Strzemiński, Władysław. "Aspekty rzeczywistości. " *Forma*, no. 5, (1936), pp. 6–13.

Strzemiński, Władysław. "Bilans koncentracji kapitalistycznej." *Wieś*, no. 24 (1948), pp. 6–7.

Strzemiński, Władysław. [Comment on a painting]. *Forma*, no. 3, (1935), p. 17.

Strzemiński, Władysław. "Do Redakcji." *Przegląd Artystyczny*, no. 1 (1948), no.1, p. 12.

Strzemiński, Władysław. Druk funkcjonalny. Łódź: Biblioteka "a.r.", 1935.

Strzemiński, Władysław. [Kaz. Strzemiński, pseud.]. "Dualizm i unizm." *Droga*, no. 6–7 (1927), pp. 211–225.

Strzemiński, Władysław. "Magiczność i postęp." *Gazeta Artystów*, no. 12 (1934), pp. 1–2.

Strzemiński, Władysław. "Malarstwo sowieckie w zwierciadle artykułu p. Chwojnika." *Pion*, no. 12 (1933), p. 10.

Strzemiński, Władysław. "O autorytetach." *Forma*, no. 1 (1933), p. 14.

Strzemiński, Władysław. "O sztuce rosyjskiej. Notatki." *Zwrotnica*, no. 3 (1922), pp. 79–82.

Strzemiński, Władysław. "O sztuce rosyjskiej. Notatki.", *Zwrotnica*, no. 4 (1923), pp. 110–114.

Strzemiński, Władysław. "Rozmowy na wystawie." *Forma*, no. 2 (1934), pp. 1–3.

Strzemiński, Władysław. "Surogaty sztuki." *Budowa*, no. 1 (1936), p. 6.

Strzemiński, Władysław. "Sztuka malarska w Łodzi." *Ilustrowana Republika* (Łódź), 7 March 1932 (no. 67), p. 4.

Strzemiński, Władysław. "Sztuka nowoczesna a szkoły artystyczne." *Droga*, no. 3 (1932), pp. 258–278.

Strzemiński, Władysław. *Teoria widzenia*. Foreword J. Przyboś. Kraków: Wydawnictwo Literackie, 1958.

Strzemiński, Władysław. *Unizm w malarstwie*. Warszawa: Biblioteka Praesensu, 1928.

Strzemiński, Władysław. [Untitled comment about a reproduction of one of his own paintings.] *Forma*, no. 2 (1934), pp. 17–18.

Strzemiński, Władysław. [Untitled comment about a reproduction of his painting *Pejzaż morski* (Seascape).] *Forma*, no. 3 (1935), p. 17.

Strzemiński, Władysław. "Widzenie Greków." *Przegląd Artystyczny*, no. 4/5 (1947), pp. 6–8.

Strzemiński, Władysław [and Stefan Krygier]. "Widzenie impresjonistów (Rozdział książki o malarstwie, mającej się niebawem ukazać w druku." *Odrodzenie*, no. 25 (1947), pp. 4–5. "Widzenie gotyku." *Przegląd Artystyczny*, no. 9/12 (1947), pp. 8–10.

Tatarkiewicz, Władysław. *Filozofia nowożytna do roku 1830*. Vol. 2, of *Historia filozofii*. Warszawa: Czytelnik, 1947.

Tiepłow, Boris Michajłowicz [B.M. Teplov]. *Psychologia*. Trans. M. Żebrowska. Warszawa: Nasza księgarnia, 1950.

Wittgenstein, Ludwig. *Tractatus Logico-Philosophicus*. Trans. D.F. Pears and B. F McGuinness. Introduction Bertrand Russell. Revised edition. London: Routledge & Kegan Paul, 2014.

Wölfflin, Heinrich. *Principles of Art History. The Problem of the Development of Style in the Later Art*. Trans. M.D. Hottinger. London: G. Bell & Sons Ltd, 1932.

illustrations

1. Defending a baby elephant against a panther (detail), engraving on a rock, Ain Safsaf, Southern Algeria, Northern Africa, early Neolithic [redrawn by Strzemiński, Department of Scientific Documentation, Muzeum Sztuki, Łódź].
2. Child's drawing [redrawn by Strzemiński, Department of Documentation, Muzeum Sztuki, Łódź].
3. Lion and horses, detail of an engraving on a rock, Font-de-Gaume, Dordogne (dép.), France, Palaeolithic, Aurignacian culture [redrawn by Strzemiński, Department of Scientific Documentation, Muzeum Sztuki, Łódź].
4. Engraving on the left: Reindeer, Bøla, Norway, Neolithic; engraving on the right: Reindeer, Hell, Norway, Neolithic [redrawn by Strzemiński, Department of Scientific Documentation, Muzeum Sztuki, Łódź].
5. Doe, engraving on a stone, Le Bout du Monde site, Les Eyzies, Dordogne (dép.), France, Palaeolithic, Magdalenian period [redrawn by Strzemiński, Department of Scientific Documentation, Muzeum Sztuki, Łódź].
6. Rhinoceros, engraving on stone, Le Colombier, Ain (dép.), France, Palaeolithic, late Aurignacian period [redrawn by Strzemiński, Department of Scientific Documentation, Muzeum Sztuki, Łódź].
7. Bison, cave painting, Niaux, Ariège (dép.), France, Palaeolithic, Magdalenian period [redrawn by Strzemiński, Department of Scientific Documentation, Muzeum Sztuki, Łódź].
8. Rhinoceros, cave painting, Font-de-Gaume, Dordogne (dép.), France, Palaeolithic, Magdalenian period [redrawn by Strzemiński, Department of Scientific Documentation, Muzeum Sztuki, Łódź].

9. Speared bison, cave painting, Niaux, Ariège (dép.), France, Palaeolithic, Magdalenian period [redrawn by Strzemiński, Department of Scientific Documentation, Muzeum Sztuki, Łódź].

10. Hunted deer, coloured drawing from the Mandan tribe (North American Indians) on a buffalo-leather coat, North America [redrawn by Strzemiński, Department of Scientific Documentation, Muzeum Sztuki, Łódź].

11. Horse's head, engraved bone, St Michel d'Arudy, Pyrénées-Atlantiques (dép.), France, Palaeolithic, Magdalenian period [redrawn by Strzemiński, Department of Scientific Documentation, Muzeum Sztuki, Łódź].

12. Two women, coloured painting from Alpera rock-shelter, Albacete Province, Spain, Paleolithic, late Magdalenian period, Capsian culture [redrawn by Strzemiński, Department of Scientific Documentation, Muzeum Sztuki, Łódź].

13. Duck, engraved bone, Gourdan, Haute-Garonne(dép.), France, Palaeolithic, Magdalenian period [redrawn by Strzemiński, Department of Scientific Documentation, Muzeum Sztuki, Łódź].

14. Mask, Nigeria, Africa [redrawn by Strzemiński, Department of Scientific Documentation, Muzeum Sztuki, Łódź].

15. Wooden sculpture, Marquesas Islands [redrawn by Strzemiński, Department of Scientific Documentation, Muzeum Sztuki, Łódź].

16. Birds on a Greek vase, Greece, ninth – eighth century BCE. [redrawn by Strzemiński, Department of Scientific Documentation, Muzeum Sztuki, Łódź].

17. Wizard, engraved bone, Lourdes, Hautes Pyrénées (dép.), France, Palaeolithic, Magdalenian period [redrawn by Strzemiński, Department of Scientific Documentation, Muzeum Sztuki, Łódź].

18. Wooden dancing mask, Cameroon, Africa [redrawn by Strzemiński, Department of Scientific Documentation, Muzeum Sztuki, Łódź].

19. Dancing mask, Kwakiutl tribe (North American Indians), northwest coast of North America [redrawn by Strzemiński, Department of Scientific Documentation, Muzeum Sztuki, Łódź].

20. Tattoo, Southern Oceania [redrawn by Strzemiński, Department of Scientific Documentation, Muzeum Sztuki, Łódź].

21. Painting from the Navajo tribe (North American Indians), North America [redrawn by Strzemiński, Department of Scientific Documentation, Muzeum Sztuki, Łódź].

22. Stylized figures of animals and humans on a Greek vase, Tiryns, Mycenaean culture, thirteenth century BCE [redrawn by Strzemiński, Department of Scientific Documentation, Muzeum Sztuki, Łódź].

23. Wooden dancing mask from the Haida tribe (North American Indians), northwest coast of North America [redrawn by Strzemiński, Department of Scientific Documentation, Muzeum Sztuki, Łódź].

24. Clay censer with the likeness of a deity, Queen Santo, Guatemala, Maya art [redrawn by Strzemiński, Department of Scientific Documentation, Muzeum Sztuki, Łódź].

25. Oreo-Oreo deity, coloured painting on stone in a cottage, Easter Island [redrawn by Strzemiński, Department of Scientific Documentation, Muzeum Sztuki, Łódź].

26. House pillar, New Caledonia [redrawn by Strzemiński, Department of Scientific Documentation, Muzeum Sztuki, Łódź].

27. Ornament from an altar, New Guinea [redrawn by Strzemiński, Department of Scientific Documentation, Muzeum Sztuki, Łódź].

28. Ornament on a vase, Cyprus [redrawn by Strzemiński, Department of Scientific Documentation, Muzeum Sztuki, Łódź].

29. Dragon, ornament, Far Eastern art [redrawn by Strzemiński, Department of Scientific Documentation, Muzeum Sztuki, Łódź].

30. Mask, Ceylon [redrawn by Strzemiński, Department of Scientific Documentation, Muzeum Sztuki, Łódź].

31. Painting on a shield, Borneo [redrawn by Strzemiński, Department of Scientific Documentation, Muzeum Sztuki, Łódź].

32. Group of people with javelins on their shoulders in front of the image of a bison, engraved bone, Les Eyzies, Dordogne (dép). France, Palaeolithic, Magdalenian period [redrawn by Strzemiński, Department of Scientific Documentation, Muzeum Sztuki, Łódź].

33. Plaque of King Ur-nanshe and family, relief from Girsu (now referred to as Tall Luh), Mesopotamia, Sumerian art, ca. 2550 – 2500 BCE [redrawn by Strzemiński, Department of Scientific Documentation, Muzeum Sztuki, Łódź].

34. Devil at the Tree of Life, relief, Assyria, ca. 900 BCE [redrawn by Strzemiński, Department of Scientific Documentation, Muzeum Sztuki, Łódź].

35. Altar plaque, Hopi tribe (North American Indians), North America [redrawn by Strzemiński, Department of Scientific Documentation, Muzeum Sztuki, Łódź].

36. Hunting, rock painting, Tortosillas, Valencia Province, Spain, Palaeolithic, late Magdalenian period, Capsian culture [redrawn by Strzemiński, Department of Scientific Documentation, Muzeum Sztuki, Łódź].

37. Cave painting, San rock art, South Africa [redrawn by Strzemiński, Department of Scientific Documentation, Muzeum Sztuki, Łódź].

38. Rock painting, Alpera, Albacete Province, Spain, Palaeolithic, late Magdalenian period, Capsian culture [redrawn by Strzemiński, Department of Scientific Documentation, Muzeum Sztuki, Łódź].

39. Rock painting, Tanum, Sweden, Bronze Age [redrawn by Strzemiński, Department of Scientific Documentation, Muzeum Sztuki, Łódź].

40. Hunting, cave painting, San rock art, South Africa [redrawn by Strzemiński, Department of Scientific Documentation, Muzeum Sztuki, Łódź].

41. Humans, boats, birds, animals, painting on a vase, Egypt, Predynastic Period [redrawn by Strzemiński, Department of Scientific Documentation, Muzeum Sztuki, Łódź].

42. Warriors, vase painting, Archaic Greece, ninth – eighth century BCE [redrawn by Strzemiński, Department of Scientific Documentation, Muzeum Sztuki, Łódź].

43. Painting on pottery found in Moulianà, Crete, Sub-Mycenaean period [redrawn by Strzemiński, Department of Scientific Documentation, Muzeum Sztuki, Łódź].

44. Painting on the top: Goats; on the bottom: Devil with horns, zebra, and half-man Oryx, detail of White Lady rock painting in a shelter, Brandberg Mountain, southwest Africa, [redrawn by Strzemiński, Department of Scientific Documentation, Muzeum Sztuki, Łódź].

45. Horses and deer, stylized animals carved on a belt buckle, found in a tomb in Koban, Caucasus, thirteenth – sixth century BCE [redrawn by Strzemiński, Department of Scientific Documentation, Muzeum Sztuki, Łódź].

46. Hunting, coloured drawing from the Mandan tribe (North American Indians) on buffalo leather coat, North America [redrawn by Strzemiński, Department of Scientific Documentation, Muzeum Sztuki, Łódź].

47. Nausicaa, vase painting from an amphora, detail, Greece, fifth century BCE [redrawn by Strzemiński, Department of Scientific Documentation, Muzeum Sztuki, Łódź].

48. Menada pouring wine, crater painting, Greece, fifth century BCE [redrawn by Strzemiński, Department of Scientific Documentation, Muzeum Sztuki, Łódź].

49. Kylix ornament, Greece, fifth century BCE [redrawn by Strzemiński, Department of Scientific Documentation, Muzeum Sztuki, Łódź].

50. Blinding of Polyphemus, crater painting, Greece, seventh century BCE [redrawn by Strzemiński, Department of Scientific Documentation, Muzeum Sztuki, Łódź].

51. Heads, relief, second millennium BCE and Predynastic vase, Egypt [redrawn by Strzemiński, Department of Scientific Documentation, Muzeum Sztuki, Łódź].

52. Mut goddess, head of a statue, ca. 1300 BCE and pottery, Egypt [redrawn by Strzemiński, Department of Scientific Documentation, Muzeum Sztuki, Łódź].

53. Servant, sculpture, and pottery, Egypt, second millennium BCE [redrawn by Strzemiński, Department of Scientific Documentation, Muzeum Sztuki, Łódź].

54. Granite sculpture, Egypt, ca. 2500 BCE [redrawn by Strzemiński, Department of Scientific Documentation, Muzeum Sztuki, Łódź].

55. Predynastic vase and a head of Ti, limestone sculpture, Egypt, ca. 2600 BCE [redrawn by Strzemiński, Department of Scientific Documentation, Muzeum Sztuki, Łódź].

56. Predynastic sculpture of ivory (detail) and a Predynastic vase, Egypt [redrawn by Strzemiński, Department of Scientific Documentation, Muzeum Sztuki, Łódź].

57. Mourning Athena, relief, Acropolis, fifth century BCE [redrawn by Strzemiński, Department of Scientific Documentation, Muzeum Sztuki, Łódź].

58. Children making offerings to parents, detail of a relief, Egypt, ca. 2600 BCE, pottery and a smooth papyrus column with closed bud-shaped ▸

▸ capitals [redrawn by Strzemiński, Department of Scientific Documentation, Muzeum Sztuki, Łódź].

59. Servant, sculpture, second millennium BCE and a multi-stem papyrus column, second millennium BCE, Egypt [redrawn by Strzemiński, Department of Scientific Documentation, Muzeum Sztuki, Łódź].

60. Princess, wooden sculpture, ca. 1250 BCE and a circular papyrus column, second millennium BCE, Egypt [redrawn by Strzemiński, Department of Scientific Documentation, Muzeum Sztuki, Łódź].

61. Shipbuilder, granite sculpture, Egypt, third millennium BCE and pottery, Egypt [redrawn by Strzemiński, Department of Scientific Documentation, Muzeum Sztuki, Łódź].

62. Clay houses and crop silos, Nigeria, Africa [redrawn by Strzemiński, Department of Scientific Documentation, Muzeum Sztuki, Łódź].

63. Ostrich hunting, cave painting, San rock art, Herschel region, South Africa [redrawn by Strzemiński, Department of Scientific Documentation, Muzeum Sztuki, Łódź].

64. Amenhotep IV, limestone sculpture, Egypt, second millennium BCE [redrawn by Strzemiński, Department of Scientific Documentation, Muzeum Sztuki, Łódź].

65. *The Flight into Egypt*, detail of a carved capital, Church of Saint-Trophime, Arles, France, twelfth century [redrawn by Strzemiński, Department of Scientific Documentation, Muzeum Sztuki, Łódź].

66. *Adam and Eve*, detail of a carved capital, Cluny, France, twelfth century [redrawn by Strzemiński, Department of Scientific Documentation, Muzeum Sztuki, Łódź].

67. Heads, detail of a relief, Egypt, second millennium BCE [redrawn by Strzemiński, Department of Scientific Documentation, Muzeum Sztuki, Łódź].

68. Kagemni official, detail of a relief, Egypt, ca. 2500 BCE [redrawn by Strzemiński, Department of Scientific Documentation, Muzeum Sztuki, Łódź].

69. *The Flight into Egypt*, detail of a capital, Church of Saint-Trophime, Arles, France, twelfth century [redrawn by Strzemiński, Department of Scientific Documentation, Muzeum Sztuki, Łódź].

70. *Adam and Eve*, detail of a carved capital, Cluny, France, twelfth century [redrawn by Strzemiński, Department of Scientific Documentation, Muzeum Sztuki, Łódź].

71. Doric architectonics [redrawn by Strzemiński, Department of Scientific Documentation, Muzeum Sztuki, Łódź].

72. Ionian architectonics [redrawn by Strzemiński, Department of Scientific Documentation, Muzeum Sztuki, Łódź].

73. Gothic architectonics [redrawn by Strzemiński, from the first edition of the book].

74. Personifications of virtues, Gothic order, sculpture from the portal, Strasbourg Cathedral, thirteenth century [redrawn by Strzemiński, from the first edition of the book].

75. Athenians, relief, Parthenon, fifth century BCE, from the frieze and personifications of virtues, sculpture, Strasbourg, thirteenth century [redrawn by Strzemiński, from the first edition of the book].

76. Farewell of Amphiaraus, crater painting, Greece, sixth century BCE [redrawn, Department of Scholarly Documentation, Muzeum Sztuki, Łódź].

77. Spinner, detail of a tomb painting, Egypt, ca. 1900 BCE [redrawn by Strzemiński, from the first edition of the book].

78. Children making offerings to parents, detail of a relief, Egypt, ca. 2600 BCE [redrawn by Strzemiński, from the first edition of the book].

79. Pharaoh among gods, detail of a relief, Egypt, ca. 2600 BCE [redrawn by Strzemiński, from the first edition of the book].

80. Ishtar bringing captives, relief on a stamp, Mesopotamia, Sumerian art, ca. 2200 BCE [redrawn by Strzemiński, from the first edition of the book].

81. Vases, Greece [redrawn by Strzemiński, from the first edition of the book].

82. Peito, sculpture, Parthenon, fifth century BCE [redrawn by Strzemiński, from the first edition of the book].

83. Nereida, sculpture, Xanthos, Greece, fifth century BCE [redrawn by Strzemiński, from the first edition of the book].

84. Fighting Man, detail of Greek vase painting, Greece, fifth century BCE [redrawn by Strzemiński, from the first edition of the book].

85. Pericles, herma, Greece, fifth century BCE [redrawn by Strzemiński, from the first edition of the book].

86. Venus genetrix, sculpture, Greece, fifth century BCE [redrawn by Strzemiński, from the first edition of the book].

87. Sculpture, Greece, fifth century BCE [redrawn by Strzemiński, from the first edition of the book].

88. Satire sways a Nymph, detail of a painting on a skyphos, Greece, fifth century BCE [redrawn by Strzemiński, from the first edition of the book].

89. Peito, sculpture, Parthenon, fifth century BCE [redrawn by Strzemiński, from the first edition of the book].

90. Slaves in a mine, pinax, Corinth, Greece, sixth century BCE [redrawn by Strzemiński, from the first edition of the book].

91. Athenian heroes, relief on frieze, Parthenon, Greece, fifth century BCE [redrawn by Strzemiński, from the first edition of the book].

92. Gods, relief on frieze, Parthenon, Greece, fifth century BCE [redrawn by Strzemiński, from the first edition of the book].

93. Toilette, drawing engraved on the cover of a mirror, Greece, fourth century BCE [redrawn by Strzemiński, from the first edition of the book].

94. Venus genetrix, sculpture, Greece, fifth century BCE [redrawn by Strzemiński, from the first edition of the book].

95. Cupids, detail, mosaic, Mausoleum of Santa Costanza, Rome, fourth century [photo: De Agostini Picture Library / G. Dagli Orti / Bridgeman Images].

96. Detail of the vaulting, Early Christian mosaic, Mausoleum of Santa Costanza, Rome, fourth century [photo: De Agostini Picture Library / Bridgeman Images].

97. Tomb portrait, Fayum, Egypt, first century CE [collection: The British Museum, London; photo: public domain].

98. Transparent vase filled with fruit and bird, detail from wall paintings in the tomb of Clodius Hermes, Catacombs of St. Sebastian, Rome, second century [photo: dea / G. Dagli Orti, De Agostini / Getty Images].

* 99. Fantastic architectures, detail of a wall painting , House of the Vettii, Pompeii, first century CE [photo: dea / Archivo J.Lange, De Agostini / Getty Images].

100. Woodcut, Japan, eighteenth century (?) [redrawn by Strzemiński, from the first edition of the book].

101. The Laestrygonians Preparing to Attack Odysseus's Ships, wall painting in the house on the Esquiline Hill, Rome, 40–30 BCE [collection: ▸

▸ Biblioteca apostolica vaticana, Vatican; photo: © 2025. Photo Scala, Florence].

102. Bowl with doves, mosaic, Hadrian's Villa at Tivoli, Rome, second century CE [collection: Musei Capitolini, Rome; photo: De Agostini Picture Library / G. Nimatallah / Bridgeman Images].

103. Perseus and Andromeda, wall painting, House of the Dioscuri, Pompeii, first century CE [collection: Museo Archeologico Nazionale, Naples; photo: © Samuel Magal, Sites & Photos Ltd. / Bridgeman Images].

104. Hercules discovering Telephus, detail of a wall painting from Herculaneum, c. 70 CE [collection: Museo Archeologico Nazionale, Naples; photo: Index / Bridgeman Images].

105. Achilles, detail of a wall painting, House of the Tragic Poet, Pompeii, first century CE [collection: Museo Archeologico Nazionale, Naples; photo: public domain].

106. Head of a Woman, terracotta tondo, Centuripe, Sicily, Hellenistic art, third – second century BCE [collection: Indiana University Art Museum, Bloomington; photo: Kevin Montague, Indiana University Art Museum].

107. Dionysian scene, detail of a wall painting, from the ancient Roman rooms beneath the nave, Santi Giovanni e Paolo, Rome, second century CE [photo: Bridgeman Images].

108. David playing the harp surrounded by allegorical figures, miniature from Greek Byzantine psalter, Byzantine, thirteenth century [collection: Bibliothèque Nationale, Paris; photo: Bridgeman Images].

109. Mars and Venus, wall painting, House of Mars and Venus, Pompeii, Roman, first century [collection: Museo Archeologico Nazionale, Naples; photo: Bridgeman Images].

110. The Three Graces, wall painting, Pompeii, first century BCE – first century CE [collection: Museo Archeologico Nazionale, Naples; photo: public domain].

111. Athlete, mosaic, Rome, first century CE [collection: Museo Archeologico Nazionale, Naples; photo: © bpk / Alfredo Dagli Orti].

112. *Three Wise Men Paying Homage*, Rhythmic motif, Byzantine style, detail of a mosaic, the Basilica of Sant'Apollinare Nuovo, Ravenna, Italy, sixth century [redrawn by Strzemiński, from the first edition of the book].

113. *Procession of Martyrs and Saints*, detail of a mosaic, the Basilica of Sant'Apollinare Nuovo, Ravenna, Italy, sixth century [redrawn by Strzemiński, from the first edition of the book].

114. From the sarcophagus of St. Chalan in the Abbey of Notre-Dame de Bellavaux, Charenton-du-Cher, France, seventh century [collection: Musée du Berry, Bourges; photo: public domain].

115. *Death of St. John the Baptist*, miniature in the *Gospel Book of Chartres*, 850–899, France [collection: Bibliothèque nationale de France, Paris; photo: public domain].

116. *Duke William goes with Harold to his Palace at Rouen*, detail from the *Bayeux Tapestry*, France, eleventh century [collection: Bayeux Museum, Bayeux; photo: Bridgeman Images].

117. *Man Playing a Musical Instrument*, miniature from the *Songbook of Auch*, France, 990–1010 CE [collection and photo: Bibliothèque nationale de France, Paris].

118. *Duke William and his Fleet Cross the Channel to Pevensey*, from the *Bayeux Tapestry*, France, eleventh century [collection: Bayeux Museum, Bayeux; photo: Bridgeman Images].

119. Head, miniature in the Gelasian Sacramentary of Meaux or Cambrai, France, 780–800 CE [photo and collection: Bibliothèque nationale de France, Paris].

120. *Last Judgment*, sculpture from the tympanum of the western portal of Notre-Dame de Paris Cathedral, France, 1220–1230 CE [photo: Godong / UIG / Bridgeman Images].

121. *Sending the Holy Spirit*, sculpture from the tympanum of the central portal of the basilica of Sainte-Marie-Madeleine, Vézelay, France, 1130 CE [photo: public domain].

122. Miniature from the Bible (Biblia Sancti Martialis Lemovicensis altera), France, eleventh century [collection and photo: Bibliothèque nationale de France, Paris].

123. *Christ in Majesty*, miniature from Tyniec Sacramentarium, ca. 1060–1070 CE [collection: Biblioteka Narodowa, Warsaw; photo: courtesy of Biblioteka Narodowa].

124. *Abraham and Angels*, mosaic, Cathedral Basilica of Saint Mark, Venice, thirteenth century [photo: © 2025. Photo Scala, Florence].

125. *Pope John VII*, mosaic, Vatican Grottoes, Rome, 705–707 CE [photo: public domain].

126. *Saint Peter* (detail), mosaic by the Venetian-Ravenna school apse of Santa Maria, Trieste Cathedral, Friuli-Venezia Giulia, Trieste, Italy, twelfth century [photo: De Agostini / Getty Images].

127. *Scenes from the Life of Saint Jerome,* Bible of Charles the Bald, Rome, Basilica of San Paolo fuori le Mura, Carolingian style, ninth century [photo: © 2025. Photo Scala, Florence].

128. *Saint Joseph's Dream*, mosaic, Cathedral Basilica of St Mark, Venice, tenth century [photo: Mondadori Portfolio / Getty Images].

129. *Scenes from the Life of Saint Castrensis*, mosaic, Cathedral of Santa Maria Nuova, Monreale, Italy, 1174 — 1189 CE [photo: © 2025. Andrea Jemolo / Scala, Florence].

130. Giotto di Bondone (school of), *Portrait of Dante Alighieri*, detail of a wall painting from the Bargello Palace, Florence, Italy, c. 1336 [collection: Museo Nazionale del Bargello, Florence; photo: Alinari / Bridgeman Images].

131. *Dispute*, detail of a carved capital from the Church of Saint-Hilaire-le-Grand, Poitiers, France, eleventh — twelfth century [collection: Musée Sainte-Croix, Poitiers; photo: public domain].

132. *Prophet's Head*, wall painting, St. John the Baptist Cathedral in Gniezno, fourteenth century [photo: © 2025. Andrea Jemolo / Scala, Florence].

133. *St. Radegund on a Boat*. Miniature from the *Life of St. Radegund*, Poitiers, France, eleventh century [collection: Bibliothèque Municipale, Poitiers; photo: Luisa Ricciarini / Bridgeman Images].

134. *The Flight into Egypt*, detail of a carved capital, the Church of Saint-Trophime, Arles, France, twelfth century [photo: © 2025. Mario Bonotto / Photo Scala, Florence].

*** 135.** Gislebertus, *Angel Warns the Magi Not to Return to King Herod*, carved capital, Cathedral of Saint- Lazare, Autun, France, twelfth century [photo: public domain].

136. *Christ's Prophecy of St. Peter's Denial*, sculpture on portal, the Church of Saint-Gilles-du-Gard, France, twelfth century [photo: public domain].

137. *Adam and Eve*, detail of a carved capital, Cluny, ca. 1100 CE [collection: Musée du Farinier, Cluny; photo: © 2025. White Images / Scala, Florence].

138. Rafael Santi, *Madonna with Child and the Infant John the Baptist (Madonna of the Goldfinch)*, 1506–1507, detail [collection: Galleria degli Uffizi, Florence; photo: Mondadori Portfolio / Electa / Sergio Anelli / Bridgeman Images].

139. Melozzo da Forlì, *Sixtus IV Appoints Bartolomeo Platina Prefect of the Vatican Library*, mural painting, Pinacoteca Vaticana, Rome, ca. 1477 [photo: public domain].

140. Domenico Ghirlandaio, *The Birth of St. John the Baptist*, wall painting, Tornabuoni Chapel, the Church of Santa Maria Novella, Florence, 1486–1490 [photo: public domain].

141. Gothic order, thirteenth century, and Domenico Veneziano, *Portrait of a Young Woman*, 1460–1465 [redrawn by Strzemiński, from the first edition of the book].

142. Leonardo da Vinci, *Mona Lisa*, ca. 1503–1519 [collection: Musée du Louvre, Paris; redrawn by Strzemiński, from the first edition of the book; photo: public domain].

143. Francesco del Cossa, *Autumn*, 1455–1460 [collection: Gemäldegalerie, Staatliche Museen, Berlin; photo: public domain and redrawn by Strzemiński, from the first edition of the book].

144. Sandro Botticelli, *The Birth of Venus*, ca. 1482–1484 [collection: Galleria degli Uffizi, Florence; photo: public domain].

145. Sandro Botticelli, *Enthroned Maria with Child with John the Baptist and John the Evangelist*, Bardich Altarpiece, detail, 1485 [collection: Gemäldegalerie, Staatliche Museen, Berlin, Germany; photo: © Tarker / Bridgeman Images].

146. Sandro Botticelli, *Coronation of Virgin*, 1488–1490 [collection: Galleria degli Uffizi, Florence; photo: De Agostini Picture Library / N. Grifoni / Bridgeman Images].

147. Rafael Santi, *St. Catherine of Alexandria*, detail, ca. 1507 [collection: The National Gallery, London; photo: public domain].

148. Leonardo da Vinci, *The Virgin of the Rocks*, detail, 1483–1486 [collection: Musée du Louvre, Paris; photo: public domain].

149. Leonardo da Vinci, *The Virgin of the Rocks*, detail, 1483–1486 [collection: Musée du Louvre, Paris; photo: public domain].

150. Nature photography [photograph included in the author's original typescript, collection: Muzeum Sztuki, Łódź].

151. Aleksander Krzywobłocki, *Portrait of Halina Hornung*, 1930 [collection and photo: Muzeum Sztuki, Łódź].

152. Rembrandt Harmenszoon van Rijn, *Scribe sharpening his quill by candlelight* , drawing, ca. 1635 [photograph included in the author's original typescript, collection: Muzeum Sztuki, Łódź].

153. Peter Paul Rubens, *Miraculous Draught of Fishes*, detail, 1610 [photograph included in the author's original typescript, collection: Muzeum Sztuki, Łódź].

154. *Nature photography [photo: Piotr Tomczyk].

155. Rembrandt Harmenszoon van Rijn (studio of), *Self-portrait*, ca. 1645 [collection: Museum der bildenden Künste, Leipzig; photo: © bpk / Museum der bildenden Künste, Leipzig].

156. Jacopo Robusti Tintoretto, *St. Mark Rescuing a Saracen from Shipwreck*, detail, 1562 – 1566 [collection: Gallerie dell'Accademia, Venice; photo: following conservation in 2011, © 2025. Photo Scala, Florence – courtesy of the Ministero Beni e Att. Culturali].

157. Rembrandt Harmenszoon van Rijn, *Path through a Bridge*, drawing, seventeenth century [photograph included in the author's original typescript, collection: Muzeum Sztuki, Łódź].

158. Jacopo Robusti Tintoretto, *The Probatic Pool*, detail, the Church of Saint Roch, Venice, 1559 [photo: Cameraphoto Arte Venezia / Bridgeman Images].

159. Peter Paul Rubens, *Supper at Emmaus*, detail, 1638 [collection: Museo Nacional del Prado, Madrid, photo: public domain].

160. El Greco, *The Holy Family with Mary Magdalen*, ca. 1590 – 1595 [collection: Cleveland Museum of Art, Ohio; photo: Cleveland Museum of Art, Ohio, USA / Gift of the Friends of The Cleveland Museum of Art in memory of J.H. Wade / Bridgeman Images].

161. Jacopo Robusti Tintoretto, *The Last Supper*, detail, Church of San Trovaso, Venice, 1566 [photo: © 2025. Cameraphoto / Scala, Florence].

162. Jacopo Robusti Tintoretto, *Pietà*, 1563 [collection: Pinacoteca di Brera, Milan; photo: © 2025. Photo: Scala, Florence – courtesy of the Ministero Beni e Att. Culturali].

163. Sandro Botticelli, *The Youth of Moses*, 1481 – 1482, detail of a mural painting, Sistine Chapel, Vatican [photo: © 2025. Photo Scala, Florence].

164. Sandro Botticelli, *The Birth of Venus,* detail, 1482–1485 [collection: Galleria degli Uffizi, Florence; photo: public domain].

165. Jan van Eyck (follower), *Portrait of a Man with a Carnation,* ca. 1510 [collection: Gemäldegalerie, Staatliche Museen, Berlin; photo: public domain].

166. Jacopo Robusti Tintoretto, *Study for a Sculpture,* drawing, sixteenth century [photo: public domain].

167. Michelangelo Buonarroti, *The Birth of Adam,* sketch, ca. 1510–1511 [photograph included in the author's original typescript, collection: Muzeum Sztuki, Łódź].

168. Rembrandt Harmenszoon van Rijn, *View of Amsterdam from the Northwest,* etching, ca. 1640 [collection: Metropolitan Museum of Art, New York, photo: The Metropolitan Museum of Art / Art Resource / Scala, Florence].

169. Sandro Botticelli, *Portrait of a Young Woman (Simonetta Vespucci),* ca. 1480 [collection: Städel Museum, Frankfurt am Main; photo: public domain].

170. Pisanello (Antonio Pisano*), Study of a Head,* fifteenth century [photograph included in the author's original typescript, collection: Muzeum Sztuki, Łódź].

171. Sandro Botticelli, *St. Augustine in His Cell,* detail of a mural painting, c. 1480 [collection: Ognissanti, Florence; photo: Ognissanti, Florence / Bridgeman Images].

172. Rembrandt Harmenszoon van Rijn (follower), *The Good Samaritan,* seventeenth century [collection: Gemäldegalerie, Staatliche Museen, Berlin; photo: © bpk / Gemäldegalerie, SMB / Christoph Schmidt].

173. Rembrandt Harmenszoon van Rijn, *Portrait of Titus,* reading, (oil on canvas), 1656–1657 [collection: Kunsthistorisches Museum, Vienna; photo: Mondadori Portfolio / Electa / Remo Bardazzi / Bridgeman Images].

174. Rembrandt Harmenszoon van Rijn, *Self-portrait,* seventeenth century [collection: Bayerische Staatsgemäldesammlungen – Alte Pinakothek, Munich; photo: © bpk | Bayerische Staatsgemäldesammlungen].

175. Rembrandt Harmenszoon van Rijn, *Saskia in Bed,* drawing, ca. 1638 [collection: Staatliche Graphische Sammlung, Munich; photo: public domain].

176. Rembrandt Harmenszoon van Rijn, *The Holy Family,* detail, 1633–1635 [collection: Alte Pinakothek, Munich, photo: © Tarker / Bridgeman Images].

177. El Greco, *The Repentant St. Peter,* detail, c. 1600–1605 [collection: The Phillips Collection, Washington; photo: The Phillips Collection, Washington, D.C., USA / Acquired 1922 / Bridgeman Images].

178. Leonardo da Vinci, *Head of Christ,* drawing, ca. 1495 [collection: Pinacoteca di Brera, Milan; photo: © Pinacoteca di Brera].

179. Rembrandt Harmenszoon van Rijn, *Self-portrait,* 1652 [collection: Kunsthistorisches Museum, Vienna; photo: public domain].

* **180.** Rembrandt Harmenszoon van Rijn, *An Old Man in Red,* 1652–1654 [collection: Hermitage, St. Petersburg; photo: State Hermitage Museum, St. Petersburg, Russia / Bridgeman Images].

181. Rembrandt Harmenszoon van Rijn, *The Return of the Prodigal Son,* 1663–1665 [collection: Hermitage, St. Petersburg; photo: public domain].

182. Rembrandt Harmenszoon van Rijn, *Self-portrait with Saskia,* 1635 [collection: Gemäldegalerie Alte Meister, Dresden; photo: public domain].

183. Peter Paul Rubens, *Crowning of the Hero,* detail, 1612–1614 [collection: Bayerische Staatsgemäldesammlungen — Alte Pinakothek, Munich; photo: © bpk | Bayerische Staatsgemäldesammlungen].

184. Peter Paul Rubens, *Helena Fourment with Children,* 1636–1637 [collection: Musée du Louvre, Paris; photo: public domain].

185. Peter Paul Rubens, *Helena Fourment in Her Wedding Dress,* detail, 1630–1631 [collection: Alte Pinakothek, Munich; photo: © Tarker / Bridgeman Images].

186. Peter Paul Rubens and workshop, Bacchanal, detail, seventeenth century [collection: Gemäldegalerie der Akademie der bildenden Künste, Vienna; photo: Akademie der Bildenden Künste, Vienna / Bridgeman Images].

187. Bartolomé Esteban Murillo, *Two Peasant Boys,* late 1660s [collection: Dulwich Picture Gallery, London; photo: © Dulwich Picture Gallery, London / Bridgeman Images].

188. Rembrandt Harmenszoon van Rijn, *Self-portrait,* 1668 [collection: Wallraf-Richartz-Museum, Cologne; photo: public domain].

189. Bartolomé Esteban Murillo, *St. Roderick,* 1646–1655 [collection: Gemäldegalerie Alte Meister, Dresden; photo: public domain].

190. Bartolomé Esteban Murillo, *La Toilette Domestique*, 1670 – 1675 [collection: Alte Pinakothek, Munich; photo: Bridgeman Images].

191. Bartolomé Esteban Murillo, *The Virgin Mary and St. Felix of Cantalice Holding the Infant Jesus*, 1668 – 1669 [collection: Museo de Bellas Artes, Seville; photo: © Museo de Bellas Artes de Sevilla].

192. *Bartolomé Esteban Murillo, *Self-portrait*, ca. 1670 – 1673 [collection: National Gallery, London; photo: Bridgeman Images].

193. Jacob van Ruisdael, *Landscape*, seventeenth century [photograph included in the author's original typescript, collection: Muzeum Sztuki, Łódź].

194. Pieter de Hooch, *Woman Lacing Her Bodice beside a Cradle (Mother)*, ca. 1661 – 1663 [collection: Gemäldegalerie, Staatliche Museen, Berlin; photo: © bpk / Gemäldegalerie, SMB / Jörg P. Anders].

195. Jan Vermeer, *The Music Lesson*, ca. 1659 – 1664 [collection: Buckingham Palace, London; photo: public domain].

196. According to Wittgenstein's *Tractatus Logico-Philosophicus* [redrawn by Strzemiński, from the first edition of the book].

197. Jacques-Louis David, *Madame Récamier*, detail, 1800 [collection: Musée du Louvre, Paris, France; photo: Bridgeman Images].

198. Andrea Mantegna, *Lodovico II Gonzaga*, detail, Decoration of the Camera degli Sposi (Camera Picta) at the Palazzo Ducale di Mantova, 1465 – 1475 [photo: Mondadori Portfolio / Electa / Antonio Quattrone / Bridgeman Images].

199. Théodore Géricault, *The Raft of the Medusa*, 1819 [collection: Musée du Louvre, Paris; photo: Bridgeman Images].

200. Peter Paul Rubens, *The Rape of the Daughters of Leucippus*, 1620s [collection: Alte Pinakothek, Munich; photo: public domain].

201. Jean-Baptiste-Camille Corot, *Recollection of Mortefontaine*, 1864 [collection: Musée du Louvre; photo: public domain].

202. Jean-François Millet, *The Spinner, Goatherd of the Auvergne*, 1868 – 1869 [collection: Musée d'Orsay, Paris; photo: Bridgeman Images].

203. Gustave Courbet, *Old Man with a Glass of Wine*, nineteenth century [collection: Mayor Gallery, London; photo: Bridgeman Images].

204. Vincent van Gogh, *Wheat Field with Crows*, 1890 [collection: Van Gogh Museum, Amsterdam; photo: public domain].

205. Vincent van Gogh, *Harvest at La Crau with Montmajour in the Background*, July 1888 [collection: Van Gogh Museum, Amsterdam; photo: Van Gogh Museum, Amsterdam / Vincent van Gogh Foundation].

206. Vincent Van Gogh, *The Night Café in Arles*, 1888 [collection: Yale University Art Gallery, New Haven, Connecticut; photo: Yale University Art Gallery].

207. Vincent Van Gogh, *Wheat Fields with Cypresses*, 1889 [collection: Národni Galerie, Prague; photo: public domain].

208. Vincent Van Gogh, *View of Arles. Flowering Orchards*, April 1889 [collection: Van Gogh Museum, Amsterdam; photo: public domain].

209. Pierre-Auguste Renoir, *Portrait of Jeanne Samary*, 1877 [collection: Pushkin Museum of Fine Arts in Moscow; photo: public domain].

210. Nature photography [photograph included in the author's original typescript, collection: Muzeum Sztuki, Łódź].

211. Pierre-Auguste Renoir, *The Grands Boulevards*, 1875 [collection: Philadelphia Museum of Art, Philadelphia; photo: public domain].

212. Paul Cézanne, *The Kitchen Table (Vessels, Basket, and Fruit)*, 1888/1890 [collection: Musée d'Orsay, Paris; photo: public domain].

213. Vincent van Gogh, *Wheat Field at Auvers*, July 1890 [collection: Neue Pinakothek, Munich; photo: public domain].

214. Władysław Strzemiński, *Only Trace*, series: *Deportations*, 1940 [collection: Muzeum Sztuki, Łódź; photo: © Muzeum Sztuki].

215. Władysław Strzemiński, *Village*, series: *West Belorussia*, 1939 [collection: Muzeum Sztuki, Łódź; photo: © Muzeum Sztuki].

* Reproductions marked with an asterisk are not identical with those published in the first edition. Since we were not able to identify the source to redraw or obtain photos from collections that currently hold these masterpieces, illustrations have been replaced with images that are consistent as to the substance with the primary version.

Photo on page 4: Julian Przyboś, Władysław Strzemiński, and Katarzyna Kobro, ca. 1930–1931 [photo: Department of Scientific Documentation, Muzeum Sztuki, Łódź]

Photos 1–94 and 112, 113, 138, 141, 142 are reproductions of the author's re-drawings.

Muzeum Sztuki, Łódź
Więckowskiego 36
90-734 Łódź
msl.org.pl

INTERIM DIRECTOR: Daniel Muzyczuk

Władysław Strzemiński: Theory of Seeing

EDITORS: Iwona Luba, Daniel Muzyczuk
TRANSLATION: Klara Kemp-Welch, Wanda Kemp-Welch
COPY-EDITING AND PROOFREADING: William Gilcher
EDITORIAL COORDINATION: Andżelika Bauer
COOPERATION: Matylda Makowska
GRAPHIC DESIGN: Printscreen | Waldemar Węgrzyn
based on the first edition design by Stanisław Fijałkowski and Stefan Wegner
TYPESETTING OF THE ENGLISH VERSION: Katarzyna Wolny-Grządziel
PHOTO PREPARATION: Barbara Kubska

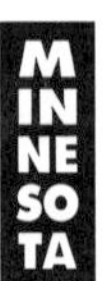
Printed and distributed by the University of Minnesota Press
111 Third Avenue South, Suite 290
Minneapolis, MN 55401-2520
www.upress.umn.edu

e-flux Published by e-flux Classics

HC ISBN 978-1-5179-2080-7
PB ISBN 978-1-5179-2081-4
A Cataloging-in-Publication record for this book is available from the Library of Congress.

ISBN 978-83-66696-62-4

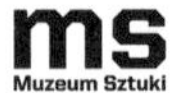
A cultural institution of the Lodzkie Region co-run by the Ministry of Culture and National Heritage of the Republic of Poland

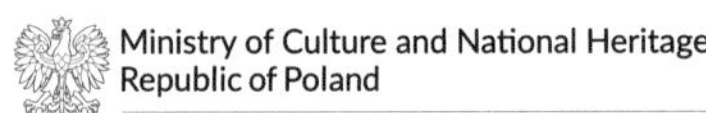

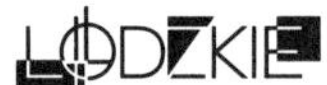

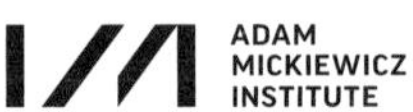

Published thanks to the support of the Adam Mickiewicz Institute